"A most valuable introduction to Taoist philosophy and ways of thought, this book shows the impact of China's tumultuous years during the civil war upon a Taoist temple high on the sacred mountain of Huashan. It is a powerful and moving account of the contradiction between the remote and aspiring monk, and the need to come to terms with violence and destruction."

–Han Suyin, author of *The Enchantress*

"Transcends the tangible and points to the mysteries we can imagine and all we cannot."

–*Los Angeles Times*

"Deng regales the reader with a feast of Taoist lore."

–*Kirkus Reviews*

"Captures the essence of a uniquely gifted and wise man whose life offers excitement, instruction, and a look into other lands and realities."

–*Natural Health*

"A fascinating, provocative history of a contemporary hero."

–*San Francisco Chronicle*

CHRONICLES OF TAO

BOOKS BY DENG MING-DAO

365 Tao

Chronicles of Tao
  The Wandering Taoist
  Seven Bamboo Tablets of the
    Cloudy Satchel
  Gateway to a Vast World

CHRONICLES OF

TAO

THE SECRET LIFE OF A TAOIST MASTER

Deng Ming-Dao

HarperOne

A Division of HarperCollins*Publishers*

HarperOne

HarperCollins books may be purchased for educational, business, or sales promotional use. For information please write: Special Markets Department, HarperCollins Publishers, 10 East 53rd Street, New York, NY 10022.

HarperCollins Web site: http://www.harpercollins.com

HarperCollins®, ☷®, and HarperOne™ are trademarks of HarperCollins Publishers.

FIRST HARPERCOLLINS PAPERBACK EDITION PUBLISHED IN 1993

Library of Congress Cataloging-in-Publication Data
Deng, Ming-Dao
The chronicles of Tao : the secret life of a Taoist master / Deng
    Ming-Dao.
p. cm.
Includes bibliographical references.
Consists of author's trilogy: The wandering Taoist, Seven bamboo tablets of the cloudy satchel, and Gateway to a vast world.
ISBN: 978–0–06–250219–3
    1. Kwan, Saihung. 2. Taoists—China—Biography. I. Deng, Ming-Dao. Wandering Taoist. 1993. II. Deng, Ming-Dao. Seven bamboo tablets of the cloudy satchel. 1993. III. Deng, Ming-Dao. Gateway to a vast world. 1993. IV. Title.
    BL1940.K93D435 1993
    299'514'092–dc20
    [B]   92–56409

07 08 09 10 11 RRD(H) 20 19 18

For Sifu and my parents

Contents

three: *Gateway to a Vast World*

Acknowledgments

WHEN I FIRST began writing in 1982, I received invaluable advice from Elizabeth Lawrence Kalashnikoff. Throughout my subsequent career, she was a source of encouragement, support, and excellent advice. It was she who first saw the possibility of combining all the chronicles into a single volume. I regret that she passed away without seeing this book, but my gratitude is undiminished.

Throughout the years, numerous people provided crucial assistance.

Clayton Carlson, Mark Salzwedel, and Amy Hertz contributed valuable editorial insights.

Lien Fung of Singapore, Su Yung Li, and Li Hsi-Chih of Guangzhou provided personal recollections of Shanghai and Du Yueshen. John Service and Frederick Wakeman augmented these memories with historical and scholarly views.

Yvonne Eastman and Peggy Gee helped with the typing of the initial manuscripts.

My parents and family were constantly supportive, helping this project in countless ways.

Finally, it was Kwan Saihung himself who provided the true substance of this book, revealing the legacy of his Taoist teachers with clarity and drama.

Introduction

LIKE MANY PEOPLE, I had heard bits and pieces of information about Taoism. It was an esoteric spiritual tradition of eccentrics and nonconformists. Some of the Beat Poets translated and found inspiration in Taoist poetry. It looked into nature for much of its imagery. Taoism had secret longevity practices. And the *Tao Te Ching* was considered by many to be a deeply profound, but highly abstruse key to Taoism.

Most surprising to me was a growing awareness that Taoism combined a staggering array of arts. I was intrigued by any tradition that went from simple fortune telling to advanced meditation, from martial arts to profound scripture.

But the stories were clear. Meditation was the fundamental way to perceive the Tao. And learning meditation required "direct transmission" from a master.

I was sure this was correct. I was unsuccessful in my attempts to follow procedures in books. Not only that, I found sitting cross legged and burning incense a boring process. This only deepened my curiosity about Taoism: Of all the great spiritual traditions, Taoism held that meditation could happen in a methodical way. But even more intriguing to me—since I admired the strange postures of a Taiji master in a park—it was said that Taoism could be learned through martial arts.

All this was of interest to me, but I didn't do much beyond study Taiji. When I heard from two friends that they were going to visit Mr. Kwan, a sixty-five-year-old martial arts teacher, I thought I'd just be meeting an old man. I went to support my friend's interest— maybe the master didn't speak English and I could help by translating. We arrived early at the secluded park where he taught. The training area was empty. We went to another section to practice while we waited, and had become deeply engaged in Taiji pushing hands when a rather large man appeared in the bushes.

He looked about thirty years old and had medium-long black hair and enormously heavy shoulders. Dressed in a gray sweatshirt and brown warm-up suit, he stood completely motionless and stared unabashedly at us. I was annoyed.

He looked like a college student, a jock out to provoke people. If he were a student of Mr. Kwan's, why didn't he go and wait respectfully for his master instead of lurking about? He disappeared, and a few minutes later one of Mr. Kwan's students came to tell us that the teacher had arrived. As we walked down the hill, she warned us that her teacher was an excellent one, but very traditional and "very eccentric."

The class was practicing *qigong* when we arrived. I was instantly impressed by the vigor and variety of the movements. The postures were forceful, yet balanced. But to my surprise, the man from the bushes was leading the class.

I turned to the student. "Is that the senior student?" I asked.

"No, that's Mr. Kwan," she replied.

"I thought he was in his mid-sixties."

"He is."

I looked closely at him. Mr. Kwan had only a very slight bit of gray hair, and one had to look quite carefully to see it. His wide face was smooth-skinned and clear, and he had large, luminescent eyes that demonstrated a sensitive awareness of his surroundings. This man was the furthest thing possible from the stereotype of an old, wizened teacher.

At a break in the class, we were formally introduced. Mr. Kwan proved to be rather shy, and after greeting us he retreated to watch his students. Toward the end of class, reassured by his students that he was approachable, I went to speak with him.

In the Asian tradition, a teacher is only as good as the lineage of his school. When I questioned him about his, I was stunned to learn that some of his teachers were among the most famous in China. He said he had trained with such masters as Yang Chengfu and Chen Weiming of Taiji, Sun Lutang of Xingyi, Fu Zhensong and Zhang Zhaodong of Bagua, as well as Wang Ziping of Mizhongyi. It was not until later that I found out that Mr. Kwan had studied a large number of other martial styles, including Shaolin, Taoist, Monkey, Eagle, Crane, Snake, and Tiger forms. I also learned that Mr. Kwan had traveled all over the world, had gone to India and Tibet to study yoga and other meditative systems, had been a soldier, a circus performer, Peking Opera performer, Beijing University political science teacher, and under secretary to Zhou Enlai.

His martial background attracted me. Most present-day masters have studied only with students of these famous teachers, and yet here was a man who represented the first generation taught by those masters. Eager to study with him, I inquired about the tuition.

Mr. Kwan looked visibly embarrassed. Money matters seemed to make him uncomfortable. He hesitantly told me that it was $35 a month. There was a pause. He added that for this sum, a student could train with him four or five times a week, if desired. There was another pause. As if he felt the cost was still insufficiently justified, he went on to explain what the money was to be used for.

Out of the $35, only $10 went to sustain himself. Another $10 was set aside for the future building of a school, and the remaining $15 was sent back to China to support his master.

I asked which master it was. All the masters he had named had passed away, and I tried to imagine what kind of master this man could have.

"My Taoist master," replied Mr. Kwan.

"Your Taoist master?" I was excited. "He must be very old."

"He is," Mr. Kwan said reluctantly. "He has long white hair and beard and is now 142 years old. He spends his time in meditation."

"142! Is that possible?"

"Of course. He's a Taoist."

"And you?"

"I am also a Taoist ascetic. In fact, I only teach martial art as a sideline."

We talked for a while more until Mr. Kwan had to leave. I returned to visit his class several times, and soon became his student. I was as interested in the rare and orthodox martial arts he taught as in his Taoism. I liked being his student and addressed him as *Sifu*.

I had seemingly endless doubt and uncertainty, which I put to Sifu in question after question. He usually gave profound answers, yet in a way that made complete sense. But sometimes he would only tell me that I had to face the problem alone. This never seemed to be an attempt to avoid an issue he couldn't discuss. Although he was generous with his guidance, he always placed squarely on me the responsibility for my own life.

I had read many books on Taoism, but as my relationship with Sifu deepened, I found that his Taoism was a complete and living tradition that went beyond theoretical book knowledge. Taoism, for Sifu, was more than a religion or a philosophy. It was a way of life. At its very core, this Taoism was the discipline of natural living and complete self-purification for the sake of spiritual advancement. Thus, although the Taoist tradition encompassed sorcery, ritual, and religious belief in an enormous pantheon, Sifu's emphasis was on ascetic practice to gain liberation from ignorance and sorrow.

Toward this goal, he of course spoke of the appreciation of nature and the noncontentious outlook about which I had often read. But his basic theme was self-sacrifice to achieve purification and perfection. This meant the seemingly simple task of avoiding degradation of ourselves, of our bodies, of others, or of the world around us.

"The gods have a test for us to take," Sifu said. "Whether we want to or not, they will test our willingness to sacrifice and reach the other side of enlightenment instead of succumbing to greed and our own degradation. The body is the temple of God, the soul is God himself. If you pollute your own body and it deteriorates, and your brain disintegrates, God will naturally leave your body. But if you know enough to sacrifice, you will reach a certain rewarding stage. Then you'll give up all that is 'nice,' easy to get, and 'fun,' and you'll eventually purify your body. That is like cleaning and repainting a temple to await God's entrance."

The avoidance of degradation meant a regulated diet, no liquor, drugs, smoking, or sexual excess. City noise, air pollution, and stress were to be shunned. I found that Sifu himself was the best example. He was celibate, fastidious in his diet, neither smoked nor took drugs, drank a single glass of wine on rare occasions, trained daily, and, in spite of a rather gruff exterior, was caring and protective of his students.

Many people wonder whether spirituality can exist in today's world. Warfare, nuclear disaster, pollution, crime, racism, social decay, sham religious leaders, and individual laziness all seem to make it impossible. Endless obstructions and diversions exist to discourage the practice of austerities. But Taoism is a methodical and gradual system. It is individually flexible and universally all-encompassing. Its approach from the physical to the spiritual implies that the religious can arise from the secular. One need only cultivate the right attitudes with sincerity.

Sifu's own Taoism was transmitted at a time when China was in great turmoil. He learned to preserve his faith through war and secular society. He is proof that in the most difficult of times, one can still be spiritual.

He frequently recounts his own experiences in order to spur us on. He told us stories of his own matches, resulting both in victories and defeats. He spoke of his master's wisdom and strictness. And he told us entrancing stories of other old masters with abilities to go into other dimensions, perform sorcery, or match fighting skills against all challengers. Naturally, our curiosity soon extended into wondering more about Sifu than these parablelike tales revealed.

But Sifu was deliberately obscure whenever we probed into details of his personal past. A Taoist master is never to reveal his birthdate, birthplace, or other individual data. Yet, because we encountered a wide range of situations where he drew from his personal experiences to teach us, and because, like a father, he indulged us in answering some of our questions, Sifu slowly revealed parts of his past life.

Reading the classic scriptures and poems about Taoism provides only some information about this great spiritual tradition. No matter how much one reads, it's hard to imagine people living in this way. It's difficult to absorb the emotional impact of its history from scholarly writings. And it's hard to see how anyone might be Taoist in contemporary times. *Chronicles of Tao* can be a good introduction to Taoism, one that will help one see Taoism beyond the fairy-tale images of immortals on cranes.

Just as the stories of Sifu's training became an integral part of my learning with him, I believe the experiences of this extraordinary individual will help people see how the great breadth of Taoism can be bound into a single, life-long path. I hope that others, though knowing the difficulties, will find inspiration to undertake their own spiritual journeys.

Note on Romanization

IT IS DIFFICULT to romanize the Chinese words necessary for this book. Although it seems best to use the pinyin system adopted by the People's Republic of China, many terms are familiar to the general reading public from other systems. The only alternative seems to be to use the pinyin system for all cases except those where a different spelling would enhance ready recognition.

Foremost among those words are, of course, *Tao* and *Taoism*. Under the pinyin system, they would be romanized as *Dao* and *Daoism*. I have retained the previous form because it is in widespread use. I have also spelled Sifu's name Kwan Saihung rather than Guan Shihong, because this is the way he himself spells it. All other proper names and technical terms have been rendered in pinyin, however; although in a few cases I have parenthetically added the Wades-Giles version of a name to ensure recognition. Regardless of how names are romanized, all surnames precede given names; hence *Guan* has been used as the surname for other members of Saihung's family, except Ma Sixing (due to the fact that a Chinese woman keeps her own surname after marriage).

Readers should take special note of several terms used throughout the book. *Qi*, *qigong*, and *Taijiquan* are the pinyin spellings of *ch'i*, *ch'i kung*, and *Tai Chi Ch'üan*, words well known to those familiar with Taoism and Chinese martial arts.

THE WANDERING TAOIST

The
Taishan
Festival

I N 1929, Kwan Saihung[1] accompanied his family on a pilgrimage up the steep slopes of Taishan. They were traveling to the Emerald Cloud Temple at the mountain's summit for the Festival of the Jade Emperor. This religious event combined weeks of ritual and devotion with a carnival-like atmosphere in the temple courtyard. The Guan family, members of an immensely wealthy warrior clan, were devout patrons of Taoism who were completing a long and arduous pilgrimage of over five hundred miles from their home in Shaanxi Province to Shandong Province. They would be guests of the temple for a month.

1. *Kwan* and *Guan* are variants of the same surname.

The final ascent of Taishan, by means of sedan chairs, was slow. Taishan's towering precipices could not be scaled in a day. But the gradual climb, divided by overnight lodging in rustic inns situated in pine groves, provided an opportunity for final ablutions. All the inns served only vegetarian foods. Cleansing the taint of animal flesh and contemplation quieted the pilgrims' minds.

12

The mountain itself made complete their otherworldly state of mind. Taishan was the foremost of the Five Sacred Mountains of China. It rose steeply above Shandong Province's vast expanse, disdaining all the other mountain ranges. It had a heavenly magnitude, an air of Imperial seclusion. Humanity was invisible from its summit. In the cool and rarifed air surrounding its high cliffs of rock, Taishan was the perfect place of solitude for the Jade Emperor.

An emperor, whether celestial or mortal, was a personage never to be seen by common people. He was a mystery, a force, an inaccessible but dominating power. But on the annual occasion of the festival, the Jade Emperor granted one exception to that rule and descended to his earthly abode to accept the supplications of his subjects.

Saihung, an energetic, mischievous, and curious nine-year-old boy, was less interested in the religious significance of the event than he was in simply having fun. His grandfather Guan Jiuyin, his grandmother Ma Sixing, and his aunt Guan Meihong understood this. They did not want to force things on Saihung but nevertheless felt that it was time for him to experience his first pilgrimage. It was with that in mind that the family faced the final approach to Taishan, the Eighteen-Twist Path.

The path was a narrow ribbon of seven thousand stone steps that followed the twisted crags of a huge cleft. Compared to the rugged granite cliffs, netted with tenacious shrubs and trees, the pathway seemed positively fragile. It was a man-made object, insignificant compared to nature. The adults were carried up in their sedan chairs, but Saihung, though he had the option of being carried on the back of a manservant, bounded up the stairs in excitement.

The early morning air was thin and cold, and Saihung was warmly dressed in a high-collared, fur-lined coat of mountain-lion skin over a suit of heavy maroon cotton. Knicker pants buttoned at the knee over white leggings, and both his shoes and money pouch were intricately embroidered silk. The shoes were felt-soled, with blue and white clouds decorating the sides and gaily colored appliquéd lion heads at the toes. His money pouch, barely visible at the hem of his coat, had a design of a frolicking lion. For good measure he wore a tiger's tooth around his neck as a talisman. All of Saihung's clothing was designed to ward off evil.

Two other items of clothing completed this outfit, and Saihung hated them both. He first pulled off his hat. It also was of mountain-lion skin, with flaps that covered the ears and two decorative lion's ears that stuck up at the crown. These protrusions were the one detail Saihung most disliked, and he took the opportunity to fling the cap away. He also removed the second item he hated, his mittens. These were, to his chagrin, impossible to dispose of. They had been securely sewn with silken cords to his coat sleeves. Still, with the hat gone and the mittens dangling, he finally felt free of encumbrance as he ran up the steps. His bobbing head, completely shaven except for a square patch of hair at the forehead, could be glimpsed as he darted among the other pilgrims.

The steps seemed endless. Saihung had stopped to rest at the side when his family's entourage caught up with him. The lead sedan chair, with its latticework windows, reduced his grandfather to a silhouetted presence. Evidently, however, his grandfather could see him perfectly well, for his deep voice soon came booming out from behind the grill.

"Saihung! Where is your hat?"

Saihung looked up innocently. "I must have left it at the inn, Grandfather."

There was a patient sigh from within the chair. One of the servants brought the hat out. Saihung grimaced at him and was preparing to kick the man's shins when his grandfather called sharply to him. With a pout, Saihung put on the hat.

Once again running ahead of the procession, however, Saihung grinned. He knew he was his grandfather's favorite, and he knew that his grandfather, though firm, was also indulgent and forgiving.

13

WHEN THE FAMILY reached the temple gates, the abbot personally came out to meet them. An old friend, he had prepared one of the temple's pavilions for the Guan family's living quarters during their stay.

Guan Jiuyin was the first to descend from his chair. Already in his mid-seventies, he was nevertheless impressively large and muscular. More than six feet in height, his size alone would have set him apart from others. The richness of his dress and his obvious charisma completed his unusual image. His fur-lined burgundy tunic and pants, black brocade vest, black cap with its piece of apple-green jade, snow-white beard, and braided hair fittingly accentuated the placid but alert expression of a warrior.

Ma Sixing, a year younger and only a few inches shorter than her husband, was the next to greet the abbot. In spite of bound feet, she walked unaided. Her slender figure was covered by expensive brocades. Over her own fur-lined tunic and trousers, she wore a long apron and a cowl, both of which were hand-embroidered in a palette of bright colors and metallic thread. Roses, chrysanthemums, fuchsias, peonies, and irises formed a complex and dazzling pattern. Long and thick, combed away from her face and pinned with jeweled ornaments, her white hair emphasized her high cheekbones and lunar complexion. Her large, almond-shaped eyes shone softly like a doe's, but this gentle appearance masked an inner ferocity.

Charm and grace had not abandoned her in her old age, and many of the other women who glimpsed her during the festival must have envied her. But unlike these conventional beauties, she always displayed a long rawhide whip coiled over her left shoulder. This was her personal weapon.

Saihung's aunt, Guan Meihong, was plainer and darker than her mother. In her fifties, she was dressed in a blue velvet suit. Although her cowl and apron were also embroidered, she had simpler tastes and usually dressed somberly. She had only recently unbound her feet, and walking, even with the help of a cane, was painful.

When Saihung was introduced to the abbot, he dutifully gave his greetings, bowing deeply. But after he saw that the adults had turned to conversation, he slipped through the temple gates.

The temple courtyard burst with a frenzy of activity and bright colors. Against a background of the temple's bronze-tiled roofs and worn red-brick walls, thousands of hand-painted silk lanterns, pinwheels, and tiny bells swung above stalls, stages, and crowds of people. Musicians, acrobats, puppeteers, magicians, and musclemen were performing throughout the courtyard. Priests, dressed in patched gray robes, strolled among the people selling incense, talismans, and votive objects. Some gave advice, while others predicted people's fortunes. But best of all, to Saihung, were the many food stands offering fresh, steaming vegetarian food and delightfully sweet candy.

Eating, for Saihung, was even more wonderful than getting into mischief, and he had a great appetite for both. Although he wanted to explore the entire festival, he could hardly refuse the temptation of fragrant food. He bought many different kinds of candies, some of which he ate on the spot, saving the others in his pockets. Only after he had found his favorite—miniature apples skewered and dipped in honey—did he go to the rest of the festival.

He squeezed his way through the dense forest of trousers and skirts to the center of the courtyard. On a high platform was a group of darkly dressed musicians performing from a large repertoire of operas, popular songs, and classical works. They had a good range of instruments, including the lute, harp, and violin, the flute and other reed instruments, and an arsenal of gongs, cymbals, and drums. Armed with this mighty array, the musicians were wholly unconcerned with the already roaring din of the festival. They played loudly and shrilly, finishing off each section of a song with wildly crashing cymbals and gongs.

Whenever another group was ready to perform on another stage, its figures would cry out loudly like carnival hawkers, promising great entertainment and unimaginable feats. Saihung was attracted by the announcement of a magician.

"Come! Come! Come! Uncles and aunts! Sisters and brothers! Elders and children! Come! Come! Come! See amazing things, magic to make the gods jealous, magic that will leave you incredulous! Come! Come!"

Saihung rushed over to see a tall, dark man with arching eyebrows and eyes that glared exaggeratedly. Dressed in red silk, he strolled forward haughtily to the stage edge and, without preliminaries, made silk scarves appear and disappear from his hands; materialized fans, bowls, and vases from behind a small bouquet of flowers; and shot flames from his sleeves. But he soon discarded the props disdainfully, as if to say that those were mere parlor tricks. He addressed the crowd.

"Elders, uncles, aunts, and children. I have spent fifty years as a magician. I've known immortals and priests, sorcerers and recluses. I have learned obscure secrets, but none so amazing as mesmerism."

In short order, he extracted a volunteer from the crowd—a fat man with a pockmarked face who openly voiced his skepticism. The magician focused his eyes on the man, who had folded his arms in utter determination. The crowd was silent. The man's arms slowly fell.

"You troublesome bumpkin!" cursed the magician. "You really should have been born as—a chicken!" The man immediately began flapping absurdly about, jumping and pecking. Everyone roared with laughter.

From another platform, loud cries announced another act.

"Hey! Hey! Come see the musclemen of Mongolia! Come see great feats of strength!"

Saihung ran to see several brutish men, grinning coarsely and grunting vulgarly. Poking at one another, they burst into laughter as they joked among themselves. The largest one came forward, dressed in heavy boots, white cotton pants, and a red fur-lined vest over his bare torso. He flexed his muscles, and his dark-skinned chest and arms inflated grotesquely.

He picked up an iron bar that no one in the audience could bend. He twisted it and straightened it. There was applause. The muscleman smiled in appreciation, showing broken yellow teeth. He held his hand up for silence. Walking over to a stack of bricks, he poised himself. With a guttural cry, his head came smashing down, splitting the entire stack.

Saihung finished the last of his candy apples before the applause had ended. He debated with himself about what to do next. There were the acrobats, the puppet shows of the Monkey King, and the *Romance of the Three Kingdoms*, and there was still plenty more to eat. He was still deliberating when someone slapped his head. He spun about angrily, but his expression immediately changed when he saw the cane.

"So here you are, running away again!" said his aunt.

"Oh, Auntie, did you see the musclemen?"

"Saihung! Don't try to get out of it. You know you are not supposed to run about alone! Anyone can see you're a wealthy boy, a child from an aristocratic family. There are always bandits ready to kidnap boys just like you."

Saihung looked unconvinced.

"You'd better be good, Saihung," warned his aunt. "Perhaps you aren't afraid of men with knives, but there are also demons!"

Saihung looked up immediately. He remembered tales his uncles back home had told him. His aunt shrewdly noticed his vulnerability.

"Yes, Saihung. They lurk around in shadows simply waiting for plump, naughty boys like you. When one comes along, they grab him, put him into a sack, and hang him upside down in their caves until they're ready to cook him in a big cauldron."

Saihung rushed immediately to her side, grateful that it was daytime and that there were few shadows. He took his aunt's hand. But he was not one to go docilely.

"Auntie," he said, looking up sadly. "I want to see the rest of the fair."

"There's time, Saihung. We'll be here many days."

"But I want to see it now."

"Your grandparents are wondering about you. We must go back, but you'll see more along the way."

"All right . . . but Auntie?"

"Yes?"

"I've not had anything to eat. Will you buy me something?"

A
Chance
Encounter

I N THE DAYS that followed, Saihung had time to explore the rest of the festival under his aunt's supervision. The temple became playground, theater, and restaurant for him and provided endless diversions. He met other children and became friends with them. Together, he and his new companions made up games, snacked, or looked at the many performances.

But the Taishan Festival was, after all, a religious event. Concurrent with all the festivities were daily rituals. The most important one was the Dance of the Big Dipper.

This ceremony was performed in stages over forty-nine days, in a specially consecrated courtyard. The purpose of the dance was to integrate humanity with the cosmos by calling to Earth the gods who lived in each of the Dipper's seven stars.

The stars were perfect worlds, and it was improbable that the gods would have voluntarily left their spheres to come to the human world. But the priests, by performing the dances and chanting invocations, could summon them, and the gods came to bestow blessings and provide divine aid. Only with the gods themselves present could the festival truly have spiritual power.

19

The priests fasted for seven days in order to purify themselves. They erected three poles and an altar before the main temple hall. Incense burners, red candles, flowers, oil lamps, and offerings were placed on the table, and a large circle inscribed around it. Within the circumference of this circle were marked seven spots in the shape of the Big Dipper.

On the day Saihung went to see the ceremony, he saw the abbot emerge from the temple in elaborate robes. Most of the priests who had been wandering in the festival dressed in worn, threadbare robes covered with patches, but the high priest was immaculately groomed. His long hair was put up beneath a black cloth hat, and he wore a robe embroidered with yin-yang symbols and hexagrams from the *I Ching*. "Windcatcher sleeves" were so long they hid his hands. He carried a date-wood plaque inscribed with his own personal incantation, and a willow-wood sword. Walking gracefully on black velvet shoes with four-inch-thick soles, he performed devotions at the altar before stepping into the sacred circle.

Surrounding the perimeter of the circle, the pilgrims pressed in closely to view the dance, one of martial movements and swordplay. The abbot stood in turn on each of the spots that represented the stars. Holding the plaque before his face because mortals were unworthy to gaze at the gods, he chanted long invocations and called each god by name.

Saihung thought the dance looked like great fun. He dashed into the sacred circle and ran behind the abbot to imitate his rhythm and twisting steps. A murmur went up among the assembled devotees.

"Saihung!" his horrified aunt cried. She stepped as discreetly as she could into the circle. Leaning unsteadily on her cane and swaying on her tiny feet, she quickly pulled him back into the crowd.

"How could you do such a thing?" she scolded. "It's sacrilege to step into the circle. Try to behave yourself. Really, you are so troublesome, sometimes I wish the bandits would take you!"

Ignoring the stares and whispered comments from the onlookers, she turned to watch the ceremony again, gripping Saihung's hand tightly.

"Auntie, I can't see."

His aunt did not reply. He tried again in a tiny voice, not daring to anger her more. She did not turn toward him, yet her grip reminded him that he was to stay with her. Saihung was momentarily grave. Was his aunt really mad this time? Had she actually meant for the bandits to take him away?

After a while, her grip relaxed, and she once more was pleasant and smiling. When she let go of him to put her cane in the hand that had been holding his, she reminded him not to stray. But no sooner had she again immersed herself in watching the dance than Saihung had quietly slipped off.

A strong fragrance of sandalwood incense attracted his attention. He had smelled it constantly during his stay at the temple, yet today it seemed to be especially strong. He decided to trace the scent to its source.

Saihung came to the main temple hall, a massive structure with a sparkling bronze-tiled roof nearly three stories above the courtyard. Saihung could see the multicolored eaves carved painstakingly with dragons, phoenixes, and other motifs. Golden calligraphy on dark wood plaques and red-lacquered pillars framed the entrance to a cool, dark interior. Clouds of incense drifted languidly toward him.

Saihung went up the steep stone steps, pausing just at the threshold. It was so dark inside. He suspected that this might be the ideal environment for demons who ate little boys. He looked around carefully. Saihung had no idea what demons might actually look like, but since he saw only a few pilgrims, he soon ventured in.

He found his way to the center of the hall. In a high, gilded altar was the life-sized figure of the Jade Emperor flanked on the left by the Queen Mother and on the right by the Princess of the Azure Clouds. The three sat behind a large, ornately carved teak-wood table set with all the necessary objects of worship. A large urn holding incense, candles, oil lamps, porcelain vases filled with flowers, vessels of rice, tea, wine, fruit, sweets, and five dishes of herbs representing black, red, yellow, green, and white—the colors of the five elements and the five directions—meant that all under heaven was being offered to the gods. It was in this spirit of reverence that each pilgrim worshiped, placing incense sticks in the large urn and kneeling down on prayer cushions before each figure.

Not one to be left out, Saihung walked up to the altar and knelt down.

He looked up directly at the Jade Emperor, who was dressed in ceremonial robes of yellow silk embroidered with imperial dragons. The headdress was a flat board set horizontally on a hat from which thirteen strings of beads hung in front and behind his head. The Jade Emperor was seated on a tiger skin and held the Imperial book of etiquette. His hands and face had been modeled perfectly of porcelain, and his hair and beard were real hair. The artistry was flawless, and as Saihung met the Jade Emperor's benevolent gaze, he completely forgot that the Emperor was a statue.

Saihung bowed low before moving to the Queen Mother. Her face had rosy cheeks and red lips, and her hair was pinned with precious jewelry. She presided over banquets where the gods ate the peaches of immortality. Each peach took three thousand years to ripen, and a single bite prolonged a life by ten thousand years.

Saihung then bowed to the Princess of the Azure Clouds. A daughter of the Jade Emperor, the Princess sat clothed in lustrous silken robes and wore a headpiece representing three birds with outstretched wings. She was a goddess who protected women and children, and women who desired children came to pray to her.

Whether they came with personal desires for healing, a good harvest, or a new child, all the worshipers had made their way up the steep face of Taishan to pray here. Only by presenting their

21

needs and offerings directly could the pilgrims be assured of a response. Although Saihung had no immediate request, he cheerfully completed his imitation prayers among the pious gathering.

He began to take his leave of the altar when he noticed another grouping of figures. The central one appeared to be a tall Taoist elder with a kindly, bearded face, silvery hair combed into a topknot held with a single pin, and a simple black robe over pristine white garments. Behind him were two figures who seemed to be young Taoist acolytes, dressed in gray robes, black hair also set up in topknots. Their beardless faces were calm and peaceful.

Saihung moved over to the group of figures, knelt down, and bowed so low that his forehead touched the ground.

He was startled by soft, amused laughter. Saihung straightened up instantly and looked around. He saw only the shadows of the pilgrims before the altar. The laughter came again. Saihung turned to face the figures. Reddening in embarrassment, he quickly jumped up to kick the old man for having tricked him. The two acolytes came forward to restrain him. Saihung struggled furiously and kicked them repeatedly.

The scene was unnoticed by the worshipers until there was a frantic scream from the doorway. Saihung's aunt, fearing that Saihung was being kidnapped, rushed across the temple hall. Renegade priests frequently descended from the mountains to kidnap children for ransom or slavery.

"Help! Police! Police!" she cried as she wrestled Saihung away. She turned angrily toward the priest and raised her cane to strike him.

The old priest only laughed merrily. He gently raised his long, flowing sleeve and passed it before her face. She instantly fell into a trance.

The priest smiled and turned to Saihung, who stared back in bewilderment. He was unsure whether the man was a festival magician, a demon, a bandit, or truly a priest. Saihung found himself as motionless as his aunt—yet he was still conscious. His mind went blank of its speculations. Time seemed to lose its ability to arbitrate events. A communication, a mystery, passed between the two of them, and for however long that moment lasted, nothing else existed. Saihung felt something deep, searing, and silent.

Saihung slowly became aware of the temple hall. In the flickering yellow candlelight, he saw the color return to his aunt's face. She snapped out of her trance as if there had been no intervening time. Seizing Saihung's hand, she ran from the temple.

When Saihung and his aunt arrived, Guan Jiuyin and Ma Sixing were sitting in one of the side pavilions drinking tea. Saihung's aunt readily recognized her mother's upright figure and her father's imposing posture, but she also saw others. She was alarmed. It was the same priest and his acolytes.

"Meihong," said Guan Jiuyin as his daughter came up uncertainly. "We've heard all about it. There's been a misunderstanding. This is my friend and spiritual teacher, the Grand Master of Huashan in Shaanxi Province." He turned to the priest. "*Da Shi* [Great Master], I apologize if she has offended you."

Meihung instantly knelt down, but the priest raised her upward again.

"It's only a trivial incident, after all." He laughed. He turned to Saihung and spent a long time looking at him. The look was thoughtful, and no one dared to interrupt.

"Jiuyin."

"Yes, *Da Shi*."

"This is your grandson."

"Yes, *Da Shi*."

"There is a blue star on his forehead. This marks him as someone special."

Saihung said nothing. He could understand neither the conversation nor his grandfather's unusual deference to the priest, but he was fascinated by the Grand Master's open smile and kind eyes.

The family waited quietly for the Grand Master to continue.

"His spirit did not need to return to this dusty world," said the Grand Master after many minutes. "He came willingly. But those who volunteer to return are given a task. If he is to fulfill his mission, he will need long training."

"*Da Shi*," said Guan Jiuyin, "would you undertake his training?"

The Grand Master looked up. His clear, bright eyes caught the brilliant afternoon sun and mirrored it perfectly. "Perhaps.

Perhaps," said the Grand Master slowly. "But I retired from the world years ago and am a renunciate. It would be difficult for me to take a student now, especially one who is so young. So very, very young."

SAIHUNG ROSE BEFORE dawn the next morning to accompany his grandparents to a scenic spot on Taishan, the Sun-Observing Peak. This vista point was famous for being the best place to watch the sunrise.

Shandong Province was overlayered with darkness and clouds. Only gradually were the crests of the turbulent, swirling clouds lit by pale light. Soon that light reddened and set streaks of clouds blazing as the intensely bright disk of the sun burned away the night.

Saihung thought over all the events of the festival. He thought of the pageantry, the ritual, the Grand Master. He turned over in his mind all the rich images of the Taishan Festival, and they became fused in the flame of the dawning sun.

three

The Guan
Family
Mansion

T HE GUAN FAMILY mansion, located in Shaanxi Province, was the center for a clan of sixty members. Situated at the base of a mountain and surrounded by two thousand family-owned acres of forest and farmland, the mansion combined artistic landscaping with classical Chinese architecture. Its conglomeration of many separate buildings was protected by a high wall that made it a virtual fortress.

This castle reflected the Guan family's martial class, but it was not a dull or grim environment. In addition to being a family of warriors, the Guan family also embraced the tastes of statesmen, scholars, and artists. The castle was a sanctuary, a retreat of quiet, tree-shaded gardens with trickling streams and blossoming flowers. It was a place of luxurious hand-crafted pavilions of wood and tile, bronze and gold, and of living quarters embellished by delicate latticework windows, their interiors rich with masterpiece furnishings and precious antiques.

More than four generations old and already imbued with history, the mansion complex was in an eccentric shape: It snaked around the base of the mountain in an undulating configuration. Aside from its strategic advantage of exposing only one wall with a single steel-studded gate to defend, the shape of the Guan family mansion reflected the planning of Taoist geomancy. The Guan patriarch who had established the estate had commissioned a Taoist priest to determine its best location and physical shape. No traditional Chinese ever built a home without a geomancer to calculate the complicated cross influences of location and orientation in relation to the cosmic forces of wind, water, earth, and destiny. Each builder endeavored to integrate his family harmoniously with the universe and, by following the flow of natural forces, to preserve his clan and make it prosperous. The Taoist who had laid the plans for the Guans had decreed that the mountainside was the most propitious location and the dragon form the ideal ground plan.

Thus it came about that the sixty family members and one hundred servants lived in a dragon-shaped citadel, with mountain cascades flowing through the estate and expansive roof lines arching to the sky. The head of the dragon—practically a separate fortress in itself—housed the current patriarch, Guan Jiuyin, and his family. The majority of the clan lived in the tail, with the servants, stables, classrooms, and martial training halls in the back and belly. The many rooftops had been constructed in such a way that an observer could see only a seemingly unbroken expanse of green tiles. These represented the dragon's scales. With their green color, unique arrangements, and camouflage of trees, the rooftops made the Guan family mansion almost undetectable from a long distance.

Guan Jiuyin had retreated to this enclosed and self-contained world when the Qing dynasty had fallen in 1911. Once minister of education under the Empress Dowager, a scholar, statesman, respected elder in five provinces, and a master martial artist, Guan Jiuyin now sought solitude. He had hoped to spend his time in the pursuit of refined arts, for he enjoyed painting, poetry, and the study of Taoism. But he was the patriarch of a rich, powerful, aristocratic clan, and he found no rest from the outside world. Even within the mansion, Guan Jiuyin could not escape China's turmoil.

The mansion was attacked periodically by a wide variety of bandits, rivals, and would-be assassins. China in the 1920s was still chaotic and lawless. Large groups of bandits regularly raided villages and the estates of the wealthy. That was one of the reasons that almost all the members of the Guan family and their servants were trained in martial skills—to fight off criminals who themselves were expert fighters. Guns were not yet in wide usage, and personal proficiency still determined survival.

Rivalry between powerful leaders and clans was also common then, and what could not be settled any other way was perpetrated by intrigue. Although Guan Jiuyin had retired, he had been an outspoken advocate during his public life, and many still harbored anger toward him. Whenever two clans came into competition over wealth, power, or prestige, assassination was a common means of gaining dominance.

The Guan family also had rivals in a more uncommon way. As a warrior family, they were members of China's diverse and deep martial underworld. This underworld had its own rules and social codes. Members of the underworld frequently challenged one another to determine who was superior in skill and therefore rank. The more prestigious one's defeated opponent was, the greater the victory. A clan patriarch such as Guan Jiuyin was a favorite target.

But Guan Jiuyin found China's social turmoil more disturbing than any physical assault. There were guards and servants who could fight, and he was still confident in his own skill. All those physical attacks were to him simple efforts at outright destruction, which could be fended off. But the domestic social decay, the encroachment of modernization, the imperialistic invasion by the West, the civil war between the Nationalists and Communists, the rampages of the warlords, and the shifting in the values of the young presented dilemmas too important to ignore, too complex for individual solution.

He felt even most of those problems could be closed out by the mansion walls except the last, and there the walls were breached by the clan's own children. Foremost among those whose values conflicted with Guan Jiuyin was his son and Sai-hung's father, Guan Wanhong.

Guan Wanhong was a man entirely different from his father's cultured character. Wanhong, a fierce-tempered, ambitious, and ruthless general in warlord and Nationalist armies, wanted only wealth, prestige, and political power. Although he had received a classical, almost scholarly, education, he was wholly uninterested in the traditional poetry and painting his father collected so devotedly. His one goal was to be a success in the modern world, and he had entered the military both because it suited his temperament and because he perceived it to be the swiftest possible means to rise to prominence.

Guan Jiuyin had frowned on Wanhong's decision to enter the military. By Chinese standards, to be a martial artist and to be a soldier were not necessarily comparable. A martial artist was not only concerned with the self-perfection of his physical skill, but was also concerned with justice, and, like a medieval European knight errant, championed the causes of the weak, poor, and defenseless. His only concern was to attain the highest possible level in the art, to fight for morality, to achieve the heroic. But a soldier did not act in this standard. He was concerned not with morality, but with slaughter. He did not seek opponents qualified to compete with him, but indiscriminately destroyed all who opposed him. He was not an individual fighting for his honorable principle, but a tool to be manipulated by powerful commanders. A soldier, to Guan Jiuyin, was a mercenary, a dupe, a hack, a butcher.

Father and son had argued for years, and the strain in their relationship became more and more pronounced. The two could scarcely meet without arguing. Before long, the strain was reflected even in the physical arrangement of the Guan family mansion: Guan Jiuyin exiled Wanhong and his family to separate houses and gardens away from his own and forbade Wanhong ever to wear a uniform or bring firearms into his presence. It was a continual struggle between old and new, between the classical and contemporary. For the moment, Wanhong was still subordinate. Guan Jiuyin was the clan patriarch who still held authority over him, and Wanhong always appeared before his father dressed in Chinese clothing. But the world that Wanhong represented progressively eroded, however slowly, the old Chinese ideals.

Saihung was caught in the conflict between the two men. Wanhong wanted to raise Saihung in his own image, and Saihung's mother, though an art and music teacher, agreed with her husband. Together they wanted Saihung to have a scholarly education but to succeed in the world by entering military life. They began to pressure Saihung, as early as the age of four, to further their ambitions. The pressure became too great; Saihung was a rebellious child, constantly condemned by his parents as too obstinate and difficult.

When Saihung was seven, he suffered a ferocious beating by his drunken father, and Guan Jiuyin took advantage of the opportunity. As patriarch, Guan Jiuyin took Saihung away from Wanhong and brought him to live in his own quarters. From that moment on, although he frequently returned to his father's pavilions to visit and play, Saihung stayed with his grandfather, and Guan Jiuyin assumed primary responsibility for Saihung's upbringing.

The
Mischievous
Student

"Saihung, isn't it time you were with your tutor?"

Saihung froze instantly where he stood behind the rock arrangement. He turned to look back at Flying Cloud, the twelve-year-old retained by the family as Saihung's companion and playmate. Flying Cloud returned his own look of surprise. How could the patriarch see them?

Seeing no other alternative, Saihung jumped out. His grandfather was not even looking in his direction but was strolling down the courtyard holding up a mynah bird in a bamboo cage. Guan Ji-uyin had two exquisitely black-feathered mynahs and, like many Chinese gentlemen, took them on morning strolls to give them fresh air and to let them learn the songs of wild birds. Unfortunately, the mynah's favorite words were "I'm hungry! I'm hungry!"

Guan Jiuyin paused momentarily, turning his face toward Saihung. Saihung saw the aquiline profile, the silvery queue, one hand holding the cage up high, the other loosely curled behind his back. Guan Jiuyin's hands were one of his trademarks. Strong, heavy, thick-fingered, they had nails shaped like talons. They were the hands of an eagle-claw martial artist.

"Saihung, go to your tutor," said Guan Jiuyin firmly.

"Yes, Grandfather."

"And, Flying Cloud . . . "

"Yes, Great Lord?"

"See that he goes now."

Saihung's tutor, a thin, elderly man, welcomed his pupil enthusiastically. The prospect of once again studying the classics he cherished so dearly excited him. Unfortunately, neither the lessons nor the tutor inspired Saihung. Old Tutor was simply not the kind of man Saihung looked up to. Compared to the other men of the clan—most of whom were warriors, not scholars—Old Tutor seemed to have transcended physicality. His already minimal body seemed to exist purely as a frame for layers of clothing and as a support for a head.

Old Tutor had a sallow, wrinkled face with such thin flesh that many details of his skull were clearly evident. His thinning gray queue and inadequate beard dangled lifelessly. His most energetic gesture was to open his eyes as wide as possible, all the while desperately trying to stabilize the wire-rimmed glasses that rocked on his bridgeless nose.

Monotonous regularity marked each morning. The program consistently began with recitation, followed by written exercises and calligraphy lessons. Whether spoken or written, the sole source of his teaching was the basic Confucian classic *The Four Books*. Although Saihung was young, the classics could not be compromised for the sake of children's understanding. He had to accommodate himself to the classics. Nevertheless, the tutor chose simpler passages, always emphasizing the Confucian virtues of self-cultivation, proper social and familial order, moral and ethical conduct, and, most important, filial piety.

31

These lessons, aside from their irksome dullness, were the object of Saihung's inward scorn. The Paragons of Filial Piety were children who seemed so lacking in independence that Saihung discounted them all. One lesson, for example, celebrated a small boy who noticed that though his parents had mosquito netting, they were still bitten every night. In order to prevent this, the boy preceded his parents into the bedroom, offering the mosquitoes his own body. He killed some, but the majority gorged themselves on his blood until they were too satiated to attack his parents. Through the boy's sacrifice, the parents were able to sleep well. Saihung, however, found the whole idea idiotic and therefore could not imagine himself as a filial son.

Compared to the lectures and recitations, Saihung found his writing sessions more interesting. Although the classics were once again the subject, to be copied repeatedly in order to assure retention, Saihung thought of writing more as drawing. Guiding the ink-soaked brush was a graphic adventure.

Patiently, Old Tutor taught him to hold his brush perpendicular, with the palm cupped so deeply that a walnut could fit in the space. The brush was first charged by drawing it through the ink and pointing the tip on the inkstone. Then the character was built up stroke by stroke, each mark following a set order, in a definite place and with proper proportion. Constancy of motion was critical. Brushing too quickly caused the bristles to drag dryly, while too slow a stroke made the delicate mulberry paper swell with blurs.

During his writing lessons, Saihung could depend on one familiar event. Old Tutor would often fall asleep. Today, as dependably as ever, Old Tutor sat gazing at the ceiling, his mind fixed on some obscure thought. Before long, scholarly musings gave way to slumber.

Saihung finished the last ideograph, a complicated structure of twenty-four strokes. Each time that the Old Tutor fell asleep, Saihung faced a dilemma of continuing his lessons or playing. It was a tribute to the Confucian system that most of the time he chose to finish his lessons and diplomatically awaken his tutor with a cough. But today he saw a tantalizing possibility. The more he contemplated it, the more appealing it grew. Possibility quickly changed to probability.

He carefully crept behind the unmoving figure. The scholar's queue dangled enticingly. Grasping it gently, Saihung knotted it to the chair.

He went to the door and looked outside. Flying Cloud was waiting patiently.

"Old Tutor! Old Tutor!" Saihung called from the doorway.

There was no response.

"He must really be visiting the sages," Saihung whispered to his companion. He turned back, and cupping his hands to his mouth, screamed out to his tutor once more.

The Old Tutor's tired eyes fluttered hesitantly. Seeing that his student's chair was empty, they blinked in puzzlement.

"Old Tutor!"

Saihung and Flying Cloud raced into the garden as they heard the tutor's outraged squawk.

"Young Lord," said Flying Cloud, after their giggling had stopped. "Aren't you afraid of punishment? He's sure to tell the Matriarch."

Saihung grinned naughtily as he reached into his pocket for some candy. "As long as I stay near Grandfather, she won't hit me."

A FTERNOONS WERE DEVOTED to playing and exploring the fascinations of the mansion. In quick order, the two boys had played games of tag, teased the maids, played hide-and-seek in the clan chapel—coming dangerously close to knocking over both the porcelain statue of Guan Gong, the God of War, and the prayer tablets of ancestors—fed Saihung's pet panda cub, and looked at Ma Sixing's black horse with the white mane. Laughing and out of breath, they found themselves sitting on the stone steps of Ma Sixing's training hall.

"What are they doing in there?" asked Saihung.

"The matriarch is training the women."

"Let's take a look. Maybe we can pick up some techniques."

Flying Cloud tried to resist. It was his duty to keep Saihung out of trouble. Mustering as lofty a Confucian expression as he could, he said with dignity, "It is not allowed, Young Lord."

Saihung scrutinized his companion. He imagined Flying Cloud as a dried-up old scholar with glasses and beard.

33

"The matriarch permits no visiting," intoned Flying Cloud somberly. "Remember propriety, Young Lord."

Saihung laughed. "Yes, but what if the matriarch didn't know?"

Flying Cloud's expression changed from Confucian severity to boyish shock. "Young Lord!"

Saihung smiled. He had cracked part of the scholarly facade. But he could still imagine a wispy beard on Flying Cloud.

"We'll climb up on the roof," said Saihung mischievously.

"Young Lord!"

There goes the beard, thought Saihung with delight. Now, he's just a boy again.

Since the courtyard doors were locked and there was frosted glass behind the latticework window, the only way to sneak a peek was to climb up and remove some of the unmortared roof tiles. Saihung began climbing a nearby tree, and Flying Cloud, caught in a conflict between his better judgment and his duty to follow Saihung everywhere, climbed with him. Stepping carefully across the roof of a lower gallery, they climbed onto the main roof. The tiles were smooth and set at a steep angle, but by clinging to the cornerline of the rooftop they inched on to the flat ridgepole. Flying Cloud was trembling. Saihung was oblivious to the height.

They crawled to the center and, lying on their stomachs, removed some of the tiling. Ma Sixing was in clear view, supervising a group of sparring women.

Ma Sixing, the daughter of a Qing dynasty prime minister, had studied martial arts from a Buddhist nun on Emieshan in Sichuan Province. Throughout Chinese history, monks and nuns living on isolated mountaintops had needed self-defense against bandits and animals and, adding metaphysical knowledge to boxing forms, had developed sophisticated fighting techniques. They added long periods of practice time to that legacy, passed it on within their sects and, on rare occasions, to secular pupils. Ma Sixing had lived in the nun's temple, mastering not only freehand fighting but *qinna* (seizing and bone locking), *qinggong* (the ability to lighten the body at will for jumping and acrobatics), and weapons as well.

Her art had been developed by women for women. Taking into account the vulnerabilities and limited strengths of women, the nuns had devised unique forms of training internal energy. They evolved a sophisticated internal alchemy rooted in female chemistry. Trained in practices forbidden ever to be seen by men, a woman could fearlessly face any attacker with ferocious strength and skill.

Ma Sixing's weapons had a feminine character, but they were nevertheless formidable. Chief among these was her whip, made of twenty-three sections of braided rawhide. Each section was capped with a steel sphere and chain-linked to the next section. Another weapon was the sash that bound her waist. It was interwoven with steel threading and had a row of steel balls dangling at each end. The sash was versatile, always available, and could be used for strangling or whipping. Finally, throwing darts were disguised as her hair ornaments, and short, slim daggers were concealed in her sleeves.

Saihung recognized most of the students as maids. On a few occasions, he remembered hearing how the women servants had killed intruders in the night by quietly strangling them with steel-threaded sashes. Now, he could see the full range of their training methods, from shadowboxing and sparring to striking sandbags and wooden dummies.

In the center of the hall were 108 pyramids of delicate porcelain rice bowls. Each pyramid was made of five bowls, four placed upside down in a square shape on the floor and a fifth overturned bowl on top. The 108 stacks were arranged one step apart and formed a plum-blossom pattern.

Two women were fighting with their feet on the pyramids. By stepping only on the tiny bowls, they strengthened their legs, perfected their balance, and trained in *qinggong* as they stepped or jumped from stack to stack. All the while they were striking and kicking, aiming especially for delicate pressure points. So sure was their footing that they neither displaced nor broke the fragile pyramids.

In spite of their expertise, the women still made mistakes. When this happened, Ma Sixing, who sat attentively in a chair at the head of the hall, displayed her own ability with *qinggong*.

Wielding a split bamboo stick, she leapt out of her chair, covering over twenty feet with gliding jumps, to mete out her punishment.

After some time of practice, the women were dismissed. Saihung looked eagerly down, expecting to see his grandmother's own practice. But Ma Sixing went into another room and closed the door behind her. Her personal practice was a secret from everyone.

THAT EVENING, Saihung sat quietly in the shadows of his grandfather's pavilion. Twilight had shimmered for only a moment before it had plunged into deep indigo, and the Milky Way was a fine spray around the waxing moon. The air had cooled, and a faint breeze set orange maple leaves dancing over the dark, rippling pond.

On a tiny island, framed by lotus leaves, stood a small gazebo. It had a peaked tile roof, red pillars, and patterned cutout windows on each side. The glow of light from the main buildings barely defined its contours, but the interior of the gazebo was lit by a solitary candle.

In its flickering light, Saihung saw his grandmother seated before her Chinese harp. She had released her uncut hair, and it formed a snowy mantle down her back. Her silken gown, embroidered with tortoises and autumn leaves against a wisteria-colored background, echoed her surroundings. Sitting completely still, she relaxed, abandoning daily responsibilities, letting moments slip luxuriously by. Then her fingers, pale as sculpted ivory, selected a string.

She felt each string against her fingertips and noticed the subtle gradations of their diameters. She plucked the first tone. It vibrated gently. Soon the courtyard reverberated with her song. Some staccato passages pierced like dagger thrusts, others spread out wide and low over the pond, and occasionally a single ending note trembled like a sob.

Guan Jiuyin sat inside the pavilion, reading a slim volume of poetry by Su Dongpo. The rhythm of the harp accorded naturally with the meter of the poetry. He was at peace. No matter what happened during the day, the cool evenings afforded him solitude. Sometimes he composed poetry with Ma Sixing. At other times he practiced painting, calligraphy, martial arts, or read. But whatever the activity, he treasured these intimate moments, sharing only with his wife and Saihung the renewing pulse of life.

"Grandfather?"

Guan Jiuyin looked at Saihung, who was sitting beside him. Saihung turned from the window. "Tell me a story, Grandfather."

"What story would you like to hear?"

Saihung looked at his grandfather's hands, thought of the times he had seen his grandfather practicing his self-created spear style, the Blood Spear, and promptly replied, "I'd like to hear more about Bai Mei."

Guan Jiuyin assented with a laugh and carefully laid his book down.

"Now listen carefully, Saihung. The last time we talked, I had just begun telling you about Bai Mei—the White Eyebrow Priest. He was a great Taoist, so accomplished in internal alchemy that neither punches nor weapons damaged any part of his body. He also created his own martial style—unique because it was patterned neither on a philosophical idea nor on imitating animals: It was a form based on human movements.

"Bai Mei was a true renunciate, but the world pursued him. No matter where he went, society chased him. Two separate groups sought him out because of his martial abilities, the rulers of the Qing dynasty and the rebels who sought to overthrow them. They all realized that anyone who had Bai Mei on their side and mastered his art would have a distinct advantage. Each side came to force him to join them or else to kill him.

"Bai Mei was not interested in either side and with pride and confidence finally responded to the threats by attacking the Forbidden City itself. Leading seventy-two of his disciples, he stormed into the palace. But it was a disaster. The forewarned Imperial troops ambushed and trapped them.

"The Emperor came out and mocked them. But he was shrewd: He would spare them, if they joined him. There was no choice. Bai Mei became the Emperor's personal guard.

"The Emperor was not the least bit afraid of being assassinated. He himself was a great martial artist, and he played one man against another. The Emperor had men even greater than

Bai Mei in his court. Mysterious men. Strange men. Men from faraway lands like Tibet and Persia.

"Meanwhile, revolutionaries trying to overthrow the empire had taken refuge in the Shaolin Temple. Living as monks and training in Shaolin-style martial arts, they continued to plan revolt. They were dedicated, expert fighters, and the Emperor was determined to destroy them.

38

"He sent Bai Mei and the royal troops to Shaolin. The temple was burned and almost everyone was killed, including the abbot, who died in a duel with Bai Mei.

"Two of those who escaped, a Crane Master and a Monkey Master, trained for ten years and then sought out Bai Mei. They were bent on vengeance. During their training, they had learned that Bai Mei's invulnerability had to have one weak point, a 'gate' that would permit entry to his human armor. But the 'gate' location varied from practitioner to practitioner, and in the ensuing fight, they couldn't find it.

"They attacked him together. They kicked his groin, but Bai Mei had succeeded in drawing his vital organs into his body. They struck his eyes; his eyelids were like steel. All the while, Bai Mei dealt one deadly counterblow after another. The two Shaolin masters were severely injured and bleeding.

"In one last desperate attempt, the Monkey Master boosted the Crane fighter into a high jump, and the Crane Master delivered a crushing blow to the crown of Bai Mei's head. That was the point. Bai Mei's armor was lost, and it became a matched struggle among the three men.

"Bai Mei was still strong enough to fight them off and escape, but he died several days later. The two monks were also critically injured. Bai Mei had ruined their bodies, and they lay bedridden for ten years before dying."

Saihung listened intently until the conclusion of the story. Laughing with delight, he told his grandfather, "I want to be a martial hero too!"

Guan Jiuyin looked patiently at him.

"There is more to life than that, Saihung. You mustn't simply decide to become a fighter or soldier. The true hero starts as a cultivated person. You must learn the 'Way.'

"Fame and fortune are predestined. Of what use is a guileful heart? Rather, constantly seek the truth, maintain your discipline, and preserve your dignity.

"Cultivate the 'Way.' Don't swim against the current. Only by swimming with it can you avoid disaster. For the bitter truth of life is this: Each person is at the mercy of the tide. Sometimes one wants to go east, but one is swept to the west. Sometimes one wants to go north, but one is carried to the south. There is no choice. Finding this truth is the Way. The Way is 'Tao.'

"Tao is the flow of the universe. Tao is the Mysterious. Tao is balance. But balance can be lost; the fragile equilibrium can be destroyed by evil. Evil must sometimes be met head-on. Evil must be destroyed, and those allied with Tao must then fight. If you learn to live with Tao and someday use your skills to fight evil, then perhaps you can be called a hero."

Guan Jiuyin patted Saihung fondly and picked up a bamboo flute. Ma Sixing's last note faded away into the darkness. She soundlessly left the gazebo; her gown of autumn colors was absorbed by the darkness like winter swallowing fall. Guan Jiuyin walked to the pool's edge, his silver-haired figure like a snow-laden tree.

He raised the flute to his lips, and his song rose in the air like a pell-mell flight of swallows. Gradually, his tempo fluttered down, his notes descended into a lower register, hovering over the water in an almost inaudible vibration. The pond before him had been a mirror of the dark heavens, but now its perfect surface was broken in a trembling response. Ripples went steadily to the far banks in overlapping circles as fish came swimming to Guan Jiuyin. Soon they were dancing before him, lifting their heads from the water. There were flashes of silver, orange, white, and black as the carp moved to every note in a hypnotic dance.

Journey
with Two
Acolytes

ARLY THE NEXT morning, Guan Jiuyin summoned Saihung to the library. A servant ushered him into the large room, whispering that his grandfather would be there in a moment. Saihung walked into the quiet of the room almost reverently; he had seldom been in it.

The library contained some of Guan Jiuyin's most treasured possessions. Superbly crafted bookcases, each one a different shape from the next, lined the walls. Some were simply rectangular, with staggered shelves, while others had been made so that the contours and arrangement of the shelves formed a gigantic ideograph. The eccentric rosewood shelves contained unusual objects: precious books and scrolls, celadon bowls, Tang dynasty horses, and jade sculptures that had taken decades to carve.

Throughout the room, more spectacular objects rested on individual polished redwood burl stands. Among them were porcelain figurines of gods and saints, and several hand-painted vases, more than five feet in height. Paintings of famous mountains, portraits, and scrolls with exquisite calligraphy were hung on the walls, part of a vast collection changed seasonally. Saihung particularly admired one painting of strange and grotesque mountains.

Every object in the room represented the achievement of a master, immortal through his craft. Many of the works were centuries old, carefully preserved by connoisseurs of the esoteric. Altogether, the volumes of ancient knowledge, the jades, the porcelains, and the paintings dominated the room with their eternal beauty and seemed to insulate it from the coarse and vulgar world.

There was the whisper of a door opening, and Guan Jiuyin came in. He sat down at his desk of ornately carved rosewood, inlaid mother-of-pearl, and pink Italian marble, and motioned to his servants. Two young men were escorted into the library.

The two were dressed like the Taoist acolytes Saihung had seen during the Taishan Festival. They wore long-sleeved gray robes over black pants and white leggings, and their straw sandals, well made but cut by the rocky roads, were a startling contrast to the rich carpet beneath their feet. Their faces were clear and serene beneath black coarsely woven hats and neat topknots.

Guan Jiuyin introduced each of them. The first was severe in expression and lean-muscled. His name was Mist Through a Grove. His fellow acolyte was larger, more densely muscled, but had a ready smile. Guan Jiuyin introduced him as Sound of Clear Water. Saihung greeted each one with a formal bow.

"I am sending you away for a while with these two young men," Guan Jiuyin said to Saihung. "You're going to meet your maternal grandfather. He will oversee your education for a while. You will meet new people and learn new skills."

Saihung was overjoyed. To him it meant two new playmates, more adventure, no tutoring, and no scoldings.

The next day, the three of them left the Guan family mansion. They walked, since horses were a rare luxury, and the two acolytes, amiable and lenient, treated him with great care. Saihung tried to extract as much playing and candy eating as possible, and he got piggyback rides as well.

Two eighteen-year-old acolytes and a nine-year-old boy together on the roads were an unusual sight, especially with Saihung carrying his bundle and a rattan rattle. But no one stopped to bother them. The acolytes' robes, topknots, and staffs were plain symbols of their position, and people respected them, still remembering the Imperial days when interference with a Taoist was a capital offense. The two advanced fearlessly as they passed the many strangers, soldiers, and travelers on the roads.

During their journey, Saihung soon identified the essential qualities of each acolyte. Mist Through a Grove was reserved, quiet, and serious. He had an abstract quality and the distant air of one who knew a great secret. A superb musician, master of most of the Chinese instruments, he carried a flute with him that he played at each day's resting place. Even-tempered and humble, he was courteous to all whom they met.

Sound of Clear Water was a skilled carpenter and had a craftsman's pragmatic outlook. Where his counterpart was more cerebral, he was fiercely and physically aggressive, earthy, and energetic. Both acolytes were renunciates and uninterested in society, but where Mist Through a Grove held himself aloof, Sound of Clear Water was vocally intolerant when other travelers occasionally or inadvertently hindered their way. When a particularly obnoxious fellow slowed the boarding of a ferry by arguing over the fare, Sound of Clear Water argued violently with him and forced him aside.

Mist Through a Grove remained silent during this outburst. Although his temperament was different, he recognized that his brother's aggressiveness was also Taoism. The two were paired, inseparable, sworn to stand by each other, and Mist Through a Grove implicitly agreed with Sound of Clear Water's view. Perfection was all that was worth achieving, and those seeking it found the insensitive and lazy offensive.

They stayed during the nights in country inns, and all three shared the large sleeping platforms. Nights were getting colder. Saihung slept between the two acolytes, beneath layers of cotton quilting on clay platforms with wood-burning chambers. The acolytes placed him thus to comfort him, so far away from home. Saihung took advantage of the situation, snuggling up to one and then the other. But one night, Mist Through a Grove noticed Saihung sitting up, looking into the room.

"What's wrong, Saihung?"

Saihung said nothing. He was uncertain about explaining his fear. But the shadows that silhouetted on the thin paper windows, the strange scratching sound against the wall, indicated a demon or possibly an ogre. His fear quickly escalated. After all, the two acolytes were still young. Perhaps a demon was coming to eat them all!

"Is that—is that a demon?" Saihung asked in a terrified whisper.

"Where?" asked Mist Through a Grove.

Saihung pointed nervously.

Sound of Clear Water also sat up.

"Hey! How can anyone sleep with you two whispering?" He looked in the direction of Saihung's finger and jumped.

"Oh no! A demon!" cried Sound of Clear Water.

Saihung hid behind both of them.

"Good thing *Da Shi* gave us a talisman to ward off evil," shrieked Sound of Clear Water. "But it only works for two!"

Terrified, Saihung clutched his tiger-tooth talisman.

"Can you see it?" he asked.

"Of course I can!" boomed back Sound of Clear Water. "Can't you? There! He's coming through the window. He's got red hair, green skin, big warts, sharp teeth, and he's drooling. He's got a big burlap bag."

"A bag?"

"Yes, you know, the kind they put little boys in? Now, Brother and I here are too sinewy. I think he wants a plump little rich kid."

Saihung screamed.

Mist Through a Grove stood up and pulled Saihung out of bed. Saihung resisted frantically as the acolyte dragged him to the shadow.

"Do you see a demon?" he asked softly.

"No," Saihung conceded. "But Brother can!"

"Let me tell you something, Saihung. Only the dying or very ill see demons. You aren't either one." He pushed the window

43

open. "Look outside. Don't you see that these tree branches make moving shadows and scrape against the wall?"

Saihung looked up at him. "You mean there are no demons?"

Mist Through a Grove smiled reassuringly. Saihung had found the truth himself.

Saihung ran back to the sleeping platform, where Sound of Clear Water was laughing, and jumped furiously on top of him. "You lied! You lied!" he shouted as he ineffectually hit the acolyte. Sound of Clear Water only laughed all the more as he lay back and let Saihung kick and punch him.

The tenth morning of their journey was cloudy and overcast. Autumn had deepened into intense cold. The trees bordering Shaanxi's grain fields were a dazzling display of reds, oranges, and yellows—as if their branches were fragments of a crystallized and shattered spectrum. Saihung pulled his jacket tightly against the stiff wind and took a look into the distance. On the horizon was the misty profile of the Huashan mountain range.

The mountains rose with a towering suddenness that accentuated the flatness of the surrounding lowlands. They were lofty, proud, rugged mountains, with cliffs so close to perpendicular that few people ventured up their heights. Its unearthly grandeur was the perfect Taoist setting.

But Saihung's childish impression of Huashan was that of a giant's forbidding citadel. He was frightened and begged to go home.

"Brothers, this isn't fun anymore," he said when they stopped for a rest. "Let's go back now and find another game to play."

The acolytes looked at each other. Sound of Clear Water went to Saihung's bag and took out Saihung's rattle.

"Here, Little Brother, why not have some fun and see what's up there?" he said.

"I want to go home," said Saihung, turning his back to the acolyte.

"How about candy apples?" asked Mist Through a Grove. "They say the best ones are made on the mountain."

"No. No, it's no fun anymore."

The two acolytes looked in exasperation at the balking boy. Sound of Clear Water sighed in frustration.

"Ah, Saihung," said Mist Through a Grove. "Didn't we tell you the secret?"

The acolyte laid a friendly hand on Saihung's shoulder. He was shrewd; Saihung's curiosity was immediately piqued.

"What secret?"

Sound of Clear Water understood instantly.

"Shh! Don't tell him! We promised *Da Shi!*"

"Tell me! Tell me!"

"No! Don't tell him!"

Mist Through a Grove hushed his brother. "No," he said seriously, "we should tell him."

"Yes! Yes! Tell me!"

"Saihung, we wanted it to be a surprise. Now we'll have to tell you: Not only your maternal grandfather but your grandfather, Guan Jiuyin, are waiting for you up there."

"Really?"

"Yes. Now come, we have to reach an inn by tonight. Tomorrow we begin climbing the mountain. Even that will take two days."

"All right," said Saihung, cheerful again. He turned to Sound of Clear Water. "Brother, will you give me a ride?"

"Me?" returned Sound of Clear Water. "Certainly not. You're nearly sixty pounds. My back's almost broken from all the other times."

"I don't like you anymore!" Saihung pouted. "I'll ask Older Brother."

"Don't look now, but Older Brother is down the road already." Sound of Clear Water laughed.

Saihung sat down obstinately. "I'm not walking."

"Suit yourself." The acolyte shrugged as he took up his bag and staff and walked away.

"I'm not moving!" screamed Saihung.

Sound of Clear Water quickly caught up with his brother. The two had barely gone a hundred paces when the trio was complete again.

Entering
Another
World

T HEY REACHED THE foot of Huashan the
next day. Sheer cliff walls soared into the
sky, and vertical faces of granite seemed to offer no opening for
travelers. There was only a single trail that led into the mountains.

It was a stiff, four-hour climb through two mountain passes
and down a long valley to reach the Qingkeping Terrace, a beautiful pine forest where several mountain streams converged.
They stayed the night in a small temple to refresh themselves.
Other Taoist priests and acolytes were also guests, and the two
acolytes chatted amiably with them.

The setting of the temple was breathtaking in its beauty. The
rest of Huashan stood like heavenly ramparts beyond silhouettes

of gnarled and ancient pines. The sound of waterfalls was a constant calming music, and the cool, pure air was invigorating. Nature reigned supreme here; no human violation was evident. The mountains stood in their original purity.

The next day the three travelers started on their climb of the first of Huashan's five main peaks, the North Peak. This high spire of granite served as the sentry peak, with the other four set far behind. It was the only access to the whole of Huashan, and the climb was arduous. Two stones with carved calligraphy alluded to the danger of the climb with the words "Change Your Mind" and "Safety Is to Turn Back." The acolytes led Saihung past that point to another rock called the Recollection Stone, where the advice changed to "Think of One's Parents" and "Advance Forward Courageously."

They scaled the North Peak in three main sections by way of a narrow path only two feet wide. Long segments of the trail were actually stairs and rock ladders cut into the cliffside, with iron chains provided for assistance. Climbing the steps of the Thousand-Foot Precipice, traversing the Hundred-Foot Gorge, and finally inching up the Heaven's Furrow took many grueling hours before the three reached the summit.

The North Peak was a blade of rock thrust straight up from the mountains below. Its clean sides presented only narrow crevices where shrubs and pines rooted sparsely. A rising spine with an apex barely wide enough to stand on, there was no plateau at its summit, only a path of eroded steps leading through two stone gates to a small temple built astride the knife-edge ridge.

Foundations extended down each side into the slope. The temple was barely twenty feet in width. Its facade was made of brick and stucco with a sloped terra-cotta roof supported by two plain red pillars. The temple, accommodating to its uneven foundation, was composed of a succession of tiny buildings, perched in a straight line like saddles on the mountain.

The three walked in single file to the temple. Turning his head from side to side was enough for Saihung to see both sides of the mountain plunge swiftly away. As they came to the front portico of the temple, Saihung saw the foundations of uneven handmade bricks and was not at all assured of the building's stability.

A cool breeze caressed them as they paused at the doorway. The sun was just beginning to set. In the far distance Saihung could see the Shaanxi basin, checkered with farmland stretching to the horizon. Through distant clouds surging like the backs of stampeding animals, the silver ribbon of the Yellow River was a twisting blur. The sun became a bright red glow, and the entire panorama was lit by its warm light. Huashan turned golden. The world was far away and it seemed as if they had attained the first level of heaven itself.

The *Da Shi*—Grand Master of Huashan—met them inside the temple. All three immediately knelt down and bowed low. Saihung was reminded of having mistaken the Grand Master for a statue, but now the Grand Master seemed very much alive. The Grand Master raised them and smiled in greeting.

The Grand Master was the patriarch of all the other abbots, priests, and ascetics of Huashan. Slender and tall, he moved gracefully and lightly. His arching brows were like wisps of snow, his beard like a cascade. His face was only slightly wrinkled around his brow, and his eyes were always serene and half-lidded as if concealing an inner light. A scar cut across the right side of his mouth, suggesting his fighting past. The Grand Master looked ancient, yet his energetic aura was readily apparent. Like the mountain, he seemed as if he had been there from primordial time.

The two acolytes shut the heavy temple doors. In the darkness of the temple interior, with three strange men, on a faraway mountaintop, Saihung grew apprehensive. He looked at the two acolytes, but they remained silent. He turned to the Grand Master, who was also quiet. The Grand Master had just returned from a month-long retreat of complete solitude and silence and did not talk easily. Breath was life's force not to be wasted. Instead, he sat watchfully.

"Where is Grandfather?" Saihung demanded.

"He's not here," said Sound of Clear Water.

"You tricked me again!" Saihung shouted. "I'll never forgive you!" As he burst out loudly, he was inwardly surprised. The two acolytes had laughed at his tantrums before, but they now stood with serious expressions.

48

"Take me home! Take me home!" Saihung exploded. In a fury, he kicked over a chair, chipping it. Sound of Clear Water, maker of the temple furniture, looked visibly pained. Saihung noticed this and continued to knock over as much as possible. The acolytes rushed crazily around, saving furniture and porcelain from his rampage. Saihung was screaming, crying, and hitting them all the while.

The Grand Master calmly left the room, leaving the two acolytes to cope with him.

49

Saihung's tantrum lasted over an hour until he had cried himself hoarse. He whimpered in a corner, completely spent. The journey, the climb, the high altitude, and his own outburst had worn him out.

He lay crumpled like a whipped animal, too weary to fight any longer. The Grand Master returned and stood over him. Reaching out, he touched his right index finger to Saihung's forehead, and Saihung's mind went blank.

The Grand Master spoke for the first time.

"You are in another world now. From this day on, your life will change completely. You shall become a vehicle to receive. You have entered Taoism."

The
Grand
Mountains

Huashan—THE GRAND Mountains—was an isolated religious and educational community. The Taoists researched and preserved special knowledge, educated coming generations, and pursued reclusive lives of mysticism and meditation.

Among the five major peaks were individual temples and enclaves with their own masters, abbots, priests, and practitioners. Although they all placed themselves under the leadership of the Grand Master, each was autonomous. Considerable variation existed over the aspect of Taoism each emphasized: Some stressed the scriptures, sorcery, or martial arts, and some, like the sect Saihung entered, stressed hygiene, internal alchemy, and asceticism. But there were still certain basic principles shared by all the Taoists, and there was much dialogue and interchange.

This rich diversity made Huashan an ideal educational institution. At a time and place where education was the privilege of a few, it functioned like a university, and boys from the age of nine were accepted as students. Some were candidates for the priesthood, but the majority were sent for a conventional parochial education. The hundreds of boys living in the temples learned all the academic subjects from scholar priests expert in their fields.

The number of students entering Taoism as monks was considerably smaller. In order to pursue some aspect of Taoism as a specialty, one had to serve and study with a master who functioned as a spiritual father. He not only passed on his own knowledge, but carefully sent his disciples to learn from other masters as well. A master naturally limited himself to only a few disciples; through them would be transmitted the full Taoist tradition.

Aside from teaching, most advanced practitioners on Huashan pursued their own research and practices. Taoism was limitless, a lifelong pursuit of higher and higher knowledge. Some Taoists devoted themselves to herbalism, medicine, poetry, calligraphy, or music. Others were spiritual mediums, oracles, diviners. Still others pursued internal alchemy in the quest for immortality. And there were also men on Huashan who were solely hermits and recluses. Genuine renunciates, some of whom were already considered immortal, they rarely associated with anyone.

Huashan's temples were all united under the philosophy of renunciation and asceticism. Other sects of Taoism were known for other specialties; the single-minded pursuit of spiritual knowledge and self-perfection characterized Huashan.

The task of initiating Saihung into this rich Taoist tradition, and changing him from a spoiled and mischievous child to a complete and spiritual man, did not promise to be easy. But the Grand Master was wise. The very reason that Saihung would be difficult was also the reason for Saihung's training to begin now: He was only a boy. A boy had to be given the chance to grow freely, but he also had to be cultivated. The tree that was to grow tall had to be nurtured from a seedling. The Grand Master directed the acolytes to raise Saihung gently.

The Grand Master knew that Saihung would gradually accept life on the mountain because the mountain, so pure and natural, so imbued with the aura of Taoists who had reached their realization there, would influence him strongly. Little needed to be forced. Saihung would absorb naturally. The first full day after Saihung's arrival on Huashan was already the beginning of his education, as the acolytes took him climbing on the peaks.

The North Peak's ridge trail was the way to the other four peaks. It was simply a narrow ledge cut into a nearly perpendicular cliff. In some places, overhanging rock made it all the more difficult to pass. The drop, veiled as it was by mist, was still dizzying to contemplate, and Saihung clung tightly to Sound of Clear Water's hand.

The twisted, swaybacked ridge dipped down steeply to the foot of the Middle Peak. Saihung passed groves of dense pines with tiny temples hidden within them. At the foot of the Middle Peak, they began another ascent on the Dragon Ridge.

That straight, acutely angled ridge had steps cut up its spine. Although it made a hard climb, the Taoists had established the trail in this difficult way because it followed their concepts of geomancy. Trails that followed the lines of the mountain, rather than violating it by switchbacks, placed the climber in harmony with the mountain. The Dragon Ridge Trail faithfully followed the ridge line to the summit, but mystic harmony or not, it was dangerous; the steps were eroded and there were no railings.

It was a two-hour hike from the North Peak to the spot where the Dragon Ridge reached the Gold Lock Pass. During that time they passed both masters and disciples. Some greeted them, others strolled in contemplation, and some were busy carrying provisions to their temples. At the Gold Lock Pass, the trail connected with a circular one that led in a clockwise direction to the Middle, East, South, and West peaks and then back to the Pass.

They went from the Middle Peak, with its single massive temple and pine forests, to the East Peak. This high point was also known as the Morning Sun Cliff, because the sunrises seen from its summit were legendary.

The East Peak Monastery was plain stucco and tile and was composed of groups of four-square buildings set in quadrangles.

There were also smaller huts of wood and clay. As they passed a hut set behind an iron bell topped with a stone cup that collected dew, Saihung saw a willow-thin man sunning himself on the terrace. He wore gray robes and a black hat with a jade rectangle sewn to its front. The acolytes told Saihung that he was a sorcerer. There were other men in front of individual shrines who sat silently and seemed as powerful. Even the acolytes did not know them all, but said that they must all be of the same stature to be on the East Peak.

Farther down the trail they stopped at a high place that overlooked a terrace on an outcropping peak, the Chessboard Pavilion. So high and isolated was that peak that only chasms formed the background behind it. In the tenth century, the first Emperor of the Song dynasty wanted Huashan for its strategic value. But the Taoists wanted to keep Huashan sacred. Chen Tuan the Immortal challenged the Emperor to a game of chess, the winner of the game to take Huashan. On that isolated pinnacle, the Emperor lost game after game. Finally, Chen Tuan even predicted the Emperor's every move, and the Emperor finally conceded. The Chessboard Pavilion was thus named; Huashan remained Taoist.

The trio came to a precipice, and there they faced the most treacherous portion of the trail, the Cliff Path. The path was over a series of wooden planks set atop iron supports drilled into the sheer cliff. There was not even a railing to bar a straight fall of over three thousand feet—only iron chains pegged to the cliff on which to clutch. Sound of Clear Water strapped Saihung to his back, and they ventured out. The boards flexed and creaked. The wind rushing along the rock face blew Saihung's sweat cold. He closed his eyes tightly. He was completely suspended in midair, and he clung in fright to the acolyte.

The South Peak was the highest peak of Huashan, a massive piece of rock with sides so sheer that no trees could grow on them, and even heavy snow found very few resting places. China stretched away in all directions from this crowning point, and the Huang, Luo, and Wei rivers were slender strands on the edge of the sky. The peak boasted a spring-fed granite basin that remained unfrozen even in winter. The acolytes also showed Saihung the South Peak Temple, where he would live.

The final peak was the West Peak. A rugged path led up the ridge to a monastery perched impossibly on the side of the mountain. This again was geomancy. The Taoists revered the "dragon's pulse," the meridians of the earth. These energy pathways had certain "power spots," like the acupuncture points of the human body. The Taoists built their temples and shrines over those spots, even though the locations frequently coincided with the very crest. The buildings were always of natural materials, primarily brick, stone, and wood, devoid of ornamentation, and were in such harmony with the surrounding terrain that they were invisible even from a short distance. The West Peak Temple was a typical example. Its halls were set on a sixty-degree slope and were hidden by rocks and trees.

The West Peak, curiously cleft, also had its share of legends, and the most romantic gave it its alternate name, the Lotus Lamp Peak. The legend recounted the love affair between one of the Jade Emperor's seven daughters and a handsome cowherd. Goddess and mortal lived together until she was missed by her father. When the Jade Emperor found that she had not only given herself to a cowherd but had also borne him a child, he imprisoned her beneath the West Peak. Her son, Chen Xiang, grew up and found a Taoist sorcerer to teach him. When his pupil was ready, the Taoist gave Chen Xiang a divine ax, which he used to fight off the demon guard and cleave the West Peak. But the reunion was interrupted by the guard's return with all of heaven's armies. The son fought with the ax, and the mother used magic and a lotus lamp as a weapon to repulse the soldiers. The Jade Emperor, touched by Chen Xiang's devotion, forgave them, and the West Peak with its cleft was known thereafter as the Lotus Lamp Peak.

Views and stories were Saihung's first impression of Huashan. He saw it as a mountain of precipitous height. A place where vistas were alternately obscured by clouds or revealed in distant peaks and valleys. A place of legend and mythology, unusual and powerful inhabitants, and tiny temples nestled on narrow ledges. Huashan was the mysterious and the sacred. Even Saihung, indignant as he was for being forced to live there, was awestruck by its beauty, fascinated by the strange men, and affected by the pervading air of reverence.

The acolytes took Saihung to the Grand Master's temple, the South Peak Shrine of the Jade Fertility Well, a large compound of buildings and courtyards enclosed within a brick and stucco wall. The architecture was at once traditionally Chinese and yet somewhat asymmetrical in its ground plan. The acolytes explained to Saihung that the rooms and buildings had been arranged to echo the patterns of the constellations.

The main hall of the temple was the Grand Master's own residence. Before it was a large bronze incense burner, symbol of Huashan. A flight of steps led to the main entrance. Two bronze cranes stood at the base of the stone steps, two lanterns at the head. The columns and lintels that supported the temple were of carved wood, and plaques with calligraphy adorned the entrance. The two plaques that flanked the main doors urged, "Leave All Worldly Thoughts" and "Only Vegetarians May Enter."

The temple, like all those on Huashan, had a plain appearance. The stone was eroded, and the wood was weathered. But the halls of material poverty were rich in spiritual feeling. Fragrant streams of incense flowed throughout the corridors, the sounds of chanting could always be heard softly from unseen rooms, and windows framed lofty views of faraway mountains.

The temple was maintained by the monks themselves. Every menial task from cleaning and cooking to repairing the buildings was shared equally among them. Rank exempted no one save the Grand Master, and the practical upkeep of the temple also encouraged cooperation between all the monks.

In the following months, the two acolytes helped Saihung adjust to temple life. They slept on the same platform, and their mornings began even before the sun came up. Monastic life was a daily succession of religious and maintenance duties that began immediately on waking. Saihung's first task each morning was to open the paper windows so that the sunlight would dry the condensation in the high mountain room, which was cold all year round.

After washing, the three made their way in the dawning light to the main hall, where all the temple members gathered to pray and recite Taoist sutras before breakfast. The meals that followed were vegetarian and extremely frugal. Breakfast was only one bowl of rice porridge, a dish of pickled vegetables, and tea.

Saihung's mornings were devoted to receiving a conventional education, either from the acolytes or in classes at other temples. Beside reading, writing, history, and other subjects, he also learned acrobatics and calisthenics.

There was another sutra recital before lunch. Sutra recital was both for devotion and for training the breath. Recitation was in itself a type of *qigong*, and all the monks were serious about recitation—except Saihung. He found it difficult to keep still, and during each session he smiled, looked around, and mumbled cheerfully but uncomprehendingly along with the others.

Lunch consisted of noodles and vegetables and sometimes bread. All the meals were taken in utter silence; the monks were not even permitted to look at one another. The direction of one's concentration, even during meals, was to be constantly inward.

After lunch, Saihung performed his own maintenance duties while the two acolytes received personal instruction from the Grand Master. By prescribing these duties, the Grand Master sought to instill in Saihung responsibility and perseverance. But responsibility was not quick in coming. Irrepressible, thoroughly disinterested in the dull severity of monasticism, and much more interested in playing, Saihung's methods frequently led to unfortunate results.

Windows of delicate latticework and paper were kicked open gleefully. Sweeping was done with exaggerated swinging. Flowers were watered by the bucketful—from upper balconies. Airing out the accordion-folded sutras to prevent mildew gave Saihung the chance to hold one end and then fling the other across the courtyard; dozens of feet of holy scripture flew through the air to land haphazardly.

Retribution was always swift whenever Saihung became mischievous in his chores. Sometimes he was denied dinner. At other times, such as after his rough treatment of the scriptures, Sound of Clear Water spanked him. The acolyte dispensed justice dispassionately.

When it came to cultivating greenhouse vegetables, raising chickens and fish and gathering wood, Saihung was given no instruction and had to talk to other masters in order to solve any problems. It was the Grand Master's way of instilling initiative and a sense of the necessity of learning.

After evening recitation, and a dinner of vegetables, noodles, and steamed bread, there was time for more study, calisthenics, or personal affairs. It was time for bed around ten o'clock.

This schedule was carried on seven days a week, and Saihung slowly accepted Taoist monastic life. He even did his best to carry out his own self-created mission by cheering up the severe temple atmosphere with jokes, pranks, and affectionate songs. Many of the temple members did seem to enjoy his bright presence. In spite of his rebellious naughtiness, they liked Saihung's cheerful and unrestrained personality. Taoism was preparing to raise another disciple, but the disciple in exchange brought a little laughter to its hallowed halls.

57

Learning from the Natural World

N ATURE ITSELF PROVIDED many learning opportunities for Saihung, and the two acolytes took these occasions not only to explain the world to him but also to convey basic Taoist concepts. Saihung had great curiosity. In the temple and in walks around the mountains, he saw many things that aroused his inquisitiveness. The explanations the acolytes gave were designed both to satisfy his interest and to prepare him for asceticism.

As the three awoke one morning to the sonorous tones of the temple bell, Mist Through a Grove pointed to a cat who often slept with them. The temple had many cats to catch mice, and this brown-and-white one had adopted the three of them.

"The Taoists are great naturalists, Saihung. They study the animals in order to understand how they stay healthy and how they remain with the divine. All that we on the mountain do is simple and natural and no more out of the ordinary than what animals do. But what common people and Taoists perceive to be the activity of animals are often two different things."

The cat was asleep on the edge of the blue quilt, her tail and nose tucked under her folded paws. Mist Through a Grove continued his explanation:

"The early Taoists wanted to remain healthy and retard the aging process. They believed that people aged because their internal energy leaked out. In order to find a way to retain it in the body, they found inspiration in animals like our cat here. They concluded that an animal sealed its energy in by sleeping curled up, effectively closing off its anus and other passages where the energy might escape. This is how our cat sleeps.

"Now look at her abdomen, rising and falling so gently. The cat's breathing is natural and easy. The Taoists also found and confirmed that unhindered breathing filling the entire abdomen was beneficial."

The cat awoke when Mist Through a Grove nudged it. She opened her eyes and pricked up her ears attentively. Mist Through a Grove continued his lesson.

"She wakes instantly, not like humans who are lazy, drowsy, and stiff. See how she stretches. Even the cat knows calisthenics and uses them to maintain her system. The Taoists know that exercise is essential to good health.

"What if our cat gets sick? After all, she eats mice and rats, both very dirty animals. She supplements her diet with herbs and grass in order to clean her system.

"Finally, the cat is spiritual. She meditates. When she sits at the windowsill or in front of a mouse hole, she is unmoving and concentrates just like our masters. You've seen her waiting for a rat. Nothing distracts her. Her mind is only on one point. She can sit for almost an entire day at one hole until the rat comes out and she catches it. Yin and yang. Perfect stillness and concentration, perfect action and strength.

"Our cat does not need teachers. The cat teaches itself. It preserves energy, knows the art of breathing, heals itself, and is skilled in meditative concentration. Study the cat, Saihung. Everything you need to learn, she knows already."

That afternoon, the two acolytes took Saihung to a densely forested section of Huashan. They walked toward a high cliff where pines clung by twisted roots to its very brink. Beneath one lushly verdant pine was a large crane that stood motionless on one leg. Although it seemed aware of their presence, it did not stir. All the animals near Huashan recognized that the Taoists never harmed any of them, and the crane stood there confidently, dominatingly.

"Early Taoists wanted to learn each animal's secret," explained Sound of Clear Water, "and practice it themselves. In the beginning, they did not understand everything. Like you looking at the cat this morning, they only suspected certain things.

"Look at that bird. How vain it is! Birds are like that. Arrogant. Posey. But look at it again, Saihung. It's so big! How can it fly? How can it stand on one thin leg like that?

"It can only be *qi* that is responsible. Breath mixed with the bird's energy lightens its body enough to fly. Filling itself up with air, it can lift off or stand on one leg.

"But why is it standing on one leg? Because, like our cat, it is locking off the body to conserve its energy. Its head is tilted back in the head lock, and its eyes stare up at the psychic center in its forehead, its chest is made full, to lock its diaphragm, and one leg is tucked in to close the anus.

"You can see other animals using the body locks to conserve their energy. The dog sleeps curled up. The deer puts one hoof against its anus while sleeping. Observe, Saihung. All nature knows the secrets of longevity except foolish humanity."

As Saihung grew older, Sound of Clear Water would carry him no longer, and he had to climb Huashan's steep paths on his own. It was difficult, and he grew tired easily. The two acolytes used the deer and the tiger as lessons to help him further.

"Whether you are moving uphill or down, you find the way tiring, don't you?" asked Mist Through a Grove.

"You don't know how to move," said Sound of Clear Water.

"You've seen many deer," continued Mist Through a Grove. "When they run uphill, they almost seem to float up, and their hooves seem to barely touch down, because the deer know how to make their internal energy move upward.

"When a deer is running, all the energy is in its extremities—at the hooves, tail, and antlers. The deer is powerful. Through its use of body locks, it maintains its internal energy and circulates it outward. Since the deer sends all its energy upward, it can easily run uphill.

"There's a special way to move downhill, too," said Sound of Clear Water. "What's the worst thing about walking downhill? Isn't it that jarring feeling on your bones? The Taoists noticed this and looked to the tiger for inspiration. Nothing moves downhill like a tiger. He is unhurried, relaxed, loose. He slinks down the hill. His every step falls effortlessly into place. He is lithe and sleek, not like a person who stumbles and descends clumsily.

"The tiger is the symbol of strength in the bones and sinews. Coming down the hill, he uses relaxed strength and flexible joints and just eases down. He never jars his bones, because he is resilient. In all the animal kingdom, the tiger has some of the strongest bones—so strong that they too can be used as tonic medicine.

"So when descending, use the relaxed strength of the tiger to slow yourself, and keep the joints loose to protect your bones. When ascending, make your body light, using the rising energy of the deer to make your climb effortless."

There were lakes and streams in the mountains around Huashan, and the acolytes had taken Saihung on a short herb-gathering expedition when they stopped beside a lake for lunch. It was late spring, the lake was alive with dragonflies, birds, butterflies, frogs, and tortoises.

Saihung splashed water at the two acolytes, and they responded playfully by almost pushing him into the lake. Saihung, struggling to get away from their tickling, fell into the mud. There was much laughter as he glumly rinsed off his clothes and sat on a sunny rock waiting for them to dry.

As he waited, he broke off a long reed and poked at an old tortoise. The tortoise withdrew its head. Saihung tapped each foot until they too were withdrawn, and finally even the tail was inside. The tortoise waited for Saihung's attention to flag and then lumbered off to another rock. Saihung watched its steady gait.

"Look at that old fellow," whispered Sound of Clear Water. "Trying to be so dignified after a kid has poked him. But do you know what, Saihung? That tortoise will probably outlive you. The tortoise has great longevity because it never rushes. Our masters always walk leisurely because they know that rushing shortens one's life."

"How about the abbot of the North Peak Temple?" broke in Saihung irreverently. "His round head's so old and wrinkled that he looks like a turtle already!"

The two acolytes laughed.

"Yes, he does, doesn't he?" Sound of Clear Water giggled. "Let's nickname him Master Turtle."

After some more uproarious speculation about whether Master Turtle could rush even if his temple caught fire, Sound of Clear Water continued his lesson.

"Look at that other tortoise sunning himself. His head stretches way out, and he looks upward at his third eye. He's meditating. All his energy travels upward. And look at that old one sleeping. Everything's inside his shell. What's more obvious? He's practicing the three locks, and all his energy remains within his shell."

Saihung studied the two tortoises.

"But I don't want to be humpbacked like a tortoise," he complained. "And definitely not fat and ugly like those frogs over there!"

"Fat!" exclaimed Mist Through a Grove. "Oho! Those frogs aren't fat and ugly. In fact, they are creatures very much adored by Taoists!"

"Ugh!" said Saihung.

The two acolytes sat down beside Saihung. The afternoon was hot and clear. Taking off their sandals and leggings, they dangled their feet in the limpid water. Mist Through a Grove pointed to one enormous bullfrog with glistening green skin and a fine pattern of black spots like a spray of flung oil. The frog squatted in a massive lump, and its contrasting white throat inflated to an impossible bulge.

"The frog," explained Mist Through a Grove, "is a master of *qigong*. He is constantly exercising the three locks. Squatting locks the anus. Inflating his chest locks the diaphragm, and his eyes look constantly at his third eye, locking his head. With its mind on the divine and its body locked in its meditation posture, it practices *qigong* and permits no *qi* to escape. The frog's *qigong* is the best of all. He can jump unusual distances, and he can store tremendous amounts of *qi*."

Mist Through a Grove splashed through the water and, after several hilarious failures, caught a frog. He brought it back to Saihung and held it by its shoulders. The frog was pitifully thin and elongated.

"You see, Saihung," said Sound of Clear Water. "A frog isn't fat. It is its ability with *qigong* that makes it appear that way. We Taoists emulate the frog—so great at *qigong*, so stable in meditation."

S IMILAR LESSONS WERE repeated over and over until the concepts began to take hold. Soon, the acolytes moved on to a critical lesson. Saihung would be approaching adolescence, and the acolytes introduced him to the topics of sexuality and celibacy.

Saihung had seen animals mating in the spring and had demanded to know what they were doing. The acolytes explained the cycle of reproduction fully and openly and even showed him human sexual function through books and pictures. Mating was a natural event, and the Taoists never denied anything that was natural. But the acolytes pointed out that continence was also natural. After they had fully explained mating, they gave this lesson:

"Animals mate only during spring," Mist Through a Grove told Saihung. "In some species, male and female do not even intermingle a great deal. All the animals practice celibacy, and in so doing they preserve their life force."

"Look at the achievements of our masters," continued Sound of Clear Water. "If you want to preserve your health, attain longevity, and pierce life's mysteries, you must seal in the life force through the three locks, and practice *qigong* and meditation to retain and circulate the life force that is rooted in *jing*, or sexual essence."

They showed him more anatomical diagrams.

"The body has different centers, all in a line," said Mist Through a Grove. "Each one, from the bottom of the torso to the crown of the head, will provide certain powers to the practitioner. Energy is needed to open these centers. The highest point is the crown, and it is difficult to refine one's energy and raise it that high. In order to do this, *jing* reacts with breath and becomes *qi*. *Qi* is circulated and transformed into *spirit*. It is spirit energy that reaches the top.

"The animals, through the practices we showed you and with the use of celibacy, preserve their *jing* and remain in the spiritual. Should you engage in sex, you will deplete your *jing*. No *jing* means no *qi*. No *qi* means no spirituality."

The two acolytes took him to the monastery schools and showed him boys of varying ages so that Saihung would know in advance of body changes that would happen to him. They wanted him to have an easy transition into puberty and prepared him thoroughly. On festival days, they took him to the North Peak Temple, Huashan's only public temple. There, they drove home their point about celibacy by pointing out married men.

"Look how wrinkled that one is," said Sound of Clear Water. "He's probably no older than forty, but his face is wrinkled, his hair is gray and falling out. Why? No *jing*. He expends too much of it and does not have knowledge of the locks and upward circulation. He's stooped over, his breathing is shallow, and his body appears stiff and brittle. Compared to any Taoist here, he is unequal to any one of them even twice his age."

Saihung could see the differences. The Taoists did seem different from ordinary men, and he began to favor the way of the celibate ascetic even before his adolescence. He now knew only the pure Taoist world, where, free of contradicting temptations, the acolytes' teachings took hold. Saihung soon aspired to the spiritual heights achieved by the masters.

S AIHUNG WAS ELEVEN when he and the two acolytes discussed the cycles of life. It was a stunning summer's day, and the air, even at the summit of the West Peak, was warm and balmy. Saihung gazed out across the deep valley, following the cadence of mountain ridges to the horizon, and reveled in the sky's sleek blue canopy.

Mist Through a Grove gave him time to enjoy the view before he summed up all the informal nature lessons they had had until then.

"Everything is cyclical," he said. "The world follows the seasons. The seasons—spring, summer, fall, and winter—follow one another.

"The animals live in harmony with the seasons. In spring, they mate. In summer, they bear their young. In autumn, they nurture their young and prepare for winter. In winter, they either maintain stillness or migrate, but everything is aimed at survival. Rodents burrow. Turtles and bears hibernate. The weak die."

"Each year, you should also follow the seasons. Spring is the time for new growth, movement, exercise, and fresh activity. Summer is the time to release your vigor fully, to work on endeavors begun. Autumn is a time of harvest but also of preparation for winter. Winter is a time when nothing moves. Everything withdraws into the earth or dies. That is when you should withdraw into yourself and meditate.

"The course of your life will also follow the patterns of the seasons. Now you are in the spring of your life. You must go forward, bursting like the buds on the trees. You must act any way you feel. You're a child, and if you didn't act mischievous or playful, you wouldn't be normal. But as you grow older, remember that the spring is also the optimum time to plant the seeds of your future.

"In the summer of your life, be a strong, proud, and able youth. Cultivate yourself, make achievements, explore, leave nothing undone that should be started. Do everything, satisfy all the emotions, but do so with moderation and within the context of your philosophy. Whether you must sometimes be active or retreating, shining or veiled, good or even evil, you must come forth and do great things in the summer of your life.

"In autumn, you will reap what you have sown. Once you're in middle age, you will have set your life's course. The consequences of your earlier acts and decisions will begin to appear. How important it is to reach this stage with no regrets! This should be the time you begin to slow down, to teach others, collect your rewards, and make preparations for old age.

"Old age is winter. You become still. Your hair becomes ice and snow. You meditate, contemplate life's meaning, and prepare for death."

Sound of Clear Water picked up the theme. Saihung was receptive, and the acolyte spoke quietly and slowly.

"Many men are afraid of death because they are ignorant of what it is and when it will come. They think death is an ending. It isn't. It is a transformation. Life does not cease. It goes in cycles like the seasons.

"No one in your family has died yet, but you've seen death. You've seen fallen trees, withered wildflowers, corpses of animals in the snows. But have they all ceased to exist? Is death to be a simple fall into immobility and decay? Whether it is a person or animal, the fact is that death is only the casting off of a shell.

"What you are, what I am, what the animals are, is something intangible, indestructible, formless—a collection of ancestral memories mixed with traces of the past cosmos. We are spirits, and each individual spirit has existed from the very beginning and will continue hurtling through space, changing and evolving, into infinity.

"What you know to be animals were not always animals and will not always remain animals. They are only taking this shell during this lifetime. They are spirits who have come into this world to learn things that are important to them as individuals, and to achieve a divine purpose. But when they come to earth they need a shield, a shell, a body. The body is not the true individual. It is only a vessel. When it is time to go on to another reality, the bodies that have been the vessels are discarded, and the spirit goes on.

"You cannot wear two sets of clothing. You cannot stay in one building and simultaneously enter another. The shell that is your body must be used up. It will get worn, broken, destroyed. But the spirit is never destroyed, and there is no need to be frightened.

"Men are also afraid because they do not know when death will come. This is just one of the curses the gods have placed on humanity. As punishment for man's perversity and evil, the gods blocked the knowledge of death's approach.

"The animals know it, though. They know when death is approaching because they are in constant communion with the gods. But the gods no longer speak with men. In our sorrow and ignorance, our arrogance and vanity, we are the only creatures on earth who live out of communion with the higher levels. Only by living a pure life can we lift this curse from ourselves.

"So don't be afraid of death, Saihung. Rather, be prepared for its coming, know its approach, and seek the knowledge in this lifetime that will guide you to a higher reality in the next. Then, at the moment of death, you will cast off your body fearlessly and enter into the next cycle."

Immortals

EVEN AS SAIHUNG continued to learn from nature, he was fascinated and inspired by the Taoists of Huashan, men who embodied the art that Saihung was only beginning to acquire. Their Taoism was as individual as their personalities and inclinations. They had isolated themselves from the mundane world's illusions and pitfalls to perfect their art and seek higher knowledge. Neither wealth, fame, family, nor official position meant anything to them.

Some lived anonymously in mist-shrouded valleys. Others made great social contributions, but still essentially were of the same traditions, because their work was always the product of inward investigation. Huang Di, the Yellow Emperor, wrote the *Classic of Internal Medicine,* still used today. Shen Nong experimented on himself with thousands of herbs, his "stomach-with-a-window" being a metaphor for his meditative abilities. Fu Xi invented the Bagua diagram that was the basis of the *I Ching* and divination. Hua Tuo perfected the art of surgery and the Five Animals therapeutic exercises. Lao Tzu and Chuang Tzu wrote important works. All these men, whether they passed through this world mysteriously or left great traces, were men who shunned the world for the sake of their science and art.

Unique among the Taoist recluses were men who sought immortality through internal alchemy. These hermits, like the legendary Ge Hong (Ko Hung), withdrew from the world in their quest for alchemical mixtures of gold and cinnabar, mercury and lead, that would grant them immortality and ascension into heaven. Taoists on Huashan still engaged in that quest, but unlike many of their predecessors, they had abandoned poisonous metallics in favor of *qigong,* herbs, and meditation.

Some of the masters of Huashan were already addressed as "Immortal." These were highly regarded individuals, ageless in appearance. Their titles meant "realized persons," signifying that the masters had fulfilled, as a minimum requirement, the completion of internal alchemy for the sake of longevity, liberation from the cycle of transmigration, enlightened perception of the nature of life, astral travel, and the total memorization of the hundreds of volumes comprising the Taoist canon. So accomplished were the immortals that they were exempt even from the Grand Master's authority. He knew they were above him in their achievements.

S AIHUNG MET THE first of Huashan's immortals one afternoon when he had gone to find his master on an upper terrace of the temple. Saihung ran up happily to him.

"Gong-Gong! Gong-Gong!" he called, addressing his master as if he were a grandfather. "Here I am!"

The Grand Master turned and smiled, placing a hand on the little boy.

"Gong-Gong, I've got some new 'mouse songs' to whisper in your ear. Just like my uncles here, I learn from the animals too! Listen!"

The Grand Master bent down, and Saihung sang his song. His master laughed with pleasure.

"That's a very nice song, Saihung," said the Grand Master.

"I've got more!" said Saihung excitedly.

70

"Perhaps later," replied the Grand Master. "Right now, I need to go and meet someone."

"Is Uncle Yang, the Taiji Master, coming back?"

"No, Saihung. This is someone you've never met before."

Master and disciple walked for over an hour until they came to a tiny stucco cottage. It was plain, with only a few square windows and an old tile roof. It was summer, and every building on Huashan had its windows propped open to admit the warm sunlight. The windows of this one, however, were tightly shut. The door was slightly ajar and, after knocking, the two stepped inside.

The small interior was dark and quiet, and a flow of cool air blew on them as they entered. Still blind from the bright sun, Saihung's vision adjusted slowly. Set among a few modest furnishings, was a large coffin.

Saihung saw his master drop down to his hands and knees, and Saihung automatically followed. He was puzzled. He had only seen his master bow during ceremonies. But there was no altar here, and his master couldn't be bowing to the coffin. Saihung completed his bow and looked up. There was a tall figure standing before them.

The figure remained standing and acknowledged their bow with a slight nod.

"Hey, you!" cried Saihung, "Why don't you bow too? Don't you know how important my master is?"

"Saihung!" said the Grand Master sharply. "Don't be rude. He is the master here, not I." He turned to the man. "Greetings to the Bat Immortal."

The Bat Immortal smiled slightly. He was tall, thin, and moved in an almost feminine fashion. His face was small, his beard and hair braided with ribbons, his skin unwrinkled, pale, and bloodless. Narrow eyes were sunken, the skin around them blackened, and they were almost closed all the time. But from the narrow slits of his eyes there seemed to shine an inner light, a hidden glow.

"I've come to ask a point about the scriptures," said the Grand Master.

The Bat Immortal acknowledged the request by stepping forward. He avoided the sunlight coming through the door, and his steps were soundless. He stopped in front of Saihung. His eyelids lifted slightly; the glow from his eyes intensified.

"Is this the boy you mentioned?" he asked in a thin and hollow voice.

"Yes," replied the Grand Master.

The Bat Immortal turned back to Saihung. Saihung looked up, and he had the uncanny feeling that the Bat Immortal gazed directly through his eyelids. Saihung's attention lapsed, and when he again became aware, the Bat Immortal had turned away.

The Grand Master sent Saihung outside to wait.

When he emerged an hour later, the Grand Master walked directly away. Saihung followed him. After a half hour of silence, the Grand Master told him about the Bat Immortal.

"The Bat Immortal practices extreme yin training. That's why he has taken the name he has and sleeps in a coffin, avoids sunlight, stays only in cold places, and never eats anything hot. He cultivates the Great Yin, and this is the source of his spirituality."

"He seems like a wicked man, with those dark circles and ghostly movements," said Saihung.

"Don't think he is evil," cautioned his master. "He frightens you because he is an unfamiliar person. Naturally. He is immortal, and immortals are rarely glimpsed."

"But, Gong-Gong, I don't understand why you bow to him. Everyone always bows to you."

"Saihung, there are always greater and greater masters, and we must always show our respect."

"Why is he great?"

"The Bat Immortal is one of the premier authorities on the scriptures. He can elucidate any point of the entire Taoist canon. In fact, he has all the scriptures committed to his infallible memory."

Saihung thought of the hundreds of scriptures. He did not like that kind of Taoism.

"But, Gong-Gong, don't you know the scriptures already?"

"My understanding is very far below the Bat Immortal's. Taoists must learn continually. When they need instruction, they must seek it out.

"Let me explain. When we assigned you to care for the greenhouse, you knew nothing about it. You had to use your own initiative and ask many people for instructions, didn't you?"

Saihung agreed.

"In the same way, even the masters must work to dispel their own ignorance. We are all seekers of knowledge, and we must all perfect our knowledge. On Huashan, there is always an answer. If we need guidance, we ask an old master. If he does not know, there is always an older one still."

SAIHUNG WAS LATER introduced to two immortals who not only had two different ways of seeking their knowledge but also shared it with other masters on Huashan through public discourses. The two lived in another small shrine and were paired together. They were known as the Yin-Yang Immortals.

On the occasion of one of their lectures, the Grand Master brought Saihung into their shrine. The two sat upon a platform side by side. One was small and dark and sat with closed eyes. The other was large and light-skinned and gazed out at the gathering audience with a piercing look.

"What an odd pair!" Saihung exclaimed.

"You turtle's egg!" scolded his master as he slapped the back of Saihung's head. "Be more respectful!"

Saihung rubbed his head and took a second look at the youthful-looking Yin-Yang Immortals.

Yin did not look at all Chinese. He was very dark-skinned. His black hair, though coiled in a topknot, was wavy. His uncut beard was curly. He sat cross-legged in loose gray robes; a white cord from his left shoulder encircled his body diagonally. Saihung had never seen such a person before.

Yang, on the other hand, was tall, robust, and ruddy-skinned. He had thick, straight, coiled jet-black hair and a massive shaven face. His gray robes were almost bursting because of the muscles of his deep chest. On closer scrutiny, Saihung remembered having seen the Yang Immortal striding Huashan's cliff paths with sure and mighty steps.

The Grand Master explained to Saihung that the Yin-Yang Immortals were peerless in expounding the constantly shifting course of the Tao, but that they experienced it in two different modes. The Yin Immortal was the master of inner Taoism. He explored innermost consciousness through days of deep meditation and returned to report his discoveries. The Yang Immortal experienced outer Taoism. In his walks around the mountain, he observed all the phenomena and changes in the stars, nature, and weather, giving detailed lectures on things to come. Both of them combined their specialties with a solid foundation in the scriptures. Coupled together, the Yin-Yang Immortals elucidated and continued to explore further the entire range of Taoist knowledge.

The seminar was about to begin, and the Grand Master, after introducing Saihung to the Yin-Yang Immortals, sent Saihung away with the two acolytes. "One should never rush in entering Taoism," said the Grand Master as he sent them away. "One must proceed step by step, never advancing to the next stage until one is ready. One need not fret. If one discharges one's tasks and proceeds with one's training perseveringly, then the transitions are virtually automatic. You are young, Saihung. For now, it is enough for you to know that such people as the Yin-Yang Immortals exist."

Walks could be long and tiring for Saihung, for his master was tall, energetic, and long-legged, but the excursions always led to something educational. The Grand Master also pointed out things in nature, but they were quite different from those shown by the acolytes. Sometimes he would point to a trail and say, "There's a mystical palace at the end of that trail. Venture down and you will never return." At another time, he paused by another trail and gestured toward the mist-shrouded ravine, saying, "This is the road to immortality."

And once he pointed out a lone Taoist with a lump on his head. "That is Master Sun the Immortal, who has seen many dynasties come and go."

73

Returning from one of their hikes, the Grand Master led Saihung to the Pool of Heaven on the South Peak, where a man squatted with his head tilted upward. This was perhaps the oddest immortal Saihung had seen. He was big and stout, and with his hands before him and head tilted back, he reminded Saihung of a frog. But the two acolytes had said that the frogs were meditating. This person seemed only to be sleeping. It did not seem to bother the Grand Master that the immortal appeared to be asleep. The Grand Master stood respectfully aside, hands folded, clearly prepared to wait. Saihung went closer to the massive figure. After several minutes he could contain himself no longer and shouted, "Hey! Hey, you! My master's here to see you! Why don't you wake up, you silly thing!"

"Saihung! You are disgraceful!" reprimanded his master.

"But, Gong-Gong! He's dead asleep and just squats there like a big lump. He's like a big toad, really. What an enormous toad he is! Hey, Gong-Gong, how will we cook such a large toad?"

"Saihung! Watch that saucy mouth of yours!"

Saihung crept right up to the figure. What a big head! It was wider at the jaws, and the face was flat. The nose was fat and bulbous, the thin-lipped mouth seemed almost to go from ear to ear, and the eyes were tightly shut. He was beardless, and his balding head looked all the more bullet-shaped.

"Why, he's quite asleep," said Saihung to himself. "I wonder if he'll feel this."

Saihung rapped his knuckles on the person's forehead. There was no response. He was about to try again when his master slapped him smartly on the back of his head.

"Behave, you turtle's egg!" roared the Grand Master.

"He always hits the same spot!" groaned Saihung softly, rubbing his head. But it seemed to be all right to look, if not to touch, and Saihung bent down again to examine the figure.

He was just about nose-to-nose when he was alarmed by opening eyes looking directly at him. The rubbery face took on an annoyed expression. Saihung jumped back hastily.

"Gong-Gong! He's awake! He's got green eyes!"

The Grand Master silently dropped down to his knees, and Saihung followed.

"Greetings to the Frog Immortal," saluted the Grand Master solemnly.

The Frog Immortal reluctantly acknowledged them with a gruff clearing of his throat. He contorted his face in a grimace of irritation but soon seemed to fall back asleep. Long moments of silence followed.

"When a master has reached the stage he has," whispered the Grand Master to Saihung, "he has 'Immortal Spirit'—complete obliteration of the self and sensory awareness. He is in total union with the spiritual. The Frog Immortal has reached the highest stage of Taoism through the advanced practice of *qigong* and meditation. He is one with the void. He appears to be asleep because he is in a constant state of realization."

75

Presently, the Frog Immortal opened his eyes again. The Grand Master bowed and said, "Immortal, this is my disciple."

The Frog Immortal seemed to ruminate and then sprang away in a twenty-foot leap, landing in the same frog position. He paused awhile and sprang back, landing lightly and soundlessly right before a startled Saihung. He scrutinized Saihung closely, and grunted.

"Did you come all this way to see me?" he asked temperamentally.

"Yes, Immortal," replied Saihung hesitantly.

"Hmmmmph! You don't understand this."

"It does look odd."

"Odd!" roared the Frog Immortal indignantly. "Odd! This is my meditation! I can leap so high because my body is filled with *qi!* I can make it lighter than air. Then I meditate beside water, or even on a wooden disk floating on the water. Water is my element. It has electricity. The body has electricity. Outer electricity excites inner electricity. Do you understand?"

"Yes, Immortal."

"No, you don't!" shouted the Frog Immortal. Saihung looked back innocently. The immortal was agitated for a moment, but then seemed to relent a bit. "Well, kid, maybe I'll teach you a thing or two someday," he muttered; then he fell motionless again.

It wasn't long before Saihung thought he felt the influence of the Frog Immortal as well as the Yin-Yang and Bat immortals.

They appeared to him regularly in dreams, speaking things that Saihung could never recall. He felt that they somehow guided him. He questioned the two acolytes, but they didn't know. Saihung asked his master whether the immortals could really appear in his dreams, but the Grand Master only turned his back abruptly and walked silently away.

Turning
Point at
Twelve

Even though Saihung's relationship with his master had grown as close as that of grandchild to grandfather, the Grand Master remained an awesome figure of authority and wisdom. He was kind and patient, but he could also be stern and strict. The Grand Master, like all Chinese patriarchal figures, raised Saihung with an absolutely firm hand, directing each stage of growth with a consistent eye to developing all of his ward's potential. Just as he allowed no questioning of his authority, he allowed no questioning of his personal background. Because he was a Taoist master, his own activities and history were not to be discussed. The Grand Master said nothing about his birth, age, learning, travels, or even where he went when he disappeared, sometimes for months, without any advance notice.

The only thing Saihung thought could be certain was something his mysterious "Gong-Gong" told him: that he had been reared on Huashan. But Saihung was surprised when, in talking to an old monk, he found that the Grand Master had come from elsewhere.

The two were working in the temple kitchen, and Saihung was chattering about his master.

"Gong-Gong says he was raised from a little boy right here on the mountain and that he's already ninety!"

"Shhh!" hushed the old monk. "Don't let him know we're talking about him."

"But Gong-Gong's far away."

"No! No! He'll know! Don't you know by now? The masters here can know anything!"

He motioned Saihung to a deep corner of the kitchen, near the great sacks of rice and the lines of dried herbs and vegetables. He glanced nervously around before leaning down. "Don't ever tell your master I told you this, but he came from another place."

"He did? Are you sure?"

"*I* was one of the boys raised on Huashan, and look at me now: gray and thin. When your master came here, his hair was already white. I was just twenty then. Now, I've grown old, but your master's appearance remains the same.

"They said that *Da Shi* has been all over China, even to India, Tibet, and Persia. No one knows all his exploits, either as a Taoist or a martial artist, but he must have wandered for decades."

The old monk was whispering so softly by now that his face was nearly pressed to Saihung's. "Remember," he said in low tones, "don't ever reveal that you learned this from me. Your master will be truly angry with me if he finds out."

ON SAIHUNG'S TWELFTH birthday, the Grand Master called him to his chambers. Three years on Huashan had changed him greatly. Saihung was less stubborn and talkative, and trusted his master's wisdom. The acolytes had encouraged his eagerness to learn, saying that he must seize every opportunity the Grand Master presented. Saihung went to see his master expectantly, and the Grand Master spoke freely. It was time for Saihung to make a decisive commitment to his training.

"One's life proceeds in stages according to the twelve celestial stems," said the Grand Master. "People believe a person is shaped by upbringing or by society. In actuality, it is the seasons, the constellations, and fate that shape a person. Life is preordained by heaven; your destiny is to live out your span on this earth, but you must still make choices. Throughout your life, you will be confronted with decisions and challenges. This is how heaven will test you. How will you respond?

79

"A person is like a cartwheel; each stage of his life is like a spoke. When the wheel hits a rock, it will either stop, shatter, or roll right over. But the rock cannot be avoided. So it is for you: No matter what happens, you must meet life head-on.

"You must proceed from one stage to another, just as the spokes of the cartwheel revolve. At each stage, you will experience new knowledge. It is only by using this knowledge and following uninterruptedly the turning of your life that you will fulfill your destiny.

"Emotion is natural. But it is right to go on, to change, to avoid stagnation. Feel no regrets. It is like the rattle you brought to this mountain. At one time, you would not part with it. Now, it has been left behind. Another day you will forsake other things of your boyhood, but neither you nor those things need be sad, for it is right that you grow.

"At the edge of each new phase, you will feel aspiration, curiosity, inquisitiveness. You will want knowledge, and acquiring some will only make you thirst for more. That is right. You are a human being, and it is human nature to seek knowledge. Therefore, pursue knowledge without hesitation or compromise.

"Remember, however, that the time to go from stage to stage is precise, just as the spokes of the cartwheel are precisely set. If you try to skip a stage, or rush to the next, your personality will warp. If you do not move on to the next stage, you will be retarded. The stages of growth can neither be avoided nor held fast. You must proceed through them. This requires guidance. Only a master can guide you, only he can perceive the stages, only he can shape you into the perfection you will need to succeed.

"Now, Saihung, you are a boy no longer. It is time for you to enter fully into your youth."

Saihung was sent to a dormitory in the South Peak monastery school, where he lived with many other students. Learning both from the exposure to other boys and the instruction of numerous teachers and often attending specialized classes in other temples, he simultaneously maintained his duties at the South Peak Temple. Chopping wood, drawing well water, sewing and washing clothes, attending his master, and cooking were just some of his tasks. Saihung no longer played his pranks, nor did he resent his assignments. Everyone contributed to the temple, and he saw that only by cooperation could those in the monastery overcome the poverty and harshness of mountain life.

When Saihung brought dinner to the Grand Master one evening, the Grand Master expressed his approval and explained his view.

"You once refused to do your chores. At other times, you misbehaved. We denied you dinner. Now, you understand. If you do not work, you do not eat. Work and reward go hand in hand.

"Everyone in the temple must work, and humility is always fostered. One who works, one who serves, cannot set himself above others. This is important, because with humility you will never become arrogant. No matter how high you climb on the path of knowledge, you will not misuse your powers but instead will help others. Through work and humility, you will know compassion.

"You will also be able to survive. If you descend the mountain and meet hardship, you must know how to provide for yourself. You will be able to take a job and have marketable skills. Work is an integral part of your training. It teaches you cooperation, humility, compassion, and skill. So work hard, Saihung, work."

Work was drudgery, but studying the classics and morality was far worse drudgery to Saihung. He attended school with a student body of five hundred boys, all strictly controlled by the priests. Classes were signaled by the temple bell. At that time, each boy had to enter the classroom promptly, bow to a statue of

Kong Ming, the Taoist strategist of the Three Kingdoms period, and take his place in the rows of students who sat cross-legged on the floor. The boys were forbidden to talk to one another or to look in any direction except straight ahead. The teachers sat on platforms and demanded absolute attention throughout tedious hours of reading, writing, history, geography, mathematics, classics, and morality.

Both the classics and Taoist scriptures were central to the curriculum. The Confucian texts were the *Four Books* and the *Five Classics,* which Saihung read, transcribed, recited, and discussed every day. Taoist books such as the *Jade Classic of the Yellow Chamber* laid out the theoretical foundations of Taoism. Far from believing in any conflict between Confucianism and Taoism, the priests demanded perfect mastery of both schools' classics, stressing morality as a consistent theme.

"Don't lie," lectured the ethics teacher. "Why shouldn't you lie? The words of the sages are: 'Wrong no one, lest others wrong you.' Take this as an example:

"Imagine that you are walking on Huashan during the night. You have a lantern, but a lost boy you meet doesn't have one. Out of mischief, you send him down the wrong path. The boy falls off a cliff and dies because you lied.

"Don't think evil things, and you will not do wrong. People do bad things because they give in to temptation. But if we don't even think of temptation, if we do not even allow ourselves to consider it, we will not have anything to which to yield."

That's easy to say, thought Saihung. If the temptation was there, it was there. He thought about the times back home when he tied his tutor's queue to the chair. . . .

"Saihung!" growled the teacher, "Are you thinking bad thoughts again?"

THE TEACHING OF ethics extended beyond the classroom. The temple was a closed, twenty-four-hours-a-day system. There were literally no temptations permitted. No outside influences contradicted the priests, and they, with their perfect realization and psychic abilities, worked single-mindedly on raising them properly. They generally tried to teach by example and persuasion, but severely punished liars, cheaters, thieves, and bullies by beating and, occasionally, expulsion.

Such strict supervision and rigorous academic standards brought up most of the students to be intelligent, precocious boys. Saihung, with his latent talents, blossomed quickly. In response, the Grand Master returned to the theme of humility in his talks with Saihung.

82

"The more you learn, the more you must use your knowledge for others," said the Grand Master. "The wiser you become, the more unselfish you must also become. As your experience deepens, and with it your humility, you will realize unfathomable depths of knowledge. You can never become arrogant and narrow-minded if you perceive how small your abilities are when contrasted to those of the greatest.

"Remember to use your knowledge in the service of others, but expect nothing in return. Never seek a reward for your labors, for that is a sin.

"You were not always yourself and will not always remain yourself—'You' who are this physical body. You come into this world with problems and dilemmas to be solved either as punishment for transgressions in past lives or because you were unsatisfied in past lives. That is why you must meet all your problems and hindrances in this lifetime. Burn all your attachments to worldly goals, purge desire, satisfy the thirst for knowledge. Never refuse any experience; overcome all your obstacles. You can then leave this world fulfilled and go to a higher plane.

"This is called purging one's *ming huan*, one's karma, and to achieve this, you must live in vital health as long as you need. You must ensure not only that you live to purge all consequences of your past lives, but also that you create no new difficulties. The proper method is to purify one's body, enter into the spiritual, and return to the void. The beginning is to train the body."

"*Da Shi*," Saihung said, addressing his master by title now that he was a full-fledged student, "why do you stay? Haven't you achieved your liberation?"

"Some spiritual people leave the earth the moment they are free of their past acts. But the Taoists believe in preserving their knowledge and helping the next generation to succeed as well."

"So you could leave?"

"Maybe not," joked the Grand Master, his eyes crinkling with humor. "Maybe you're my curse."

Saihung reddened. "Really, *Da Shi?*"

The Grand Master laughed and patted Saihung comfortingly. "I teach you because it is my duty. I have a task in this lifetime. I'll depart only after it is accomplished."

"Do I have a task?"

"Of course you do."

"What is it?"

The Grand Master roared in amusement. "You're rushing. That is not for you to know yet. If you want to find out, you have to start at the beginning."

Wudangshan

IN HIS EARLY teens, Saihung began traveling extensively to learn from martial
artists. "These men have something unique," said his master.
"They are master fighters, but they are dying without anyone
else reaching their stature. You must study with them now. Boxing will improve both your spirituality and fighting."

The influence of both the Grand Master and Guan Jiuyin,
men famous and highly respected in the martial world, enabled
Saihung to study with many great teachers. Martial arts excited
him passionately, almost becoming more important than Taoism,
and he often entered provincial tournaments. His boxing teachers guided him strictly, and he learned both in private and in

classes. An important place to which he journeyed was Wudang-shan, the center of Taoist martial arts in China.

Wudangshan was the sacred mountain of the Pole Star Sect of Taoism; internal alchemy combined with martial arts was its specialty. For centuries, great boxers and spiritual men had emerged from its seventy-two peaks, including Zhang Sanfeng, the four-teenth-century creator of Taijiquan, and Bai Mei, the nemesis of Shaolin. Wudang styles were supremely effective, and Saihung learned from four main teachers.

The four masters were not priests but fighters who had taken refuge on Wudangshan. Seeking spiritual redemption, they came to the mountain to learn Taoism in repentance for their years of killing in the martial world. In return for the mercy of the Taoist priests, the Iron Luohan, Crane, Monkey, and Snake masters taught their arts to the students.

The Iron Luohan Master was in his forties, and was a competent and accomplished boxer. A member of the Shaolin tradition, he had enormous muscles and an idealistic temperament. Wanting very much to identify with the image of a heroic knight, he was a paragon of chivalry and always championed the causes of the weak. Many martial artists looked down on him, for they were interested only in the practice of killing, and were not idealistic, weak, or compassionate. But the Iron Luohan Master maintained his principles and sought to teach his students heroic aspiration as well as his boxing system.

The Iron Luohan system—consisting of several styles: Spring Leg style, Long Fist, Iron Wire Fist, and the Eighteen Luohan Fist—emphasized muscular strength. The master taught that all the body should be as tough and hard as iron and that the most critical part of training was the forearms. Unless the forearms or "bridge hands" were toughened, blocks were ineffective, grappling was weak, and punches lacked power. Training the bridge hands was excruciating. With his arms straight at the sides, Saihung lay on two chairs that supported only his head and heels as progressively heavier sandbags were added to his wrists. Then he had to whip through exercises with extensive jumping, stretching, springing, crisp blocks, and power punches. Only with this grueling daily training did the

Iron Luohan Master feel the students could achieve the proper degree of hard strength.

The Crane Master was a thin man in his fifties. His long face and pointed chin framed two inquisitive eyes with irises so large that almost no white showed. He had thin, black hair braided into a queue. His arms were like stalks, and he walked like a crane, in a long-legged, toed-out, syncopated gait.

86

The White Crane style made extensive use of *qi* and posture. Balance and energy circulation were essential. In contrast to the Iron Luohan Master's emphasis on muscular strength, the Crane Master urged the students to inflate their limbs with *qi* to achieve the same effect. If that were done, he said, one need rely only on posture to win a fight.

The master personally proved his point in endless sparring sessions. Saihung, confident in his Luohan training, went forward. But to his frustration, he was unable to strike the master, who never blocked but only evaded, in a succession of beautiful birdlike poses. Sometimes he looked like a flying crane, and at other times, he eluded Saihung with one-legged postures.

"The crane is a bird," lectured the master. "Birds are proud and arrogant. They strike poses. Show off. This is the characteristic of the style. Your opponent attacks, but you are interested only in maintaining your best profile. Let him attack. You need only move into your posture. If his arms get caught in your 'wing,' if your 'beak' strikes him, it is from your posture, not from a premeditated effort."

The Crane Master soon showed his devastating attacks. He favored the Crane Fist, a beaklike formation of the thumb and fingertips pointed together. The strike was sophisticated. All the force was directed onto a small area, increasing its impact. The attacks came from unexpected angles in a battery of bewildering hooks and zigzag strikes. The Crane Master could abruptly change directions and always succeeded in penetrating Saihung's defenses to peck at eyes, ears, throat, or pressure points.

The Monkey Master was a clown. Seldom serious, he laughed and chattered constantly. Living in a mud-walled hut set in a tiny sun-dappled grove, he really looked like a lone ape. He had short, stubby legs, grotesquely long, dangling arms, and a pleasant round face that seemed all the larger for the closely cropped hair. He loved to joke with his students and did dozens of flips and monkey imitations to entertain them.

The Monkey style employed acrobatics, *qinggong*, a loose body, concentrated mind, and external strength. Flexibility was paramount, and the Monkey Master felt that relaxation was imperative not only to the physical and mental states necessary for monkey boxing, but for spirituality as well. He explained by using monkeys as an example.

"Look at all you Taoist boys." He giggled. "Someday you'll grow up to be priests with long lives of meditation. The monkeys have you beaten. They know meditation already.

"If you look quietly in the forests, you can come across a monkey sitting by a stream, just staring. He's not moving, he's not doing anything. He's just sitting. He's in complete stillness. Just think—he didn't need a Taoist to teach him.

"Or you might look up and see a monkey perched on a high treetop, completely lost in himself. He might be a hundred feet off the ground, but he won't fall because he has complete, one-pointed concentration. Just look at you fellows. Why, you can hardly stand properly!

"The monkey is totally relaxed. He is unafraid because he knows his intelligence makes him superior. The monkey knows strategy, instinctively comprehending the saying 'I move after the enemy, but arrive before him.' Attack a monkey. He'll roll away, take a watchful posture. He'll stay there for hours or days until your next move. You can't catch him off guard. The instant you move, he'll respond more quickly than you anticipate."

Strikes in the Monkey style were unique and varied, including double-knuckle punches, bitelike pinches, slaps, arcing fingers that caught eyes, nostrils, or lips, and devious overhead raps. Saihung also learned the unusual monkey stances, bowlegged off-center walks and jumps, because, as his teacher said, "A monkey cannot stand straight up, so he is always moving. You must use this mobility in your fighting."

Sparring with the Monkey Master was both hilarious and terrifying. In the beginning of each match, he jumped absurdly around, mockingly allowing Saihung to strike him. He had the singular ability to take strikes anywhere on his body, including his kettlelike head. Saihung punched with abandon, and all the time the master bobbed ridiculously. Once the master decided to hit back, however, Saihung knew true terror and invariably ran away. But the teacher pursued him relentlessly, pounced on him with a monkey leap, showing Saihung that only the master was impervious to pain.

Saihung's fourth Wudangshan teacher was the Snake Master, a cold, evil man. He did not want respect or warm regard from others. He wanted only to be feared, and all the other masters avoided him. A tall figure as flat and massive as a tombstone, staying ever in shadow, glaring unwelcomingly with reptilian intensity, and eating only cold food, the Snake Master was a terrifying presence.

Out of all his teachers, Saihung genuinely feared only him. The Snake Master was brutal during sparring, and when he broke his normal graveyard silence to speak, it was only to deliver a short, cutting remark. Ostensibly, he corrected his students, but in reality he always seized on their weakest personality flaws.

The primary Snake attack was an openhanded strike with the fingertips. The Iron Luohan punched, the Crane pecked, and the Monkey pawed, but the Snake pierced. The Snake Master wordlessly established his credentials with Saihung and the class by leading them to a butcher shop and repeatedly stabbing his hands through a side of beef.

"In order to have piercing strength," said the Snake Master, "you must have internal energy that is as pliable as a blade of grass. A blade of grass gives with the wind. Even a hurricane cannot uproot it. It is so soft; yet it can cut your hand. It is this pliable energy you seek. No matter what your opponent hits you with, yield, slither, give way to his attack. Absorb his energy until the full extension of his strike, and then at that moment, when he is weakest, whip back ferociously."

His eyes glittered as he invited Saihung to attack. He evaded with a flexibility that made his body appear boneless. Saihung attempted grappling and locking, but the master's arms were like rubber. Then the Snake Master lashed back with sadistic pleasure, his arms coiling around Saihung's head before a flurry of strikes left fingertip bruises all over Saihung's body.

"Your defenses are too open," announced the Snake Master derisively. He noticed Saihung rubbing his sore spots. "If I don't hit you, you won't remember. This way, your body feels the pain, and you'll never forget to guard your vulnerable points."

The ultimate strategy of the Snake system was to attack vital points. Strikes to these spots could cripple, damage internal organs, and even kill. Each day for a hundred days Saihung trained with fingertip push-ups and hundreds of strikes to a hard sandbag. The Snake Master insisted that the right effect could be achieved only if the fingers could be inserted into the opponent's body to a one-inch depth.

89

"A snake kills in several ways," said the master. "It bites, it chokes, and it hits vital spots. A snake catches an animal in its coils, and while the animal struggles, the snake's tail hits the animal's vital spots. Our art is derived from watching this.

"The strike is not only physical, it is internal. The mind commands the energy into the fingertips as they hit your target. The precision is pinpointed." He struck Saihung lightly, and Saihung began to gasp desperately for air. The master let the class watch him struggle for several minutes before he released the effect by massage and a slap on the back.

"This is my system," he said. "It is dedicated to complete domination."

The great martial ability he acquired, combined with his quick temper, made Saihung pugnacious. But his ever-watchful Taoist teachers constantly reminded him to be humble. At the end of summer, he and his class left Wudangshan and were making their way back to Huashan, when they stopped at a teahouse. The priest escorting them summarized this Taoist viewpoint.

"Learning martial arts means self-assurance, not arrogance. Your confidence should make you the meekest, most humble person on earth. If you are secure in your techniques, nothing anyone can do has any meaning. It is impossible for them to annoy you because you know they cannot harm you. You know you can fight, but you do not exercise that ability. You remain free of violence.

"It is not the boxer who is dangerous; rather, it is the weakling. Insecure, the latter must constantly 'prove' himself. His weakness and ignorance make him arrogant."

"Hey, look at those Taoist boys!" cried out a man in the teahouse.

"Teenagers who have never known women!" His companion laughed.

Saihung's temper flared up instantly. The priest looked over at the men and smiled warmly.

"Walking away from a confrontation makes one superior," continued the priest to the class. "You have not been taught martial arts to kill, to win glory for yourself, or to exalt religion. Rather, the purpose is self-discipline and self-defense."

"You mean they're all virgins?" shouted the man to his companion.

"I suppose," replied the other loudly. "In fact, maybe they don't even have any balls! Hey! Hey, little Taoists, do you have any balls?"

"Even if they do, I bet they're smaller than this peach pit!"

"Do you suppose they've ever seen a woman? Do they know what one looks like?"

"Hah! They probably wouldn't even know what to do with one!"

Saihung was ready. His muscles tensed for a fight. He looked to the priest for a sign. The priest only turned lazily around to gaze kindly at the two laughing men.

Fixed by the priest's steady but nonaggressive stare, the two men gradually became quiet with embarrassment. When several minutes of silence had elapsed, the priest motioned the class to leave.

"Meeting people who demonstrate their ignorance is not an invitation to fight. Since you can remember your abilities, you can understand their plight. Rather than hate them, you should feel compassion."

twelve

The
Grand
Master
Challenges
Saihung

S AIHUNG, EVEN BEFORE he had reached the age of fifteen, was a strong fighter. When his martial masters entered him in provincial tournaments, he won his share of the matches. In his wanderings around the countryside, he was a dramatic figure, handsome, lean, and well muscled. He had a wide, smooth-skinned face and braided hair that had been uncut since his first arrival on Huashan. He was a proud young man, brash and reckless in his challenges.

Passing through a town, Saihung had seen a notice in the village square announcing the arrival of the White Crane Society. The large sign had said, WHITE CRANE: UNDER HEAVEN WE ARE THE FIRST and WHEN WE ARE HERE, THERE IS NO SECOND PLACE.

Saihung had promptly written on the notice, "When I am here, you are second."

The next day, the White Crane Society left the note, "If you dare, you'll be here tomorrow."

"I'll be here," wrote Saihung.

Five young men in the fanciest silk clothing were there the next day. Saihung appeared in his coarse gray Taoist robes.

"What? You? Why, you're just a kid," exclaimed the twenty-eight-year-old leader. "You are stupid for talking so big. Besides, I see you are a Taoist. I cannot fight a monk."

"I'm not a Taoist," responded Saihung. "I'm a wandering herbalist and martial artist."

"You kid! Even asleep, I know more than you!"

"Hah! Only in your dreams do you know more than I!"

"Watch your mouth, kid!" roared the tall leader.

"How many will attack?" responded Saihung casually. "I'm only asking so I can tell the undertaker how many to expect."

"Don't talk so arrogantly. Only I need fight you. Tell me where you are from, little Taoist, so we know where to ship your stinking carcass!"

"That won't be necessary. Fight, if you are a man!"

The Crane boxer sprang forward. Saihung was still, gathering his *qi*. Just as the Crane boxer was almost on him, Saihung threw himself on the ground and brought a kick straight up into his opponent's groin. He hooked his other foot around the Crane boxer's ankle and tripped him.

Saihung jumped up and with his full weight crushed down on the man's abdomen. The he flipped the Crane boxer over and, spreading the boxer's legs into a frog's legs position, ripped the hip muscles.

"Didn't I tell you?" Saihung said mockingly as he strutted away. He felt completely triumphant and rejoiced in the superiority of his skills.

IT WAS TIME for him to return to Huashan, yet he was reluctant. The pleasures of the world fascinated him. He enjoyed the wealth and prestige of his family; beautiful clothes; rich surroundings; and feasts of river fish, goose, and bear paws. He constantly savored his victories and began to yearn for the glories of a fighter. By comparison, the frugality of Huashan, its absolute discipline and life of extreme denial, seemed unbearable. But he was committed to return. Saihung began his ascent with a sigh.

The Grand Master summoned Saihung as soon as his disciple had returned to the mountain.

"You think you're talented, don't you?"

Saihung nodded confidently.

"You're not. You've been lucky. If you want to be good, you need meditation. Your internal system must be perfect. It is the internal that is the source of power, and you must go deep inside and use the totality of yourself in order to develop."

"I have won tournaments and challenges."

"You can be better if you meditate before your practice. It will unleash unusual energy."

"I already know internal martial arts. I can fight."

"But you do not go deep enough into meditation, and the spiritual, after all, is higher than fighting."

"Perhaps I'm not interested. It's great fun out there. I have, in my wanderings, been in the Peking Opera, joined a circus, and learned from many boxers. I would never have been able to do this if I had not been a wandering Taoist. Members of a holy order can't learn the most brutal parts of martial arts. I want to learn the ultimate in techniques, and I'd never be able to do that here on the mountain."

"You think your skill is so great?" asked the Grand Master casually.

"Yes, I do."

"Then fight me. If you win, I will introduce you to many masters. You'll be free to enter the outside martial world. But if you lose, you return to your studies. Agreed?"

Saihung looked at his master. Standing on a terrace overlooking a vast view of mountain ranges, they seemed alone at the top of the world. Saihung asked himself why he had climbed all that way simply to talk with this recluse who lived such a spare and severe life. Life seemed better down below, and in spite of years of training, the Grand Master looked like any other old man. Saihung judged his master's weight. Saihung knew he outweighed him.

93

"I agree," said Saihung with a confident smile.

"All right," returned the Grand Master. "Fight!"

Saihung attacked immediately with strong and sure whirlwind strikes so swift that most men would have fallen simply because of their slower reflexes. The Grand Master, however, only retreated calmly before Saihung's advance. He let Saihung try all the boxing techniques gleaned from his many tournament bouts, but not even a single blow touched the Grand Master's robes.

Saihung grew angry, and gathering in his full might, charged his master. The Grand Master gracefully launched himself in a spinning leap over Saihung's shoulders. Saihung turned and struck out, but a whipping force sped by his face. A moment later, a devastating slap turned his head. It was the Grand Master's sleeve.

His master now took the initiative, and Saihung backed frantically away from his spinning arms. Through his blocks, he could see the Grand Master glaring ferociously at him as sleeve after sleeve came. Before long, his arms had been whipped numb. He dropped his guard. His master struck him with a palm blow, and Saihung flew across the terrace.

Saihung lay stunned on the stone pavement. The Grand Master came over to him. He was kind and smiling again. Helping Saihung up, he patted him reassuringly.

"You've lost," the Grand Master said softly. "You lost because you do not have enough concentration. I won because my concentration is complete. Concentration is impossible without meditation."

Saihung stood up and caught his breath.

"I'd still rather be a wandering Taoist. Look at you. Yes, you're a holy man. But what has it gotten you? You're starved. You live in damp rooms on a lonely mountaintop. You're a nobody. Are you successful? Do the gods listen to you? Will you go to heaven? How do you know there's even such a thing as heaven?"

"You can only see the gods and heaven by mastering this world," replied the Grand Master patiently. "Then you can see the next world.

"I admit that if I were to see heaven, I might believe, but how can I go to heaven? Wouldn't I fall out of the sky?"

"Not the body," laughed the Grand Master. "Your spirit travels to heaven and returns. That is the way."

"Your spirit? Can it come out from the body?"

"Oh yes. But you must control the senses. When you realize that this world is an illusion, you can control the senses, master the world, and travel on."

"The world is an illusion?"

"Yes. Nothing is real."

"What do you mean, 'Nothing is real'? Of course this world is real!"

"It isn't. It's illusion. Once you master your senses and the five elements, you will know that too."

"I don't believe you. How do I know what 'mastering the senses' and 'mastering the world' mean?"

The Grand Master looked at Saihung placidly. "This, Saihung, is mastery of the world." He pointed dramatically across the terrace at an unlit stick of incense. It lit immediately. Sandalwood fragrance drifted toward them.

"And it is also this," said the Grand Master.

He pointed at a heavy brass teapot on a table six feet away. It floated up and moved slowly in the air to another table. Saihung was dumbfounded.

"Master the five elements and then you can see the other world. But you have to study if you want to achieve this. Contemplate this. Make a decision. Some things must be begun in youth to achieve success later. A tree grows from a seed. I know it's difficult for you to believe. You're young. You haven't seen fruit. That's why I show you. But you cannot always demand complete proof before you begin something. In some things, you must have blind faith. The gods are supreme. They will let you know."

"Meditation is not simply something you do by itself, casually," said the Grand Master. "Other disciplines complement it and must also be mastered. Martial arts generate mighty strength, and the raw energy for meditation, but the mind must be cultivated through music, calligraphy, painting, and metaphysics before you can be ready for contemplation.

"Music is the direct link between the soul and the divine. The body is like a hollow reed, and music fills it with the song of the gods. Music will calm you, soothe your nerves, tell you of other-worldliness. Even in the midst of great turmoil, music can bring peace to your heart. No one lives without music. You must learn to play music, to experience not only the sounds but to accept its physical benefits as well. Playing the flute, for example, trains the mind and *qi* to act in unison and stimulates the meridians in the fingertips. Whether you listen or whether you play, music refines your soul. It is peace, emotion, expression, and the sound of the sacred.

"Calligraphy is calming and unifying. The brush is an extension of the hand, and moving it stimulates the meridians, moves the skeletal system, soothes the nerves, relaxes the mind, and develops the ability to absorb poetry. By copying poetry, you ponder the nuances and subtleties unnoticeable in reading. The original intent of the poets and sages are absorbed by tracing their exact strokes. Viewing and copying calligraphy will tell you what the scriptures mean. The actual act of calligraphy makes you calm, gentle, rational, and intelligent.

"Painting can be an expression of an artist's inner workings, but it can also be a method of taking the outside world directly into the psyche. As expression, art is the exercise of beauty. It comes from the heart, not the mind, stimulates compassion and joy, and nourishes the beauty of your inner soul.

"Beauty implies appreciation. The painter expresses his appreciation of nature's beauty, but he also absorbs natural beauty through painting. What the eye sees goes directly into the soul. In this regard, spiritual diagrams are also painting and can lead one to the divine. Thus, both in presenting nature and other art, painting directly affects the personality."

Saihung was assigned classes in music, calligraphy, and painting in addition to a heavy curriculum of philosophy, anthropology, archaeology, astronomy, meteorology, and the classics. All his courses were designed to expand his mind, discipline him, and refine his temperament. The Grand Master also gave instruction on the metaphysical arts of talismanic writing, the summoning of spirits, and divination. Added to the pillar of his physical training, the arts and metaphysics were the second and third pillars; these three areas together were the foundations for meditation.

Divination familiarized Saihung with Taoist cosmology and provided him with a way of receiving the words of the gods. The Grand Master understood Saihung's reluctance to believe in something unseen and unheard. The Taoist answer was to communicate directly to the spirits and gods through visualization and divination in order to prove their existence. The *I Ching*, a holy book characterizing the universal cosmological principle as change through the interaction of yin and yang and the transmutations of the *Bagua*, was based on sixty-four hexagrams that embodied all cosmic states. The *I Ching* itself was a codification of an even earlier system of divination devised by Fu Xi.

But to simply expose Saihung to such a difficult and ancient holy book was something the Grand Master was too wise to do. He wanted Saihung to understand divination and the philosophy of the *I Ching* more directly, so he took him to see the Ancient Oracle.

As they had in years before, master and student trekked together into the remote mountains. During the journey, the Grand Master told Saihung the story of the Oracle.

"Five hundred years ago, the Taoists of Huashan chanced on a man nearly dead of exposure. No one knew where he had come from, and the man revealed nothing of his past and pointedly disavowed any connection with Taoism. He was too weak to be moved. They nursed him back to health on that mountaintop.

"He recovered and simply announced that he would stay on that spot to 'practice his art.' What that art might be was a mystery even to the oldest Taoists. The man sat down at the foot of a large cypress tree on the edge of a high ledge. He never moved again.

"The Taoists supplied him with food and water, but the man stopped eating entirely. His hair grew directly into the tree, and he gained all his nourishment from that.

"'Never cut my hair, it is my lifeblood,' he said. But one day, a curious young acolyte crept up from behind and cut several strands, whereupon the man froze the intruder with magic. The man became severely ill, and the tree withered.

"'So, you tried to take my life. I'll take yours instead,' said the Oracle. He transformed the boy into a tree, and over the centuries his hair continued to grow until it pierced into the trunk which was the transformed boy. They say it's still the boy who stands there, sheltering the Ancient Oracle.

"The Oracle has memorized the entire *I Ching* and can attain the applicable hexagram not by tools, but by going into a trance and receiving the hexagram directly from the spirit of Fu Xi, the originator of *Bagua*."

Saihung and his master made their way up an overgrown path. There was indeed a figure sitting against a cypress tree. They prostrated themselves before him.

Saihung looked up at the wizened man. His eyes were closed, his skin dry, his beard scraggly and uncut. Someone had draped leopard skins on his shoulders and lap, covering his faded and tattered clothes. His hands and feet were bare, the long nails curling. Saihung noticed incredulously that the Oracle's tangled white hair did disappear into the tree trunk.

The Ancient Oracle opened his eyes. Saihung asked a question. The Oracle closed his eyes for a minute and then, opening them again, verbally revealed the hexagrams and their changes. From their formations, he interpreted an answer.

Saihung returned many times. The Ancient Oracle not only knew in advance of Saihung's coming, but also knew his questions. Whenever Saihung went to him, the Ancient Oracle had already prepared his answer.

Eventually, Saihung learned to use the *I Ching* by himself, and this gave him a pragmatic experience with the application of Taoist philosophy in everyday life. The *I Ching* gave its answer after Saihung constructed a hexagram from coin tosses. He put three coins into a turtle shell; these were Fu Xi's original tools of divination. He shook the shell until the coins fell out. Depending on the pattern into which the coins fell, a certain line was implied. It could be Yin, Yang, Changing Yin, or Changing Yang. From six tosses, the hexagram could be constructed. Saihung would consult the *I Ching* about that hexagram, and if it had changing lines, he would also look up the hexagram made by the change. Change was the central theme of the *I Ching,* and how life changed was its most important lesson. Through his study and practice, Saihung learned the wisdom of *I Ching:* that change was natural, that yielding and action were both important, that there were certain personal requirements the gods demanded if ill consequences were to be avoided, and that whenever an event reached its zenith, it automatically began to change to its opposite.

THE GRAND MASTER finally introduced elementary meditation to Saihung. As in all his training, the learning proceeded from the simple to the complex in cumulative stages strictly controlled by the Grand Master. Nothing was to be left to chance. The Grand Master explained the procedure to him and warned him in advance of what he would experience. There was always a task to be achieved in his meditations, and Saihung was required to report all that happened to him in the process. The Grand Master then either confirmed the validity of Saihung's experience or rejected it as hallucination.

"In our tradition," said the Grand Master, "meditation is impossible without a pure body, open meridians, and *qi*. We've explained to you since childhood: Without *qi*, there is no spirit. We require also that the trainee have a refined personality. Otherwise, a monster could emerge. Finally, the trainee must know something of cosmology, which provides the right context.

"You begin meditation upon these foundations. There are three kinds of meditation: moving, standing, and sitting. You have already experienced moving meditation by learning Xingyi, Bagua, Taiji, and the Five Animals of Huado. In moving meditation, the external is dynamic, but the internal is still. In standing meditation, the external is static, but the inside moves. This is where you shall begin."

Standing meditation was a series of static postures combined with specific hand gestures. Although the body position was a factor, the crucial force was the mind. Standing meditation developed concentration with pinpoint accuracy.

At the end of his meditations, Saihung performed a series of dispersals. This was a hallmark Taoist procedure that dispersed the energy accumulated during meditation. The Taoists felt that meditation concentrated blood and *qi* in various centers, but primarily in the brain. Unless the accumulation was released and the entire body made neutral again, headaches, loss of hair, nervousness, insanity, heart problems, and hemorrhaging could result.

This philosophy completed the explanation of meditation. Meditation was an activity to be undertaken only after long years of preparation and the attainment of perfect health. It unleashed great forces in the body and accelerated the circulation. Unless a body had been strengthened, it could not withstand the shock. Sometimes breathing slowed so much that it stopped spontaneously. Without *qigong* training, the practitioner would pass out.

"Now you see how you've changed," said the Grand Master, a year after he had "challenged" Saihung. "You see that meditation is supported by the three pillars of your previous training. You find yourself of a calmer temperament, and you believe it because it works. It gives you measurable results. Now you have an inkling of what it is to be an internalist. Nothing in the outside world compares. It is the basis of your life, and you must go deeper and deeper."

A
Decision
Made
Alone

S AIHUNG'S SUCCESS IN his practices brought
on a period of self-evaluation. He had come
to the point where, as an ordinary adept, he would automatically
have taken vows of renunciation. But Saihung was not an ordinary adept. He had received special consideration and had been
allowed to travel regularly. Guan Jiuyin had expected that
Saihung would return to the outside world, and the Grand Master's primary concern was to raise this difficult boy and educate
him to the standards of his clan. Now, the course had come to a
culmination. Saihung had to make a decision: return to society or
enter fully into Taoist asceticism.

In China, a sixteen-year-old was already an adult. Saihung was to decide alone. He trusted only his grandfather and master, but neither one wanted to influence him. He was free to do as he wished.

The Grand Master bade him go down from the mountain and return to his family for deliberation. As Saihung left the mountain, he suddenly felt that the Taoists of Huashan remained as mysterious and unfathomable as when he had first met them. The Taoists were ascetics. Ascetics were not in need of anything from society, and life and death were the same to them. That unique independence from everything that normal people craved or feared was both appealing and frightening. Saihung had followed twin paths throughout his upbringing. He knew the ascetic path and the worldly one of his family and martial society, and although he had never before considered the implications of his anomalous situation, he now had to choose his future.

Saihung walked into the countryside of Shaanxi. He was an unusual figure, exuding the pure physicality and inner confidence of his training. It was uncommon to see such a healthy youth on the poverty- and war-stricken plains, and many of the travelers could barely keep themselves from gawking.

In the 1930s, the province had seen great strife and had never recovered from the recent Communist and Kuomintang battles in her northern section. The land was ruined; the populace was starving. Saihung had seen the devastation in his previous travels and had felt as helpless as the rest of the people. With the necessity of his imminent decision, he was careful to observe everything and eager to learn the latest news. He constantly asked himself if he wanted to be a part of this world.

He crossed the plains of Shaanxi, the land where much of Chinese civilization began. Centuries of history sprawled outward from the silk road that ended at Xian, like flower blossoms at the end of a long stem. It was an area that had seen culture, politics, warfare, and natural calamities come and go as regularly and inexorably as the flooding of the Yellow River.

What he saw and felt over the following days became a convolution of experiences without the perspective and artificial organization of secondhand history. Because he deliberately absorbed everything, the insane paradoxes of Chinese society its extremes of wisdom and ignorance, wealth and poverty, benevolence and slavery, abundance and famine, power and helplessness, branded themselves into his mind.

He constantly tried to imagine his fate if he were to reenter society, and naturally began by trying to compare himself with other men his age. There weren't many among the peasants. Famine and conscription had decimated the population. Many of those left had joined such illicit warlord-sanctioned activities as pimping, gambling, and slave dealing.

The peasants' life was one of desperation. They were simultaneously ennobled by their attempt to wrest a meager yield from the parched land and degraded by their exploitation. The peasants depended on their ancestral lands, but they tilled overworked earth. Their mud homes were falling apart. Many buildings had been wrecked by soldiers who took doors on which to sleep and framing for fuel. The weather did the rest to destroy the small rooms into which families crowded as chaos increased. Snakes, lizards, and roaches crawled through at will. Rats, desperate for food, regularly attacked unattended infants. Pigs and farm animals, brought inside to prevent theft, left their filth everywhere. Disease was rampant. It was surprising that as many people as there were survived, to repeat the next day the wretched experiences of the days past.

Communist and Nationalist agents regularly tried to recruit reinforcements from a population desperate for relief. The Communists appealed to anti-Japanese sentiment and expressed ideals of agrarian reform. The Nationalists voiced anticommunist sentiments and praised the glories of the existing central government. Only the young listened to them. The old had heard too many promises already.

In some ways, the Communists were preferable to the Nationalists. Although they were repetitive in propagandizing their idealistic programs, they did not, like Nationalists, shoot opponents in wholesale lots. But when soldiers came instead of cadres, Saihung saw little difference. Soldiers, whether Communist, Nationalist, or warlord, caused universal suffering. Seizing homes, food, and supplies; trampling crops, garrisoning in temples, using

103

shrines for stables, raping, looting, torturing, and killing—not just the enemy but anyone they wished—were all commonplace practices. The cruelty inflicted on the people simply for the perverted enjoyment of the soldiers occurred with such monotonous regularity that the survivors took horror for granted.

Many tried to adapt, like organisms adapting to some new environment, becoming opportunists so far from human that Saihung could barely contain his revulsion. Some people sold their babies for slaves. Others sold human flesh and hearts as pork. Every sort of ugliness and villainy was in plain view. Cheating merchants, dishonest officials, unrestrained soldiers, overzealous white missionaries, European slave traders—all preyed regularly on the rotting society. Even "paragons" of virtue and justice turned to exploiting the population.

Saihung saw that scholars and aristocrats, people who had appeared formerly as examples of righteousness, were now the most hypocritical and despicable of all. Insensitive to the miseries of the villagers, they strolled about in fine silken clothing, casually fluttering their exquisite fans. Purposefully conspicuous on streets lined with beggars and the lower class, they almost seemed to welcome the suffering. In their shortsighted way, Saihung thought, they enjoyed this state of affairs, because it highlighted their status and gave them continuing opportunities to exact profits. They were self-centered and repressive. Nothing seemed to matter as long as they could continue to stand on the backs of the peasantry.

As Saihung journeyed on toward his home, the sight of a predatory society feeding on itself became overpowering. He was a participant in a mad carnival. It was a walk with death never out of sight. A parade with dogs and crows presiding over corpses. A march of girls sold into prostitution, or coerced into arranged marriages. A line of pathetic human caricatures with open sores, bulging tumors, severed limbs, tubercular wheezes, hunchbacks, and mutilated faces. Saihung gave away what money he had, but it was minuscule in proportion to the overwhelmingly grotesque needs. He remained a helpless walker, a part of the procession of terror, until he reached his ancestral home.

HE HEAVY GATES closed behind him, and the family and servants received him enthusiastically. With great fanfare, he
was welcomed back into the Guan family mansion. Saihung felt
the familiarity and security of his childhood home. The beautiful
architecture, serene gardens, and the high walls were all intact.
But as he walked beneath wisteria-laced archways, over hand-
carved footbridges, and past trees planted by his ancestors four
generations ago, he wondered whether it was he or the world that
had changed. He tried to reconcile the turmoil through which he
had traveled and the paradise of the mansion. Had the contrasts
existed before? Had he simply been unaware?

He reflected that he had never really taken a long-range view
of his life. He had allowed his master and grandfather to set a
course for him and had followed it. But now he saw himself torn
between extremes—between wealth and poverty, between duty
and want, between renunciation and worldliness. He had closed
his mind to all social problems, when immersed either in his
training or in the diversions his family status provided. On
Huashan, he knew the thrill of new knowledge; while at home,
he could claim his legacy of fine clothes, purebred horses, delicious feasts, attentive servants, art collections, and rare weapons.
Until now, he had ignored the contradictions of his unusual upbringing, the demands of his parents, and the responsibilities of
his clan. He had, in fact, deferred all responsibility.

He sat down before the pond and gazebo where he had spent
so many evenings with his grandparents. No memories, precedents, or inspirations came to him. He had to find his own way.
After he examined thoroughly his possible alternatives, Saihung
decided he would leave the Guan family mansion.

He knew that his grandparents would continue to support
him spiritually and financially. He admired both of them, but
he also knew that their time was declining. Saihung was also
sure his parents would oppose him but dismissed them because
he resented their standards. As for his uncles and aunts, he was
tired of their petty squabblings and devious intraclan intrigues
and had no qualms in walking away from them. Saihung braced
himself for the furor his decision would create. Although he was
certain that his grandparents would eventually accept his

choice, he already felt the disapproval of all the others in his collective clan.

Renunciation and entering a religious order was considered a disgrace. The words for renunciate literally meant "one-who-has-left-one's-family," and to do this in a Confucian society, with its heavy emphasis on filial piety, was a sin. When one renounced, one became a nonperson. One's name, place in the clan records, representation in the family temple—every possible trace of one's identity was expunged. There would be no one in his place to carry on the clan, beget heirs, or increase its wealth and status.

Saihung went to see his grandfather, entering the library where he had first met the two acolytes. He quietly announced his decision.

Guan Jiuyin sat back in his chair and thoughtfully stroked his beard. He looked at his grandson for a long time before articulating carefully chosen words.

"I sent you up to the mountain to learn, build your strength, and be disciplined, acquire an unbreakable principle and will. But I expected you to return to the clan."

Saihung was silent. He thought of his many classmates who, having graduated from Huashan, had indeed returned to secular life to become scholars, artists, martial heroes, or simply eccentric wanderers. Each was without a doubt a singular man, but few had disavowed all worldly attachments. Out of all the thousands educated on the mountain, few chose, or were eligible, to become ascetics. Saihung vacillated.

"You are a member of a great clan," continued his grandfather. "Wealth, prestige, and power are your birthright; one might even say, duty. You can enjoy it. When you are here, you have no trouble. Do you truly want to walk away from it all?"

Saihung felt the glory of the mansion, that enormous dragon sprawling on the hillside. He considered again. But instead of regret, he only felt a curious dullness, an aloof elation. Saihung looked down and finally replied, "Yes."

Guan Jiuyin sighed and gave his approval.

The news of Saihung's decision went through the mansion swiftly. Even though Saihung tried to spend as much time as possible alone in the gardens, he was acutely aware of the disapproving stares.

He could not avoid a confrontation with his parents, however, and they clashed with him every day. Although they realized the futility of arguing, since the clan patriarch supported Saihung, they nevertheless protested his decision—the mother arguing because Saihung would not be a scholar, the father angry because Saihung would not be a soldier. They argued even on the day of his departure.

"You don't care about me as a person," Saihung finally said. "You only want me to succeed because it would bring prestige to you and the clan."

"That is your duty as a person," retorted his mother. "Have you, in your unfilial thinking, forgotten what duty is? You have to be a productive member of society and live up to the family name. Think of the responsibilities you are neglecting."

"Yes, think about it!" broke in his father emotionally. "Instead of meeting your obligations, you want to run off and become a wretched priest! What's so good about following some old, man around barren mountains? What does a damn priest do but sit around all day pretending that he's mumbling to the sages? All those fellows are bums, burdens on society, beggars who don't work. Carrying on their ostensible spirituality depends on the goodwill of others. Priests make their living skimming off the top of society's labors."

"Entering religious life disgraces the family," said his mother. "You should think of returning to your family if only because of the debt you owe them for raising you from a miserable child."

Saihung jumped up. His parents watched him from where they sat stiffly and formally. Saihung tried to voice his feelings, but he had no clever retorts, no simple, irrefutable explanation. He felt pressure build in his head until he burst out with a heated farewell.

"Look, I only came to say good-bye. If I were uncaring, like you two, or like my brothers. I wouldn't even have returned to say anything. I would have just taken my vows and let all you worldly opportunists go to hell! Instead I came back. Doesn't that show I am doing my last duty as a son? My mind is made up. I'm leaving!"

He broke from the room to curses from his angry father. A wave of panic swelled within him. He wanted to leave the mansion immediately. But he was still in the prison of obligations. He had still another gate through which he must pass: He had to talk to his betrothed.

When he was five years old, Saihung had been engaged to a girl two years older than he. The girl had then been taken into the Guan family at the age of nine to be reared and nurtured by the family of her future in-laws. This was an accepted custom to ensure complete compatibility with her future husband's family. She was already weeping when Saihung came to say good-bye.

"I'm going to be an old spinster if you abandon me," she sobbed.

Saihung looked at her. Dressed in her finest gown, her hair perfectly combed and pinned with flowers, she sat in the beautiful reception room of his home. He could see that her entire world extended no farther than the women's chambers. She was the daughter of an extremely powerful general, and the marriage had been arranged to tie the two families together. He knew that all she wanted was to be his wife. That had been her sole upbringing.

"I'm already eighteen," she pleaded. "No man will want me now. I may even lose the protection of your family."

"I'm sorry," said Saihung. "You can always marry another man."

"I'm too old. I've been betrothed to you. How can you break our engagement so cruelly?"

Saihung tried to answer. His desperation to leave churned inside him. He tried to think. If his life had gone normally, he would already have married, at the age of fifteen, a girl he did not even know. He attempted another explanation, but she only wept more.

How to cope with a crying girl had simply not been covered in Saihung's extensive education. While he felt sympathy, he also felt the urgent need to leave. He asked her to stop crying, but she couldn't. Finally, his helplessness overcame him.

"You're free to marry anyone else. I hope you can find happiness with him!"

He bolted from the room, slamming the inlaid lattice doors, hoping he could close out her hysterical cries. It was too much for him. Saihung went immediately to get his belongings.

He fled the mansion to curses, mockery, and accusations of betrayal from his entire clan. No one came forth to congratulate him or express support. He walked through the heavy date-wood gates. As soon as they shut, he was alone with his doubt.

TWO WEEKS LATER, Saihung knelt down in the main hall of the South Peak Temple, the Hall of the Three Pure Ones (the Taoist trinity of Lao Tzu, the Jade Emperor, and the Original Being). It was a large, high-ceilinged, ornately decorated room sparkling with hundreds of slender burning tapers. Plain wood pillars supported partly gilded and partly painted carved archways depicting scenes of the Monkey King in heaven and his exploits in fighting demons. At the head of the hall was an intricately carved, ceiling-high facade behind which were three statues of the Three Pure Ones. Behind them was a painting of other gods. They had all been painted to look directly at the viewer, and the perspective gave them the appearance of floating off the picture plane. It was a grand, overwhelming vision of the heavenly host descending toward a single point, and Saihung knelt at that exact place.

The heavy rosewood altar table was set with all the necessary offerings, but it had several ritual objects different from normal altars. A gourd, symbol of renunciation; a horsetail whisk, emblem of a Taoist master; and a comb for the ceremony were special implements.

As he awaited his initiation, doubt still consumed Saihung. But all the members of the South Peak Temple, the Grand Master, the two acolytes, and his grandparents were all in attendance. Every time he panicked, he looked around at them. They had been with him constantly from the beginning. Saihung trusted them and hoped that faith would carry him through.

The elders were solemn and sat stoically. It was a momentous occasion, but their seriousness also seemed to include an awareness of Saihung's conflicting feelings. Only the two acolytes, still youths themselves, showed expressions of kindness and compassion. They smiled and gave him surreptitious looks of encouragement during the ceremony. These two were sympathetic; they knew his inner conflict.

The ceremony began. The assembly joined the Grand Master in a responsive recitation of the scriptures, punctuated by strikes on the bell, the gong, and the wooden fish. The smoke of the incense filled the hall, and the undulating flames from the oil lamps and candles gave a golden glow to the room. A hazy, otherworldly feeling came over Saihung as he recited alone.

He bowed nine times to the altar while offering incense, bowed to the past grand masters, and bowed nine times to his own Grand Master. He then made offerings of food, tea, and wine.

The Grand Master walked behind Saihung and combed his long black hair. This represented the combing away of all his past *ming huan*, all the consequences and attachments of his past lives. The Grand Master continued to recite and put Saihung's hair into a coil on his head and then pegged it expertly with a wooden hairpin. Saihung had now left his family.

The Grand Master taught Saihung his personal Taoist name and verse. These words were taken from the *Thousand Word Text*. According to the sequence of characters, Saihung's name identified him immediately to other Taoists. The verse was a code that authenticated his membership, generation, rank within his sect, and rank of the sect itself.

The two acolytes presented Saihung with neatly folded gray robes, cotton shoes, and prayer mat, copper begging bowl, and a special sutra for the next twelve years of his training. There was more recitation before Saihung went alone to worship in five separate shrines honoring the gods, immortals, and ascetics particularly related to his school. Afterward, he rejoined the assembly for a huge vegetarian feast.

He was committed, but privately he still harbored doubts and fears. Uncertainty and insecurity made him wonder if he had irrevocably chosen an unhappy path. But he had seen China and he had known his family home—neither held any appeal for him. Saihung knew that this was his only real choice.

Internal
Alchemy

As an initiated Taoist adept, Saihung began training in the esoteric practices of his sect. His practices of internal alchemy, including hygiene, therapeutic movement, and meditation would lead to a very special culmination.

Hygiene reflected the Taoist desire to purify the body, cleansing it of toxins that inhibited spiritual growth. In spite of their meticulously scrupulous diets and *qigong* exercises, the Taoists still felt that the body accumulated poisons.

"Every day while you breathe," stated his master, "your body collects dust, dirt, and other particles from the air. When you sleep, those substances remain in your lungs and enter your bloodstream. In addition, your body itself creates waste gases. All these things must be purged daily."

The Grand Master instructed Saihung in even more vigorous *qigong* exercises and introduced special herbs to flush out his system. An herbal tea made up of five different flowers cleansed his digestive tract; another of roots and leaves cleansed his blood. Other formulas dissolved clotted blood, dispersed trapped *qi*, or relieved unbalanced organs.

Purification was followed by tonification, using ginseng and other herbs. These were even more powerful than the herbs Saihung had received during his earlier training and were intended not only to maintain or strengthen the body, but to alter it permanently. This use of herbs and the accompanying training in meditation were integral to the sect's practice of internal alchemy.

"There is no such thing as immortality in its true sense," stated the Grand Master. "Immortality means longevity. Through correct practices, you can prolong your life to an unusual limit and remain free from illness. But no one lives forever. Even the gods must die.

"We can only taste immortality, but the practices can never be interrupted. Never neglect your body. If you train your mind but ignore your body, it will atrophy. If you neglect your mind and train your body, you'll never advance. The secret is that mind and body are united and that one can combine their energy to transcend this mortal plane."

Saihung's practice of internal alchemy took place in a small hut set aside solely for meditators. He was to stay there for forty-nine days to achieve the goal of opening his meridians in a process known as the "microcosmic orbit." The hut was a tiny mud-walled structure with a tile roof, a single shuttered window, and a "Dutch" door. Its only furnishings were a bed, a candlestick, and a low, square bench. When the Grand Master led Saihung inside, Saihung wondered if he would feel claustrophobic. The room was so small that he could have touched all four walls without moving from the center.

Saihung placed a woven-grass mat on the bench. Over that he laid down a deerskin, followed by his own prayer rug. The grass mat was an insulator, the animal skin contributed the psychic energy of the deer, and the prayer rug was his own meditation aid. Saihung was to sit there for several hours every day of the forty-nine.

The Grand Master showed Saihung the proper seated posture. Saihung sat on the edge of the bench with his feet resting on the floor. He relaxed completely, keeping his spine perfectly straight, head raised with chin tucked in, and hands clasped in a special prayer gesture.

Then the Grand Master left Saihung. Closing the door, he pasted a paper strip over the bottom edge of the door's lower half. The seal was both a talisman to drive away evil spirits and to prevent either Saihung from leaving or anyone from entering. Saihung could open only the top half for sunlight and for food and waste to be passed back and forth.

L IVING IN SILENCE, reading sacred books, exercising, having a regulated diet, taking herbs, and meditating gave Saihung a deep inner contentment. He never experienced claustrophobia. His all-consuming task and the strength of his inner vision opened up new vistas. His world had turned inward and, as he had seen with the Yin Immortal, the inner world could be infinite.

Completing the microcosmic orbit and continuing its practice did not make him superhuman. Rather, it was the cultivation of human potential. He felt extraordinarily vigorous. At this point, the manuals stated, he was on his way to developing the "golden body"—a healthy mind and body nearly impervious to illness and natural calamity.

On the afternoon of the forty-ninth day, he sat breathing the clear mountain air. He had completed his task. Although it had been a difficult one, he felt the rewards. He had changed, made his breakthrough. Saihung was elated.

Sunlight was streaming through the top half of the door when his master appeared. There was a smiling exchange of greetings as the Grand Master broke the seal and released him. Saihung spoke for the first time in weeks and recounted his experiences. The Grand Master nodded in approval.

The two of them left the meditation hut and hiked through the mountains. Huashan's natural beauty flooded Saihung's mind once again. Breathtaking vistas of rock, pine, and cloud, accented by falling water and pleasant breezes, combined to offer him joyful congratulations. He treasured his achievement, and it was his alone.

The master took his disciple through a gate on the East Peak and into the Two Immortals Cave. In its depths, Saihung would receive his vision.

The Two Immortals were two boys who had been playful acolytes on Huashan. As they romped along a path one morning, they had met a stout, muscular, white-haired man dressed in peasant clothing. Slung over his shoulder was a branch, with several enormous peaches.

He was Dong Fengshui, a disciple of the Northern Sea Immortal. Before he had become a disciple, he had been a thief. The impulses of his former profession had been difficult to suppress. Anxious to attain immortality, weary of austerities, and impatient with internal alchemy, he had gone to the garden of the Queen of the West and had stolen some peaches of immortality. He was just returning when he happened on the two boys.

He liked them immediately and spent the day playing with them. Intrigued by their wit and intelligence, he asked them complex riddles, and to his surprise the boys solved them with ease and flair.

"Little ones," Dong Fengshui addressed them as he stood to go. "I like you, but have nothing to give you in parting. How about taking one of these peaches? One bite and you shall live forty thousand years."

The boys clapped their hands delightedly and, after the man left, ate the entire peach. They instantly became immortal, and their spirits ascended to heaven.

The Jade Emperor was surprised by their sudden appearance.

"How is it that two boys have acquired immortality?" asked the Emperor.

"A stranger gave us a magic peach," they answered.

"Ahhh, the stars must have been right for you to have such fortune," said the Jade Emperor. He ordered his ministers to investigate. They returned with a thorough account and confirmed that the Book of Life listed the two boys as predestined for immortality.

"I sanction your attainment," decreed the Jade Emperor. "Since you became immortal as children, you will remain children forever. And since you are such good friends, you shall be known as the Two Immortals." He touched their third eyes, opening them to perception, and bestowed divine wisdom on them. Then he gave them special scriptures and bade them return to earth to teach humanity.

The Two Immortals returned to Huashan and lived in the very cave Saihung now entered with his master. The Taoists believed that the psychic energy they left there, or perhaps their actual presence, would aid in other acolytes' quests.

Deep and wide, the cave was a tunnel filled with stalactites and stalagmites that had grown one by one over the centuries. Their eerie, grotesque shapes glowed with luminous minerals. It was a cave of eternal night lit only by iridescent pinnacles.

Saihung carried a torch, and its undulating flame cast jagged shadows. In spite of its light, Saihung could see no limits to the cave. But as they walked through the rock formations that dwarfed them, he saw a faint, skittering reflection. It was an underground river—an indigo mirror that doubled the stalactite ceiling—and so deep and mighty that it seldom rippled.

They went aboard a split bamboo raft that was in readiness at the bank. Saihung stuck his torch at the head of the raft and, taking up a long pole, pushed off.

Only the sound of his pole broke the silence. They went deep into the earth, where the rock smothered all sounds, where the river flowed on in complete quiet like a giant artery.

The river branched off into many different caves, but the Grand Master set an unerring course. The effect of the torch, shadows, reflections, and glowing rocks was mesmerizing, and their frail craft was engulfed in a tunnel of whirling colors.

They disembarked at a grotto. Walking to its end, about fifty paces from the water's edge, they came to a large stone couch. The sides were carved with strange anthropomorphic figures and an indecipherable cursive script. The Grand Master gestured. Saihung put down animal skins and his prayer rug and lay down.

The Grand Master directed him into the proper position for dreaming. Saihung lay on his left side with his head resting on the crook of his left elbow with the hand cupping his ear. The right hand cupped his genitals. His left leg was straight, his right one bent with the ankle resting on his left knee. He would await his vision in this position.

The Grand Master left. He would return the next morning to bring Saihung back and interpret the vision. Until then Saihung was to sleep, and dream.

Everyone who had lain on that couch had had a vision; it was a certainty. The visions revealed different things. Some dreamers learned that they should go no further in ascetic training but should return to society. Others were shown a horrible future crisis they had to face. Some were given a special task. But no matter what came, both the acolyte and his master were bound to accept the omen. In most cases, the personal vision became the lodestone of the adept's life. It was a treasure, a jewel that shone only for him and guided him through the darkness of life.

Saihung lay still and quiet. His breathing became slow and regular. Mystery enveloped him, and he fell swiftly asleep.

The next morning, his master appeared on the indigo waters, poling the frail raft alone. Saihung told him his vision. The Grand Master nodded.

"This is your vision, Saihung. It is the climax to years of effort. Tell no one of it. It is your secret source, the inspiration that will guide you in your future life of austerity and sustain you in times of adversity."

SAIHUNG WENT TO live in a compound with other adepts of his age and level of accomplishment. Although he still participated in the communal maintenance of the community, his only task was religious study. He read many sacred books and scriptures, continued to train his body, learned healing, and mastered more complex meditations.

The compound was a quadrangle of buildings, set on one side of a spacious mud-walled enclosure, within a large horseshoe-shaped meadow. Old pines grew from crevices in the stone walls, and an abundant spring splashed down a gully of broken rock.

Calligraphy was carved on the cliff face. A number of meditation caves were visible on the high stone wall.

Several priests presided over the compound and supervised the students. They taught during the day and held discussions at night about scriptures, past Taoists, or the progress of the students.

Each adept had his own master and particular individual training. But the compound was to teach them certain basic subjects, giving them companionship and mutual support. A strong camaraderie existed among all the boys.

Medicine—one of the most important group subjects—was taught by Master Shifting Wind. Master Shifting Wind ate a diet of herbs and only a handful of rice. He approached his work reverently by worshiping Shen Nong daily before class at a shrine in his herb room. When he taught, he indicated that he possessed an amazing store of knowledge. He never used books—he had memorized them all. Medicine was based on the knowledge of organs, meridians, and body structures. It was the perfect complement to meditation. The meditations were concerned with points within the body, and medicine simultaneously improved visualization while teaching healing.

Self-knowledge preceded giving knowledge to others. Just as the Emperor Shen Nong had experimented with herbs on his own body, so the aspiring adept also observed the effects of medicine on himself. Saihung's knowledge of massage, herbalism, and acupuncture was always based on experience with others and on his own experience as a patient.

Saihung's studies began with massage, since this skill was simply one body dealing with another. He learned that even with intermediate tools such as herbs and needles, direct healing was medicine in its most fundamental form. The most knowledgeable healers used only meditation.

Massage familiarized Saihung with anatomy, pressure points, and meridians. He learned to project his *qi* into his fingers to strengthen his grip, and the ideal was to control his patient completely and relax him by the methodical grasping of the spots. If the patient was reluctant, tense, or apprehensive, Saihung used methods to open immediately the muscles and bones, making the body receptive to the kneading, slapping, or pressing treatments.

A wide range of illnesses could be healed with massage. He learned to treat dislocated and broken bones, bruises, some hemorrhages, muscle spasms, twisted veins, poisons in the bloodstream, clots, twisted nerves, neuralgia, and dislocated organs.

The second stage of massage required learning to project *qi* directly into a patient's body, and it was frustratingly difficult. Projecting *qi* could bring deep poisons or clotted blood to the skin surface for dispersal or, as a life-force transfusion, could save a life. Saihung experienced its feeling when the teacher demonstrated on him. An electrical field of prickly heat penetrated his skin. But when he tried this on a classmate, he could not make the energy rush forth. Master Shifting Wind instructed Saihung to leave his hands on his classmate, and then the master put his own hands on Saihung's shoulder blades. Using Saihung's arms as conductors, he projected his *qi* through to the classmate. Saihung felt a surge of energy pass through his arms, and the master told him to try to reproduce the feeling to make his own *qi* come forth.

Diagnosis, an essential tool of medicine, was accomplished primarily through interpreting the pulse. This alone was a ten-year study. Diagnostic pulse reading was an outgrowth of the holistic view of the human body. Positing that the five organs and six viscera determined health, the physicians found that the organ's conditions could be read in the six different pulses at each wrist.

These pulses could be differentiated only by great sensitivity, subtle nuances of pressure, and by projecting *qi* through the healer's fingertips and into the bloodstream. His *qi* entered the body almost as a sonar, so that the echo of his own energy and the way it bounced back helped him reach his diagnosis. He used the "Eight Standards" in analyzing the state of each organ and viscus. By determining whether its condition was yin or yang, hard or soft, inner or outer, hot or cold, or a combination, he tried to ascertain the illness.

The teacher first took the pulse of the subject and then asked each student to diagnose. Master Shifting Wind was strict. A system that demanded such a sensitive balance between subjectivity and objectivity inevitably led to many student mistakes. In his severity, Master Shifting Wind accused them repeatedly of lying or fantasizing. As he was a martial artist, his slaps were stinging. Saihung could not remember having heard himself called a turtle's egg or having been slapped so frequently even in his youth.

The Taoists did not like to treat illness; they preferred to prevent it with tonic herbs. Medical classics stated that treating an illness after it had begun was like "waiting until one is thirsty to dig a well" or "suppressing a revolution after it has begun." Saihung was familiar with preventive medicine all through his apprenticeship. But in serious cases, the doctors could choose acupuncture, surgery, healing with talismans, and (the highest and most dramatic type of healing Saihung witnessed) healing with the mind.

ONE DAY A portly man was admitted to Huashan. He was dying. He had a bluish pallor, and a tongue so swollen that it threatened to choke him.

The man was an extraordinarily rich aristocrat and yet had been unable to find a doctor to save him. In desperation, he ordered himself carried to Huashan and begged for help.

Master Shifting Wind went to see him. He diagnosed the symptoms as poisoning and, after questioning the man, surmised that a rival must have done it. "You will either choke to death, or, if the poison reaches your heart, die of a heart attack," he concluded.

The Taoists decided to heal him. Master Shifting Wind sat behind the aristocrat, laying his hands on the man's back. He was in constant concentration for two hours until he suddenly fell over. His face was pale, he could not move, and his palms were black.

Two other doctors dragged him to a stone. Master Shifting Wind drew himself up and placed his hands on the rock to expel the poison. Two black handprints were left there when he was done. The stone was buried.

He was exhausted and was sealed in a shrine for three months of meditation in order to regenerate his life force. The patient survived, and both he and the master recovered with normal herb therapy.

Saihung deeply admired the master's sacrifice. It was an inspiration and high standard. He still thought often of the physician's simple dedication and tried to apply it to his own life. After he entered into another regimen of meditation and gained greater skill, he was constantly reminded of his teacher's selflessness.

ONE OF THE highest meditations that Saihung learned, the *ling qiu* meditation, opened the psychic centers. The body centers, situated in a straight line from the base of the body to the top of the head, had specific healing and spiritual powers. Meditation aimed at bringing the life force straight up through each of the centers to the crown. Paralleling the Indian Kundalini meditation, the Taoists opened each of the centers until, at the very top, they reached what the Hindus called Samadhi, the Buddhists called Nirvana, and the Taoists called Stillness. Saihung began to practice the attainment of that Immortal Spirit.

Each center, according to its anatomical placement, controlled and healed the adjacent body structures and organs and yielded particular psychic powers. The Grand Master continually warned Saihung that the abilities that would come to him would be gifts from the gods and were not to be abused. Many ascetics, having come this far, had fallen because they had grown obsessed with the importance of their centers. Instead of reaching the spiritual, they remained fascinated with the use of their lower centers and became trapped in the abuse of their powers.

Before he meditated to awaken each center, Saihung studied that center's colors and response to invocation, and looked at a diagram of its shape. Each center was imagined as a lotus bud that could be opened by the specific sound of the invocation. Within the flower was a certain pattern of colors. While he concentrated on that pattern in meditation, Saihung produced the invocation. The blooming center lit up, and its powers began to emanate. Saihung felt whirling sensations and heat whenever the center was activated. When the meditation was complete, the center closed and became dormant again.

The first center was actually outside the body and was the source of energy. Saihung brought the life force into his body at the base of his spine. Both this center and the next one at the navel controlled life and reproduction. Meditating on them brought lightness, increased physical energy, and sexual desire. The Grand Master warned him that feelings of physical and sexual power would become so strong that he might be reluctant to go on. He said that many adepts remained at those two centers, cultivating massive strength and sexuality for all sorts of deviant purposes. When Saihung opened the centers, he found it was true. Deep sexual cravings and the realization that he could develop the power of an almost unbeatable martial artist tempted him and strained his discipline.

As soon as he opened the solar-plexus center, his ordeal ceased. He had passed into the spiritual centers. The solar plexus was a source of vitality for him and gave him increased power to heal. Saihung realized that it had been this center that Master Shifting Wind had drawn upon.

The heart was compassion, skill, appreciation of beauty, and artistry. Opening it developed artistic ability and supported the arts. The Grand Master emphasized that creativity arose from this center and that people like Mist Through a Grove, an unusually talented musician, naturally had theirs open.

The throat center, not surprisingly, aided singing, but was also responsible for clairvoyance. Used in combination with the third eye, it interpreted the perceptions of other realities seen by that center. Often Saihung did not understand his spiritual experiences until the throat center poured forth verbal understanding.

The upper *dan tian*, or third eye, perceived other dimensions. The Grand Master stressed again that most people, and Saihung, had agreed to see the world only in a certain way and had called that "existence." In actuality, it was not real. Reality was the shifting of different illusions, because many dimensions coexisted. Using the third eye, Saihung could pierce through the illusory world for the meaning behind it.

Ascending the body centers symbolized the whole of Saihung's training. He had developed his body powers; learned martial arts; secured his health, longevity, and vitality; become versed in art, literature, science, and divination; and had perceived extrasensory realities and spiritual wisdom.

Now, he entered his final center. He was on the threshold of a level that was at once a culmination of many arduous years and the foundation for higher states: the Crown Center. The Thousand-Petaled Lotus bloomed. His senses dropped away. There was no external reality, no internal reality. He felt nothing, thought nothing. He merged completely with Voidness.

War

N EWS OF THE Sino-Japanese War in 1937 came to Huashan with the monthly supplies. The students who had gone down for provisions had rushed back up the mountain with the report that Japan had swept across the Marco Polo Bridge outside Beijing, overrun the iron- and coal-rich mountains of Shaanxi Province, and had begun a second drive from Tianjin toward Nanjing. Attacking at their own pace, the Japanese had advanced steadily into the Chinese countryside, meeting only badly organized and poorly supplied resistance. The disunited warlord armies and the civilian population of the northern provinces had been crushed by superbly trained, tank-led, air-supported columns.

The exceptionally gruesome stories of the fighting and atrocities shocked everyone, including Saihung. Resentment and hatred fueled nationalism, and controversy spread to all the temples of Huashan. Every priest, acolyte, and student had a different opinion. Some were excited and emotional, others calm and aloof, but all condemned the war. Daily routines were disturbed, and soon the Taoists of Huashan did not need to read of the war but instead saw it in the distance: They heard the bombing, watched fighter planes overhead, and saw dull red flashes give rise to fattening columns of black smoke as the Japanese attacked Xian sixty miles away.

A large number of Taoists advocated noninvolvement in the war. They insisted that they as "people-who-had-left-their-families," should not return to worldly affairs and break the purity they had so long cultivated. The world was a place of war, deceit, dishonesty, money, killing, politics, and danger. They did not want to break their ascetic commitment.

Patriotic Taoists disagreed, saying that if China was overrun or destroyed, ascetics would have no place to practice their arts. Moved by indignation and righteousness, these people urged some involvement. Renunciates or not, they were needed by their country and people.

Controversy split the community until the Grand Master called a public assembly. All the priests and students from Huashan's five peaks came in steady streams. Many engaged in heated discussions as they crowded anxiously into the courtyards of the South Peak Temple to await the Grand Master's instruction.

He walked out to the portico of the main hall, his tall figure standing out against the ancient wooden temple. Lifting a battered megaphone to his lips, the Grand Master addressed them in an authoritative voice.

"We are Taoist renunciates. We have all left the world and should remain unconcerned with the insignificant and petty squabbles of small-minded men. Entering the world again is to forsake the purity we have cultivated on this holy mountain: It is impossible to be in the world and remain untainted.

"Yet we are also Chinese. A foreign power is invading our country, and every person must do his part in defending it. There is more to life than spirituality.

"Aiding the war effort need not mean fighting. Each man must contribute in his own way; each man must ask himself how he can best help China. Some may go down and feed the people, some should give medical aid, and some should properly preserve the ancient traditions for the future. Even if you will not kill, you can still contribute.

"For those of you trained in the martial traditions, you must defend in that way. You are warriors, and the business of a warrior is war. . . ."

The Grand Master continued his speech, but Saihung's mind was already racing. He was young and outraged. He wanted to defend his people and homeland. He wanted to seek revenge for the atrocities committed against helpless people. He wanted to fight.

That evening he and the two acolytes discussed the future.

"We have been trained thoroughly. Our martial skills are unusual," said Saihung passionately. "We must offer our skills to our country."

His two former guardians listened seriously. Mist Through a Grove rarely expressed his inner feelings, and Sound of Clear Water, though outspoken, was equally taciturn about his personal decisions. There was a long period of silence after Saihung had stopped talking. Sound of Clear Water simply announced that he was leaving the mountain.

"We are martial artists. We fight," said Sound of Clear Water. "When I think of the inhuman acts forced upon women, children, and the elderly, I cannot contain myself. I cannot stand by. I shall kill."

"And I too," said Saihung.

They turned to Mist Through a Grove. He said nothing but returned their look steadily. He had not argued. They knew he would go.

"It is impossible to fight and be in the sect," continued Saihung. "It will be impossible to keep the precepts on the battlefield. I shall be entangled in the world. I am leaving the sect."

"Saihung," said Mist Through a Grove. "You musn't abandon your path."

"I'll become a wandering Taoist unaffiliated with a temple. Look, sometimes I can't stand it up here. I never have enough to eat, and training seven days a week can be depressing. Every day, it's wake up and recite sutras; eat breakfast, recite sutras; eat lunch, recite sutras; eat dinner, recite sutras; go to sleep, recite sutras. I tell you, I'd rather be a lone ascetic."

"You took your vows," Sound of Clear Water reminded him.

"I know. I remain a Taoist. But even if I could recite sutras on the battleground, it would be hypocritical. I'll be scheming, fighting for my life, eating meat, thinking evil, killing. How can I honor the precepts? I need all my energy and strength to concentrate on fighting."

The two acolytes glanced at each other.

"Do as you like, Saihung," said Mist Through a Grove. "But I shall try to keep the precepts."

"I shall, as well," said Sound of Clear Water.

"How can you?" asked Saihung hotly. "You'll be killing. Don't the priests say that those who kill shall be punished in hell?"

"They say," stressed Sound of Clear Water, "that to kill another human being is a sin. Would human beings commit those atrocities?"

"Besides, Saihung," added Mist Through a Grove, "we must fight evil and defend ourselves. We do not kill for pleasure, but we've all fought bandits and animals who have attacked us on the mountain. Even holy men must defend themselves. We have been attacked without provocation. It is our right to defend ourselves."

The next day, Saihung went to see his master. He was dressed not in his robes but in black martial artist's clothing bound at the wrists and ankles. He bowed and requested permission to enter. The Grand Master nodded a silent acknowledgment.

"I'm leaving the mountain," said Saihung.

The Grand Master's eyes narrowed. Before he could reply, Saihung swiftly added, "And I'm leaving the sect."

The Grand Master slammed his palm loudly to the desk. He glared angrily at him. It was the first time Saihung had seen his master angry, and he was surprised.

"You and your saucy mouth! Think! Don't speak carelessly with me!"

"I cannot keep the precepts on the battlefield."

"Who says you're going? Where did you get such impudent ideas? You are not to run around following your ridiculous whims; you are supposed to follow your training."

"But I must fight. If I fight, I must eat."

"The precepts must be observed!"

"You say the body is the temple of the gods," said Saihung defiantly. "Am I to fight without nourishment? What will happen to the 'temple' then? The body must be nourished. The gods won't remain in an ill-repaired temple."

127

"You are filled with unwholesome ideas!"

"If the mind is not allowed to be independent, we're no better than vegetables."

The Grand Master stood up and fixed Saihung with a stern look. "You're young and know no better. A little learning and you are ready to tell the world what to do. Think carefully before you take this irresponsible plunge."

"I am becoming a wandering Taoist," replied Saihung steadily. "I won't be tied to a temple."

"If you leave," said his master sharply, "don't come back!"

Saihung was stunned. But there was nothing more to be said. "*Da Shi*, I am leaving."

The Grand Master sat down and simply waved him away in dismissal.

THE ADEPTS OF Huashan were famous for their martial abilities and were eagerly accepted into the warlord armies. Saihung and the two acolytes separated, and each entered guerrilla units that had no restrictions on movement. The conventional armies were limited by the rules of war, but Saihung's units under Cai Tingjie and Bai Songqi fought in any way they pleased. Often they roamed behind enemy lines or acted as advance scouts, harassing, sabotaging, and gathering intelligence information against the enemy. Skilled and capable, Saihung and his expert unit preferred traditional weapons and carried guns only when they joined an army for conventional warfare.

Saihung's primary weapons were a single-edged saber and a spear. He dressed completely in black cotton clothes tied at the wrists and ankles, walked on straw sandals, and coiled his braided hair beneath a black cloth wrapping. He was a fiery and idealistic soldier, as energetic but as temperamental as a stallion. He specialized in isolated attacks, picking off men one by one. Attacking at dawn, twilight, or even in broad daylight, Saihung hid in tall grass and became expert at killing passing soldiers. He pierced throats with his spear so that his victims died soundlessly.

128   In close-range fighting, he favored the saber. Saihung lured enemy soldiers close to himself so that they were forced to depend on bayonets and knives rather than on bullets. In that situation, Saihung's heavy saber, honed by blades in the scabbard each time it was drawn, was a superior weapon. With whirling motions and mighty leaps, Saihung parried with ease, using the momentum to sever limbs in single swings. He remembered the philosophy of his saber instructors about piercing, slashing, parrying, and hacking: A shallow cut is used to torture a victim; decapitation is merciful.

Saihung released all the power of his youth and training in hand combat. His palms were devastating; his kicks had an iron hardness. His meridians were opened, his internal energy was conserved by celibacy, and his techniques were forged by his spartan training. He was a wild fighter. It became easy for him to dispatch a man with a single strike or break a neck with a simple twist.

His idealism slowly wore away in the climate of warfare, and Saihung found himself motivated by something new: hatred. The intellect grew dumb on the battlefield, and compassion was lost in the stark contrasts of wartime realities. He had learned many things on Huashan, but it was not until he saw enemy atrocities with his own eyes that he learned to hate men. Whenever he entered villages abandoned by the enemy, he saw bloody testimonials to human depravity. Torn bodies left mute histories of raped women, whipped flesh, bayoneted babies, mutilated boys, staked and burned genitals. The horror became so redundant that his eyes grew weary. But for his heart and will the repetition was a constant refueling of a fire that forged hatred in him and sharpened it to a razor's edge. The war atrocities seared his companions' souls of all sensitivity; they fought firmly and stoically. Not so with Saihung. He lived from day to day, powered by a flickering alternation between commitment to his cause and pure madness.

Battle after battle shook his psyche. He was wounded and scarred in body and mind by sounds that always seemed like questions. They haunted him. The ominous thuds of exploding bombs, the mad percussion of machine-gun fire, even the whisper of flesh parted from flesh as his blade made its absolute division became familiar. But it was when human sounds reached him--the anonymous whimper of a frightened child, the scream of a dying comrade, the last moan of his enemy—that he felt the sound addressed his soul directly. He yearned for those rare moments when the battlefield was quiet. In those fleeting moments, the sounds of warfare that all asked the question "Why?" faded. But he then took up the refrain within himself. During lulls in the cacophony of destruction, he tried to sort out his own thoughts and resolve the apparently monstrous dichotomy between Taoism and the war.

The purity of Huashan was undeniable, its focus on asceticism strict and absolute. There was no temptation, if only because little opportunity existed on the peaks to practice sin. It was a community of dedicated individuals, and whether saint or beginning acolyte, all were completely given over to spirituality. The most there was to hate was the dull regularity of monastic life.

Huashan seemed like heaven compared to the filth and degradation of the battlefield, where both the mountain and heaven seemed distant and inaccessible. Now Saihung lived a wretched life of anger, killing, and intrigue. He had to steal his food, eating whatever he could scrounge, and poured his intelligence into setting traps. He had to put his spirituality completely aside in order to throw the totality of his being into slaughtering other men. The old Taoists were right. It was impossible to live in the world without being entangled.

But for the time being, he *was* fully entangled. Each time he saw the mounds of rotten flesh that were feasts for the dogs and crows, his passion welled up for revenge. Battle cries drowned out the whispers of scriptures. Fury pushed aside morality. He had to fight to save his people. Since childhood he had been told that to kill was to incur eternal damnation. He accepted it. He would go to hell with no regrets.

At times, his thoughts of Huashan became bitter and cynical. If the Taoists were so great, why didn't they stop the war? But each time he could also answer himself in the words he had so often heard: The Taoists were renunciates. The world was not real; the world did not matter.

But weren't they men? Weren't they Chinese? Couldn't they stop the senseless assaults with their extraordinary powers? He realized soberly that even if they could, they wouldn't. Every person had his destiny, everyone had to choose between good and evil, and humanity had to find its own way from savagery to divinity. War was destiny, and destiny was inescapable even for the gods. Spirituality offered no obvious way out. The renunciates remained on the mountain; others struggled on the plains. But spirituality was only human aspiration crystallized. It could not work miracles. The Taoists, Saihung realized sadly, were only men after all.

Ordinary human beings. It was true that they had turned their backs on the self-destructive and self-indulgent tragedies most people called their lives. A person on the Taoist path sought his own liberation, secured it, and tried to help others all he could to gain their liberation too. But humanity was composed of individuals, each one born with the same free will and opportunity of choice between sacrificing for higher consciousness or plunging toward degradation. That was the human task. That was human meaning, individualized. If there were no evil, there would be no consequence and thus no choice. Humanity always had a choice, and ultimately one's freedom could be attained only by one's persistent conscious effort. The Taoists could not rescue all of a nation or the whole planet. That would have been an act of grace. Divine intervention of that sort was beyond the power of even the Jade Emperor himself.

Saihung's contemplations gave him perspective. He thought of reincarnation. Human life was the halfway point between upper and lower states of consciousness: Humanity had not yet resolved this dilemma in its evolutionary progression. The war, as activity during a moment of this evolution, suddenly seemed petty and insignificant.

But these philosophical flights were taking place on a battle-field. He was here. Death surrounded him; the dichotomy and the dilemma could not be resolved. He had to go on now. He didn't want to die; he didn't want to be killed. Despite his introspection into moral considerations, he formulated a simple conclusion. He would kill anyone who tried to kill him. Only then could he succeed in his present task.

Homecoming

T WO YEARS OF war life, whether horror or adventure, began to wear on Saihung. His training and a certain acquired ruthlessness had preserved him thus far. But as the war reached a frustrating stalemate, he began assessing the situation and thinking of his future.

By 1939, military conflict had reached a standoff when the Chinese, driven into the heartland by the advancing Japanese, had entrenched themselves along the foothills and valley rims. Supporting industry had been reestablished behind these lines. The Japanese attacked in small battles designed to terrorize the countryside and keep the Chinese disorganized. They struck deep into the fronts, marauding and plundering before turning back.

The Chinese responded by retreating, then attempting to pinch off the withdrawing Japanese units. But they could never destroy the superbly fortified Japanese garrisons, and a wide zone of desolation developed between the two forces. The Japanese returned again and again. Town after town was razed, peasants died by the thousands, and the dry soil was soaked with blood.

Saihung grew tired. Men were entrenched in foxholes dumbly awaiting the next attack, nursing infected sores, and expiring from fever. The war grew meaningless. He realized that there was still a world beyond the war, and that he had much to learn about that world. In Shandong Province, where the Yellow River finally ends its journey to the sea, he decided to disband his guerrilla unit and strike back to Huashan, westward in China's interior.

In the back of his mind, however, he was uncertain that he would be welcomed on the mountain. When he had broken away, his master had forbidden him to return. Saihung wondered whether he would be permitted reentry.

During that long trek to Huashan, he detoured toward the Guan family mansion. He knew that his grandparents had first taken refuge on Huashan but that both his grandmother and his grandfather now lay ill in a woodcutter's hut. His father was fighting, the rest of his family had fled to the interior, and the Guan clan had scattered. He knew that the mansion had had to be abandoned, but he wanted to see it again. There was no one to greet him. He arrived at his ancestral home alone.

A seasoned veteran, he nevertheless felt a deep sorrow when he came to the ruins of his family structures. The dragon estate, the gardens and pavilions that had been the culmination of four generations of the Guan clan, lay shattered in the scorched fields.

It was evident that Japanese troops had occupied the mansion before either leaving or having been driven out. Bullet holes were scattered like black scars on lavender walls. Cannon fire had torn gaping holes in the sides of buildings. Violent blows had splintered fragile lattices. Fire had consumed pavilions and ancient trees. Poison had polluted the streams and wells. Horses had been stabled in the family chapel. All art objects had either been plundered or smashed.

A wan and pale light sifted through the wreckage, lighting up dozens of bodies. Some were of Japanese and Chinese soldiers, but most were of servants caught in the attack. The remains of people, some of whom Saihung had known since birth as vital personalities, now lay twisted and still. He saw the body of a raped boy, blood still encrusted on his loins. In the shadow was a young girl, hair tangled, teeth broken, legs bare. An old stableman still hung from the rafters, his flesh sliced from his body in dangling strips. On each and every corpse, the faces were frozen in the terror of their violent deaths, their eyes still uncomprehending of their last moments.

Saihung walked stoically through the courtyards and hallways, trying to replace the present with the past. It was useless. Putrid flesh overcame scents of incense and jasmine in places where families had strolled. The charred ruins that represented former slender polychromed columns were characteristic of the shell that had once protected the glory and vigor of a clan. Life would never rise again here. No future could breathe that would not be tainted by the smell of men and women who had been destroyed, unaided and unpitied.

He stood in the garden where Guan Jiuyin had played his flute. Now, the fish lay belly-up on the surface of the stagnant pond. His family home was no more. Saihung turned his back on it and left. It was useless to weep. It had been the will of heaven.

S AIHUNG CLIMBED UP Huashan's steep trail. The air was still and cool, the light direct and clear. What a different place Huashan was! It was sacred. He felt acutely aware of the contrast between its austere serenity and the filth of the battlefield. Saihung stopped twice to wash himself in the mountain streams, but the bitterness and grime were hard to cleanse. He felt as if he were defiling the holy.

In humility he continued the climb toward his master. Perhaps he had never really appreciated Huashan. The first time he had been carried up and tricked. In subsequent times, he had looked at it as a tedious boarding school. Even when he had returned for his initiation, his faith had been incomplete and his heart filled with doubt. Now, he had chosen to return, ready to commit himself to austerity and knowledge. Stained with blood, racked with injury, he sought his solace, and the mountain seemed to accept him.

A group of monks saw him and came out to greet him. They happily exchanged their experiences. Some, due to their vows, had not gone down. The rest had gone either to heal or to fight. Saihung inquired about his master. He suspected that the Grand Master's anger had been merely a formality, but he mentioned it anyway.

The old temple cook burst out laughing.

"*Da Shi* disappears all the time," he said. "He doesn't say where he's going. He only says, 'I have business,' and is absent for months. We know that sometimes he went out and fought."

"How do you know?" asked Saihung.

"The newspaper clippings with the monthly supplies periodically mentioned an old Taoist with a cane. Only *Da Shi* carries that cane. We asked him about the news. Of course, he denied everything."

"What did the clippings say?"

"We know *Da Shi* went to Shanghai and Beijing to accept challenges from Japanese martial artists. The last time was in 1936."

"I was still here! Why didn't he take me?"

"Probably because your bad temper would have gotten you killed."

"Oh."

"The Japanese called us 'Sick Men of the Orient,' and *Da Shi* went to accept their challenges. He defeated a sumo wrestler in Shanghai with two fingers to the throat. He used just his sleeves and palms in a Beijing match where two karate masters, an aikido master, and a judo master attacked him simultaneously."

"So *Da Shi* isn't above getting involved himself!" cried Saihung.

"Apparently not," returned the priest. "Then there was another time that this same Taoist appeared in Sichuan."

"Sichuan!" exclaimed Saihung. "What was he doing there?"

"Just so," said the priest dryly. "How do we know why *Da Shi* was there? There was a teahouse there occupied by Japanese troops. Their commander was reputedly fourth dan black belt in karate. Well, the old Taoist walked right in and nonchalantly sat down for tea. The frightened waiters didn't know what to do but serve him. The commander boasted of his skills and the inferiority of Chinese warriors, until the old Taoist put his teacup down and laughed mockingly. The commander attacked, but the old Taoist threw him with one hand. A big fight erupted, and only the Taoist walked out of the teahouse."

"That old windbag!" cursed Saihung. "Giving me that sham rebuke! I'm going to get even!"

"Better not, Saihung." The priest chuckled. "*Da Shi* always has the last laugh."

"That's true," admitted Saihung with an embarrassed smile. "He certainly did this time."

They came to the entrance of the South Peak Temple, and the monks all urged him in. Saihung sought his master and found him in the study. Saihung knelt down.

The Grand Master looked down at him noncommittally. Saihung saw that his master had not changed. The quiet, observant eyes that could gaze unblinkingly, the snowy hair and beard, the upright posture, were so familiar. Saihung waited for his master to speak.

"So you managed to come back?" inquired the Grand Master softly.

"Yes, *Da Shi*."

"Since you're here, you should begin the next stage of training."

That was all. The Grand Master accepted and dismissed him with a gentle wave.

The
Labyrinth

A WEEK AFTER HIS return, Saihung vowed before the gods to practice austerities until he made a breakthrough. The Grand Master selected an auspicious day and walked with him to the West Peak. They paused at the stone slab at the opening to a cave. His master turned to him and said, "This is the place where you will discover your true self."

They descended along a tunnel that was the entryway to a labyrinth of passages and chambers. Saihung would live in a cluster of five chambers deep in the mountain, where countless corridors and holes remained to be explored. They wound their way into the mazelike hollows. The air was immediately chilly; the only sounds were of their footsteps. At times, the passage narrowed so much that they had to inch through sideways. Some parts of the cave were smothered in darkness, others glowed with luminous minerals. There were stalactites, drooping as if the stone itself were fluid, descending to meet stalagmites that rose in piercing peaks. A wide stream flowed by them and led the way to the five chambers lit by torches and oil lamps.

138

Several of these chambers had natural holes in their ceilings, and these were not only vents for the coal-burning cast-iron warmer, but also admitted some sunlight. By the skylights and the torches, Saihung saw his few possessions: a stone bed, incense stand, oil lamp, books, water gourd, hourglass, musical instruments, writing utensils, diary, and another robe.

There was a separate chamber devoted solely to meditation. The stream ran into it, pooling deeply in its center before flowing on. A heavy wooden meditation platform standing on feet modeled as dragon claws and carved with ancient ciphers was flanked by two iron incense burners shaped like cranes. A perfect circle incised into the sand-covered stone floor consecrated the whole platform.

Saihung laid a grass mat, leopard skin, and prayer rug on the platform. The Grand Master gave him a *Bagua* mirror, tied a talisman around his neck, and gave him last-minute instructions.

"Many Taoists have gained their realization on this very spot," said his master as he turned to leave. "All your elders have preceded you here. Study and persevere, Saihung, and you too shall succeed."

Saihung watched the Grand Master flicker into the shadows. He was alone.

Each day was based on four practices: morning meditation, astral travel, sutra recitation, and evening meditation. Around that framework was time for three hot meals brought in by classmates, practice of martial arts, reading of scriptures, playing music, writing, painting, and exploring the cave.

Rising in the morning, Saihung ate his breakfast, bathed, and did body-cleansing and strengthening exercises before going to the meditation chamber. Sitting within the sacred circle, he drew a special diagram in the sand. The complex pattern of circles, squares, lines, and angles invoked all forces on heaven and earth, called forth the ten directions, and conjured the five elements.

Every stroke was drawn with an invocation, and each one represented a god. The laborious ritual put him into a state of contemplation and created a diagram that protected and supported him. Saihung stepped into its center and sat down.

Both the pattern and his talisman would guard his body against possession once his spirit left his body. Lacking this protection, Saihung's physical shell was vulnerable to the many evil spirits and demons who readily sought an available shell. They could enter any one of the nine apertures of the body and prevent the return of Saihung's spirit.

139

Now in a quiet state, Saihung performed a series of twenty-four prayer gestures—complex hand positions that isolated thought, deepened concentration, and prepared his spirit to leave his body. The gestures represented the whole course of evolution: Saihung's meditation was the imagined culmination of the creation of the very universe.

He felt wholly otherworldly. He quietly read the sutra laid on a stand before him. The words had power. They induced his journey.

He invoked the gods with the sutra. Saihung called out their names and visualized them before him until he had reconstructed the entire Taoist pantheon. All of heaven, headed by the Three Pure Ones, was before him.

His spirit left his body, mounted on a dragon, and ascended to heaven. Once there, he prostrated himself before the gods and sat in meditation awaiting instruction. On occasions when the gods did not speak, Saihung asked his own questions of the gods.

After two hours, he repeated another part of the sutra and returned to consciousness. He ended by performing dispersing exercises and erased the diagram stroke by stroke, each time reciting sutras to release the god called by the diagram.

Before his noon meal each day, Saihung recited a sutra that appealed to the gods to purge the consequences of his past lives. The entire pantheon was invoked twice each day. The yang gods were called at noon, the yin gods in the evening.

At midday Saihung meditated again before free time in the afternoon, when he explored the mysteries of the caverns.

The cave was a complex and irregular network that twisted around on many levels. Some parts were reached only by crawling through narrow tubes in the rock, swimming underwater, or walking across naturally formed stone bridges. Previous hermits sequestered in the caves had explored and noted many parts, but many sections were unknown and even considered dangerous. Some of the tunnels had stone plaques set above them warning against entering. Other passages were favorite places for Saihung, but when he ventured into the unfamiliar, he frequently met with mysterious and sometimes frightening experiences.

Early in his stay he crawled down a rock vent and found a long corridor. Venturing several yards into it, he came on the opening of a shaft that plunged straight downward below the cave floor. Peering into the shaft, Saihung saw that ancient steps had been cut and an iron chain pegged to the walls. Grasping his torch, Saihung began the descent.

He counted the steps as he made his way down. The light from the cave above quickly dwindled into a pale dot before disappearing entirely. His torch was his only light source. He went on counting.

The rhythm of his steps became hypnotic. The darkness was disorienting. Only the shaft, with its remarkably straight progression, presented any solid context. He counted past five hundred.

He paused at a thousand steps. He thought he heard a faint sound. One thousand two hundred. Was that a voice? One thousand three hundred. Definite voices. Strange muffled shrieks and cries. He looked upward. The darkness was absolute. His courage began to falter even as he crept down to step one thousand five hundred. He heard voices speaking in an unknown tongue. As he looked down, the steps and chain disappeared from sight. The voices approached him. Now thoroughly frightened, he climbed quickly back up. He did not stop until he reached the surface, panting.

He never went near the shaft again, but the fright he had experienced wore off quickly. The next time he decided to make a horizontal exploration to find the limits of the cave dimension. He pressed himself through a narrow crevice in the granite toward a faint light. As he came to the end of the fissure, he saw daylight and mist through the opening and emerged expecting to see Huashan.

Instead he saw a forest stretching to the horizon. Confused, he tried to orient himself. As best as he could calculate, there was no forest in that direction. And even if there had been a place he had somehow never seen, it was impossible for such a wide expanse to exist anywhere around the Huashan range.

He was reluctant to venture too far away from the cave, so he carefully gazed at and examined the scene. The trees were primarily thick, gnarled pines. There were no broadleaf trees, and this gave the forest a primeval quality. No bird raised a song, nor was there the sound of wind or stream. The ancient forest was completely still.

Saihung returned to the crevice and made his way back to his chambers. He noted everything in his diary and later questioned the Grand Master. He had seen the Forest of Infinity, said his master. No one had seen its end. Even the realized masters did not venture there, for once a person lost his way, he could never return.

On another afternoon, Saihung chanced on an opening he had never seen before. It was high up on the wall of a narrow cavern. He climbed up to the opening and onto a sunlit ledge. The rock shelf was a small indentation in the sheer cliff face, wide enough for Saihung to stretch out and enjoy the warmth of the late afternoon. Across a plunging crevice, he saw another cliff topped by forests. He relaxed and gazed appreciatively at the lush scenery.

In a moment, an animal appeared and began prancing before him. It was about the size and shape of a pony, but it was unlike any other creature Saihung had ever seen. Although it had hooves and a body shaped like a pony, it had a deer's head, a fluffy tail, and scales on its body. Excitedly, it pranced and circled, stood on its hind legs, pawed the dirt, and whinnied like a horse, all in apparent urging for Saihung to come and join it. But Saihung could do nothing. The chasm made it impossible for the two to meet. The animal left periodically, only to peek out coyly from behind a tree and rush forth to frolic again before him.

Saihung watched the animal's dance until the sun began to set. He turned to begin his evening practices. The animal seemed disappointed and stood sadly at the cliff's edge. Saihung turned for one last look. It seemed so beautiful as it tossed its head slowly in the flaming light.

At the next weekly visit from his master, Saihung asked him about the animal.

"*Da Shi*, I am beginning to see unusual creatures. Two days ago, I saw an odd pony, and today I saw a rabbit."

Saihung described the animal. His master replied tersely.

"That scene and everything you experience is something meant for you. It's up to you to try and understand the meaning yourself."

"At least the animal was there, but the rabbit was even more strange."

"What happened?"

"I regularly go through a grotto that has grass on its floor. Today I was startled to see a ring of mushrooms and a rabbit. I went through the grotto and returned less than five minutes later. Both the rabbit and mushrooms were gone. Could the rabbit have eaten the mushrooms? Even if it had, there should have been holes in the grass, or chewed-off stalks. Instead the grass was completely intact."

"Perhaps the gods are sending you a sign," said the Grand Master.

"But what does the sign mean?"

"Find out yourself. If you can't do it, ask the gods yourself, in your dream state."

S IX MONTHS OF practice had elapsed, and Saihung, writing in his diary, tried continually to assess his experiences. He now genuinely enjoyed meditation. He laughed in amusement. Huashan had trained him for a decade before he had reached that point. Now, the serenity, the joy, the feeling of absolute health, and the thrill of learning had literally become addicting.

There was no boredom. Meditation had made him sensitive. Far from missing human beings, he relished the solitude. His senses and feelings had become so sharpened that there was more than enough stimulation. Art and music were diversion enough. Self-discovery was learning enough. And his unusual experiences, real or visionary, were wondrous enough.

Saihung puzzled over his experiences. They were riddles, enigmas to him. Were the shaft, the Forest of Infinity, the pony, and the rabbit real or hallucinations? Had he seen these things only out of madness? Or did they exist with or without his perception? Perhaps it was only his point of view that was wrong. Perhaps his assumptions about reality were wrong. The sutras always emphasized that different things were illusory. Realities co-existed. Dimensions could interface at any place or time. Maybe everything existed at once. Or maybe the pony was real and the world of people wasn't.

Yet he had no doubt that he could have been lost down the shaft or in the forest, or fallen into the chasm. He continued to wonder whether these things existed independently or whether they were merely projections of his own psyche. In the months ahead, he experienced events so powerful that the question became more and more indistinct. No matter where the source of reality lay, he knew that it could affect him physically, mentally, and spiritually.

Temptation
and
Knowledge

W HEN SAIHUNG ENTERED the cave, he expected to be there for nine months. But nine months had long since passed, and he had stopped inquiring about leaving. The Grand Master's response was always monotonously the same.

"Not yet. You haven't completed your task."

His master's weekly visits fortified him with contrasting guidance: the imparting of the sages' knowledge and the consistent dictum to face things alone. The Grand Master introduced Saihung to the *Tao Te Ching*, the *Jade Pivot*, the *Yellow Court Canon*, the *Tea Classic*, and deeper meditation techniques, but urged Saihung to confront his inner self constantly with his own resources.

He instructed Saihung to remain open to mystical experiences that might come to him, but to distinguish between those that could impart true knowledge to him and those that could disrupt his progress.

The Grand Master often reminded Saihung of what was at stake. Saihung knew of some men confined to cells for life because they had been driven insane by the strain of the cave—whether they had lost their mental balance from loneliness, mistakes in meditation, or from some outside source was difficult to say. Others had committed suicide. Some had become lost in the maze of tunnels. But the Grand Master encouraged Saihung by saying that those who succeeded emerged with unshakable faith.

One and a half years had passed calmly. Saihung even had regular companions now. He fed birds with rice saved from his meals, and he had also befriended a monkey who traded fruit for portions of Saihung's dinners. The two became very close, and the monkey periodically sat on Saihung's broad shoulders to ritually pick nonexistent lice from Saihung's hair. Nothing more unusual happened until Saihung one day looked up from his meditation platform and noticed the pool. There was a man's head in the water.

One side of it was greenish, and the eye was large, black, and round. The other side was human, but with a bitter look to it. The left side seemed definitely reptilian. It might be an apparition, Saihung told himself. The face stared at him unblinkingly. Stubborn and not to be intimidated by what was probably only an illusion, Saihung glared back obstinately.

"*I* am the resident of this grotto," said the head. "What are *you* doing here?"

"I am an ascetic practicing austerities," replied Saihung.

"How could you be practicing austerities? You're just a kid. You can't know very much. I have been cultivating myself for five hundred years and have five hundred more years to go."

"Oh, stop pretending!" shouted Saihung. "I'll squash you with one kick!"

The head's eyes opened wide in surprise. Saihung saw the naked man leap from the water onto a rock in one movement.

His body was short and thin, with dangling arms and long fingers. His hair hung to his knees.

The man stood laughing. Saihung was taken aback at the man's nakedness, and the man noticed right away. He turned a circle and was instantly clothed in Taoist robes. He giggled.

"I am the Toad Taoist," he announced. "Who are you?"

"I am Kwan Saihung, Zhengyi Sect of Huashan."

"Zhengyi Sect, eh? Who's your master?"

"The Grand Master of Huashan."

"I know him." The Toad Taoist laughed. "He's a silly old fool. Why don't you give up this nonsense?"

"Why don't you shut up? You're not even real!"

The Toad Taoist went into a fit of laughter. Saihung decided to ignore him and began his sutra recitation. The Toad Taoist jeered at him, laughed at him, and insulted him for four hours. He had no shortage of breath, and the walls of the rock chamber resounded with his heckling.

Eventually, when he saw that Saihung wasn't to be provoked, he gradually subsided. When Saihung completed his last recitation, the Toad Taoist addressed him in a somewhat more conciliatory tone.

"All right. No one meets me unless they're destined to. What do you want?"

"Nothing."

This set the Toad Taoist laughing again, and he leapt froglike over the pool, landing right before Saihung. Saihung stood up. The Toad Taoist rushed up behind him and stood mimicking Saihung's stance. Saihung stepped to the left. So did he. Saihung walked in a circle. The man shadowed him exactly. Wherever Saihung walked, the Toad Taoist duplicated his very move. Saihung looked back in exasperation. The Toad Taoist grinned and looked at him with an insane expression.

Saihung sat down. The Toad Taoist leaned over Saihung's shoulder and rolled his eyes up at him. After a minute more, he spoke again.

"You're sincere, I'll admit," said the Toad Taoist as he sat down. "There is some substance to the Zhengyi Sect after all. Listen, my boy, do you know why I'm here?"

"No."

"Centuries ago I got into a big fight, and as punishment I was sentenced to this grotto for a thousand years. Well, I'm halfway through now, but I am still cultivating myself continuously. Now what about you? What are you practicing?"

"I am practicing Taoist alchemy and meditation."

"Is that so?" said the Toad Taoist thoughtfully. "Then you must meditate on the *ling qiu*."

"Yes, I do."

"As I said earlier, no one meets me unless the stars decree it. You must have been destined to meet me. I should tell you something as a gift.

"You must realize that, as a student of Taoist alchemy, the *ling qiu* meditation is essential to your progress. But did you know that those psychic centers don't exist? They're only patterns that you imagine at a certain place in your body, imagined patterns that activate the subconscious and release power. In actuality, it is not some psychic center, but purely the mind. Do you realize what I'm saying? The mind is everything. Everything!"

He walked up to Saihung and in a smooth movement brought his palm before Saihung's face.

"Here's a bowl," he said, "and some fruit. An orange, grapes, peaches!"

Saihung tried to think carefully. He touched the fruit. They were real. But he was suspicious. Perhaps the Toad Taoist was presenting him with a puzzle. He thought back and realized that the preceding few moments had been blocked from his consciousness. Fleeting images of the Toad Taoist bending down came to him.

"Those grapes are a twig," said Saihung. Instantly, the grapes reverted. "That orange is a rock. The other fruit are leaves. The bowl is a flat stone." As he mentioned each item, it changed back to its original state and fell from the Toad Taoist's hand.

"I'll admit you're intelligent," said the Toad Taoist, smiling broadly. "You can see how powerful the mind is. You could have eaten that fruit. But would you have been eating a rock or a fruit? The mind decides that. Take the cave itself. We agree this cave exists. It wouldn't if our minds willed otherwise. But what does it matter? The *ling qiu* don't exist, and yet they work!"

The Toad Taoist floated into the air.

"I am using the *dan tian* combined with the throat center," he said. "How can I do it if the *ling qiu* don't exist? It is the mind. I tell you, nothing is real, nothing exists except the mind."

He instructed Saihung in deeper *ling qiu* meditation before saying good-bye. The Toad Taoist jumped into the water and slowly sank until just his head bobbed at the surface. Then that too sank until he was gone. He would return to visit Saihung regularly, but he always arrived and departed in the same odd way.

"Remember, my boy," he called just before he submerged completely. "Nothing is real!"

ONE DAY, SAIHUNG, leaving the chamber, crossed a large stone bridge that vaulted the stream. He noticed an old man and an old woman at the other end. They were dressed in country clothes. The man's snowy hair was put up in a topknot, and he carried a long pipe. The woman had white hair that hung down to her heels, and she carried a straw broom. They greeted him.

"We are bamboo trees over two thousand years old."

"Two-thousand-year-old trees are possible," said Saihung, "but bamboos cannot be people."

"I see by your clothes and talisman that you're a Taoist," said the woman. "You should know such things are possible."

"Anything that is ancient," explained the man, "can be anything it wants. Things need not remain fixed. Take you, for example. You're an ordinary human being. How long could you live? A hundred years? A hundred and fifty? You don't understand the powers of ancient beings."

"You're a Taoist," said the woman, smiling, "and we know all Taoists seek immortality. We can confer immortality on you, and you can see for yourself the power of ancient things. You will have abilities to do things you cannot even imagine now."

"Nothing is free," said Saihung. "What do you want in return?"

"Aah, a straightforward fellow!" exclaimed the old man. "You would only have to be a bamboo for a short period in our service. We can transform your healthy body into a vigorous bamboo that would reproduce and cover the earth with bamboo forests. After you had propagated bamboo everywhere, you would not only be immortal, but you would be able to fly, transform objects, become invisible, enter other dimensions—why, you'd rival the gods themselves! Follow us. Believe in us, and you'll become immortal."

"Thanks for the entertainment," said Saihung mockingly. "However, a person's life span is predestined. Longevity is a gift only from the gods, not something to be bargained for. I don't want your powers. They're only delusion."

The old man rushed forward with an angry roar and struck at him. Saihung warded off the blow and counterattacked, but the old man dodged his blows. The woman leapt on him, clawing at his face. Saihung jumped from the bridge and drew a talisman in the sand before him.

The infuriated man drew a deep inhalation from his pipe and blew a thick cloud of smoke toward him. His wife raised the broom to fan the vapor toward Saihung.

"You are demons!" shouted Saihung as he pointed at them. "I'll recite the Demon Catcher sutra!"

The old couple stopped in fright. Saihung recited the first line, and they fled.

SAIHUNG SAT COMFORTABLY on the meditation platform reading his evening sutra. He had almost memorized the entire scripture in the two years he had been in the cave. The oil lamp burned brightly, and he was almost completely immersed in his contemplation when something caught his eye. On the opposite bank was a young woman with a basket. She was a willowy figure, dressed in a peach-colored silk gown and a diaphanous cape. Her presence was a rich contrast to the roughness of the cave. Saihung looked more closely at her face. She had large brown eyes that radiated a hypnotic feline quality. Her skin was as smooth as satin, and the trace of blush on her cheeks was a fainter echo of her full red lips. Her lustrous black hair, perfectly coiffed, was like a cloud pinned with gold.

Seeing Saihung, she placed her basket aside and shyly pulled a rose-colored scarf from her sleeve. Veiling her nose and mouth, she stood at the water's edge.

"Oh, sir!" she cried out. "How fortunate I am to have met you. I'm afraid I've lost my way."

Saihung looked at her in alarm. He put his hands into a protective prayer gesture. She paused almost imperceptibly when he did that.

"Oh, sir! Won't you please help me?" she repeated.

Saihung recited a sutra for protection. The woman stepped back.

"Why recite that?" she asked in a hurt tone. "There's no need. I won't harm you. Here, I'll entertain you with a dance. Perhaps that will reassure you that I'm only an innocent girl."

Singing in a clear voice, she began a graceful dance. Her every note was perfect, her movements flawless. She seemed to be the very embodiment of femininity. When she finished her dance with a gentle bow, however, she saw that Saihung was immobile and still reciting.

"Aah, you're an ascetic, I see," she said. "If that's what you're interested in, let me tell you that I have achieved power far beyond what you can ever hope for with all this dreary sitting. I can control the five elements. I can command wind and rain. Limitless wealth is mine at any moment. I have everlasting youth and beauty. And I enjoy the boundless pleasures of love.

"Doesn't that far surpass your tradition? A Taoist remains poor, and even if he manages to acquire immortality, he loses beauty and youth. Your tradition also includes celibacy, believing that abstinence will maintain vitality. But I, far from weakening with love, become stronger—as do my lovers.

"Look at yourself. You're muscular, strong, and handsome. It's obvious that it isn't your destiny to remain a begging, ash-covered monk with matted hair, but to become a great prince instead. Come with me. Be my lover. Not only will you know for the first time the pleasure of a woman's love, but you shall gain powers far surpassing your master's."

Saihung continued reciting. The woman sighed.

"Why put on this silly show, sir? Don't you believe me? Or are you the type who only believes what he sees?"

Saihung broke into a sweat from the effort of recitation. He tried to bring his resolution to the fore as he apprehensively watched the woman.

She turned away from him, unpinning her hair. As if the cloud of her hair had burst and rained perfume, Saihung breathed in an exciting fragrance. She turned toward him and slowly removed her cape and outer robes until she stood only in her underrobe. Never taking her eyes from his, she slowly undid its ties. Saihung saw the translucent skin at her neck sweep downward into an expanse of warm nakedness.

Her body was perfect. From the soft slope of her shoulders to her full breasts, over her slender hips, down to her long, shapely legs, she could have been made of jade and gold. She used her flowing hair to veil herself, but it was the contrast between that curtain and what lay boldly open to Saihung's gaze that made the dance of her limbs the most maddening.

151

"They tell me," she said breathlessly, "that men desire all kinds of women. What woman do you crave in your innermost fantasy? What woman makes your loins blaze with want? I can be that woman. I can fulfill your every fantasy.

"I know all styles of love. Come and embrace me. Embrace eternal youth. Love me. You'll be a prince of the greatest stature. Take me. You'll command magnificent powers. Possess me. I'll be yours for eternity. Enter me. Love me over and over. I'll bring you pleasure that will burn, consume, satisfy your innermost hungers, and still arouse a passion that will leave you ever eager for the infinite variations of love."

Saihung sat in stony stiffness, hands pressed together, lips reciting endlessly.

The woman grew angry when she saw that he was not to be moved.

"How dare you scorn me!" she shouted. "No man does that. You stupid monk. You sit there mumbling inanities while the ultimate in the world's riches, powers, and pleasures is yours for the taking! All that idiotic chanting will get you nowhere—and it certainly won't defend you."

She whirled in a circular dance, and where she once stood as a voluptuous nude, there was now only an eerie, trembling pillar of long green hair. It shook frighteningly, emitting a loud cackling that echoed sharply in the cavern.

The pillar revolved slowly, and Saihung saw the woman's face at the top. Her face began to elongate as it turned green. The eyes expanded into black orbs. The hair became a smooth scaly skin. Legs appeared. She metamorphosed into a six-foot lizard.

The lizard slithered into the pool and swam across. Rearing up before the sacred circle, she hissed loudly and flicked her tongue. But though she lunged terrifyingly at him, she couldn't penetrate the power of his sutra.

Saihung was miserable with fear. His hands were wet with perspiration; his robes were soaked. He recited continually. To break his sutra was to lose everything.

152

The lizard disappeared abruptly, and all was temporarily quiet until a dot appeared in the sublime darkness. It expanded into her face. The once-beautiful visage was now a cruelly laughing woman; her soft hair now writhed like snakes around her. She darted at him. Each time she reached the perimeter of the circle, he felt a blow in the pit of his stomach. His body broke into a fever as she maintained the attacks for an hour. Mournful sniffing sounds and pitiful wailing filled the air. He was close to nausea.

She disappeared. He did not dare stop reciting. A howling wind blew on him, extinguishing the torches and knocking over his oil lamp. The glass broke, and the oil flashed into an uncontrolled fire.

A darting flame rose and sped around the cave like a bat on fire. It fluttered maddeningly around him and struck his psychic shield repeatedly. He noticed that her attacks had now penetrated the sacred circle and were closing in. He was hysterical and almost on the verge of tears.

The flame exploded before him, and her face was there once again, her hair rooting itself into the nocturnal air. She laughed mockingly and opened her mouth. She edged toward him, and the mouth grew in size. She would devour him.

Saihung heard the temple bells almost inaudibly; dawn was coming. She pressed toward him. He could feel her hot breath as her lips and teeth opened.

A ray of light edged through the rim of one of the skylights and struck her face. She retreated and reappeared in the beautiful form that she first had come to him. The grotto brightened, and she faded with a moan.

Saihung stopped chanting only when it was definitely day. He stood up in relief. His arms ached, and his legs were stiff. He looked down in sudden awareness. Embarrassed, he realized that he had been so frightened that he had wet his pants.

He took off his clothes and dived into the pool. On the far end, he saw a nose rising. It was the Toad Taoist.

"I see that she tried to get you," he said as he swam over.

Saihung nodded, smiling at the thought that he had overcome the ordeal. The Toad Taoist giggled, splashed him, and spat water at him.

"You have a strong mind," congratulated the Toad Taoist as he dunked Saihung. "That's good. Someday there will be a crisis involving the whole world. It will be a confrontation between good and evil. You'll need this strength to survive."

Internal
Gazing

S AIHUNG LOOKED WITHIN his body. It was transparent.

Meditation, after all, was not stillness. The body always moved: The heart pumped, blood flowed, electricity fired the nerves, energy coursed through the meridians, the organs pulsated in concert, and the lungs, even if they slowed to an apparent stop, still breathed on in an exaggerated timeline. The human being never stopped moving, never stopped changing. A human being was a cosmos. A mysterious progression. A sacred equilibrium.

Saihung looked deeply into himself. He was completely immersed in that which was inner. Inner became everything. Inside and outside became one. Plunging deep within, he came to the perfect realization. Inner and outer became one in infinity.

He was a focus. A pinpoint in the cosmos. A place where infinity had congealed into one mass of movement and experience. *Qi* had become the five elements, had become yin and yang, had become a human being. He was a microcosm of eternity.

Saihung imagined the Big Dipper Constellation.

Silence. Space. Everything was real. Nothing was real. Both were equal. Time and space doubled back on each other in serpentine layers and lost their distinction. What went beyond duality?

The Big Dipper descended.

Humanity was a microcosm of the universe. They were one. One was everything. The organs were planets. The psychic centers were novas. The meridian points were stars. The meridians were pathways to heaven.

The Big Dipper came to him. He called it. He willed it.

He entered it, and it lifted him past the highest clouds, through the sleek canopy of the azure sky into blackness. All was dark save the scatter of stars. The universe was night, but day exploded and burned in its folds.

He hung there floating. It was soundless. He had projected the stars into himself, and now he himself was projected like a star. He was a body in space. Like a planet. A meteor. A sun.

But there was a deeper state. He still was a body. Why was it here, but not over there?

His body expanded in a silent explosion. His perfect mechanism unwound and shot itself in a thousand directions. The body was gone, but an intention still lingered. A memory, distant and shimmering—a strange streak of individualism still floating in space.

The streak dissipated. Beyond stars, planets, and dimensions, beyond any kaleidoscope of reality, piercing infinite layers. Gone. There was only Nothingness.

Saihung sat in the cavern. He felt small. Humble. He was the speck that was everything and nothing.

Solitude and contemplation were all he wanted. Why had he had to return? The gods had willed it. He had a task, and until he fulfilled it, he was in bondage on the earth. But the gods had let him glimpse the other side. He had seen it. He would have stayed had he not been returned.

He didn't want to be here. Nothing on earth was real. What passed for civilization, that supposed massive cultural search for perfection, was only the glorification of grotesque human narcissism. What passed for emotion was only the visceral exercise of perversion. Nothing beckoned to him.

He sat in stillness. He knew he had a task. He was put here for it. Something glimmered in him like a childhood memory. It was compassion: He had been returned not only for his own quest but to help others.

He heard a sound. He saw a moving torch. It was his master.

"It's time for you to leave." The Grand Master smiled as he placed a gentle hand on Saihung's shoulder.

He blindfolded Saihung to protect his eyes from the sunlight and led him to an enclosed shrine. Saihung soaked in herbal baths to cleanse his skin, which had turned blue from living in the earth and bathing in mineral waters. He put an herbal solution in his eyes to strengthen them. Gradually, over the course of a month, he and the Grand Master widened a skylight. But Saihung could see only blue through it.

The day came for him to emerge. He heard his master break the seal and enter. In the semidarkness of the hut, Saihung knelt down before the Grand Master.

"You have been tested thoroughly. You have made great strivings. Only today do you finally glimpse what it is to be a Taoist.

"All that matters to a Taoist is that one is in harmony with nature. In one's character, one is like heaven and earth, as bright as the sun and the moon, as orderly as the four seasons.

"When one has attained Tao, one can even precede heaven, but heaven will not act in opposition, for one will act only as heaven would have at the time. One is not destroyed because one harmoniously follows only the cyclic motion of the Tao, avoiding the aggressive, extravagant expenditures of energy. Efforts to achieve strength and power may lead to short-term success, but such excessiveness ultimately results in an early death.

"The *Tao Te Ching* clearly states that when things reach the pinnacle of their strength, they begin to grow old. Therefore, excessive strength is contrary to Tao, and what is contrary to Tao will come to a speedy end.

"Thus one seeks not to build up one's own power, but to unite with Tao. One is not aggressive and mighty, but rather humble and peaceful. One seeks not to go the way of other men but rather to follow the cycles of nature. Only then can one know renewal and rejuvenation. Through returning and going forth, expansion and contraction, one knows infinity and perhaps even immortality. For at that point, one is wholly integrated with the Tao. One gives undivided attention to its vital energy, responding with the utmost pliancy. Then one can become like a newborn infant."

The Grand Master opened the door. A crack of light expanded into complete brightness. Saihung went into the light of a new world.

two

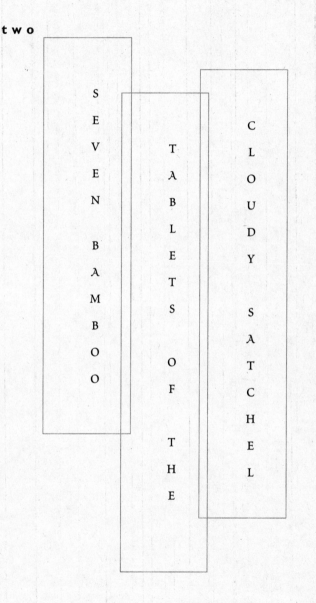

SEVEN BAMBOO

TABLETS OF THE

CLOUDY SATCHEL

Master
and
Student

BEFORE THE DYING night would be bleached by a lavender dawn, Saihung grasped a wooden bucket and held it over a well. The world would be awakening soon. The temples of Huashan would soon be stirring with priests and acolytes. China in early 1941, torn by civil war and soon to be drawn into global war, would awaken to another day of confusion and conflict. But there in the darkness it was quiet, and Saihung single-mindedly applied himself to his task.

He dropped the bucket down into the jet blackness of the well and heard a sharp, cracking sound. In the high mountains, the nights were so cold that ice formed nightly over the pure well waters. He pulled up the bucket again and released it.

His hands were still numb from the water he had spilled on them as he tied the gourd to his body and picked up a basket that contained some firewood and fresh clothing for his master. He retrieved the lantern from where he had casually stuck it into the low eaves of the well's pavilion and made his way toward his master's temple. The light of the candle flickered in its paper sphere, a dancing spot at the end of a slender bamboo handle.

He followed the path around the crest of one of Huashan's many precipices. The surroundings were lost in black, and he could barely see the far mountain ranges through corpulent silhouettes of old pines. Individual pinnacles were smeared in the dye of night; the landscape was a simple division of rough, jagged land and a sky that still had stars and a crescent moon. He had been in these towering mountains for many years, yet he had neither explored them all nor known them fully.

Saihung climbed quickly up the steep, rocky trail, his breath condensing into vapor before his face. He had to hurry. His master would soon be completing his nightlong meditations. He ran up the stone steps to a tiny temple, and walked between two bronze cranes. The words "Hall of the Immortals" were carved above the gate. Its heavy doors were taller than a man by four or five feet. Their top halves were latticework, the lower sections inlaid with mosaic flower designs. He pushed them open with some effort and walked quietly down the tiled hallway to his master's chambers. He paused at the heavy wooden doors.

"Master! Master! Master!" he called out to announce his presence. As always, there was no response. He slowly pushed the door open.

Saihung stood at the threshold. His lantern barely lit the room. The brick walls and stone floor held the cold night air, the large bronze brazier had almost gone out, the morning mists had penetrated the walls of the simply furnished room. There was only a desk, a bookshelf, a bed, and a meditation platform facing a tabernacle. His white-haired master sat there, cushioned by a magnificent tiger's skin. He was erect and unmoving. In the uncertain light, with the swirling mist, his master could have been some ancient and mysterious votive object in a stone chamber. Saihung waited.

The dawning light slightly bleached the open skylight. The master's thin figure moved a little, and soon Saihung could hear breathing other than his own. His master was ready to begin his day. Saihung laid out clean clothing and quickly applied himself to his routine. He carefully opened lattice and paper windows, propping them open with wooden sticks. Then he heaped wood chips and coal into the brazier and fanned the pile to a small but intense flame. Walking quietly across the room, he reverently drew the curtains on the intricately carved tabernacle. There were three beautifully fashioned figures inside. The central one was a Taoist saint and personal patron deity to the Grand Master. The flanking figures were the saint's acolytes. One carried a sword, the other a seal. All three were painstakingly painted and lit by an ever-burning oil lamp.

163

He checked to see that the flowers and fruit were fresh, the teacups and wine cups full, and that no dust had accumulated on the altar. Then he tied the drapes back and lit the incense. The sweet fragrance of sandalwood filled the room, and smoke drifted up into the blue light like tiny gossamer dragons on the chase.

"Altars are for the weak," whispered the Grand Master behind him. He seldom spoke to Saihung directly in these early morning meetings. If he did, it was only to utter a few terse phrases. Sometimes it was an order to bring a certain tea, a specific book, or to prepare for a journey. At other times, he would read aloud or simply make a few philosophical observations. Today he continued briefly on.

"Only those whose belief in themselves is inadequate must have some external image upon which to fix their attention. In actuality, heaven and hell are right here on earth—within each of us."

Saihung turned from the tabernacle, but his master's lips were motionless. The sepulchral silence returned as the Grand Master raised his right elbow and, with a smooth, languid motion, laid it upon a teak armrest. He nodded, a signal for Saihung, who stepped behind him to undo his hair.

The white strands, thick and full, fell down in a mass on the platform. Saihung combed it gently, tenderly. He remembered how the roles had been reversed during his initiation ceremony at the age of twelve. Then, as he had knelt before the altar, his master had combed his hair—symbolically purging attachment to worldliness—and had pinned the Taoist topknot for the first time. In the years since, Saihung had combed his master's hair many times, and each time it had strengthened a tie to the man who guided his life.

The Grand Master, it had been said, had been handsome and dashing in his youth. He had applied himself to the mastery of military arts and strategy, and had also excelled in scholarship. He had gone to the court of the Qing dynasty in Beijing, had entered into the Forbidden City itself to take the Imperial examinations. Within the high red walls and airy halls of the palace, he had been tested over and over. He had completed essays, answered tests in history, mathematics, literature, astronomy, political theory, and dozens of other subjects. He had demonstrated his skills in poetry, calligraphy, horsemanship, archery, and physical combat. After days of trial in the grand capital, he had been awarded the title "Civil and Martial Double Talent." It was one of the highest ranks, and he had been employed as an Imperial tutor.

He had thus walked the halls of royalty itself. He had absorbed the courtly etiquette and directed the mental progress of princes. Not long after his acceptance into the royal house, he had married a beautiful woman of noble background, thereby completing his success.

But a tragedy struck him, and he lost it all. Saihung's curiosity about this pivotal event had never been satisfied. No one could say what this event had been. Had it been court intrigue, the manipulation of vicious eunuchs? Could he have fallen into disgrace, advocating an unpopular viewpoint? Or had martial rivals murdered his family? Whatever the unknown circumstances had been, they had been traumatic enough for the Grand Master to have fled the world itself. He had sought solace in a life away from society. He had become a Taoist, by studying under two masters, and had entered into the priesthood. Two classes of religious life had then been opened to him: to become the resident priest of a temple, performing all public functions of ritual, divination, marriage, and funerals, or to become a renunciate following the tradition of monastic hermits. He had chosen the latter path.

He had gradually risen in the Taoist hierarchy until he had reached his present position. His title implied not only a supreme mastery of Taoist doctrine and ascetic practices, but a high temporal power as well. The acquisition of that power had taken decades, and the Grand Master was rumored to be more than one hundred years old.

165

The worlds that formed the Grand Master's background were unique social structures with only vague parallels to world history. If one imagined a surreal combination of medieval Europe—when sword, sorcery, church, throne, and alchemy all coexisted; and classical Greece—when a pantheon of gods ruled the universe, philosophers headed up their own schools, and the Spartans were the standard of warriors—then perhaps one would have some inkling of the culture that had shaped the Grand Master's life. Nothing in the universe was ever really destroyed; people drew no distinction between ancient and modern. From the oldest methods of agriculture to the latest technological invention, everything had its place in the vastness.

The Grand Master embodied a sea of tradition, history, culture, and religion, and was a purist and strong theologian. He administered the temples with a firm and broad-minded policy and tried to teach his disciples with the wisdom and strong sense of order and purpose that he had developed over his many years.

Saihung often compared himself to his master. He too was lean, severe, and grave. But his muscles were inflated and hardened by weight lifting and martial arts, his black hair was thick and coarse, and his skin was darkened by years of exposure to the sun. He could see that he was markedly different. He was temperamental, impulsive, and without his master's deep serenity. He let out a soft sigh. In his eyes, his master was a lofty figure. An inspiration, but perhaps a living ideal that he would never succeed in emulating.

Saihung wordlessly gathered his basket and his master's discarded clothes for washing. He noted with satisfaction that the room was warming and the mists had been dispelled. He placed the gourd of springwater at his master's side so that it would be available to quench his thirst after heat-building meditation. Saihung paused at the doorway to glance back. His master had crossed his legs, touched his fingers together, and closed his eyes. Within seconds he was again as motionless as a statue. As dawn finally rose on the mountain, Saihung saw the first ray of morning edge into the skylight and light his master's face.

Saihung left to wash, attend morning devotions, and eat a simple vegetarian meal with fellow monks. Afterward, he went to fetch his master's breakfast. All along, he pondered his master's few whispered words. If heaven and hell were on earth, there might be neither reward nor retribution. If that were so, then there might be neither good nor evil. Furthermore, then, why should he worship and attend boring devotional services? As he walked toward the kitchen, he resolved that he would have to question his master more closely.

The kitchen was a hell of heat. Woks large enough to bathe a child in sat on roaring, wood-burning brick stoves. Young monks fed the insatiable fires, while others stirred the boiling rice. Some chopped vegetables or prepared them for pickling. They were all under the direction of a senior priest, who was known only as "the Old Cook."

A stubborn man whose spine and shoulders seemed fused, he was as thick and squat as the inscribed stone stele in the courtyard. His head was big and solid, the cheeks fat, and eyes round—dark, but registering a surprising awareness for someone of such a boarlike countenance. He was an impatient supervisor.

The abbots had long tried to calm his bursts of temper, as deeming them sacrilegious and a poor example, but even Taoism could only do so much.

"You're late," grumbled the old cook with a bad-humored expression. "The vegetables are cold. Your master must be starving."

"This little one recognizes his sin," apologized Saihung. He seized the covered wicker tray, the dishes clattering within, and rushed out the door to his master's chambers. None of the high-ranking priests ate in the dining halls. They were served by their students.

"Master! Master! Master!" he called at the door. Silence. He went in, and his master smiled at him. Saihung bowed and set the basket down. He took out the covered porcelain dishes and set them on the table. There was a tofu and gluten dish, freshly sautéed vegetables with mushrooms, peanuts and pickles, rice, and steamed bread. The fragrance—rich, clear, and fresh—burst like a cloud from each dish. Saihung could scarcely contain himself, and his mouth was watering as he poured tea and placed chopsticks delicately on their porcelain holder.

"How are your studies coming?" the Grand Master asked as he began to eat. Saihung adjusted quickly. Sometimes his master would say nothing for days. He had to seize the opportunity whenever his master was inclined to talk.

"It is hard to perfect oneself," replied Saihung modestly.

"There is a saying, 'The mind of a holy man is like a mirror. It neither grasps nor resists. It receives and returns. It is for this reason that the sage encompasses the world without hurt.' This is something which you must strive for. You must purify yourself. Do not occupy your mind with trivialities."

"Great Master, is there such a thing as good and evil, right and wrong?"

"Why do you ask?"

"You have said, 'Everything we do, we do ourselves,' and 'Heaven and hell are right here on earth.' Does that mean that there is no external authority? And if not, who is to define right and wrong?"

"I will tell you a story to explain," said the Grand Master. "Once a beautiful and richly dressed woman appeared at a house. Naturally, the owner of the house welcomed her. He was dazzled by her ethereal loveliness.

"'May I ask who you are?' he said.

"'I am the Goddess of Fortune,' she replied. 'I bring luck to unhappy children, heal the diseased, grant children to the barren, bring untold riches, and fulfill every wish and supplication.'" The owner of the house immediately straightened his robes, bowed low before her, and personally gave her the honored seat in his home.

"Before long, another woman came. She was bent over and hobbled. Her face was desiccated, misshapen, wrinkled. Her hair was as tangled as dry rice grass. She stank. The owner was indignant and rudely demanded to know why she was trespassing.

"'I am called the Dark Lady. Wherever I go, the rich go bankrupt, high officials fall in disgrace, the weak die, the strong lose their might, women weep endlessly, and men mourn.'

"The owner immediately seized her staff to drive her away.

"But the Goddess of Fortune stopped him, saying, 'Those who would honor me must also honor her, for wherever I go, the Dark Lady inevitably follows. We are as inseparable as a shadow to a body. We cannot live apart.'

"The owner understood immediately and urged both goddesses to depart, now very much afraid that both might stay. The wise lead their lives in this way."

The Grand Master looked at Saihung to see if he had understood the parable. He saw only a quizzical student. The Grand Master picked up his chopsticks and ate quietly. After many minutes of thoughtfulness, he continued.

"Good and evil do exist. There is bright Tao and dark Tao. There are demons and gods. There are good and bad people. But there is no evil in nature, the constellations, nor in animals. These things are allied with Tao and have no volition of their own. They follow the Tao with no resistance. This is what is meant by the mirror that neither grasps nor resists, that perceives and returns simultaneously. But humanity and gods differ from plants, stars, and animals in one crucial respect: They have intelligence. They have rational, calculating minds. They have free will. It is because of their scheming that people have good and evil. They can make a choice, and there would be no choice without both good and evil.

"Yin and yang are the fundamental duality of the universe. Neither is mutually exclusive. For darkness to exist, there must be light. For day to come, night must precede it. If there is a right, then there must be wrong. This is the first meaning of the parable.

"The human race was created from yin and yang. We are both. If we had no tension and interplay between polar opposites, there could be no movement within us or in the universe. There would be complete stagnation, a supreme stasis. Sterility would be the sole reality. Thus, we must accept relativity. We must accept good and evil, because they are part of the fundamental process of creation. If you can comprehend this, then I must tell you one other thing: You must accept both good and evil within yourself."

"Great Master," broke in Saihung, "I am a Taoist. My endeavor is to live a decent life. I wish only to improve myself and to be a force for good."

The Grand Master laughed sarcastically. "How pious you are! There is nothing more disgusting than the pious."

"I don't understand. Isn't this what I've been taught since childhood? Is there anything objectionable to living a moral life? Why should I not yearn to live as a hero of justice?"

"Morality and ethics are for the stupid and unthinking. Such people may lack discrimination but nevertheless possess scheming minds. The sages invented morality solely to control such fools. Those who understand the Tao should not heed such things."

Saihung paused. He could not quite bring himself to accept the Grand Master's words. Surely, he was not being told that morality and immorality were indistinguishable. "I am quite confused by your words. Please instruct me. You cannot be saying that to be evil is as valuable as to be good."

"I am only saying that morality is not for the discriminating," said the Grand Master in irritation. "The pious and moral person lives his life in fear of doing wrong. Whenever he commits a 'sin,' he rushes to the temples to beg the gods for forgiveness and strength. He sees depictions of hell's retribution and trembles at the thought of falling so low. He reads scriptures, gives alms to the poor, and works himself into constant anxiety about doing 'good.' All this praying and mumbling is useless. He lives his life a babbling, idiotic slave of superstition. The gods are not in the least attracted by someone who bows and scrapes his way through life."

"Can I stop going to devotional service then?" asked Saihung mischievously.

"Rebellion!" exploded the Grand Master. Saihung shrank back. "You are a monk. You must do this as a type of etiquette, even a duty. But inwardly, you should understand the actual nature of what you are doing. For the public, you are performing an important service. For yourself, you must use this for self-control and self-discipline. In this way, you reaffirm the good and do nothing to support evil. You are destined to be a holy aspirant.

"Those who have some wisdom accept that they embody contradictory elements. Thus, even while they cleave to the good, they know that they will inevitably do bad, but they understand themselves when they do. Committing evil should not be intentional. Do not say, 'Today I must do my quota of bad deeds in order to fulfill my destiny.' That is an utter mistake. Rather, you must always strive to understand a situation before you act. You must perceive what is required of you and then fulfill it. You must take this action whether or not it conforms to petty morality. This is the way of the sages. That is why the owner sent the two goddesses away. He understood relativity, and the inseparability of opposites. He chose the way of the wise: He chose neither good nor evil, but a transcendent path instead. A smart-ass hears the doctrine that he's both good and evil and thinks it a license for him to act as he pleases. He'll never understand that in doing so he will bounce eternally between the two poles.

"Take yourself, for example. You commit enough mischief for a hundred demons. I accept this as natural. But don't think you can use Taoism to justify it. Because you intentionally plunge into reckless behavior, you have still not escaped duality. The sage seeks to transcend duality."

Saihung was scarlet with embarrassment. He tried to ask another question to divert the conversation away from himself.

"If 'Everything we do, we do ourselves,' and if good and evil exist solely inside beings of volition, then there can be no retribution. Then there can be no higher discriminating authority."

"You are a tricky one, I admit," said the Grand Master. "But such sophistry will get you nowhere. Let me explain. Good and evil are not as simple as heroes and villains in an opera. Good and evil exist as destiny and fate."

"Destiny and fate?" responded a puzzled Saihung. "Aren't they the same?"

"No, they aren't. Destiny is that which you must fulfill in this lifetime. You are born with a task. During your life, you must continually strive to identify it and complete it to its last detail.

This is no simple errand, mind you. It is a terribly intricate and unique enigma for each person that must slowly be brought to fruition. The issue at stake is nothing less than transcending the consequences of past lives in order to be reborn in a higher state or, better yet, to escape all together. That is destiny.

"Fate is an active agent that exists solely to deter you from fulfilling your destiny. It struggles against you, impedes your progress. Fate functions through illusion. It is responsible for mirages that lead you astray. It is temptation. It tricks you, fills your mind with grand notions and proud thoughts. Fate would like nothing better than to deter you from your goal. Whenever you think of doing wrong or playing a trick, and you become aware of yourself, you have instantly found fate. Give and fate has won. Resist and it has lost. But it will be there, tirelessly waiting to distract you once more.

"This is what 'Heaven and hell are right here on earth' means. Don't look outwardly for heavenly beings and hellish denizens. Look within you. Pursue your destiny and you are closer to heaven. Yield to fate and you slip toward hell. If you ultimately fulfill your destiny, you transcend human existence. If you fall to Fate, you suffer in a quagmire of delusion and ignorance.

"Don't naively think that gods and devils administer you and the cosmos. Again, this is folk superstition. The gods *do* exist, but they don't look like the figures upon the altar. Furthermore, they have little interest in humanity. There is nothing we can do to gain a visit from the gods anyway; they cannot bear our human stench. No, don't rely on gods and don't be afraid of devils. They have their own problems, for even they must struggle with destiny and fate.

"If you understand good and evil as destiny and fate, you understand that your actions alone move you toward one or the other. Nothing else enters into your life equation. Solve a bit of your destiny and you triumph. Give in the slightest to delusion and your vision is all the more obscured. You used this saying to argue against a metaphysical authority, but the case is quite the opposite.

"There is no demon to punish you if you're bad. Hell doesn't exist after death unless you believe in it; the mind is strong enough to create exactly the place you envision and imprison your entire being in that dimension for an eternity. Retribution only exists within the mechanism of consequence. Consequence is not a being. It has no mind. It's not a thing. It is a force.

"All your actions have consequences. Put water over fire and it boils. Jump up and you will come back down. Action and reaction. In precisely the same way, your every action simultaneously has a commensurate reaction. In a person's life, the strands of consequence can become hopelessly tangled, imprisoning him in a matted and thick web. Such a person will be reborn a thousand times. But a net can also catch fish. The strands can be knotted into a net of good. This is the consequence of the devout person: The web of his past good actions continues to grow and generates more good, but he will still have to be reborn. The highest level is to transcend good and evil and erase one's consequences altogether. Then one leaves the wheel of life. So there is such a thing as divine retribution. It is neither the punishment decreed by the Jade Emperor nor by the King of Hell. Divine retribution is your simple interaction of destiny, fate, and consequence. That is all."

Saihung tried his best to memorize and comprehend the words.

"Don't strain your mind," commented the Grand Master dryly. "You've not completed your life of mischief yet."

"I'll still try to understand." Saihung grinned.

"Good, good." The Grand Master laughed. "Keep trying."

As was his habit, the Grand Master ate only a very small bit of millet and a bird's sampling of the dishes. Saihung urged the Grand Master to eat more.

"I eat only to maintain my tie to this earthly plane," responded the Grand Master. "I could live on air and drink only the dew from trees, but I am not ready to relinquish my identity as a man. Sages who do not eat food already live half their lives in a divine state. As for me, I can only glimpse the divine, and I accept that I have more to do in order to complete my task on earth. I do not want my body to deteriorate. The body must be maintained in an absolutely perfect equilibrium. It must be in peak health to function as one's spiritual vehicle. I eat only enough to satisfy my body. Please take these dishes away and complete your kitchen duties."

"As you wish, Great Master," said Saihung with a bow. He cleared the table and left the room.

Once around the corner, he glanced up and down the deserted hall. The white light that came through the lattice and paper window gave the wicker basket a warm glow. He set the basket down on the gray tile floor and opened it. He touched the lid of a dish. His hand felt the smooth blue-and-white porcelain. Saihung quietly set the lid aside and removed the dish. He brought it to his lips, and the pickles and peanuts were gone instantly. One by one, he devoured every morsel of food in the basket before returning to the kitchen.

173

"Was the Grand Master pleased?" asked the old cook eagerly. Like any cook, he wanted his creations to be well received. Saihung wordlessly brought out the empty plates and displayed them triumphantly. The old cook's shiny face expanded in a joyous smile.

"He ate it all!" the cook marveled. "Tomorrow, we should send more. He's so thin! He musn't go hungry!"

"As you say, Master," said Saihung humbly.

S AIHUNG WALKED REVERENTIALLY up the steep granite steps toward the temple in which he had been initiated, the Hall of the Three Pure Ones. The stone was so hard that countless processions had failed to soften the edges. He saw small puddles of water here and there, for the steps and portico had been thoroughly washed only an hour before.

The temple facade was set back from the mighty cinnabar-colored wooden pillars that supported the beamed ceiling. The hall was at least fifty feet high at the ridgepole, and its colors were brilliant in the sun. The lintels were painted in geometrical designs of red, green, gold, and blue surrounding small vignettes of holy scenes. Above the red-lacquered doors was a huge black plaque with the temple's name flowing in raised gold calligraphy. The doors of the temple were heavy and extended high enough for him to have walked straight in with another man standing on his shoulders. Avoiding the latticework, he placed his palms on the center, away from the inlaid floral design, and pushed the doors open with great effort. There was a rush of cool air.

The sheer verticality of the doors was matched by the soaring proportions of the hall's interior. Like most Chinese sacred halls, the ridgepole paralleled the front entrance; the hall was wider than it was deep. The lines of the roof sloping down in the rear, and the supporting pillars, which were naturally shorter toward the back, created an exaggerated perspective. Combined with the raised platform and larger-than-life-sized deities, the illusory perspective gave the hall a surreal sense of space.

The breathtaking architectural proportions were matched by the dazzling richness of color. All the supporting beams were carved and painted in a manner even more complicated than the exterior beams. The patterns formed intricate screens and kaleidoscopic backdrops.

Three altars were placed side by side, and each had a god framed by gilded archways. On closer inspection, one could see that the gold filigree screens were formed of thousands of figures no larger than a finger's length.

The gods were painted to look as if they could be flesh and blood, giving a clear impression of substance beneath the robes, the contours of firm muscle or a swelling chest. The faces were painted a skin color, eyes and lips rendered in perfect detail. The hands of all three were exposed, but each was held in a different gesture. Lao Tzu, on the left, held a fan. The Original Being, in the center, held an orb that represented the universe. The Jade Emperor, on the right, held a scepter. All three had clothing so artfully carved that they draped like real cloth. The robes and prayer rugs were depictions of the wealthiest brocades. The lacings of gold leaf formed beautiful highlights that caught the worshiper's eye from any angle.

The thrones on which they sat cross-legged were worthy of emperors. They too were carefully carved, as if every stroke of the sculptor's knife and every mark of the painter's brush was a gesture of devotion.

In any other context, the Three Pure Ones would have been considered sculptures of the highest quality. Any connoisseur of art would instantly have recognized not only the imagination, vitality, and craftsmanship, but also the epiphanatic element that is part of all great art. They had that mysterious ability to evoke reverence and awe, and to provoke thought and introspection. They had a sense of aliveness that transcended the physical reality of wood and paint.

Saihung walked toward the high altar, which was already laden with huge vases of purple, yellow, and red flowers, unblemished fruit, food offerings, and fragrant sandalwood. Oil lamps were ready to be lit. The many ritual implements, such as bells, wooden knockers, gongs, and a jade scepter lay waiting. The red candles had been lit already, and hundreds more awaited lighting on the side. Saihung knew his master was purifying himself in preparation for the ritual before Taoism's supreme trinity. Soon the hall would be filled with solemn holy men, the fire of devotion within them burning as brightly as the hundreds of flames in the temple. Saihung didn't want to miss a single moment. He looked for a good vantage point in anticipation of the great event he had planned. He would be able to see every corner of the hall from the beams some twenty-five feet above the floor. The only way up was to climb the gilded archways that framed the Three Pure Ones. He quickly put his fingers into the carvings. His toes found other openings, and he climbed up, stepping on the heads of the God of Longevity, the Goddess of Mercy, and a host of Immortals, Sea Dragons, and demons.

He swung himself in great glee onto the wide beam. He saw that it wasn't even painted on top, but there were decades of dust and incense soot in a grimy layer. Streaks of dark gray smeared over his clean blue ritual robes and dirtied his hands. Saihung didn't care. His excitement took him over completely.

He inched out to the very center of the beam and waited for the procession's approach. The mighty bronze echoes of the temple bells reverberated through the mountains. Every stone, each pine, even the flowing streams, responded to the command of those mighty strikes. This was one of Huashan's holiest of days. There had been neither classes nor chores that morning, only ablutions and private devotions.

Saihung heard the procession approaching with the gentle sounds of gongs, clappers, and chanting. The temple doors were opened by young novices. The regular monks entered first, each one in blue gowns and pants, white leggings and straw sandals. Only the hats differed in shape, some round, others square, some with two peaks, to denote the rank of the wearer. The residents of Huashan filed in with solemnity and order. Their very steps were measured, and their hands were clasped as a sign of discipline and preservation of holy energy.

176   The higher priests were dressed in more colorful clothes, embroidered with the same plethora of colors that decorated the temple interior. The Grand Master, as the leader, was dressed most colorfully of all. His black gauze hat had nine peaks, the symbol of the highest office of any Taoist monastic order. An oval piece of green jade was sewn to the front of the hat. His beard was full and dazzling white in the sunshine, and it flowed like a river down his chest. The robe's predominant colors were purple, red, and gold, although many other colors had been employed to form embroidered symbols of cranes, bats, the word "longevity" in some of the "Ten Thousand Variations" and the trigrams of the *I Ching*. The satin surface of the robes was exquisite in its sheen, and brilliant in its color as only silk could be.

The Grand Master gracefully stepped over the eight-inch-high threshold of the temple doors. He hitched up his long, trailing sleeves and full hem with a subtle, unobtrusive gesture, and walked closer to the Three Pure Ones. At no time did he glance down. His mind and soul were fixed on the objects of his worship with complete concentration.

All the candles had been lit, and the dark temple interior glowed with hundreds of pinpoints of golden flame. The incense from the central altar—a smoldering stick of pure sandalwood—wafted up in twisting clouds. The Grand Master lit three long sticks of incense and prostrated himself at each altar before offering the burning lengths on behalf of the entire mountain. Behind him, the other priests maintained their soft chanting. The long phrases of devout words formed currents of adoration that intertwined with the fragrant smoke. It was by that chain, raised ever heavenward, that the Taoists hoped to link heaven and earth.

The Grand Master returned to the central altar and opened the sacred scripture. Each Taoist deity had its own scriptures, and Taoists firmly believed that the figures of wood and paint could be awakened by the chanting of the appropriate texts. If the supplicants were sincere enough, the offerings sweet enough, and the place pure enough, the gods could be coaxed from the perfection of heaven.

The Grand Master's nasal voice rose like the sound of an oboe. It was reedy, yet full of deep and subtle resonances. It was an almost operatic ceremony; the gongs and wooden clappers maintained a steady pulse that punctuated appropriate climaxes in the reading. As the Grand Master's voice grew louder, and the incense had burned furiously to half its length, the sanctity of the ceremony was suddenly interrupted by a horrendous noise.

The priests broke their concentration. Although nothing was supposed to have the power of distracting them when they faced the gods, they turned involuntarily. One of the teak doors came crashing to the cold floor, sending up clouds of dust from the cracks. It fell at an angle, and the impact sent a split like lightning down its length. Three men stood in the doorway.

The light from the south-facing doors was glaringly bright, and many of the priests' eyes were dim from the darkness and smoke. Sentry priests rushed in, while the others shrank back in panic toward the altar. The three men now charging to the temple center were clearly fighters.

Moving pugnaciously, their muscles bulging like melons in the sleeves of their corduroy clothes, the three glared viciously at the puny holy men. Their queues—which, like most martial artists, they still wore not as a symbol of allegiance to the long-dead Qing dynasty, but as a sign of their elite class—swung about them like live snakes. They planted themselves before the altar and simultaneously wrapped the braids around their necks. They had come to fight.

"Who is the Grand Master?" thundered the tallest.

"It is I," said the Grand Master gently. He came forward with a courteous bow. "Have we offended you worthy patrons in some way?"

"Damn you! Didn't you send this?" One boxer pulled out a thin sheet of mulberry paper. Jet-black calligraphy showed through the translucent fiber. "It says: 'You three dare to call yourselves Heaven, Earth, and Man. These arrogant titles are more than I can tolerate. In all my years of wandering in the red dust of the world, I have never seen more pathetic caricatures of human beings. Your presumption to call yourselves martial artists on the basis of insignificant brawls with children is even more laughable. If you've any ounce of true courage, meet my challenge at the place and time I designate below. Only by eliminating you from the world can this life be cleansed of your foul presence.'"

"I assure you I never wrote that!" said the Grand Master hastily. "I am a humble and poor priest. I would not dare to compete with heroes such as yourselves. This is a great misunderstanding."

"Shut up! Isn't this your signature and seal?"

The Grand Master looked down as the letter was thrown to the floor. It was the only time in his life that Saihung had seen his master shocked. The old man's eyes were wide in disbelief, and his mouth dropped open. The signature was his. The seal was genuine.

The tall man who represented Heaven took the Grand Master's surprise as an admission of guilt, and squared off for his attack. The Grand Master saw that talk was useless. His face became suddenly fierce; his body began moving warily. Even his robes seemed to bristle with electrical energy.

Heaven, dressed in dark blue corduroy tunic and pants, moved with pantherlike energy into the salutation of the Golden Arhat system. He would not be fighting with fists and kicks, only with his palms. His dark face was lined and had a somewhat skewed appearance; his nose had been broken in his youth.

"Today is your funeral, old man," he snarled.

"Life and death are preordained by the gods," replied the Grand Master fiercely. "If I am to die, I am happy to do so before the gods. But you will not be the one to send me to King Yama."

"Raise your hands, old fool. I do not want gossip that I killed a defenseless man."

"Why cling to a nonexistent honor?" replied the Grand Master without raising his hands. "Attack when you please. If I use more than three moves to defeat you, I will consider myself dishonored."

"Die, then!"

Heaven lunged forward with a low growl. But the champion of hundreds of matches only managed a single strike that was blocked with the same hand that turned his head in a devastating slap. He fell unconscious.

Saihung could not contain himself and began giggling. The Grand Master looked up, and the face that was fierce for fighting became red with fury. But before he could speak, Earth attacked him.

Earth was a fat, pockmarked, and coarse man. His moves, derived from the Shaolin style, were not fancy. They were awkward and simplistic. But his sheer weight and strength had always been technique enough. Outweighing the average man by sixty pounds, he was a squat and ugly menace.

He closed in on the Grand Master with a reckless charge that the thin old man sidestepped. He came again. A look of regret flickered on the Grand Master's face. It would be like a pig before the butcher, but the martial code demanded fulfillment. He dodged and stepped forward. The sound of his fluttering sleeve was like a flag in a hurricane. He brought his palm slicing down on the kidneys, and a kick then dislocated the knee.

Man was a thin, wiry creature with an ugly scar down the right side of his rectangular face. His salute showed him to be a Wudong stylist. Again, the Grand Master allowed his opponent to attack first. The attacker made a feint to the midsection before a rapid jab to the eyes. The Grand Master's hand slid out of his full sleeves, grasped the wrist, and, with a twist, threw Man to the floor. A flick of his toe knocked him unconscious.

The Grand Master stepped back and ordered people to carry the men out. Doctor-priests were sent to revive them and reset dislocated bones. The Grand Master had wanted only to incapacitate them momentarily. He knew they had been duped into the attack.

"Beast!" he shouted at Saihung. "Come down here!"

Saihung quietly slid down a pillar.

"Go to your quarters until you're called."

It was another three hours before the Grand Master's personal attendants, the two acolytes, escorted Saihung to his master's chambers. The Grand Master was still in his ceremonial costume.

179

He walked slowly around his desk until he was face-to-face with Saihung. Saihung could sense a sudden acceleration in his master's body. His master slapped him sharply on the cheek.

"Kneel!" he commanded. "You evil child! This blasphemous act would have been unimaginable for any normal person. I knew you forged my name as soon as I heard you laugh. Only you, with your constant penchant for mischief, could have conceived such a scheme."

Saihung was quiet. He did not dare reply. But inside, he still reveled in the sheer excitement of it all.

"You made a serious error," the Grand Master continued. "You made a fool of yourself, dishonored me, and violated the sanctity of consecrated ground. Your sin is heavy indeed."

"But they deserved it." Saihung smirked. "What better way to humiliate them than to beat them before the Three Pure Ones? After all, the Trinity is even higher than Heaven, Earth, and Man."

"You are forgetting yourself by talking so freely!" interrupted the Grand Master. "You will be punished. But first, tell me how you arranged this shameful incident."

"I was begging for alms," recounted Saihung, "when I happened across their school. I went in to challenge them myself but saw that I could not beat them. So I came back and sent the letter. Anyone so arrogant that they take such a high title deserves to be taken down a notch or two."

"You are wrong," scolded the Grand Master. "It is you who deserve humbling. Take him away."

The two acolytes took Saihung to a cave that ran far below the surface. The air was chilly and moist. Kindly, they had brought some padded clothing. All three were silent—the two acolytes because of solemnity, Saihung because he was still reliving his delight.

They came to a water-filled chamber. The place where a stalactite and stalagmite once met had broken centuries ago, leaving a jagged point over a round plateau about five feet in diameter. The rock platform was in the middle of a wide underground pool, and it was about ten feet above the surface. A heavy wooden plank stretched from the outcropping where they stood to the tiny island. The acolytes thrust the clothing and a gourd of water into Saihung's hands and ordered him across. Once he had seated himself, they withdrew the plank.

Saihung watched them turn, and he saw the glow from their torches fade in the darkness. His sentence was to sit in meditation for forty-nine days in order to contemplate his crime. During that time, he would have only rice gruel and water. Saihung closed his eyes, and the frigid air made him cough. The murmur of the water was a constant disturbance, and he heard uncomfortable shuffling noises from bats above. He knew he would suffer, but every time he recalled the day's events, he would laugh. Repentance would not come easily when he found the delicious results from the crime so wonderful to savor.

A few jagged openings high above him threw tiny pale spots of dim light on the surface of the pool. He could see only a slight reflection of the drooping stone formations and grotesque iridescent cauliflowerlike mineral deposits. The black liquid moved slowly and deeply.

He grew unhappy. There was no escape but memory. As he looked into the water, he remembered the pools of sparkling aquamarine in the pine forests of his family estate. He recalled how, as a young boy, he had learned to swim. Third Uncle had tied two enormous gourds to him so the water would buoy him up rather than swallow him. The experience had been one of his happiest childhood memories.

Painful remembrances came as well. Sent at the age of seven to the village school to supplement his home tutorials, he had been beaten up daily. He had fought back but could never overcome the apparently magical onslaughts of his tormentors. Ashamed to tell anyone, he had stoically borne his suffering until Third Uncle had noticed some bruises while they had been swimming.

"I fight, but they do strange things with their hands and legs, and I always lose," Saihung had lamented.

"You silly boy," Third Uncle had scolded. "They're using martial arts."

"What's that?" he had asked. Only then had he begun to learn not just techniques to defend himself, but a pivotal fact:

His family was of a warrior class, descended from the Manchus of the Qing dynasty and of the God of War, Guan Gong. Until then, he had known nothing. All practice of technique and all weaponry were kept hidden even from the clan children.

He felt there were answers in the past that the temples preserved. The wisdom of ancient times was not, for him, in the realm of archaeology. There was splendor, inspiration, and treasure. He felt a comfort in the antique, a hint of stability, an air of survival. In the worn buildings on high cliffs so close to heaven, he felt a resonance within his soul. He could reflect on the lapsed glories of old civilizations, muse on the passing of mortal things, and ponder the eternity of spiritual endeavor. Taoism spoke of immortality, and he had committed himself to its study not so much for the sake of longevity, but rather for the sake of finding the immortal poetics that would transcend his feelings of conflict, decay, and temporality.

But for the time being, he was condemned to the cave. He did see how his own faults had not only landed him there, but had interfered with his goals.

Saihung's initial attempts to make this a time of formal fasting and meditation gave out at some vague point halfway through his term. He quit the pretense. He was cold and hungry, and his thoughts were distorted. He spent much of his time sleeping—or perhaps simply lapsing from consciousness. He was oddly intrigued to find that the hard rock had become an acceptable sleeping surface and that he barely cared anymore if his cheek was powdered with dust.

Forty-nine days later, his awareness trapped in a frigid stupor, he saw a wooden plank slide across the floor of his tiny world. It pushed a small heap of dust and dirt before it and made an unpleasant scraping noise. He tried to look up, but it was difficult to make both his eyes focus on the same point. He saw flashes of flame, heard stepping noises, and felt a viselike grip on his arms. The fingers squeezed him painfully, the muscles that he had once flexed so proudly now yielding flaccidly.

He coughed, but nothing came up through his dry throat. The smell of smoke made his cough worse. He found himself negotiating the flexing plank. The flowing ink below him was a molten night sky. The reflected torches were like dying suns, dissolving in rivers of spent gas and exhausted flame. He heard moans and whimpers from those expiring stars, but then he adjusted his consciousness and realized that it was the creaking wood. He was wobbly. His muscles disobeyed the orders to stabilize his movements. His adrenals had long ago run dry.

Saihung finally made out the faces of the two acolytes and managed a half-smile.

They tenderly supported him as he stumbled through the tunnel to the outside. It was a cold dawn, but the breeze felt warmer to Saihung than the subterranean air. He opened his mouth to speak with what seemed like a gargantuan but ludicrous misaligning of his jaws. The acolytes only whispered to him to be quiet. They would take him to their own cell to nurse him back to health.

His dirty hair hung like withered roots; his face was gray with grime. Saihung's beard had grown into a chaotic jumble of black lines. He could have been a troll from the earth. He was a creature, a wretched, depleted, crumpled beast. Obstinate, rebellious, and proud, Saihung reflected that he was barely sorry for the prank that had led to this denigration.

He saw again the mountain beauty of Huashan, the towering vistas, the azure perfection of the sky. The legends, inspired by Huashan's gigantic tripod shape, had said the mountains were the very support to heaven's vault. As Saihung breathed in its clean air and tasted the bitter restorative given to him, he knew that the splendor of nature would hasten his return to normal life.

Two
Butterflies

S AIHUNG, NOW BACK to a regular routine, still found morning devotions utterly boring. When his master spoke, he found the words alive and full of relevance. By contrast, he found all this mumbling quite dreadful. These words were hundreds of years old, formed by sages in the intricate patterns that would lead the aspirants to divine heights. But to Saihung, they were only a barrier to breakfast.

He could barely remain reverent as he entered the refectory with the sounding of another bell. Silence was absolute. Not only was talking prohibited, but even glancing at one another was punishable by a healthy stroke from the prefect's cane. The prior filled a bowl, while Saihung and his fellow monks stood in devotion, and offered it at the altar of a Taoist saint. Flanking the altar were two long trestle tables built from heavy timbers.

Saihung spooned up his bowl of rice porridge from the large wooden tub and sat down. There was a plate of pickled cabbage, turnips, and cucumbers for every two monks, and Saihung scrupulously ate only his half. He returned for a second bowl— the maximum amount allowed—and washed it all down with boiled water. "A pity it isn't a festival day," Saihung lamented to himself. Then at least he would have had a piece of fried wheat bread too.

After breakfast Saihung went to wash himself. The open-air washing pavilion had a series of enormous ceramic urns with holes at the bottom to drain the waste water. Two lengths of bamboo lined with copper tubing were fixed above the urns. The left-hand one carried water directly from an artesian well, while the right-hand one carried hot water. Everything in the mountain was done by human labor. Two young monks heated the water in a large boiler over an open flame before diverting it into the pipe. Saihung undressed and stepped into the urn. The bottom was cold, and the air was frigid. He splashed himself quickly and rubbed himself with sandalwood soap. He noted with satisfaction that his muscles were still hard and defined. Philosophy was fine, but physical prowess was tangible.

The hot water was too hot. He didn't know which was worse, cold water in the frigid morning air or the contrasting torture of the hot water. Saihung got out, dried off, dressed, and thanked the two boys. This morning he was scheduled not for lectures, but for class in the staff and sword with the Sick Crane Taoist. He started out in anticipation not simply of the class, but of seeing his friend as well.

The Grand Master had thirteen disciples, of whom Saihung was the youngest. The next-oldest student was named Butterfly, and he was in his late twenties. The other classmates were much older than Saihung. They had all been ordained and had become accomplished men before Saihung had even been accepted as a student. Such men had had little interest in him as a child, but accepted him solely because he had become part of the Grand Master's inner group. Only Butterfly was within seven years of

Saihung's age, and it was natural that the two formed a friendship through their growing years. If the Grand Master was like a father, Butterfly was like Saihung's elder brother.

He was the sibling Saihung could never have at home. Butterfly was warm, giving, and concerned. Saihung's own brothers were all intensely competitive, the result of his parents' high demands and ambitions. Each brother had been separated from one another and raised by different teachers in order to create extremely successful men. There had been no such thing as brotherly love to Saihung, only familial criticism and brutal comparison. He always felt short, ugly, and stupid when he went home. His brothers were great scholars, brilliant military men, rich merchants. Saihung was only a monk and would never bring prestige and fame to his parents and clan. It had thus been with the Grand Master and the thirteen disciples that he had finally known a family that accepted him as an individual. It had been with Butterfly that he had found a brother to look up to.

Apparently by coincidence, Saihung's given Taoist name was also Butterfly. The Grand Master had given Saihung the title for three reasons. First, Saihung was fascinated by beauty. He was attracted to fine art objects, scenes of nature, and exotic flowers. Second, Saihung became bored easily. He went from one subject to another, one infatuation to another, sometimes in moody swings. Finally, butterflies themselves seemed to like Saihung. They often hovered around him or even alighted on him. Saihung had thus been named the Butterfly Taoist. Like that insect fluttering from blossom to flower, he was drawn to beauty; but he never stayed for long in any single aspect of life. Huashan thus came to have two Butterflies: Saihung because he loved beauty, Butterfly because he was beautiful.

The elder Butterfly seemed to embody everything that a young man aspired to achieve. Intelligent, witty, and articulate, he was able to enter into a discussion with anyone from the most learned scholars to worldly state ministers. He could take part in contests where the participants spontaneously composed poetry—and this was only a hint of his command of literature, history, and philosophy. His skill as a musician was renowned, and even the grizzled old monks who supposedly did not care for earthly stimuli smiled when Butterfly played the lute.

186

He was handsome, with a physical perfection sculpted by years as a martial artist. His smooth-complexioned face glowed with athletic discipline, and his eyes were always vigilant. He usually had a charming smile for all who met him. People would turn to stare at him on the street in admiration; elders thought him good-natured and ready with sound advice. The youth of Huashan idolized him even more because he was not a monk: He had been an orphan adopted by the Grand Master and thus had the best that both the temple and worldly lives could offer.

When Saihung arrived at a small meadow, he saw that Butterfly was already there among the seven other students. Staff in hand, he tutored a few of his classmates. He learned quickly and wasn't selfish in helping friends.

"I'll never get this technique," sighed a slender youngster from Shaanxi Province named Chrysanthemum.

"Nor will I," complained another with a heavy Shandong accent. "I had it, and then Master changed some of the movements. Maybe he's forgotten."

"Yes, yes," agreed the first. "The Sick Crane Taoist is getting old. Maybe he's getting senile."

Butterfly laughed. "The Sick Crane Taoist is more vital than the three of us in the prime of our youth. He wins poetry contests and succeeded in the Imperial examinations."

"Yes, yes, we know all that," said Chrysanthemum. "But he still can't remember. We would have finished learning this set if he wouldn't keep meddling with it."

"Remember? Finish? You two have no classical background!" exclaimed Butterfly.

"Classical? In this day and age?" retorted the Shandong student. "Wake up, elder brother, it's 1941!"

"Haven't you heard the old saying?" asked Butterfly patiently. "'Sailing upon the ocean of knowledge, one cannot reach the shore.' He remembers many different versions. What he is actually doing is taking you through different stages of development. When you have absorbed one technique, he will refine it and make it more sophisticated. The set remains the same, but the movements acquire deeper subtlety. In this way, your form is fresh, and you will not lose interest. Since you never know exactly what will happen, your curiosity will be stimulated, and you won't be bored.

"There must be variety in every kind of activity. Dance, drama, music, painting, and of course exercise must stick to the major themes yet still express the individuality and thought of the moment. The master changes things according to your understanding. He waits until you're ready to let go. He perceives when one version has become stale and is ready to give you a new little twist to move you forward."

"Hush!" broke in another classmate. "The master is coming!"

The students hurriedly fell into line. As they did so, Saihung looked at the two younger students and saw that Butterfly's talk had inspired them. But when he turned to look at the master, his heart dropped. He could see that the master was in a temperamental mood.

In his early sixties, the Sick Crane Taoist had thin, dry hair streaked with white and tied into the traditional topknot. His skin was a deep copper. The darkness made his gray mustache startling in its contrast. The mouth was small but still showed broken teeth.

A thin, aquiline nose divided two narrow eyes that seemed like two strokes of a Chinese brush. The corners came to sharp, narrow, downward-turning points. Though he had no bags under his eyes, there were wrinkles from squinting, the result both of sunlight and hours of reading under an oil lamp at night.

The master's name was inspired by his looks. As slender as a stick, his back was slightly rounded, his chest hollow, almost caved in. His neck was noticeably longer than average. In fact, he seemed little more than a scarecrow. But Saihung had been invited to touch the master's body in order to feel a demonstration of particular muscle movements. The flesh had been tough and hard. One couldn't squeeze through to the bone.

The Sick Crane Taoist habitually held his hands behind his back. His gray robes had long sleeves that fell to his sides, and he sometimes appeared altogether limbless, as a crane standing quietly appears to be little more than a head and body perched on spindly legs.

The master walked back and forth before the class, eyeing each student.

"Good morning, Teacher," said the class in unison.

"Humph! Don't call me your teacher! You have no discipline, talking and chattering like that. I could hear your noise all the way up the trail."

They said nothing. Talking was forbidden.

"Master," broke in Butterfly. "It was my fault."

The eyes like brushstrokes flared into onyx orbs. The hand came swiftly down. Tough as he was, Butterfly's cheek turned red.

189

"How dare you speak?" demanded the Sick Crane Taoist.

"I apologize, Great Teacher," said Butterfly with a bow. "This insignificant one is solely at fault."

"You are the eldest. You are responsible."

"Yes. I engaged them in conversation. I am the only one to blame. Please punish me."

The master relented.

Saihung watched him admiringly. "He takes the blame, but he knows the old man likes him too much to really punish him. He's crafty!"

"All right," ordered the Sick Crane Taoist. "Ready . . . begin!"

The class instantly launched into a unison performance of the staff set.

When the class completed its performance, the Sick Crane Taoist nodded. He gave neither words of praise nor reproach. He had noted their level of accomplishment, and his teaching would begin from that point.

"This is the proper execution of this technique," he said, picking up a staff. "The stick must not be held rigidly in the fist but must be manipulated with the palms and fingers. When you bring the staff on a downward strike, you emphasize the pressing movement of the forward palm."

He motioned to Saihung. "Little Butterfly, come forward. Show me this part of the set."

Saihung performed his movements with his utmost strength and skill. He was confident, for he had won boxing tournaments in the cities. The set itself was a routine of stances and fighting postures performed with lightning speed. Each was a distinctive collection of the style's hallmark techniques. Saihung proudly completed his movements.

"Barely acceptable," pronounced the master with a sigh. "Shouldn't it look more like this?"

The Sick Crane Taoist now jumped rigorously into the center of the meadow. Gone were his eccentric posture, the quirky walk, and the impression of pathetic thinness. His muscles snapped into lines, his limbs moved with tangible liveliness. The staff whistled angrily through the air, and its ends flexed from the sheer force that propelled it.

When he stopped, there was no panting for breath. The Sick Crane Taoist returned to a casual posture that made it seem as if he had been no more than an old gentleman twirling an umbrella. The ferocious power that had been called up was withdrawn.

"Get into position," he said to Saihung. Saihung took a low stance, and he felt the master come up close to him. It was an eerie feeling. He moved from posture to posture, but, with the Sick Crane Taoist touching him and gently directing his arms with nudges and pushes, Saihung felt that he was not moving of his own volition. Instead the master's own life force had entered into him.

"There, isn't that better?" asked the master. Saihung had to admit that the subtle adjustments and the odd feeling of having something inside him had changed his performance and understanding.

Saihung became aware of a new attitude toward the staff. He felt its smooth surface against his palm and fingers, noted its rotation and changes in pressure as he directed it in different directions. It was hard, unyielding to his grip, yet flexible along its length. The staff vibrated almost imperceptibly to the force that he exerted through it, forming a response to his strength. This dialogue—made up in part by its obedience to his command, in part by the resistance of its weight—gave Saihung an added awareness of his own body. Moving the heavy staff, a thing outside himself, seemingly directed his attention inward. Saihung noted the stretching and contracting of his arm and shoulder muscles, the exertion of his chest, the contribution of his back. He noticed the rapid, bellowslike rhythm of his lungs and how they accelerated to meet the demands of the set. All this was somehow different, a change from his earlier knowledge. He wondered if it had been the Sick Crane Taoist's touch. It was said that there was such a thing as direct transmission of knowledge, and this might have been it. But such speculation was brief for Saihung as he returned his full attention to completing his set and immersing himself in his newly discovered awareness.

They practiced on for an hour, drilling over and over, reviewing, perfecting, and absorbing the movements. The Sick Crane Taoist watched them closely and gave corrections and instructions individually. When he noticed his students finally tiring, he said jovially, "Today I want to teach some philosophy to you. Isn't that ironic? You, a bunch of aspiring holy men, needing more philosophy."

It was a joke, but since laughter wasn't allowed in class, a daring few smiled.

"Let me tell you something further about the staff and sword," he continued.

"I want to give you an image to help you understand the staff's inner essence." The master paused. "The staff should be compared with the umbrella."

Saihung was puzzled. How could a stick be like an umbrella?

"Be a little imaginative," the master urged, delighted at having mystified them. Even Butterfly, with his greater experience, had never heard the comparison before. The Sick Crane Taoist revealed the secret.

"The proper execution of the staff requires that the stick be frequently angled away from the body. It is extended from the practitioner. It has reach. The body is like the shaft of the umbrella, while the stick itself represents the movement and extension of the ribs of the parasol. Sometimes a parasol is opened, sometimes it's closed; sometimes the stick is close to the body, and at other times it is thrust outward. But, just like an umbrella, the action is caused by the hand's leverage. The shaft and the ribs are distinctly separate parts. They always work at opposing angles to one another. This is the principle of the staff.

"Now, we are about to shift to the sword. There is also an image for that. The sword may most properly be compared to a dragon. Its characteristics are virtually opposite to the staff. Where the staff is always a separate implement, the sword must have total unity with the practitioner. There is no distinction between man and weapon here. They are one. Together, they must twist, turn, coil, leap, and fly like a celestial dragon in the clouds. Take up your swords now, and don't treat them like sticks. You and the sword are a single unit. Your limbs are part of that unit. All concentration comes brightly to bear on the very tip of the sword. Let the blade shine! Here is the dragon seeking his way! Begin!"

192   As the master had emphasized, the sword was seldom extended all the way, and it certainly lacked the reach of the staff. The movements were predominantly whirling ones, with the blade held close to the body. Inspired by combat, parries were executed at close range, the body and legs turning frequently to lead the edge in angled, slicing cuts. When the sword was thrust outward, it returned by cutting its way along a different angle rather than simply being pulled back. The set had a liveliness that was indeed reminiscent of serpentine motion.

Few movements in this particular sword style were two-handed, and the free hand was never allowed simply to wave around. It too had precise movements to make, all the while maintaining a prescribed hand gesture of the index and middle fingers straight and the ring and little finger curled beneath the bent thumb. This gesture was not simply an imitation of the sword for the sake of symmetry; it was thought to be a talismanic protector. The early swordsmen believed that each time the blade passed near or above the head, the mystical power of the sword could injure the soul. The hand gesture protected the practitioner from harm.

The sword had been an integral part of life. Emperors and officials always had beautiful swords inlaid with jewels. Noblemen fought with swords rather than coarser weapons like maces and axes. Even a poet like Li Po was expert in swordsmanship. Swords were believed to possess individual personalities, supernatural powers, and even their own destinies. A peach-wood sword was considered so magical that the Taoists used it in exorcism.

He sprang into the set. It felt good. He wasn't simply smashing his way through. The sword nature is refined and demanded grace and sensibility. He felt it draw upon different muscles, too: not the long ones, or the large groups, as the staff required; the sword needed the dozens of little muscles deep in the arm and body. It needed fine motor coordination. Performing the staff was like painting a wall. Using the sword was like writing an essay in intricate and exquisite calligraphy.

He felt the sword take root in him, and he felt his breathing extend to the tip of the blade. He gave himself up to the speed and momentum of the set. His feet moved automatically, and he experienced one of those rare moments in any performing art or sport: The postures flowed on their own, effortlessly.

The Sick Crane Taoist noticed Saihung's performance but said nothing. Praise encouraged egotism. He only said, "Not bad," and instructed the class to review again and again.

After two hours, the Sick Crane Taoist brought the class to a close and allowed his students to rest. But that was not the end. They all went for a walk through the mountains.

The Taoists had a thorough rationale for every activity, and hiking was no exception. It was of physical benefit because it increased stamina and resistance to disease. The stimulation to the circulatory and respiratory systems, as well as to the strength of the legs, was undeniable, but there were religious overtones as well. In the swift walking, one was allowed to trample neither plants nor insects. By walking in perfect silence, the students were expected to contemplate the beauty and meaning of the landscape they traveled through. Nature and the Tao were not wholly identical, but nature was a paradigm of the Tao. Thus, a student who could sharpen his perception and understand the subtle inner workings of nature could also enhance his awareness of the Tao.

As they began walking, Saihung was filled with impressions. He heard the crunch of his straw shoes on the dirt-and-gravel trail as he established his stride. He felt his leg muscles flex, the long bands of his thighs contracting and expanding, the movements of his hamstrings as he planted one foot firmly after another. The path began to lead uphill, and he noted the corresponding shift in the interplay of his muscles as his quadriceps joined in the effort to carry him forward. He increased his pace, eager to walk and see.

A tangle of weeds grew beside the trail; grasses, vines, young, tight green shoots of yarrow thrust themselves above the competing thicket. Small red flies, and gnats that were like incandescent flecks in the sunshine, buzzed around in their own spiraling patterns. Saihung filled his lungs deeply. Although it seldom got hot on Huashan, especially in springtime, this day was warm with a slight breeze. He welcomed the fresh pure air, and he smelled the grassy fragrance of the field.

As they climbed toward a ridge, shadows began to fall across his vision. Trees began to shade the sunlight. He looked upward to see the beginnings of the spruce, fir, pines, and broad-leaved trees that forested the area. Some rose straight up in stately magnificence. Some had broken branches, limbs torn off by storms, pruned in ways that a gardener would have called ugly, but beautiful because it was natural.

The sound of water came to him. It was a brook that made its rocky tumble beside the trail. Loudest, almost orchestral, were the falling and splashing noises as the water overcame fallen trees or piled rock. The song of birds was a chorus above the water's sound, the percussion of branches moved by the wind, the sweeping rhythm of a thousand leaves. Above that background were occasional solos: the high, delicate whine of insects, the buzzing of bees.

The smell of the wet earth mixed with pine awakened thoughts of past walks. Saihung recalled the excitement of exploring the world, making new discoveries of different plants, the odd antics of insects, the wreckage of storms. He never tired of walking in the forests. Not once in his life had the mountain groves been unchanged. There was infinite variation, yet the forest always obeyed the seasonal cycles.

They climbed higher. Huge boulders, their undersides encrusted with moss and lichens, their upper surfaces bleached to bare grainy stone, began to dominate the land. The underbrush was beginning to be choked out. The richness was not possible amid the rock and dry earth. Only the larger trees and plants could invade the rock crevices, thrust their roots deep into soil, and increase their height to survive in the more difficult environment. A few other plants took advantage—like the wood ears and parasitic ivies—but it was still the tall timber that was the major plant life. The trees stood higher than pagodas, and their branches spread out mightily. But there wasn't the canopy that there had been in the lower valley. The sky shone through in large, beautifully abstract patches. The color was an intense cobalt blue—a hue so vivid that the sky, not the trees, seemed in the foreground.

The rapid ascent nevertheless had its rewards in incomparable views of the far mountains. As the group climbed higher onto bare rock mountain, the previously invisible horizon came to stretch grandly across Saihung's field of vision. Clouds, lower than his feet, galloped by like stampeding animals. Mountain range after mountain range stretched to his left in a succession that finally merged with the hazy blue. Before him he could see the thickly wooded foothills punctuated by the white line of a waterfall. He saw fields, the small patchwork evidence of humanity, and a few villages thousands of feet to his right. The mountain dwarfed him ridiculously as he climbed toward its summit; the scale of nature made the evidence of civilization below seem totally insignificant. There was something about being high up, standing on a distant vantage point, that always aroused in him an otherworldly feeling. He was totally divorced from society, and yet on that towering platform he could still see its traces. Even the brown meandering course of the Yellow River, which snaked across the land, was puny, and the human world was already less than that mighty river.

They walked on for another mile before circling back to their practice field. It was nearly noon, and Saihung was hot and thirsty. His hips and legs were sore, tired in a good way. He walked to the shade of an old pine tree, picked a spot in the midst of bark chips, pieces of pinecone, and soft grass, and sat down. The Sick Crane Taoist began talking, the first words anyone had spoken since the beginning of the walk. But Saihung, uninterested, began to examine a ladybug that had happened to crawl up his pants leg.

"Who noticed a special plant?" asked the master.

"I did, Master," said the Shaanxi youth.

Good, thought Saihung. Just launch into your usual lecture, and I'll rest. He sat back to enjoy the warm sunshine. There was always discussion at the end of the walk in which the Sick Crane Taoist asked questions or solicited their observations. He wanted assurances that his students were being observant. The Shaanxi monk was a poor physical performer but an ardent talker, and his classmates let him satisfy the master.

"Little Butterfly!" The intrusion was so abrupt that Saihung instantly realized how lost in his own thoughts he had become.

"Yes, Master," he replied quickly.

"A yellow-orange leaf fell as we passed. Tell me about it."

A falling leaf? In spring? Saihung thought desperately back. He could remember no leaf. His embarrassment was reply enough.

"You didn't notice it?" asked the Sick Crane Taoist with a shake of his head. "You who so pride yourself on being a fighter. What if it had been a dart thrown at you?"

The master paused to let him think it over. All Saihung could think was that he hated being made to look so foolish. But, he reminded himself, he was there to learn both humility and awareness. He suppressed his pride and looked up at the master.

"One should notice these things," said the master softly and kindly. "Upon noticing such a thing, one should inquire why. Did it survive the winter? Was the tree diseased? Was it lacking for water? Had something knocked it down? Even to have noticed its exquisite color as it came down, a golden flicker against a mass of browns and greens, would have been acceptable. Not to notice it is insensitivity.

"We live on this mountain to be in nature. We shun the foul deeds of humanity, their pitiful lives, the mental pollution of what they vainly call civilization. We isolate ourselves from their loud noise, their stink, their obscene laughter, and their self-pitying laments. We withdraw to nature in order to purify ourselves and lead holy lives. Nature and its animals are innocent. We may think nature cruel and unmerciful when we find a deer's carcass or see a tree torn by a thunderstorm. This is nature's way and nature's logic. Nature lacks the wishful thinking and stupid sentimentality that humans possess. This purity and innocence is in tune with the gods, with the divine, with the Tao. Nature's way is the way of the Tao. If we want to attune ourselves with the Tao, we must place ourselves in an area that is in itself aligned with Tao.

"But it is of no use to live in a natural place if you fail to notice its gift. Nature is full of messages, though we often fail to see; and even if we do see, we fail to comprehend. There are ten thousand sacred messages for you everywhere you glance, only you've not the eyes to see. That leaf could have been a sign to you, even a message from the gods. But you failed to notice it."

CLASS WAS OVER, and Saihung began climbing the hillside for midday devotions and lunch. He was glad when Butterfly joined him.

"Little Brother, I'll be leaving again in a few days."

"So soon, Elder Brother? You've only been here this time for a month." Saihung felt a disconcerting emotion.

"Yes, but I'm growing restless. Besides, I have business to attend to in Beijing."

"And, of course, your lady friend."

"Yes, yes." Butterfly smiled. "Though there are many, she is more special than the rest."

"I envy you," said Saihung with a pout. "You roam the whole land in search of adventure. You see wealth and beauty. People adore and respect you. Your life is so full."

"Such a life is not for you, little one. Your destiny is to be a monk. It was meant to be. All can tell you were born for this role."

"But this is not life. I'm cold and hungry. Each day is completely regimented. Sutra recitation and meditation are boring, and physical practice is utter drudgery. Besides, all my efforts meet with constant disapproval. Nothing satisfies the teachers. They don't know how to praise."

"No one forced this on you."

"It's true," said Saihung with a sigh. "I was ordained at the age of sixteen. Though I made a choice, I still think about secular life and wonder if I'm doing the right thing. Did you ever have doubts?"

"Yes, of course I did. Every man has his own doubts. That's why I travel so relentlessly in search of meaning. I learn as much as I can from the wise Taoists and live life as fully as possible out in the world."

"You are lucky. You have the best of both worlds. When you want to rest, seek yourself, or recover from wounds, you come back to the temple. But when it suits you, you dress in the finest silks, wear precious jewelry, ride expensive horses, eat at lavish banquets, gamble all night long, and know the love of women."

"Aah, I knew I never should have brought you to pleasure halls like the Red Peony Pavilion," said Butterfly with a smile. "If the Grand Master ever found out, he would punish us both."

"It was I who asked you to take me."

"Perhaps I should not have consented."

"I'm glad to have seen such places," said Saihung. "Nothing short of direct experience would have been adequate after all your exciting stories. But I found that that world wasn't for me. I don't like drinking, I don't like opium, I don't feel the need to break my vows of celibacy. Still, I wonder if this severe life of restraint and austerity is best."

"I know you are not interested in the outside world. But perhaps you should consider how it could affect you. The Japanese have enormous pieces of the country. Chiang Kaishek and the Nationalists are desperately trying to run a government from Chong Qing, fight the Japanese, and stab the Communists in the back at the same time. Beyond Asia, Germany has attacked Poland, and the whole world is slipping into war. People are killing one another in numbers that have never been used to count corpses before."

"I fought in the Sino-Japanese War two years ago. I saw the horror. I fought to defend my people."

"The atrocities continue."

"What do you want me to do? Join Mao in Yenan? Align myself with warlords as you have done? I'm a renunciate. Politics never last."

"Can you deny that China has had war every day of your life? Now, it isn't just China but the whole world that teeters on the edge of instability. All of Europe enters into the fighting. The fighting may spread to the United States and maybe even South America. While the whole world is destroyed, you sit on your meditation rug."

"Taoism is a philosophy of the heart," Saihung replied steadily. "It cannot be eradicated. The Tao is perpetual. Even the destruction of the planet cannot affect it. I can see our master. I can see our classmates. Observing the levels that they've achieved inspires me to reach for their level. I know that their achievements could not be touched by war or any other adversity, for they are triumphs within. I may have my own doubts, but politics is not the way to purge them."

"You are steadfast in your faith?"

"Yes, I am," said Saihung.

"The world may be coming to a final apocalypse, and you do not consider changing."

"Through all my austerities, I feel that I am gaining results. I do not want to be like ordinary people. I want to be something more, something greater. Those people lead wretched lives, buffeted around by the whims of fate. That is not the life for me. I want to perfect myself."

"I believe in perfection and discipline too. Otherwise, I could never have come this far. Don't be taken by the outer trappings of my life. Women and gambling are only a small part of it. I want to do something great, something heroic. The world will not come to an end. If you did not recognize that, you would not be so calm. But it will take great men to bring order to this planetwide degeneration. I want to be one of those men. That will take as much discipline, courage, intelligence, a drive for perfection—and in a way, purity—as a monastic life."

"Are you saying that we're equal?" asked Saihung. He was pleased with the comparison.

"I encourage you to study hard, Little Butterfly. The monastic life and worldly life are two edges of the same sword. They are inseparable. Neither could exist without the other. Neither is better than the other. But it behooves each of us to understand our destinies. Only by following our innermost predilections can we find success. I urge you to remain persevering in your asceticism. It's true that physical and social needs are ruthlessly denied, but your spirit will find satisfaction. Little Butterfly, you should not allow discouragement to make you falter."

"Elder Brother," said Saihung, greatly moved. "You are so eloquent. Why do you not become an initiate as well?"

"Perhaps I will," said Butterfly with a pensive look, "when I finish my earthly wanderings. That's why I must travel to complete my experiences. The masters say, 'Taste the world before renouncing.' When I've had my fill of worldly life, I will come back to stay for good."

"Then we could all be together—always."

"Yes, little one . . . always."

The mighty bronze temple bell reverberated throughout the mountainside. It was time for devotions. They said good-bye.

Saihung stood near one of the temple's antique bronze incense burners and watched his elder brother leave the courtyard. Saihung wondered if he would ever leave his worldly life. He knew that Butterfly had lived in the world for a long time, and his life had been scandalous. His membership in a secret society, his time as a warlord's bodyguard, and his work as a protection escort for a drug-smuggling operation had brought frequent complaints to Huashan. The Grand Master did little, however, and Saihung puzzled over this.

While he himself had been punished many times for pranks, mischief, and laziness, he had never seen Butterfly punished. The Grand Master and the other priests continued to love him as a son, and Butterfly responded in the same way: He came back for the unwavering support of his adopted family, attributed his good achievements to his upbringing, and regularly supported Huashan with monetary donations. But Saihung wondered if that was enough to compensate for the many times provincial elders had climbed Huashan to report his misdeeds and demand his arrest.

Saihung walked through a series of gates before coming to the South Peak Shrine of the Jade Fertility Well. He entered, joining the ranks of blue-robed monks for the service. In the front of the group were the presiding priests in embroidered silk, reading aloud the divine words of sages. Musicians provided hymnal accompaniment.

Beyond the elaborate altar, Saihung saw the object of their devotion: the figure of a past Huashan ancestor who had become immortal through a lifetime of self-cultivation. Even from a distance, he could see that the figure was covered with dust. But somehow, as the chanting and singing intensified, Saihung imagined that the god heard them and that his eyes seemed almost to open in response. A feeling of sincerity arose in him. As this ascetic had attained salvation through cultivation, so Saihung hoped that he and Butterfly would succeed together in their destinies, and that, somehow, his older brother would reform.

Nocturnal
Lessons

W ITH RENEWED DETERMINATION, Saihung readied himself for the meager meals, the four periods of scriptural recitation per day, the variety of classes, the hard work, and the intensive meditation. He renewed his commitment to master the challenge of temple life and gain for himself unbreakable will and spiritual perception— qualities he knew could come only from cloistered cultivation.

One of the most important forums for the Grand Master to transmit his knowledge was an evening class with a few students.

Saihung, the two acolytes, and one other student met in the Grand Master's chamber a few nights after their return. They sat on floor cushions while the Grand Master sat upon his meditation platform.

He delicately pulled back his sleeve and rested his right arm on the meditation crutch.

"Tonight," began the Grand Master, "I want to begin a little differently. You students always ask me questions. This time, I will ask *you* a question:

"What is Taoism?

"Little Butterfly. You have been here with me since the age of nine. Surely you can give me an adequate answer. Please respond."

Saihung flushed. He felt nervous being put on the spot and struggled desperately to put together a coherent reply.

"There is something that pervades all things," Saihung said. "It is a movement, a force, a progression to the vast universe that is so mighty even the gods are subordinate to it. This power is so great that humanity can only perceive its minor manifestations. The constellations, the seasons, the changes of nature, the history of civilization—all are manifestations of the Tao, yet none of them can be seized upon as the Tao itself. The metaphysical components of the universe—the ten thousand things, the five elements, yin and yang—are parts of Tao, yet they are not the whole. A human being cannot know the Tao in its entirety, but one can learn its principles and live in harmony with it. In this way, one can follow the stream of life and attain immortality.

"Tao*ism* is a system that was handed down by the gods, sages, and realized beings. Humanity, in its ignorance of the Tao, engages in vain striving. The sages gave us the doctrines of the Tao in order to show us the way to liberation. Taoism has developed internal and external alchemies, scriptures, and meditations in order to sustain the devotee in his quest. This is a brief summary of my understanding of Taoism."

The Grand Master sat with his eyes closed and listened intently to Saihung's discourse. He was silent for a few moments, and then he opened his eye and fixed his gaze on his young disciple.

"Is that all?" he asked.

"This is all I can muster at this time," said Saihung hesitantly.

"What you say is acceptable, but perhaps not quite deep enough. I agree with you that our discussion should begin with the Tao itself. But let us be sure that this Tao is indeed that which underlies the whole universe. We can begin by observation. We see an order to the world of phenomena. In the regular cycles of the stars, planets, and seasons we discern a cosmology. No serious thinker would think that this is all there is. We must inquire further: What animates these things? Where did they come from? Some might answer that the gods created and govern the universe. But this is not a satisfactory answer, for then we must ask, 'Where did the gods come from?' In addition, we know from scripture and even mere folktales that the gods are themselves subject to causality. There must thus be something beyond the gods in our search for the underlying force of the universe, some force that is in itself related to the cause of things.

"Notice that I said *force*. The universe cannot be reduced to matter. Rock, no matter how finely ground, cannot account for life, movement, time, and the dimensions. No, neither nature, the gods, nor matter are the ultimate fabric of the universe.

"The scriptures say, 'Being was produced by Nonbeing.' Examine this. The only possible, totally irreducible origin of the universe can be Nonbeing. Only it is irreducible.

"In the beginning was Nothingness. Out of Nothingness came a random thought. A thought caused a movement within the stillness that generated infinite ripples. Movement gave rise to *qi*, vital breath. Breath congealed into the five elements—metal, water, wood, earth, fire, symbolic of matter. Then this chaos became organized by yin and yang. Breathing knew inhalation and exhalation, the universe was ordered according to duality; for only in the interaction and tension between polar opposites could movement and evolution arise. The interaction of all these things finally brought forth the gods, humanity, and all the myriad phenomena. That first thought was like a stone dropping into a pristinely still pond. All that came after that may be called the Tao.

"The Tao is therefore not that which is totally irreducible, for only Nothingness qualifies for that definition. But the Tao is only one shade away from Nothingness, and one could say it has a very intimate interaction with Nothingness. In Tao's changes and hidden permutations—the ripples on the pond—heaven and earth and the ten thousand things issued forth and are all still inseparable from the Tao.

"Words do not serve a mystic well. I can only indicate, point the way. You must perceive this yourselves. Do not accept my words or even those sayings of enlightened creatures as a satisfactory substitute for experience. When I say these things, I am describing those phenomena I have seen in meditation. This is why the holy ones say, 'Without going out of the door, the sage knows heaven and earth.' If you would have such wisdom, you must meditate.

"Now, what does Taoism mean?

"Taoism is the method of studying and bringing ourselves into harmony with the Tao—or, still further, it is the procedure for uniting with the Tao itself. The sages say, 'Tao is forever, and he that possesses it, though his body ceases, is not destroyed.' However, there is no one simple method. People are different, and the Tao is never static. Different ways of life must be tailored according to the needs and destinies of individuals. This is why the *Seven Bamboo Tablets* catalogue three hundred sixty ways of self-cultivation.

"Taoism is a spiritual system of many levels. Where other religions strive to totally define their beliefs to the exclusion of all others, the vast, sprawling range of Taoism embraces the whole universe. One of its most fundamental points of philosophical origin is to accept humanity and the world as they are.

"Starting with humanity itself, the Taoists appreciated its intrinsic characteristics of sin and aspiration, wretchedness and nobility, savagery and artfulness, emotion and intelligence, perversity and purity, sadism and compassion, violence and pacifism, egotism and transcendence. Unlike other sages, the Taoists chose not to reject humanity's evil impulses. The duality had to be accepted and worked with.

"Once both sides of dualism were accepted, the Taoists clearly saw that individuals combined good and evil in varying proportions. Taoism therefore evolved into a system large enough to satisfy the needs of all the different people. Taoists gave morality and piety to the common man; faith and loyalty to the hero; martial arts and sorcery to the power-hungry man; knowledge to the intellectual; and, for the rare few looking for even more, they gave meditation and the secret of transcendence. Then they turned everything inside out and said, 'Not only are these segments of the world's people, but by the principle of microcosm and macrocosm, they are also inner realities of every individual.'

"The Taoist is always a pragmatist, not an idealist. His interest is always to deal with what is there before him, rather than to impose his will upon reality. Perhaps it is for this reason that Taoism is sometimes accused of being too slippery and elusive to define. Some might even say it is an opportunist's doctrine. But actually, all Taoism cares about is dealing with the situation before it, the one that always changes, the Tao.

"Historically, there are five major antecedents to Taoism. Shamanism, philosophy, hygiene, alchemy, and the school of Peng-Lai were the components of what would develop into a massive spiritual movement.

"Shamanism was Taoism's earliest beginning. The primitive peoples believed in a world of gods, demons, ancestral spirits, and an all-powerful Nature that was mysterious and even unresponsive to humanity. They turned to their leaders, shaman priests who used magic to cure the sick, divine the hidden, and control events. The priests intervened through their personal power between their constituents and a hostile world.

"Cults of divine beings sprang up to further make life understandable. Chief among these cults were the worship of ancestors—for the joint work of agriculture made the family unit essential—and the worship of nature gods of the earth, mountain, lake, trees, harvest, and so on. Indeed, every conceivable feature of the landscape and agricultural life was believed to have its divinity. The Yellow River, for example, was called the Count of the River, and he was believed to ride a chariot drawn by tortoises. The people sought to placate his cruel and temperamental flooding by human sacrifices equally as terrible. It was only through the intervention of enlightened sages that the people gradually progressed in their consciousness. Emperor Huang-Di was known for his discourse on medicine. Emperor Fu Xi taught divination and formulated the Eight Trigrams. Emperor Shen Nong experimented with herbs upon his own body. Emperor Yu tamed the floods. These emperors of prehistory shaped shamanism and originated elements of Taoism that still persist today. Many of our traditions of nature worship, divination, geomancy, talismanic art, exorcism, and spirit oracles harken back to the centuries that preceded recorded history.

"The philosophical school of Taoism, the pure Conversation School, can be held to have originated during the Zhou dynasty. Lao Tzu was such a Taoist. When he left Luoyang to renounce the world, he came for a time to Huashan. But because of his discourses in the court with Confucius, his philosophy took a twin course: It became part of Taoism, and it gradually became a somewhat secular philosophy for the literati. In the third century A.D. schools of thought, centered around such thinkers as Chuang Tzu and Lieh Tzu, advocated a Taoism that propounded noncontention, theories of government by virtue, relativity of opposites, and the search for the Tao through meditation. The schools that arose from this period may therefore be considered to have advocated an intellectual class of Taoism that paid little attention to divinities, shamanism, or physical practice.

"Physical practice arose with the hygiene school, and our sect in large part is descended from this tradition. The essential premises of this lineage are that both the physical body and the mind must be disciplined and cultivated as a means to spiritual attainment. From the first to fourth centuries A.D, the school's teachings were codified first in the *Jade Classic of the Yellow Chamber* and then the *True Classic of the Great Mystery.* It was in these early centuries doctrines arose of the three *dan tian* vital centers: breath circulation, diet, meditation, martial arts. All this was united in a principle postulating the existence of thirty-six thousand gods within the human body. Given the assumption of the person as divine receptacle, it is easy to see how they believed that the body should be kept pure and strong—for it was believed that the gods would abandon an unfit body. There was a strong leaning toward asceticism. Wine, drugs, and all external means were rejected, since they could potentially offend one's resident gods.

"The goal of the hygiene school was initially physical immortality. But they gradually became aware of the doctrine of reincarnation, and their priorities shifted to the creation of an immortal soul within the earthly shell that could transcend death.

"The alchemists, by contrast, continued to believe in physical immortality. Their origins were in the Five Element School of Tsou Yen, who came into prominence about 325 B.C. It was from this lineage that the *fang shih* originated. The *fang shih*—Formula Masters—were so called because they experimented constantly to find the formula for immortality. They engaged in endless combining of herbs, minerals, and chemicals, and all sorts of smelting processes. Unfortunately for their health, most of their early efforts concentrated on such minerals as mercury, sulfur, and lead. Eventually, they adjusted their research—if only in the interests of self-preservation—toward the use of herbs, ritual, sexual alchemy, meditation, and magic. It is this division of Taoism that inherited the early shamanistic concerns of demon enslavement and sorcery.

207

"We come finally to the cult of Peng-Lai, the school that is most unabashedly concerned with simple physical immortality. Sometime around the fourth century B.C., a legend arose about magic islands somewhere in the Pacific where the Mushroom of Immortality grew. Expedition after expedition was launched to find the islands. By the time of Emperor Qin Shi, who united China in 221 B.C. and ruled a mere sixty miles from Huashan, the cult of Peng-Lai combined with the alchemist-magicians. Along with their arts of spirit possession and witchcraft, they advocated the cult of Peng-Lai. Emperor Qin Shi wanted to live forever, and the man who ordered the Great Wall built became a fanatic about Peng-Lai and alchemy. The Emperor sent ten thousand girls and boys to search for Peng-Lai, with orders to succeed or be punished with execution. The ten thousand found the islands of Japan, but no Mushrooms of Immortality, and opted to stay rather than be executed. The Emperor's efforts at alchemical preservation of his own Imperial person were no more successful. In fact, it is rumored that the illness that killed him was brought on by ingesting some poisonous formula.

"From the fourth century A.D. to the present, there has been enormously complex cross-pollination of these five basic aspects. Sixteen centuries of the Taoist movement have generated endless combinations and recombinations. All the thousands of later sects and forms of Taoism can be distinguished as either left- or right-handed Taoism. On the left are sorcery, alchemy, sexual practice, and demon enslavement. Roughly, it is a path that believes in external methods. The right-handed path advocates asceticism, celibacy, and meditation. Roughly, it is an internal path. Somewhat common to both are studies in scriptures, worship, meditation, divination, chanting, pursuit of immortality, geomancy, talismanic art, vision quests, and so on. All ostensibly seek union with the Tao; they only differ in their methodology and interpretation of Taoist principles. All are considered valid and orthodox methods. All yield results, and high masters of any sect can demonstrate supernatural power and manifest great spiritual insight.

"But I am rigorously opposed to the left-handed path. There is too much temptation. Admittedly, one can practice asceticism sincerely and honestly and gain only contentment, tranquillity, and piety. One is not necessarily freed from tribulation. The left-hand path grants great power with a simple incantation or ingestion of pills. But the results are not honestly gained, and the adept, not having undergone the struggle to gain his position with a sound set of values, finds it too tempting to abuse his power. Levitation, transformation, seeing into the future, and controlling demons are all instantly available on the left-hand path. But nothing is free in life. Consorting with the dark side requires payment, and one's only form of barter is the human soul. Each time the force of dark Tao is tapped, it feeds upon a small bit of the human essence. The whole person is eventually transformed into an agent for the dark Tao. Immortality and power are yours for eternity, but you have sacrificed your soul for it.

"In conclusion, I say that the Tao is awesome and transcends human conception. Taoism, with its centuries of great minds seeking to know the Tao, has expanded into a labyrinthine sprawl of different doctrines and schools. There are Taoists for every facet of the Tao—even if it is Tao's evil side. But I say to you that in spite of this staggering amount of human effort, the Tao remains an enigma and mystery that nevertheless inexorably surrounds our lives and destinies." The Grand Master paused.

"Are there any questions?"

"Master, how does one properly follow the Tao?" asked Saihung. "There are so many methods that it is quite mind-boggling."

"It's true," replied the Grand Master. "In fact, Little Butterfly, you must fully master and surpass the *Seven Bamboo Tablets* before you can consider yourself firmly on the way."

"But I have neither seen the books nor had their contents explained to me. How can I master them?"

"Not the books, not the words," said the Grand Master. "The teachings."

"Why can't I see them?"

"You're not ready yet."

"But surely the books set down a course of study to follow," said Sound of Clear Water. "Wouldn't it be more efficient if we knew what to do?"

"Course? Do?" The Grand Master laughed. "There is no set course to the Tao! You must use your own initiative to set your own course. How you end up is how you end up. Act on impulse. Whatever you feel is right. You might want to be a recluse. That's Tao. You might want to live in a big city. That's Tao. If you have joy in the world, that's Tao. If you get angry, that's Tao. You are looking deeply into life."

"Then one may act freely?" asked Mist Through a Grove.

"Why not? The Tao has no fixed pattern. The Tao is free! Flexible! Constantly changing! Followers of the Way should do no less." The Grand Master giggled at his confused students.

"Imposing any rigid pattern, even if it's derived from the Taoist canons, is wrong," he continued. "Wearing priestly robes, a topknot, saying sutras, praying every day, are all worthless. You can burn incense day after day, and the gods may not listen. It's only you yourself who make things happen."

"So why shouldn't I just indulge myself?" asked Saihung bluntly.

"One should have purpose, conviction, and goals. Self-indulgence is Tao too; but is it freedom? In your self-indulgence, you could destroy yourself recklessly. In the pursuit of your self-indulgence, you might have an impulse to do something, but you would not be able to achieve it because you lacked ability. Therefore, you would have no freedom, and I would judge freedom better than mere self-indulgence."

"So there's no getting out of temple life?" asked Saihung.

"Not if you want to achieve any goals. If you do not want to live a life solely devoted to gratifying your baser instincts, then you should try to achieve something great. If you have a goal, then you will gladly sacrifice lower things for the sake of gaining something higher."

"It does seem that the Taoist life is one of sacrifice. It's paradoxical," commented Mist Through a Grove.

"Not just sacrifice," reminded the Grand Master. "I am not advocating blind self-denial. Pure asceticism can be mentally and physically dangerous if it is unbalanced. Vegetarianism without the tonic herbs to balance it is wrong. Celibacy without technique is insane. This is the test of your mastery: How do you attain balance? You must always ask yourself this.

"Asceticism is only to fulfill your potential. Strictness develops you quickly into special individuals. Then you will fulfill your destinies and be in a position to help others. That is also the Tao."

The Grand Master heard the low reverberation of the temple bell. He ended the class with a prayer, and his students went home.

The night air was cool and slightly damp. Smells of moss and pine mingled with the respiration of the trees. Saihung walked quietly along the covered temple walkway. The spaces between pillars divided the gardens into perfect views of balance and poetry. He went to a lone meditation cell and lit a candle.

Night came as a blue-blackness flooded over the faded wooden temple eaves, and sight and sound ebbed. All the day's endeavors were past and any cares that still existed could be put off until the next day. The quietness that gradually grew in the holy interiors was a neutral ground, a passive space. Saihung's mind projected brief flashes to fill that stillness. There were worries, but worrying achieved nothing. There was loneliness and longing, but he pushed that aside. There were plans and just mental talking, but he put no stock in those words. It was quiet. Perhaps the teachers were right to insist on silence. It was inevitable, they said, that man would utter something impure and blasphemous and thus drive the gods away. Only in soundlessness might there be sufficient tranquillity to attract the divine. Saihung turned away from his emotional vexations, his internal dialogue, even that which he considered duty and responsibility.

He turned away from memories that floated up through his consciousness in an apparently random sequence: walking in his grandfather's garden, a restaurant he'd been to in Beijing, the night's lessons, a smile from one of his master's friends, a fight with an opponent. He turned away from the traces and shadows of his life and instead looked within.

He wondered if any man could sense his own destiny, or whether any man could defeat an impulse from a higher source. Saihung sat down and crossed his legs. His spine automatically straightened to assume the position he'd known for years. The neutral darkness of the room changed to a feeling of positive serenity. Self-dialogue had given way to introspection. Introspection gave way to contemplation. His attachment to the day faded. Contemplation focused on the gentle rhythm, the high and low tide of his breathing. He noticed his pulse, and it seemed he could even hear his blood flowing, his nerves firing, without any direction on his part. But he soon plunged deeper within himself, and his awareness reached beyond his own body functions. It was true that spirituality was rooted in the body. The body could even be said to be indivisible from the spirit. In the soft viscera, pungent body fluids, viscous blood, tangled veins, grainy bones, and foul excrement, spirituality rose up.

From deep in his subconscious arose something his master had told him long ago.

"The heart of the perfect man is pure. Even in a swamp he remains unsullied. Though thunderbolts destroy mountains, and winds churn the four oceans, he is unafraid. He flies through the clouds, sails above the sun and moon, and transcends the world. Life and death cannot sever his unity with the world. His heart is with all things, but he is not one of them."

This last shimmer of conscious memory dissolved in light.

A Quest

ONE DAY THE Grand Master summoned his disciples before him.

"I have a quest. Who is willing?"

"I am, Master!" said Saihung quickly.

"It is true that I need a man captured. But I'm not sure if you're the one."

"A martial quest is even better!" said Saihung enthusiastically. "Who is the man?"

"It is someone I have forgiven nine times. I can forgive him no longer. Really, my hand has been forced. The provincial governor himself came to me and threatened to level every temple on Huashan unless I did something."

The Grand Master paused and looked directly at Saihung.

"This man has been dubbed the Heaven Soaring Spider. He recently robbed a government gold convoy, killing many guards. His acrobatic skill, which can carry him from rooftop to rooftop or over walls, is almost supernatural. He fights with two daggers and is an Eagle Claw boxer."

Saihung mentally tabulated this data. He wanted to fully understand his quarry.

"He is a notorious playboy," continued the Grand Master. "A pimp, a drug smuggler, and a member of the Green Circle Gang. In fact, the governor is after him precisely because this libertine seduced his wife. He is now in Beijing, making a spectacular exhibition of himself in the papers. Every week there is news of his criminal behavior."

"Master," asked Saihung respectfully, "why are you interested in such a man?"

The Grand Master sighed for a moment. A look of resolve set his face firmly.

"I raised this man from childhood. He is your elder classmate, Butterfly."

Saihung was solemn.

"Are you sure your personal feelings won't interfere?" asked the Grand Master. "Even Guan Gong let personal feeling interfere with duty."

"No, Master," said Saihung. "He has gone too far and has betrayed you and our sect. I will not let him go."

"You speak like a young man."

"I will not fail, Master."

"Then you must go. You leave tomorrow with Wuyung and Wuquan, two sentry monks. You will pursue Butterfly and bring him back quickly."

WITHIN A WEEK Saihung, Wuyung, and Wuquan were on a westbound train. Saihung was dressed in the flamboyant manner of a rich martial artist: a green silk brocade, high-collared gown, a sash of heavy black silk embroidered on the ends, and black cloth boots; disks of precious jade hanging from his belt symbolized his aristocratic class. His long hair was tied in a queue, illegal in Republican China, and hidden beneath his gown like the weapons he carried.

Saihung looked at the brothers Wuyung and Wuquan seated across from him. Both in their forties, they had come to Huashan to renounce the world and become novitiates. They were sullen, large, and mean, and Saihung suspected that the two had had a rough past. Somewhere along the way they had been given sad names that had stuck with them even in the temple. Wuyung meant "useless," and Wuquan meant "powerless."

214 Wuyung, the elder brother, had a head shaped like an old melon. His skin was rough from some childhood illness, and his brows were often tensed in his most typical demeanor of pensive melancholy. He was hard-muscled, with shoulders like a bull, and his heavy body swelled his black-and-purple gown.

Wuquan had more angular features. His dark brown face was like a bronze mask; the slits for eyes were narrow, uneven, and shadowed. Belligerence had been worked into every fiber of his face and body, and there was barely a trace of mercy to alloy it. His brown and gray gown was vainly tailored to show his titan frame.

The brothers were close in a rough and unsentimental way. Theirs was the silent alliance of blood and of men who had faced life and death together. The years of battle had made the sad-eyed Wuyung superstitious, while Wuquan was slyly cynical, especially regarding his older brother's outlook. They rarely exchanged words. They were two journeyman warriors. Saihung realized that his master was not a gambling man. He was sending two hulking killers after a nimble-footed one.

They stayed on the train day and night, enduring the unyielding benches, the constant swaying, iron cacophony of wheel to rail, and the even louder human noise of fellow travelers. The smelling, chattering crush of people packed on at each stop, stuffing their squealing bodies and makeshift luggage into the narrow confines of the train. They pushed, jostled, hung out the windows, screamed in peasant voices down the cramped, shaking car. But they shrank away in fear from the three warriors. They saw the clothes, noticed Saihung's aristocratic insignia, and spied the wrapped swords. Although it had been almost two decades since the collapse of the Qing dynasty, the fear and awe for the elite noble and warrior class was deeply ingrained into their simple outlook. Everyone knew the old saying: "A swordsman only carries a sword to kill. A sword can never be resheathed until it has tasted blood."

They transferred to a train on the Beijing-Shanghai line at a filthy and crowded station where the tracks were littered with debris. Saihung was glad to board the steam-engined train. It only unnerved him a little bit to watch a man stroll nonchalantly down the tracks and begin to bang away at the wheels with a hammer. This seemingly random pounding on the train made the whole contraption seem more ridiculous. Wuquan explained that the tie rods were being tapped back into place.

Their train headed northward, and in a few hours it passed into Japanese-occupied territory. Butterfly's gang connection and his presence in the war zone would make the task of capturing him more difficult. They would have to try not to alert his confederates or meet any Japanese patrols.

As Saihung's train lurched on its twin rails, he passed mud-brick houses, farms, orchards, and towns. But he also saw old bomb craters, devastated villages never completely repaired, and sleek dogs fattened from scavenging the dead. The war had settled into ineffective and bumbling skirmishes between the Chinese and Japanese, and the territory was a confusion of Japanese military administration, remnants of Chinese bureaucracy, soldiers, guerrillas, and gangsters. The fighting had evolved into a grim ennui where the Japanese occupational forces traded freely with Chinese gangsters and opportunists. Opium and heroin were the chief commodities, and thousands of pounds enriched both sides. China, from the Yellow River to the coast, was a surreal mix of death, cruelty, narcotics trade, and fumbling militarism. Heroism had long ago vanished as the rare and volatile quality it was.

THEY ARRIVED AT the train station for Qufu in Shandong Province in the afternoon. The skies were a dense gray-purple pall that dissolved into a heavy downpour upon their arrival. The air was hot. It let up after a while, but the roads were already a quagmire of brown sludge. They still had nine-and-a-half miles into Qufu. Since the town was both the birthplace and burial site of Confucius, geomancy and respect for the Great Sage would not permit the line to go directly there. The three of them hitched a ride on a farmer's cart.

They passed under a stone archway, the old drum tower, and found their way through the broken-down streets and lanes to an address the Grand Master had given to them. It was an herb store with a dark interior rich with a pungent aroma.

216 The proprietor was a stocky man in his fifties. Balding and bespectacled, he was nevertheless energetic and forceful. He greeted them from behind a counter.

"What would you like to buy?" he said.

Seeing that they were strangers, he waved his hand to direct their attention to his wares. Hundreds of tiny drawers lay behind him in cabinetry that went from floor to ceiling. There were no labels. He knew where each herb was.

On the opposite side, a display case showed such esoterica as ginseng, tiger bone, rhinocerous skin, *lingzhi* mushroom, deer antler, dried lizard, goat forelegs, and various dried organs of bears, deer, and sea lions. A pair of middle-aged men sat in chairs nearby. This in itself was not suspicious—an herbalist's cronies often came to chat the day away. But these two looked like murderers.

"I come with an introduction," said Saihung.

"Is that so?" responded the herbalist noncommittally.

Saihung pushed the letter forward.

"Come back tomorrow," said the herbalist after he read the letter. "Your master's prestige is great. I won't refuse you."

When Saihung returned the next day, he was told that he could meet the people he wanted. The herbalist had discussed the request, and there was an agreement. In two days, there was to be a council meeting. The three of them would then have an audience with the elders of the martial world.

There were two great underworlds in China: the criminal underworld, and *Wulin*, the world of martial artists. Whether good or bad, they considered themselves bound by chivalry, honor, and principle. They obeyed a King of *Wulin* and councils of elders and policed themselves by their own law. The outlaw martial artists were particularly interesting. They viewed themselves as champions of justice. Rewarding the loyal, punishing the traitorous, and generously helping those who caught their fancy were hallmarks of their style. Though they were still criminals, they were part of *Wulin*.

Of course, some of these people also fell into the second underworld. That underworld was controlled by secret societies like the Green Circle Gang, the Red League, the Trident Society, the White Lotus Clan, and the Iron Shin Society. Many of those gangsters did not belong to any tradition of masters, schools, discipline, or honor. They were hoodlums, pure and simple; greedy sycophants, brutal sadists, and strongarm masterminds obsessed with bullying and riches. It was true that many of the secret societies, such as the Red League, had begun as patriotic anti-Manchu organizations dedicated to the overthrow of the Qing dynasty. But over the years, the underworld societies concerned themselves more with opium, heroin, prostitution, gambling, graft, extortion, assassination, and political manipulation.

Both underworlds formed a crisscrossing net of contacts throughout China, and to almost all parts of the world where there were overseas Chinese. Both would be essential to the successful completion of Saihung's task. For now, Saihung had to begin with the martial world. Only they could guarantee that Huashan would be spared until he could catch Butterfly.

The martial world was administered in territories by a head patriarch and a group of elders, and all martial artists were obliged to follow the council's dictates. The elders settled disputes, sanctioned duels, directed collective actions, and ordered the execution of those who violated the code of chivalry. It was to such a council that the three monks went to present their petition.

The meeting was held on a hot and humid afternoon in a private mansion. In one dark hall, chairs were set up in rows like a theater, and the various members of the martial world sat in audience. At the head of the pillared hall was a round table where the ten elders sat. They each wore long Chinese gowns except for two men. One, with graying hair, wore the olive-drab uniform of the Nationalist army. The other was a man in his fifties dressed in Buddhist robes. Together, the ten represented religion, government, and business, as well as martial arts. If it concerned power, the martial world had a hand in it. The Buddhist monk was the patriarch of the martial world. His name was Qingyi, which means "Pure Mind." He had a smooth-shaven skull, although his face had begun to sag and wrinkle and his eyes were slightly puffy. His goatee had forgotten how to grow long or thick, but his shoulders hinted at a past broadness. His robes were a khaki color and a shawl of deep brown with a golden pattern like mortar between bricks angled over his chest and a shoulder. He wore a rosary of 108 beads around his neck, punctuated every thirty-six beads by one of brilliant Imperial jade.

Qingyi called the meeting to order.

"I call the three monks from Huashan. Step forward."

They stood up and approached the table. Some of the elders did not even bother to look at them but remained smoking cigarettes disinterestedly.

"Speak."

"I am the Butterfly Taoist of Huashan, student of the Grand Master," said Saihung. "I come to petition the elders to stay the hand of the Shaanxi governor. He wants my classmate who seduced his wife. Unless we turn him over immediately, he will order the army to destroy all Huashan."

Qingyi glanced at the Nationalist officer. He smiled derisively and looked at the tip of his burning cigarette. Why trifle over a mere woman?

"In my master's opinion," continued Saihung, "it is an internal matter for Huashan to settle. We will resolve the issue within the context of *Wulin*. We ask the elders to intercede on our behalf."

Qingyi looked around the table. No one spoke. There was only nodding and hand gestures. Saihung saw one man shake his head no. The rest agreed. Qingyi looked up.

"We will give you one hundred days only. After that, we cannot protect you."

"We thank the elders," said Saihung with a bow.

They left the meeting and hurried back to their inn to prepare for their trip. Saihung was satisfied. He knew that the elders would use their considerable leverage to enforce their rule. The army officer would send formal governmental orders; the businessmen could withhold money and supplies. Saihung had no doubt that Huashan would be safe from troops for one hundred days.

T HEIR TRAIN DREW nearer to Beijing. The sun was a flaming sphere, parching the barren land. The fields were scratched pitifully from the dusty soil. Laboring peasants, tied emotionally to the land in spite of warfare and natural calamity, worked for hours to pull crops of corn, wheat, millet, and potatoes from the chunks of clay. Bent over, hobbled, they stained the hot earth with whatever moisture they could divert to their fields, and endured the sandblasting brawn of the wild desert winds.

Dynasty after dynasty, generation after generation, year after year, Beijing stood at its chosen location. It was supposed to be an ideal geomantic site, the center of the world itself, yet it was no paradise. The clouds of hot yellow dust blew over the city like cavalry; the sun made the air dry and hard to breathe. Grit accumulated quickly between the lips and the corners of the eyes. Trees, crops, pack animals, and people alike withered in the climate of Beijing. The magic that the founders of the "Capital of Swallows" had used to establish the very pivot of Chinese civilization had diminished. As the train rushed toward its terminus, Saihung thought of the many armies that had, over the centuries, charged across the plains to sack the city and usurp its emperors. The tramp of marching armies, the pounding of hooves, and the crushing of tank tread had been heard throughout history as attackers from the north, peasant rebels from the south, European armies from across the globe, and Japanese invaders from the ocean sought to breach the vermilion walls of the Forbidden City.

The train terminal was outside the old city walls, and the three began walking toward the center of the city. For once they were glad of the hordes of people, since they could use the crowds to camouflage their presence from the occupying Japanese and the ever-watchful underworld spies. They made their way through narrow, crowded streets, between mud-and-brick houses that seemed as if they would sink into the earth with a good rain or heavy earthquake. It was like being in a maze. Because of an old decree that no building be higher than the Forbidden City, and because the old-fashioned population refused to distance themselves from the earth, the city had become a sprawl of low buildings, gray walls, and dusty lanes.

Walls were the major surface presented to the eyes in Beijing. Most homes and compounds had a wall around them. Some were weathered and broken, with yellow grit and coal dust caking the crevices where mortar once cemented the brick. Others had irregular patches of eroded whitewash and stucco, showing the brown rammed-earth blocks beneath. Windows were seldom seen on buildings close to the street, and those that were visible were usually translucent paper or a glass so dirty that they might have been clay anyway. Bright sunlight failed to enliven the utter dinginess of the walls, even though its rays occasionally caught tatters of old New Year's couplets or progressively faded cheap woodcuts of door gods.

All travelers entering Beijing's walls were required to register with the city magistrate. They went immediately to a brick building with red pillars and tiled roofs and found an empty reception hall with a stage and heavy rosewood desk and chair. A doorway on each side and a mural of two cranes above a frothing ocean made the room completely symmetrical. Except for the absence of chairs, it could have been a tiny theater.

A red drum on a high stand was adjacent to the open doors. At the center of the taut yellow drumhead was a large red dot. Sai-hung grabbed a stick and struck the drum loudly. This was an unrefusable demand to see the magistrate.

Soldiers in olive-drab Western-style uniforms and rifles filed out of each doorway at the end of the room. They walked silently and expressionlessly down the steps and turned to face each other. The attendant, a desiccated coat-rack of a man, came out in an ill-fitting blue gown. He had tiny glasses and a mustache and goatee that looked as if they had been scribbled on.

"The Magistrate of Beijing!" he announced pompously. Sai-hung and his companions dropped to their knees. The stone floor was hard and cold.

The Magistrate made his entrance with all the drama of an opera star. A squat, tough, no-nonsense bureaucrat dressed in black brocade, burgundy vest, and black skullcap, he sat down formally and with such an upright posture that a carpenter might have measured a plumb angle with his spine. His red face was like a boar's. His beard bristled like a scrub brush. His eyes were round but heavily lidded, conveying an uncaring, cynical outlook.

Saihung, Wuyung, and Wuquan kowtowed three times, each time touching their foreheads to the floor.

"The supplicants will state their request," ordered the assistant.

"We request permission to enter the city in search of a man," replied Saihung. He looked at the floor as he spoke—it was considered discourteous to look at the Magistrate.

"Your papers!" demanded the attendant imperiously.

Saihung offered his identification with both hands held above his head. He was still looking down. The attendant walked down the steps and took them to the Magistrate. Two soldiers took the others.

The Magistrate unfolded Saihung's passport, a long, accordion-pleated piece of paper bound between two hard covers. On one side was an oval photograph of Saihung along with his address and signature. There was a text signed by the Grand Master of Huashan telling the purpose of Saihung's business. The enormous square seal of Huashan was stamped at the end along with the Grand Master's own seal. Further along the passport were panels for official inscriptions along the way.

The Magistrate grunted noncommittally. The attendant and the guards watched him intently. Every facial expression, every utterance, every gesture, meant something. This was the way he communicated. It was beneath him to talk to his minions, let alone those who came to petition him.

The Magistrate stroked his beard as he considered and then seized a brush from the stand. The attendant obsequiously weighted the passport down with bars of white jade and eagerly scrutinized the five dishes of ink on the desk. It didn't matter what the Magistrate wrote. The color of the ink itself would convey his orders.

Black meant no. Green meant yes. Blue signified that the matter would be taken under consideration. White meant that the request had no merit and did not deserve comment. Red meant immediate execution. Saihung anxiously watched the tip of the brush poised above the dishes. Finally, to his relief and the attendant's disappointment, it plunged into the green ink.

The Magistrate beckoned to his attendant and whispered something.

"The Magistrate knows your master," said the attendant. It was intriguing to hear how his voice conveyed both a cowardly obedience to his master's orders and yet his complete distaste for them. He continued: "He wishes you the best in your search."

The Magistrate got up without any further comment and left the room. The attendant followed like a dog, and the soldiers filed out. Only one remained behind to return the passports.

They went to a teahouse and, by paying a higher price, were able to go to the second story. From that vantage point, they could see the whole city. Out of the haze and the infinite block-houses of the people's homes, Saihung could see the outlines of the Imperial City with its cinnabar walls and golden-tiled roofs. The heat was oppressive, but the sandalwood-lattice windows scented the air whenever a breeze wafted in. The waiter rushed up, inquired what kind of tea they wanted, and took their order for food. As they waited, Saihung squinted against the light and wondered how they might find his elder brother.

They were in the right place to begin. The teahouse was a universal gathering place. Open from dawn until the late hours of the night, people went there to socialize and spend their time. Tea and food were readily available and, in the fancier places, entertainment was provided by lovely women musicians or strolling storytellers. The customers were usually a cross-section of Chinese society: Scholars indulging an outrageous fetish for tea, businessmen talking over deals, middlemen arranging marriages, uncomfortably formal relatives entertaining visitors, students exchanging ideas, friends celebrating their cherished ties, or old men relaxing in their unhurried retirement.

By far the most colorful were the martial artists. They were often giants, almost mutant aberrations. They came from all over the north, and one could see by their dress which were warriors from Manchuria, Shandong, or the far west. They sat with their feet wide apart and firmly planted on the ground, always in readiness to spring up. Etiquette dictated that their weapons remained unconcealed. Shorter weapons like swords, fans, daggers, and clubs lay on the table top. Maces, spears, and staffs were propped against the table.

222

Wuyung saw an old acquaintance. A thin man, dressed all in black, with a broadsword lying within easy reach, he greeted the monk enthusiastically. After some conversation, Saihung saw a brief flash of silver coin. The man smiled even more broadly and saluted as Wuyung returned to the table.

"I dislike bribes," said Saihung in a low voice.

"Consider it tea money for an informer," replied Wuyung simply. "Anyway, it was luck that we ran into him. I got some information."

"What is it?" asked his brother.

"Butterfly lives with his wealthy mistress, a woman in her early thirties named the 'Powerful Tigress.' She herself is a formidable fighter. Her fingers can pierce a body as easily as if they were steel spikes. Her father was an Imperial Shaolin knight who had only two children. The older was the Tigress, the younger now a teenage boy. Since the Tigress was older, the father taught her his art unreservedly, but he died before the boy could be fully trained. The sister has probably finished his education, and Butterfly has probably added to her technique."

"We'll go to her mansion," said Wuquan quickly.

"Not so fast," interjected Saihung. "We should find out more. There are many women fighters who can be more dangerous than men."

"Exactly," agreed Wuyung. "That's why we'll go to the coroner's office tomorrow."

Saihung, Wuyung, and Wuquan went to the city mortuary the next morning, a grim brick building smeared with coal soot and grime. They showed their papers to the coroner and persuaded him to let them see a body collected two days before. The coroner was an odd man—stranger than one might expect for someone who worked constantly with the dead.

His brow and eyes were vaguely canine, while his lips were always smiling to reveal a terrible overbite. He was cheerful and showed himself every bit to be a man who loved his work. Once he had ascertained their legitimate interest, he led them down a hallway with all the excitement of one about to show off his greatest accomplishment. He had a habit of wringing his leathery hands, not so much from nervousness as from anticipation.

He led the way down into a basement, his white-haired head bobbing like a fish in a dark sea. Saihung might have enjoyed the respite from the Beijing heat were it not for the smell of formaldehyde and the stench of opened bowels. The staircase led into a narrow, vaulted hall with cribs and coffins inadequately lit by oil lamps. An assistant was about to dissect a woman's body, but the coroner dismissed him and almost tenderly covered the body with a greasy sheet. He led the trio into a dark corner where they uncovered a coffin. A foul stench billowed up.

"Fortunately, we have not yet covered him in lime. I thought there might be an investigation, so I waited one more day. But no one cares who gets killed anymore."

Saihung examined the body. It was a large and stout Buddhist priest, his shaved head as massive as a cannonball. The brows were black and thick. The two nostrils seemed like simple holes, and the mouth was parted, a purple-rimmed gape that revealed clotted blood on his broken teeth. Heavy iron rosary beads, each sphere an inch and a half in diameter, hung around his neck. He wore a gray vest and pants that exposed a barrel chest and tree-trunk arms. Wuquan unsheathed his sword and with the tip pushed the vest aside. There was a brown spot beneath the end of the right collarbone, another under the left ear. The most obvious wound was a purple bruise in the shape of a human palm over his heart.

"We don't know who killed him," said the coroner in an academic tone. "But it was fast, and his weapon was broken."

They looked at a shattered weapon that had been carelessly thrown beside the corpse. It was a moon spade, a long, heavy weapon that was the specialty of Buddhist monks. On one end was a large blade, a derivation of the shovel needed to dig herbs. On the other end was a crescent-shaped blade. Both ends had steel rings hanging from the shaft that made a ringing noise during a fight. The sturdy teakwood shaft had been broken and splintered by a powerful force.

Saihung asked the coroner to leave them in privacy for a few moments and turned to Wuyung.

"What did your informer tell you, and how does this relate to Butterfly?"

Wuyung picked up a hurricane lamp and rested it on the coffin's rim.

"Two days ago, this monk came to Beijing with a goal very much like ours. He wanted to stop Butterfly and his mistress from committing more crimes. His strategy was to draw the Tigress out through her brother. He knew from underworld informers that the boy usually left the mansion at a regular time. The monk met him and barred his way. He threw two lead balls into the ground with such force and weight that they sank deep into the dirt. The monk jumped onto the two spheres and issued a challenge: If the boy could push him off, the monk would teach him his art. Naturally, the boy charged. Confident of his own skill and, like all martial artists, obsessed with the urge to learn more, he attacked carelessly. The monk slapped him over the heart. The boy spit up blood and fled.

"He showed his wound to his sister, who recognized the imprint of an iron-palm master. She went immediately to avenge him. The monk was waiting. He fought her bare-handed at first; but, surprised at her strength and ability, he had to resort to his weapon. Even then, the witnesses say, she succeeded in depriving this veteran boxer of his moon spade. In her fury, she snapped the shaft and returned the same blow that had wounded her brother. The monk's years of training were insufficient. Her deadly fingers broke the slender thread of his life."

Saihung looked at the stiff body. The wounds and bloated areas were as clear as words. They were a distinct warning of a fighter who deserved her name.

"Let's go," he said. "Butterfly may already know we've arrived in Beijing. We'll attack her mansion this afternoon."

The two monks agreed. They gave the coroner some "tea money" and began their walk across town to the northwestern quarter.

"It's such bad luck to visit a mortuary on the day of a duel," muttered Wuyung.

Wuquan cursed his brother's superstition. "Who cares about such ideas? Now, the stench—that was real."

"It makes this city smell good by comparison," said Saihung.

225

Wuyung took a deep breath. The smell of coal smoke—that harsh odor like burning oil and pig grease—was heavy in the air. He coughed.

"Hell," he complained. "It's not that different."

The three companions walked through one of the oldest sections of Beijing. The swaybacked gray buildings and crumbling walls formed twisting narrow lanes—simple, almost accidental corridors left over after building. Although Beijing had at one time been carefully laid out by geomancers on a precise grid, entropy and the chaos of individualism had long ago taken over. It was thus all the more a contrast when they turned a corner to see a long, unbroken expanse of immaculate gray brick. The wall surrounding the Tigress's estate was over thirty feet high and topped by green glazed tile. The gate was flanked by red pillars, and the vermilion doors were of timber heavy, enough to withstand a tank. There was no easy way in. They had to use a rope to scale the wall.

Saihung was impressed by the beauty of the gardens within the outwardly grim enclosure. A piece of paradise in the most colorful splendor had been neatly inlaid into the monochromatic dreariness of the aged city. The beauty of the gardens and home had the air of long cultivation. Such refined taste and careful balance of architecture and landscape came only over many years. The Tigress's father must have hidden this jewel from the emperor. Had the ruler known, he would have killed his knight out of jealousy.

A man-made pond fronted the house, and a long stream appeared to wind to the west and back of the home. The water was a muddy green, but its opaque surface mirrored the many weeping willows that grew at the banks. The shores were no simple mud; instead they were lined in an irregular arrangement of the most eccentrically weathered stone available.

They crept to the brick mansion, a massive two-story arrangement of traditional latticework, sturdy pillars, and upturned tile roof corners. A neat row of glazed pottery planted with cactus stood at the edge of the stone portico. The doors were lacquered red and inlaid with mother-of-pearl that marvelously recalled marine colors.

Saihung withdrew from the splendor of his surroundings and took his outer gown off to reveal a tighter shirt. His body was tied with a rope that had a blade on one end. Saihung looked at his companions, a signal to draw their swords. The naked blades, so straight and sharp in a heaven where smooth and round were the main characteristics, seemed gratingly bright. The Tang scholar Li Quan was right, thought Saihung, "Weapons are tools of ill omen." A sword begged to be used.

227

Saihung faced the door again. He kicked it in crudely, and it fell with a loud crash. The lacquer chipped and burst from the impact.

Saihung and his companions walked into the room and looked around. They saw a classically symmetrical main reception hall. There were two rows of ornately carved and silk-cushioned ebony chairs with tea tables in between, and an extravagantly large silk rug in a pattern of flowers and symbols for longevity. The walls were lined with precious scrolls and ceramics. At the head of the hall was an enormous horizontal scroll of bright red peonies, and a pair of chairs faced the doors. The room light was dim, and there was a faint musty trace in the air. The monks heard a frantic running sound and a woman's voice ordering servants away.

Three people soon emerged from two doors on either side of the far end. The first was clearly the Tigress. She was of medium height and walked gracefully. Dressed in gold-and-blue silk tunic and pants, her shapely figure was lean and athletic. Her feet were strong and unbound. Her skin was like translucent jade. Her eyes were large, dark-lashed, and came to thin trailing points at the outer corners. For a moment, Saihung nearly forgot his reason for being there and his rude entrance. As he savored the gentle perfume, he reflected that he, too, might forsake mountain life had a woman like the Tigress ever tempted him.

Behind her was her brother. A slender teenager with shaven head and inquisitive eyes, he seemed untroubled by his recent wound. Dressed in red silk, he was carefully tucking up the hem of his gown into the black sash to allow for quick footwork and kicks. He carried a spear about his own height, and its red tassel tossed as he leveled the point at them. He smirked, showing teeth that were even and white.

Sister and brother advanced to the center of the room, but the third person lingered close to the door. It was Butterfly. Instead of the swaggering, self-confident Butterfly Saihung knew, his elder brother seemed reticent, his glance at them almost fatalistic.

"We've come for you, Butterfly!" Saihung shouted across the room.

Butterfly looked up, and then away.

"Master wants you. You've gone beyond what he can tolerate. Come with us now!"

"This is my house," said the Tigress. "You are in no position to give orders."

"Stay out of this, or I won't be polite," replied Saihung hotly. He looked at Butterfly, who took a step back. "Attack!" shouted Saihung as he charged forward.

The Tigress met his onslaught with ease, and Saihung found himself in an unfavorable position. Her skill was greater than his. It wasn't simply a matter of strength. Instinctively, he sensed the overwhelming superiority of his weight and brawn; but she was exasperatingly elusive and quick. She dodged his strikes and did not even bother to block. When she counterattacked, Saihung had to retreat desperately. Striking with her fingertips made her reach longer. She was a lethal opponent.

Saihung leapt to one side and dashed for Butterfly, who retreated calmly. The Tigress leapt at Saihung. He sidestepped, and she drove him back, finally connecting with a devastating kick to his chest. There was a flash of metal and both opponents paused momentarily in surprise. She had a blade in the toe of her boot; he was wearing a steel breastplate.

"You cowardly monk," she said in disgust.

Saihung only grinned sheepishly. He wasn't one to take chances. In that brief moment, he tugged at the slipknot and whirled around. The rope dart uncoiled and he flung it at her. She was too good a boxer to be picked off, but he at least hoped to keep her off balance.

The rope dart had a whistle on it, and it whined at a high pitch. The rope had to be kept taut and brought back after each strike. As it returned, Saihung could wrap it around different parts of his wrist, elbows, or legs, and then send it flying out at some unpredictable angle. He could also whirl it in all sorts of arcs to cut horizontally. The Tigress was completely unimpressed and pressed her attack. Fifteen feet of rope and a razor-sharp blade were all that kept her at bay. He hoped that Wuyung and Wuquan were doing better.

The two sentry monks were a good two feet taller than their opponent, and each probably outweighed the youth by fifty pounds. But the boy made up for these disadvantages with nimble speed and the long reach of his spear.

Two swordsmen were an easy thing for him, and their devious spinning movements and precise thrusts were countered by a special feature of his weapon. The shaft of his spear was cut from a certain vine that retained its flexibility due to lengthy soaking in special oils. If he hit one of the monks along the length of the spear, the shaft would still whip around and embed the blade into the body. At the same time, the spear could still be used to butt, parry, cut, thrust, and smash in all the same ways as a staff. Saihung saw that the teenager was a master of fighting.

The Tigress charged Saihung. He fought back ferociously and hurled the dart straight at her. She sidestepped quickly, but he still cut her shoulder slightly. He stepped forward as the dart came whistling back. The rope flexed powerfully in his palms; he felt the burn of its rapidly shooting fibers on his fingers. He had to keep it moving yet redirect it. One loop, then another, a rapid spin to gain momentum as he turned his back to her. Just as she came within range, he hit her with a backward tiger-tail kick and sent the dart shrieking madly out. It struck the boy so hard that its five-inch blade sank from sight. Saihung leapt forward and mercilessly threw a loop around his neck. Without hesitation, the two brothers thrust their blades in for the kill.

The Tigress was wild with grief and anger and threw herself at them with her full fury. She had no reservation now, no careful strategy, no graceful moves. A treacherous and magnificent force emerged from her, and she struck Saihung with a blow as powerful as any he had felt from a man. He twisted quickly to reduce the force, but was still thrown off balance. He stumbled back as she came with a finger strike aimed at his throat. He caught a glimpse of her glaring eyes, red with hatred and tears. He heard the quiet hiss of her exhalation as the full force of her internal energy was directed with pinpoint accuracy.

But before he could feel her sting, in a blurred flash he saw Wuquan sever her hand. The deadly hiss became a cry of agony as her precious weapon dropped to the floor and her hot blood burst from the stump. She backed out of range with a look so violent that the three monks paused.

She controlled her breathing with great effort and stood up. She saw her dead brother. A look around the room told her that her lover had abandoned her. Even worse, she had lost her hand. She was insulted, dishonored in a way no other form of degradation could have done. Her fingers were famous; her fighting ability was her pride. Now, she had lost everything. If nothing else, a martial hero or heroine never compromised pride. She made the only move she could.

The Tigress could harness her full energy, and had mastered the ability to direct *qi* and blood instantly to any part of her body. Now, she raised it all to her tongue—the junction of the *Du* and *Jen* meridians. As her whole life force rose to this single point, she bit down on her tongue with a ferocious finality. Her throat welled with blood, and her spirit burst through her self-inflicted wound. Saihung watched her body swing around and fall like an animal brought down by a hunter.

Saihung unwrapped his rope from the boy. The body was heavy, animated not by life but by gravity. Saihung coiled the stained rope up—he'd have to get it replaced—and carefully cleaned the blade. A raw odor filled the room, a pungent counterpoint to the lingering perfume. Saihung walked to the door and found an oil lamp. In a second, the burning fluid soaked into the carpet, and the broken bodies turned orange on a lawn of flame.

IN THE FOLLOWING days, Saihung, Wuyung, and Wuquan pursued Butterfly by inquiring into the great network of underworld spies. They lost precious time chasing down untrue rumors and false leads. After five days of searching both cities and countryside, they came to a village called Dahong in Hubei Province. There, in a seedy wineshop, they found an informer—

a small-time racketeer and thief. After a generous payment, he told them what they needed to know.

"Your classmate is in the company of the Hubei Three Tigers. The first is a master of the Eight Trigrams Palm named Li. His teacher was a Zen monk, and his lineage is descended from Yin Fu, the master who protected the Empress Dowager when she fled Beijing in 1900. The second is named Wang. He is a disciple of the famous Sun Lutong and is a master of Form and Mind Boxing and the Six Harmonies Sword. The third is called the Flying Cat. A small man, he is nevertheless quite formidable, having been thoroughly taught by one of the last Qing dynasty knights, the Divine Flying Leopard. These men are all in their fifties and thus in the prime of their abilities. You're all too young to beat them."

"Nevertheless," replied Wuquan, "please tell us how we can find them."

The thief considered a moment and then laughed. "Fine, fine. This way, I'll know where to send coffins for you."

They left the still-smirking crook and made their plans. This was now solidly an affair of *Wulin*. As such, the only avenue was a personal challenge—and only one person could challenge the three. For all of them to gang up on each of the Three Tigers would be dishonorable. Saihung volunteered and sent out letters of challenge immediately.

THE WEATHER GREW hotter. Saihung became temperamental and impatient to catch Butterfly. In two days, he met both Li and Wang and had beaten them both. He beat Li's graceful and elusive Eight Trigrams style with the savage grappling and merciless falls of Mongolian wrestling. A fifty-year-old man simply couldn't endure too many throws to the hard ground. Ironically, Saihung used Li's very own style against Wang. The twisting movements and circular strikes were the perfect counter to the straight, crushing advance of Form and Mind Boxing. In neither instance did he kill his opponent. This was a case of martial honor. They had sheltered Butterfly only out of friendship.

Saihung clarified the misunderstanding after Wang conceded. Only then did the two masters realize the trouble Butterfly was in. They told Saihung to hurry southward. The Flying Cat was escorting Butterfly to the Yangzi River.

The three companions hurried to the train station but missed the train, an event that Wuyung immediately took as a bad omen. It was four hours to the next. They could do nothing but wait and catch the next Nanjing-bound train. It was twenty-four hours before they arrived on the north shore of the Yangzi River. There was no bridge across the impossibly wide gulf, and it would take hours to ferry the train across. The three of them rushed to the banks and hired a small boat to take them across.

The Nanjing piers were swarming with people trying to get onto the makeshift wooden junks, steamers, and freighters. Crates were piled everywhere, as were baskets of produce and cages of ducks and geese. The docks stank with gasoline, oil, garbage, and sweat.

Even at that early morning hour, the weather was sweltering. Saihung dragged his sleeve across his forehead, and the sweat soaked through. As he squinted against the sun, he was startled to see Butterfly, a dazzling figure on the drab docks dressed in a suit of rich sky-blue silk. Beneath his tunic was a pristine white shirt, open to the chest. He was smiling and walking at a leisurely pace. Beside him was a man in black.

Saihung pushed his way rudely through the crowd, and the immediate squawking that his rush provoked alerted the Flying Cat. As Saihung pushed the last bystander aside, a shrieking whistle came flying at him. The Flying Cat, master of the rope dart, had made Saihung the target of his weapon.

The screaming crowd backed off immediately, but they did not scatter too far. They paused halfway between fear and curiosity. Saihung and the Flying Cat squared off in this human arena. The Flying Cat circled him warily. He was a thin, short man. His face was shaped like an olive pit; the skin was brown and leathery. His jet-black hair was thickly pomaded and his eyes sharp and narrow.

The rope dart came bitingly, but Saihung produced his weapon, a steel fan. He snapped it open to shield himself and launched his counterattack. He quickly closed the distance, but to his astonishment the Flying Cat not only dodged his punches but jumped with terrific gymnastic skill over Saihung's head. He kicked Saihung in midair and then renewed his efforts with the rope dart.

Saihung fell to the wooden planks and felt several searing slivers penetrate his palm. He jumped up angrily in time to deflect the rope. The Flying Cat did nothing to retrieve the dart all the way. He could jump after it, loop it in midair, and send it dive-bombing down. The next time he jumped, Saihung cocked the fan back and with a snap brought it open before him. As he did so, he pressed a secret button on the fan's outer rib. Thirteen slender needles propelled by Saihung's rapid wrist movement and a spring-loaded chamber hit the Flying Cat in the leg.

Wuyung and Wuquan joined in. It was too crowded to draw their swords, so they fought bare-handed. Though wounded, the Flying Cat fought bravely on, but his opponents soon left him unconscious on the pier.

Saihung pushed through the crowd and ran to the end of the pier. A boat was already pulling away with Butterfly on the deck.

"You know why I'm after you!" shouted Saihung furiously. "I swear I'll get you!"

He was surprised to see Butterfly's impassive look. His elder brother seemed distracted and tentative. Saihung watched the boat drift away and strained to hear any reply. Nothing came. Damn! Why was it that no one in his life talked when it mattered?

THE BROKEN-DOWN STEAMER they took in pursuit was crowded, and Saihung chose to stand at the railing to watch the water. The Yangzi coursed powerfully in its channel. This body of water was too large to be given a ridiculous label like "river." It was an ocean—deep, treacherous, wide, and mighty. All sorts of garbage thrown from boats floated on its opaque, mud-colored surface. As the boat slowly pulled away from shore, the brown expanse became greater and greater. There was a feeling of freedom. Adrift in the smooth expanse of water, great adventure seemed possible.

Saihung watched water curl away from the sides of the boat. The white foam barely frothed. The world took on a very simple

233

composition. Three horizontal bands comprised everything: blue sky, verdant fields, brown water. He watched the green band flow steadily by. Sometimes it was a gentle beachlike bank; at other times it was an eroding wall of loose earth, with little chunks tumbling to the water. Occasionally, a rock formation stood in weathered defiance to the undercutting currents. They passed fields and some mud-brick homes. Towns were mere aberrations to the impassive bands of blue, green, and brown.

Another steamer passed them going upstream. It was crammed with refugees fleeing the occupied zones. Saihung stared at them. They were rough, desperate, and afraid. A surprising number of people were going downstream to look for relatives or to find work. "A job is rare these days," he overheard a man say. "Even if it's in the occupied area, it's better than starving."

There was a flurry of excitement on board as a corpse floated past them. It was surprising how fast it moved. Before long, another one came. The water flowed so quickly, but the figures were still.

"Did you see that?" asked Wuyung excitedly. "A bad omen!"

"Yes," said Saihung. "Was that last one a man or woman?"

"Do you know how to tell?" asked Wuquan. "If it's floating facedown, it's usually a man. Faceup it's usually a woman."

"How did you collect this strange fact?" asked Saihung.

"Somewhere in my travels," said Wuquan casually. "A woman's hips are heavier, so her bottom pulls her down, and her face floats up. But a man is more top-heavy, with a heavier head. He'll float facedown."

Soon another corpse floated by, and they tried to test Wuquan's theory. Unfortunately, this one's head was half shot away.

Saihung pushed his way through the noisy crowd toward the bow of the boat. There, braving the occasional spray of mist, he continued to stare downstream at the great watery brown triangle of the river. The waves were hypnotic. Somewhere in his lessons his master had told him that water was a special element for him, advising him to gaze at its surface to bring calmness and introspection.

He had killed in Beijing. Who knew how many he had killed in his life? He had been born into a warrior's family, the art of killing was his heritage. He had fought often in his youth to defend his home from bandits, he had dueled in martial challenges, and he had fought as a guerrilla soldier. Besides, just as Saihung and all martial artists understood, so the Tigress and her brother would have understood the ultimate price of fighting. But their death nevertheless struck him as tragedy and waste.

He had killed Butterfly's lover. That seemed to make this time different. Now, he felt like a destroyer, not a hero. He was a fighter who mowed down those who opposed the fulfillment of his quest. No longer was he an idealistic monk. Instead he was a man who had been challenged to complete a mission, and he suddenly saw that there was another morality to challenge.

The ethics of challenge were success, and challenge was the heart and soul of the code of chivalry to which he was bound. But hidden within *yiqi* was the sorrow of sacrificing all other principles. Throughout time, men had lived by the quest, but the bards never told the real reason that boys became men: It was by sacrificing nicety and elegant ideals that they finally understood the irony of ethics and reality. As a martial artist, a modern knight, Saihung knew that he liked challenges. There was something about the conflict between principle and circumstance that he craved. But each time he took on a challenge, he had to learn anew the same lesson of sacrifice and compromise. Standing at the boat railing, he accepted again that he had killed, accepted again that his soul would suffer for it, accepted again that he would pay a great price to catch his brother. He felt a feeling of finality as he turned to the boat's side. This was what it was like to be a champion of a chivalrous cause.

He watched the brown water flowing effortlessly by him. He was still too emotional, he thought. Saihung thought back some ten years to a question he had asked the Grand Master as he was trying to understand the concept of *wu wei*.

"What does *wu wei* mean?" he had asked.

"It means," his master had replied, "that everything you do seems spontaneous, natural, and complete. Nothing affects you.

Nothing stirs up the emotions to interrupt the precious tranquility that you have constantly cultivated."

"Nothing affects you?"

"Nothing."

"What if you were meditating and someone tries to kill you?" asked Saihung.

"If they come to kill me, fine. I shall kill them first."

"And then?"

"And then I sit back down to meditate."

"That's all?"

"Yes."

"Wouldn't you suffer for killing another?"

"Not in this case. They came to kill me. I merely interrupted them."

"Wouldn't you suffer within?"

"No. That's *wu wei*. One event happens, then another. If you are truly *wu wei*, then you are always placid."

Another corpse floated by. A woman this time. The Yangzi River seemed full with them, and he had a sudden image of being in a procession of the dead. The dead go to hell, he thought. He and the corpses were all going to the same place at the long river's mouth: Shanghai.

Shanghai

WAS THIS HELL? Saihung asked himself on the docks of Shanghai. What he saw was so alien, so astonishing, it might as well have been. As he made his way down the swaybacked gangplank, through the shouting, spitting, stinking throng of people, he saw the Shanghai skyline. A veritable milelong rampart of sky-scraping steel and concrete buildings stood along the famous Bund. They were taller than anything he had seen, except mountains, and with their straight lines, precise rectangular windows, echoes of Greco-Roman architecture, and imposing gray columns and walls, they were stranger than anything he had known.

It might have been a pretty spot once, he reflected. The sky was a pale blue with high floating clouds, and ocean breezes swept over the flat, open delta land. The richest agricultural lands lay to the west of Shanghai for miles; though they were marred by warfare, they provided fresh produce and bits of green beauty. With the clear light that fell on this city, whose name simply meant "By-the-Sea," Shanghai might indeed have been lovely. But instead, with its clock towers, hotels, and office buildings, Saihung saw it as ugly.

238

As he stepped onto the dock, he and his two companions became like small children in a parade. The crush of people was maddening. Walking was almost as futile as prying open a hydraulic press. Even by elbowing his way through the crowd, Saihung could make only slow progress. By the time he made his way to a street corner, his senses had been overcome by smell and noise. Where was that fresh air he had breathed on the river? Now, he only smelled an odor like burning oil. He looked at the streets—a mad race of pedicabs, those rickety contraptions pulled by bronzed men. But Saihung was almost killed by a few of the other vehicles: cars. It was they, he discovered, who smelled like burning oil. Terrifyingly roaring, smoke spitting, gleaming metallic carriages, ominously black, they sped their well-dressed occupants carelessly through the crowded boulevards.

Saihung, Wuyung, and Wuquan were bombarded with the sensory images of the city: massive doorways of colonial power. Barred windows of the Hong Kong and Shanghai bank. A Russian woman stepping immodestly from a Rolls-Royce. Prosperous shipping brokers in teahouses. A corpse stiff in the gutter. Old hawkers selling candy apples. An Asian banker dressed in top hat and morning coat. A sniffling heroin addict. Drunken sailors. As Saihung pushed his way up the urban riot that was Nanjing Road, these impressions multiplied exponentially as he walked each block.

He could see gangsters on almost every corner—young, arrogant, and coarse men who would molest anyone they pleased. Dressed in bright colors, they had their tunics unbuttoned immodestly to reveal opened undertunics. Where normal people had their sleeves rolled down, theirs were rolled up. They affected bits of Western clothing with their traditional Chinese suits. Porkpie hats, apple hats, dark glasses, wide leather belts, and leather shoes were all considered very fashionable. But beneath their clothing were the traditional tools of thuggery: knives, brass knuckles, blackjacks, and pistols.

Saihung took great interest in these hoodlums. In fact, nothing was possible without approval from the gangsters. They dominated the city, controlled its banks, government, and police, and preserved themselves between the cracks of the European settlements and the disintegrating wartime society. The millions of dollars that went through the city in a flow mightier than the Yangzi was almost completely tainted by the underworld. Whether it was industry, shipping, opium, heroin, or slavery, the gangsters controlled it.

239

No one in Shanghai escaped contact with the Red and Blue gangs and the foremost mob of them all, the Green Circle Gang. Famous people like T. A. Soong, H. H. Kung, the Soong Sisters, Sun Yatsen, Mao Zedong, and Zhou Enlai had all been involved in one way or another, and it was said that Chiang Kaishek remained in power precisely because of the money, intrigues, and strong-arm tactics of the godfather of Shanghai, Du Yueshen. It was he who represented the city at its highest sophistication and deepest debauchery.

From the hotels, they could hear music, laughter. They could smell savory food: baking bread, roast ham. Once in a while there were sweet traces of opium smoke along with breezes from the sea, and the more pungent odors of the streets. The foreigners even smelled different, Wuyung told Saihung, though they never came close enough to tell. They were supposed to smell of flowers and spice, leather and wood.

Over the course of many decades, Wuquan told him, the foreigners had carved the city into the famous foreign concessions. The British had occupied the choicest land at the tip of the Bund, while the French took the area between them and the old walled city to the south. Across Suzhou Creek in the northern district was the American concession; but, unable to administer their territory with any of the grandeur of the English, they had merged with the British to form the International Settlement.

Both had their own police forces, but these were purely tools of colonial mentality. The arrangement actually was a boon to crime. A few miles could put one easily into a different jurisdiction, and gangsters exploited this continually. The police found it more profitable, literally and figuratively, to cooperate with the criminals who dominated Shanghai.

The grandeur of the foreigners had tarnished when the Japanese invaded the city in 1937 and herded the majority of Westerners into the ugly high rise called the Shanghai Mansions. Once Japanese had settled themselves, they had been compromised by the beguiling corruption and wickedness of the city, and the era of colonialism had begun to molder slightly around the edges. The city now belonged to politicians, assassins, spies, militarists, gangsters, and moneymen.

Japanese soldiers were still a dangerous presence—bullying, carousing, raping, looting—and the monks would have to be careful. But more important still was to avoid the uncanny power of Shanghai to make all who came follow her ways.

Over the next few days, Saihung and his companions made contact with the street-corner hoodlums. Bribing and cajoling their way through the criminal hierarchy, chasing down leads in the opera houses, entertaining at teahouses, and fighting to prove their ability, they finally wrangled an audience with the Gray Swan, one of the kingpins of Shanghai's underworld. But Gray Swan was a careful woman fearful of assassination, and she would only see one person. Saihung insisted that he be that one person.

The day of his appointment was sunny but muggy. As he walked through the French concession, Saihung's clothes stuck to his skin; the sweat trickled down the nape of his neck. He clung to the shade afforded by trees planted along the street. The air was hard to breathe. It was almost liquid. The villas were walled and stuccoed with a gray mixture. Behind them he could see wood and brick mansions that were so large they would someday be used for schools and offices. Their style was alien to Saihung. He had not yet been to Paris, London, or Berlin, where these homes would not have appeared so strange.

They came to a heavily guarded walled compound. The men at the steel gates all had holstered pistols. They carefully searched Saihung for weapons and then escorted him down a

curved driveway to a squat and ugly brick building. The facade
had been built only with a consideration of sturdiness and osten-
tation. Fake stone columns framed the door of heavy oak. As he
stepped into the carpeted front hallway, Saihung noticed a dis-
agreeable odor, like camphor mixed with mold.

Six men accompanied him to the living room, which was decorated in the finest Chinese style. Saihung was surprised. He
knew many gangsters affected a show of art and culture after
they had established themselves, but their taste usually ran to
gaudy and big. Here, however, the porcelain, jade, and scrolls
were of museum quality. They were fragile and ephemeral bits
of beauty next to the rough men who stood all around the room.

"The Gray Swan!" announced a bodyguard.

There at the head of the cream-colored room full of art and
murderers sat a slender woman. Her hair was perfectly coiffed, a
fragrant sable-colored mass pinned with silver, gold, and jade.
Her face was a well-formed oval with high cheekbones, arching
brow, and thin lips. She wore heavy makeup, giving the impression of a woman slightly past her prime. Her shoulders were a bit
wide, but her breasts were well rounded and full. Her legs, showing at a slit in her tight brocade dress, were long and smooth. She
had an affected habit of playing with a dangling earring.

"Ai! What a handsome boy you are!" exclaimed the Gray
Swan.

Saihung blushed.

"Just looking at you makes my legs go weak! What a fine
body! Oh! My mouth just waters!"

She turned to a bodyguard with the proportions of a Frankenstein.

"I like him." She smiled. "His skin is so soft, not like you ruf-
fians!"

The bodyguard grinned. Saihung noticed quite a few missing
teeth.

"Tell me, have you come to play with me?" she asked insinuatingly.

"I'm sorry, but no," stammered Saihung. "I'm seeking a classmate who is part of the Green Circle Gang."

"What a formal fellow you are!" She pouted. "That's the trouble with men. They always want to get right down to business!

Of course I know why you're here. If you want this man so badly, we can tell you where he is. But what will you give me in return?"

"What do you want?"

"A night alone with you would be ecstasy!" said the Gray Swan. "I can just imagine how it would be. Give me one night of pleasure, and I'll give you your classmate."

Saihung could feel the veins on both sides of his neck throb in nervousness.

"I'm sorry, but I am a renunciate. I have my vows," he said. "I'm a Taoist."

"So? Why not be a gigolo for the Tao?" she said smiling coyly.

"This is out of the question!"

The Gray Swan laughed. "It's so refreshing to see such an upstanding youth. You bullies take a good look. There was never anyone in Shanghai like him."

The bodyguards all laughed sarcastically.

Saihung spoke first. "You don't have my classmate, so it wouldn't be an even deal anyway."

"True," she said, her eyes narrowing. "You're shrewd as well as handsome."

"I can see I'm wasting my time. Permit me to take my leave."

"You couldn't leave unless I said so," cooed the Gray Swan. "But actually someone else has an interest in your case. I'm supposed to introduce you."

"Who is it?"

"Mr. Du Yueshen."

Saihung paused. Du was the king of the Shanghai underworld. It was not necessarily a good thing for him to be interested, yet Saihung knew that nothing significant happened in Shanghai without his knowledge.

"What do you want from me to see him?"

"You and I are both members of the martial world. I'll chalk it up to chivalry."

"Is that all?"

"Yes. Don't assume that truth lies only in greed."

"That seems to be the rule in Shanghai!"

"Yes, yes." The Gray Swan laughed. "But we'll just say I had too much to smoke today."

Saihung cursed her silently. He knew Du had probably given precise instructions.

"You may go," she said. "You meet Mr. Du tomorrow. They'll take you there."

Saihung agreed and turned to leave.

"Good luck!" called a man's voice.

Saihung spun around. He looked back to see the Gray Swan's laughing face. He was shocked. It was a man's laugh. The Gray Swan was a transvestite.

243

"I said good luck," he repeated. "Oh, what fun it would have been to take you to bed!"

BLINDFOLDED, SAIHUNG, WUYUNG, and Wuquan were taken by limousine to a three-storied mansion with balconies. It was built of concrete and stucco, and the window frames and balustrades were painted a Venetian red. In the narrow front courtyard were parked several more limousines. Saihung glanced around. The walls were about twelve feet high. The gate was bar steel covered with heavy plate. In a corner was a small, wilting garden with an incongruous Chinese gazebo painted red and green. Beyond the walls were more French-styled buildings.

They walked up some steps to the main portico. The front was lined with potted plants, succulents, cacti, and palms. The whole front entryway was a grid of varnished oak and beveled glass plate. Inside, the interior was dark, with walls of stained mahogany, hardwood floors, and a deep carmine carpet. The ubiquitous bodyguards were dressed in dark colors, standing like suits of armor in a haunted house. Unlike the street-corner pimps, thieves, and playboys, these men were grizzled and stoic professionals. The bulges in their clothes signaled both muscle and guns.

A bodyguard opened a sliding set of double oak doors to reveal more men stationed around the perimeter of the big room. It was furnished with large, overstuffed Western sofas and chairs, all with the same shabby brown slipcovers. Photographs and a few murky oil paintings decorated the wall, and a mirror in a rococo gilded frame hung above the cold black fireplace. A few potted palms stretched for light at the windows, but the heavy drapes were all half-drawn. An electric crystal chandelier dangled from the high ceiling. Next to a green lamp at the far end of the room sat Du Yueshen.[1]

He signaled them to come closer. Saihung examined him. Du Yueshen had a rectangular face. His hair, closely cropped in a crew cut, had receded slightly into a half-circle around his face. The forehead was high, but the brows jutted out, and the eyebrows were thick, dark, and arched in the middle. His eyes glittered with an instinctive ruthlessness. The nose was a straight wedge that flared out into large nostrils, and his mouth was wide, with sensuous lips. His ears stuck out and had earned him the hated nickname "Big-Eared Du." The skin was tight, the flesh hard from years of opium smoking. Most compared his face to that of an ape.

His shoulders had once been heavier, but now they had thinned. There was no young muscle beneath the high-collared gown, only a tough, sinewy, and hardened body. Du Yueshen was forty-five years old then, and he was experienced, accomplished, and could still claim to be at the height of his power. Whether it was in Hong Kong, Chongqing, or Shanghai, he controlled everything from the loading of opium in the harbor to the secret-society machinations that maintained Chiang Kaishek in power.

In his expressionless face, it was difficult to realize Du's vast history. He had been born in Pudong, across the Huangpu River, and had begun as a small-time drug-runner and pimp in the heyday of Shanghai's lush world of pleasure and corruption. He became the protégé of Huang Jinrong and soon rose in the ranks of the Green Circle Gang. He had helped to centralize the opium traffic and all criminal activities, making pacts with other gangs or eliminating them outright. By 1927, his power supported Chiang Kaishek's takeover of the Chinese government. Du was a dedicated anticommunist. It was he who masterminded the infamous 1927 massacre, where his men killed five thousand Communists in the streets of Shanghai.

1. Most Western sources and scholars believe that Du Yueshen left Shanghai in 1938 with the first invasion of the Japanese. However, Kwan Saihung distinctly remembers having met Du in mid-1941; in addition, two other residents of Shanghai, both daughters of prominent bankers, agree that Du was in Shanghai until he fled to Chongqing around the autumn of 1941.

At the same time, he became a leading figure in respectable banking circles. This was not necessarily an anomaly in those days, since corruption and the abuse of wealth and power were the standard in Shanghai's money circles. He dressed in fine silks, tuxedos, and top hats, and was chauffeured in expensive two-tone limousines with bodyguards riding on the running boards. He was the head of the Shanghai Civic Association, a director of the Bank of China, sat on the Currency Reserve Board, founded a school for boys, and established a fraternal organization called the Constancy Society.

Du was an ardent Nationalist and hated the Japanese, although this hardly stopped parts of his sprawling gang from cooperating in the drug trade with the occupying forces. When the Japanese invaded Shanghai in 1937, he offered to sink an entire fleet of his ships to block the harbor. Even now, parts of his gang engaged in an underground resistance against the Japanese.

Some people found it difficult to reconcile Du's many facets. Ruthless killer. Opium smuggler. Respectable banker. Shameless womanizer. Dedicated Nationalist. Drug addict. Opera afficionado. Wealthy socialite. A key to Du's personality could be found in his belief in the martial code. As a martial artist, indeed, elder and godfather of the martial world around the Yangzi River valley, he believed in *yiqi* justice, honor, principle, chivalry, and generosity. Du felt that he treated others fairly and punished those who thwarted his code. A paladin does not question his lord but merely destroys his challengers. Du's lord was an unholy trinity of power, opium, and money, and he was their champion.

Du's sense of justice was primitive, savage, and unalloyed. But it was this sense of honor, no matter how warped, that made him more than a gangster. Although later accounts would paint him as a cartoon villain, a man of pure evil, Du Yueshen was an infinitely more complex mixture of generosity and gangsterism, idealism and opportunism.

There was no doubt, however, that he was fearsome, and Saihung could feel the man's cruelty as he gazed at him.

"You are seeking a man," stated Du flatly.

"Yes," said Saihung. "In the name of the martial world, will you help me to find him?"

"Perhaps."

There was a long moment of silence. Saihung could not tell whether Du was contemplating or merely slipping into a stupor.

Everyone stood around respectfully. Du seemed shrunken. Some great men exude glory and charisma, but this was not Saihung's immediate impression of Du Yueshen. He sat for a long time, a cadaverous, unmoving figure. When Saihung looked at his eyes, however, they were alive, shrewd. Aware.

"You are a martial artist?" His voice seemed a little stronger.

Saihung nodded.

"Show me."

Saihung tucked up the hem of his gown. He launched into one of his specialty sets, the famous Willowleaf Palm. As soon as he completed the salute, he saw Du's eyes quicken. He knew he had to impress him.

Saihung felt his muscles flex, the feet firmly forming a steady base for his whirlwind strikes. His waist twisted mightily, his shoulders propelled his quickly arcing arms. He felt a rush of joy, emotion, and heat rising in him, and he proudly gave himself over to the pantomime of battle.

"Excellent! Excellent!" shouted Du as Saihung concluded the short set.

Saihung was startled. The cadaver was coming alive.

"What about you two?" Du asked Wuyung and Wuquan.

The two complied by performing a prearranged sparring set of Xingyi—Form and Mind Boxing. An internal system of martial arts, it featured crushing direct strikes. There was little retreating, only sidestepping or turning. Every move was a direct and vicious attack; every reply was counterattack. Du got more excited and motioned for a water pipe. An attendant packed it with what looked like a blob of black tar and gave it to him. Du lit a match, and the black opium glowed red. As he inhaled, the pipe made a gurgling sound, and blue-white smoke rose up around him. The unique smell of opium—fragrant, sweet, tasty—filled the room.

By the time the brothers finished their set, Du was energetic and excited. Saihung could see that he was a martial-arts enthusiast, a member of the class of people whose appreciation bordered on the fetishistic and irrational.

"I salute you young heroes," he exclaimed, clasping his hands in salute. He was smiling, almost boyish. "Let me demonstrate too!"

A bodyguard brought forth two sheathed broadswords. Du Yueshen grasped their handles and drew out two gleaming blades. Saihung could hear a rasping sound, which meant that there were sharpening steels in the scabbards. Whenever a broadsword was withdrawn or returned, its blade was honed.

"Eight Trigrams Double Broadsword!" announced Du, and he proceeded to show a unique set.

The set began with the two broadswords held in parallel as they cut to each side, twisted, and cut again. They sliced vertically, horizontally, and in wide arcs. Gradually they began cutting, stabbing, and piercing in different directions, or one would block while the other attacked. At times, both would chop down at once. Du's long arms, like the wings of a big bird, gave him a reach from tip to tip of nearly eleven feet. This made him a formidable fighter, and any opponent would find it difficult to penetrate the blades that swung like propellers. Even if he could, the kicking, jumping, flying kicks, and midair cuts would have discouraged all but veteran opponents.

The pace of his set quickened, and Saihung could see a thrilled look on Du's face. The smoke had got into him, blood flushed his face, and the pure power of the rapidly slicing blades gave him obvious pleasure. The whirling blades became a blur, cutting so quickly that they made sounds in the air like abruptly ripped bedsheets. Only occasionally did the bright flashes congeal momentarily into an expertly thrust point, a precise block, or a double scissorslike attack in tandem with almost balletic kicks. Grace, speed, and strength were wedded firmly to an absolute homicidal impulse. A faint sheen of moisture appeared on Du's skin, followed by a tight grin of satisfaction.

It was now Saihung's turn to be excited. He himself had learned the Eight Trigrams Broadsword style, but only for a single broadsword. This was a spectacular but cruel set that offered no quarter. He wished that he could learn it.

As Du finished he noticed the gleam familiar to all martial fanatics in Saihung's eyes.

"Did you like it?" he asked.

"Yes, indeed!" responded Saihung.

"Would you like to learn it?"

"Of course!" For a minute, his quest was forgotten. It was Du, ever thorough, who brought the conversation back to reality.

"You want Butterfly. I will let you seek him in my territory. But I want something in return."

"What is it?" asked Saihung.

"Huashan martial arts is famous, as you three have just demonstrated. I know there is a secret manual in five volumes, written by a man who thoroughly mastered the *Seven Bamboo Tablets of the Cloudy Satchel*. It reveals deadly martial-arts techniques through the cultivation of internal energy. Get me that manual, and I will let you have Butterfly."

"I will have to send for it," said Saihung hesitantly. It was a high price, and he wondered if Huashan would approve its release.

"Good. Have it for me within a week. In the meantime, you can learn this set."

THE DAY THAT the books arrived in Shanghai via a special courier was gray and overcast. The clouds, dense inkstains on sleek, pale silk, threatened to dissolve not into a heroic storm but a gloomy drizzle. The air was a moist, furry presence outside the dirty windows of Saihung's cheap hotel room. He put the parcel on the square table and opened it. The cloth case was faded purple silk with ivory pins to keep the cover closed. Inside were five volumes. As Saihung opened the book, the wan light fell on yellowed pages with jet-black calligraphy.

It intrigued him that Du Yueshen in Shanghai would know of these esoteric manuals in the custody of Huashan's priests. It was a measure not only of Du's position, but the rumors, legends, and information that shot through the communication networks of the martial world. Saihung began reading the manual and immediately saw that Du had not been misinformed. The book laid down profound theoretical principles for internal cultivation and then showed how the superhuman power could be projected into an opponent's body during fighting to rupture internal organs. It was clearly a tremendous risk to allow such murderous techniques to fall into the hands of a killer like Du. Saihung realized that Huashan elders were so desperate to capture Butterfly that they were willing to gamble the books.

Saihung arrived at Du's mansion by pedicab, and found Du Yueshen engaged in his regular habit of opium smoking. He seemed to be having trouble breathing—he was a lifelong asthmatic—and the rims of his eyes were red and teary. Opium was a pleasure and vice with him, but it also helped to mitigate the wheezing and shortness of breath. Without a smoke, Du was unable to call forth his martial abilities. It was for that reason that plenty of armed bodyguards accompanied him everywhere, and that he always sampled from the river of black powder that surged through his territory.

Du looked darkly at Saihung when he opened the case.

"There are only three volumes here." The man who sent a coffin and pallbearers to visit people with whom he was displeased was clearly upset.

"Surely, you don't think me naive," replied Saihung, boldly. "I give you three volumes in good faith. But where is my classmate? When I capture him, you shall have the other two."

"I would not suggest you double-cross me," hissed Du.

"Of course not. But a deal is a deal: the books for Butterfly. I would not think that you would expect payment without the merchandise."

"All right," said Du, after scrutinizing Saihung. "I will expect the last two volumes to be delivered to me when you complete your quest. Otherwise, I will forget our friendship; I will find you and burn your temple."

"I understand," said Saihung with a diplomatic smile. "Can you tell me where to find him?"

"Shandong Province," revealed Du. "He is at the home of his teacher, the venerable Divine Eagle. This is all the information that these three books will buy."

"It is enough. Thank you."

"I am leaving for Chongqing tonight," continued Du. The Japanese are getting suspicious. I do not know if I will return soon or if we will meet again. But remember that the Green Circle

Gang surrounds all of China. I am everywhere. Remember that I want those books."

"A deal is a deal. If I catch Butterfly in Shandong, you will have what you wish."

"Yes. I will have it," said Du in a low voice. "I will always have what I crave."

Saihung made his final good-byes and rushed back to the hotel where Wuyung and Wuquan were waiting. They gathered their things and set out that afternoon. But Saihung told them only that Butterfly had been sighted in Shandong and nothing else. He suggested that they split up, and that they meet at Taishan, the premier peak of China's Five Sacred Mountains. The mountain was considered to be a sacred place for Taoists, and every Taoist was supposed to make a pilgrimage at least once in a lifetime, much like Moslems visiting Mecca. As initiates, the two brothers had never been to the summit, and they readily agreed. They never suspected that Saihung knew all along where Butterfly was hiding.

THE HOME OF the Divine Eagle was an isolated and palatial walled villa in the mountains of central Shandong. The peaks did not have the ascetic expanses of rock that Huashan had. Instead they were older, rounded, weathered, and broken. Splintered, battered, crumbled into heaps of rock and dirt, they were covered with a net of dense woods that thrived in the misty atmosphere. The landscape formed an ethereal backdrop to a place that was a virtual fortress. No villages were nearby. The towering walls were a solitary presence in the phantasm mountains.

The Divine Eagle was a friend of Saihung's grandfather, so he welcomed him warmly. A man with the proportions of a legend, he had strong shoulders and hands with fingers that looked like railroad spikes. His white-bearded face was wrinkled, with a bump on his forehead and a hooked nose with a somewhat bulbous tip. There was no space between his thick eyebrows; and his dark, glaring, intense eyes were disquieting and unemotional.

He had received Saihung's letter and, while he did not wish to involve himself in the trouble, had suggested that Butterfly remain to meet with Saihung instead of fleeing again. It was the

Divine Eagle's opinion that nothing could be gained by prolonging the chase. Everyone would benefit if the two brothers resolved the difficulties.

The pursuit had lasted two months and had taken Saihung up and down China. Finally, he was about to catch up to his elder brother. He washed himself and changed into a dark burgundy silk gown and went out into the gardens.

Through the round opening of a moon gate in a pristine white-washed wall, he saw the complete composition of an inlaid rock courtyard, weathered rock, and a massive upthrust pillar of petrified wood surrounded by peonies. He walked through the gate, turned to his right, and came to a hexagonal archway. Above it was an inscription that read THE ETERNAL FRAGRANCE OF ANTIQUITY.

An inlaid slate pathway led into a lush garden of turquoise pools, gray rockeries, weeping willows, and old pines. Saihung followed the path upward to another wall and then through its oval gate past a pavilion. A large pond, with an artificial island about fifteen feet in diameter, shimmered in the hazy light. There was a zigzag stone bridge over the water and a red-and-green gazebo to one side of the rock island. Standing with his hands folded behind his back, and immaculately dressed in vibrant cobalt silk, Butterfly stood gazing at the distant peaks.

The bridge was composed of solid slabs of granite a foot thick. It felt hard and unmoving as Saihung walked with quickening steps toward the island. The bright colors of the gazebo and Butterfly's still figure were mirrored on the pond with a background of green willow. In a moment, Saihung merged with the vivid reflections.

"I've finally caught up to you," began Saihung bluntly.

Butterfly turned around slowly, gracefully. Saihung saw that his face was as smooth-skinned and handsome as ever. He did not look troubled at all. Quite the contrary; he was calm, composed, and had an open smile.

"Yes, and you know why," Saihung continued. The Grand Master wants you. You've caused a great deal of trouble."

"Have I?" Butterfly motioned to the octagonal marble table that stood between Saihung and himself. There were four stools of fine-textured milky marble carved in the shape of drums.

Even details like the nails that held the drumhead and the handles were carved in. A finely painted porcelain tray from the Ming dynasty held a *Yihsing* teapot in the shape of a pine stump and two small cups.

"Will you have some tea, Little Brother?"

Saihung and Butterfly sat down opposite one another. Butterfly placed the teacups delicately down and poured a tea perfumed by narcissus flowers.

252

"You're ignoring the issue, Elder Brother," said Saihung directly. "You've committed many sins. You've killed many people. It's an abuse of your talent. How outrageous that I never really suspected the scope of your wrongdoing."

"Haven't you also killed? Didn't you kill my lover and her brother?"

"They were martial artists. We all accepted the possibility of dying in a duel when we became members of the martial world."

"Surely, as a Taoist, you understand that taking a life is still just that, regardless of the reason."

"Don't twist things around. You are only trying to divert attention from yourself."

"Myself? I've nothing to hide."

"Nothing? You are shameless! You stand in this garden and ignore the women you've seduced and sold into prostitution, the people you've ruined with narcotics, the innocents who have died simply because they had the misfortune to be in your path. Don't you feel any remorse at all? Don't you feel any guilt?"

Butterfly drained his teacup thoughtfully and put it down. He looked at Saihung with a steady gaze.

"Guilt?" asked Butterfly. "You've become quite a flamboyant orator. Do you really know what guilt is?"

The question stopped Saihung.

"Guilt is a veil that the inferior hide behind. They commit some supposed transgression and then whine that they feel guilty. Is this supposed to purge the consequences of their misdeeds? They say they feel remorse and then they repeat the same acts all over again. Their guilt becomes heavier. Unable to change, unable to accept themselves, they feel inferior because of their continual guilty feelings. This process becomes a lifelong pattern and cripples them totally."

Saihung was confused. The issue had been so clear to him before. He did not quite understand why it was so complicated now. Butterfly's argument was logical, but the end result did not seem acceptable.

"Guilt comes when a person accepts that his actions were wrong. But guilt is an illness," continued Butterfly. "The only medicine for guilt is to look ahead and persevere. It is inevitable in life that one will commit some wrongs. The average person hides his embarrassment. But the superior one accepts that actions were wrong and then never does them again. Such a one not only purges a weakness but eliminates the necessity of guilt as well."

"Look, cut the crap," said Saihung awkwardly. "Why don't you admit that you've done wrong?"

"Now you're judging me. Who are you to judge me? Does any person have the right to judge another?"

"There are laws and rules."

"Law is a human conception. It is an artificial and arbitrary standard. I see no reason to accept its yoke. Let the commoner have laws. Let those without imagination accept convention. A herd needs confinement. But I cannot accept such a false thing as morality."

"You've turned into a monster, perverting the very ideas of right living." Saihung was angry.

"All you do is sit there and hurl accusations. If you lived my life, you could not say such things. Those who accuse and judge should ask themselves if they have some special right to see themselves as higher than the next person. In truth, all persons are created equal. Don't be so quick to judge another."

Butterfly stood up with a sigh.

"All that matters to me is to experience life deeply and fulfill my destiny," he stated.

Saihung thought a minute. That seemed a perfectly valid goal to him.

"We are all born into this life with a destiny," said Butterfly, as he gazed at the still waters. "All that matters is that we fulfill our destiny. That requires total honesty. Above all, I've tried never to be dishonest. I accept myself. I do not trick myself into some artificial conception of myself. I don't take some ideal lifestyle

253

from the sages or some book like the *Seven Bamboo Tablets* and try to bind myself to it. How absurd! The scriptures were written by men, not gods. Why should I accept their word? No, I am determined to live life honestly. I will not violate my nature with the conceptions of others. I will accept my destiny, no matter what it is, and I will live my life only on the basis of my own identity. That standard is my only right and wrong. Let me explore it, contemplate it, coax its meaning out. Only then can I feel that I am living my life unadulterated by delusion."

"Brother, what you say is quite worthy. But that hardly justifies killing, robbing, and seducing."

"Am I to shun my destiny because it isn't a nice and respectable one? An actor mustn't complain about the role he's given. It's only a petty drama. When the opera is over he changes to another role."

"But the killing!"

"I've seldom met a martial artist so fastidious about killing. The legends are full of stories about sentimental swordsmen. They always die early."

"Elder Brother, I can agree with what you say. But it comes too late and as a justification for an evil life."

"You're young. So young. All I can say is that I never seduced a woman against her will. I never killed a man who did not want to kill me. I never robbed anyone who could not afford it and who had not acquired their gold by graft and corruption."

Saihung was quiet.

"Does this satisfy your petty morality?" asked Butterfly sarcastically.

Saihung admitted to himself that it did, in a way. But he said nothing.

Butterfly turned emotionally to Saihung.

"Little Brother. You hold my life in your hands. I appeal to you to let me go. If I am imprisoned on Huashan, I will never rest easily. My spirit will be broken."

A wave of feeling rose up in Saihung. This was his brother, his closest friend since childhood.

"Think, Little Brother. How much in life are we actually free to choose for ourselves? The seasons affect us. The stars direct

us. Circumstances hamper us. Destiny guides us. You are the way
you are because of what has come your way in life. You made se-
lections, but usually there wasn't much real choice: Out of all the
things that came your way, you decided to do what was right for
you. Now think about me. A different flow of the Tao came my
way. Women fall in love with me. Riches come easily to me. Martial prowess is strong in me. I did not ask for this. They came to
me as part of my destiny. I accepted responsibility for it. We are
both named Butterfly. We must fly free or die. Give me the
chance to fly free. Let me pursue my destiny."

"It will lead to your death."

"That's a farmer's mentality. You and I should try to live like
heroes. We will all die. And I know I must come back in future
lifetimes. But this is my role now, just as you have yours. Let me
continue to play out my role."

Saihung poured himself another cup of tea in a play for time.
He agreed with Butterfly, and was impressed all over again with
his elder brother's insight. He saw no reason to curtail such a special person's life. Butterfly was a unique and unusual person, Saihung thought. This gray and mundane world needed such
spectacular humans.

Saihung stood up and faced his brother. He savored the solitude and the tranquility of the moment. He realized how much
he loved him.

Saihung clasped his hands and bowed slightly.

"Will you stop your life of crime?"

"I understand things better now. I assure you I'll stop."

"Elder Brother, please take care of yourself. Try to lie low for a
while."

"I shall, Little Butterfly."

"I will leave first."

"Please walk slowly."

Saihung crossed the bridge and began down the path. He
looked above the waving crowns of venerable trees and saw the
celadon-colored crest of a distant mountain range silhouetted
against a deepening lavender sky. He thought of his master, so
far away on a nearly unattainable mountaintop. How distant he
was, how like a fairy tale seemed his life on the mountain. He

255

wondered how he would tell his master what he had experienced on the plains. But he resolved that he would. Surely, there would be an alternative open to them.

He reached the garden wall at the corner of the pavilion. A bed of roses was just beginning to bud. Lush blobs of red and pink stood at the end of dark green branches. A breeze stirred them slightly and a strong emotion pressed behind his sinuses. He resisted the impulse to look back.

S AIHUNG ARRIVED AT the Taishan Railway Station and took a battered bus to the foot of Taishan. Four days had passed since his meeting with Butterfly, and he considered the matter settled. All that remained was to collect the brothers and return to Huashan. He felt satisfied with his quest. He had traveled much, seen much, met unusual people, and had won several difficult duels. This was the life he loved. He truly felt himself to be a martial artist, a man who lived for adventure, a knight who fought for righteousness and justice. In time, he could become a part of that exclusive brethren of unusual men like his master or those he had seen in a Beijing teahouse.

It was cloudy and hazy. The summit of Taishan was obscured by a diaphanous veil. Saihung had agreed to meet Wuyung and Wuquan not at the summit, but on a lesser peak. On the less-traveled eastern route to Taishan was the Triple Yang Temple. It was there that Saihung met his companions and told them about his meeting with Butterfly. They could go back. Huashan was safe, and they had only used up a little over two months of the time Qingyi had set.

"Are you mad?" Wuquan burst out rudely after hearing Saihung's account. "You had that bastard in your grasp and let him go!"

"You've made a serious mistake," added Wuyung.

"What are you talking about?" asked Saihung. "It was a misunderstanding. He was accused without complete justification. Besides, he has given me his word to live in obscurity."

"You stupid kid!" cursed the older brother. "He'll never change. You let him bewitch you."

"Bewitch me?" Saihung blurted out. "Impossible. I've been meditating for years. My mind is strong."

"Then open your eyes, you dumb meditating monk," said Wuyung caustically. "You still cannot distinguish between black and white."

"Our orders were to bring him back," continued Wuyung. "You botched it. Now we'll have to begin again."

"No!" shouted Saihung. "Give him a chance. He's promised to stop. I've known him since childhood. He wouldn't lie."

"You've naive!" said Wuyung incredulously. "Even if that were true, he must still be punished for his past transgressions."

257

"That's past now," said Saihung emphatically.

"That makes no difference to me," Wuyung responded. "I must fulfill my orders."

"I agree," said his brother.

"Let's go back and let the Grand Master decide," said Saihung desperately.

"Show up empty-handed?" asked Wuyung with a sarcastic look. "Then you'll know punishment!"

"And what about Du?" asked Wuquan. "You made that deal with him. Now we'll have him on our trail, too."

"I only gave him three books," shouted Saihung, "and since I didn't bring Butterfly back from the Divine Eagle mansion, it doesn't count."

"But he has the books."

"I've kept the other two. They have the techniques. The first three are purely theoretical. I'll return those to the elders. We haven't lost much."

"Except time and Butterfly, you stupid kid!" burst out Wuyung. "Don't you realize that you've made a terrible mess of things?"

Saihung was quiet and suddenly felt embarrassed. For the first time he wondered if he had been wrong to let Butterfly get away. It had seemed so simple there in the garden. Now he was uncertain.

Wuyung scrutinized him and softened somewhat.

"Look, we'll do it this way: We'll track him through the activities of the Green Circle Gang. If it looks like he has reformed, we'll go back to consult with the Grand Master. If not, then we can still capture him before the time limit."

Wuquan agreed. Saihung also nodded, but said nothing. The more he thought about it, the more depressed he became.

Luck seemed to desert them in the following days, for the railway system was quite off schedule and no trace could be found of Butterfly. They drifted southward toward the Yangzi on the desperate theory that Butterfly might gravitate toward Green Circle Gang activities. This approach brought more information.

China seemed to be a nation of snoops. It was something Saihung had always hated about people, but now he was grateful for it. The countryside was so crowded, and people so nosy, that there was always someone to witness everything that anyone did. In the underworld, such curiosity was an essential method of intelligence. Getting that information only required buying it.

It soon became increasingly evident that Butterfly, far from reforming, was redoubling his efforts. In Yangzhou, where the trio had settled, there came disturbing news. Butterfly had assassinated several politicians in Shanghai, and was escorting a shipment of opium up the Yangzi by way of escape.

Saihung took this news with a heavy heart. There was no romance now. He had to accept that his brother was a simple gangster. He had fooled himself before. Somehow he had looked upon it as a righteous crusade. Now it only seemed like a gritty police job. This was not only mundane, but it brought everything down to a horrible reality.

Butterfly was heading toward Chongqing. Once there, he would be impossible to seize. Both Du Yueshen and Chiang Kaishek were there, and it was certain that the three monks would be killed in that city. They had to get him right away. The spies said that Butterfly would be staying for one night in Nanjing. That was where the three would set their ambush.

Nanjing was a large, spacious city on the southern bank of the Yangzi River. It was an industrial shipping center and a great historical capital as well. One of China's Eight Ancient Capitals, it still had parts of its city walls, and the Ming Tombs were adjacent to the city. It had also served for a time as Chiang Kaishek's capital, though the Japanese had driven him out ignominiously in an atrocious and bloody battle in December 1937. It had been the last time that Nanjing, the "Southern Capital," had sought to compete with Beijing, the "Northern Capital."

But a great deal of the city was wrecked in a way Beijing never was. The war had decimated entire city blocks. The rubble and

258

carnage were still clearly in evidence. Burned-out shells of buildings, homes blasted into dirt and sticks, bridges and rails bound in barbed wire, trees shot to splinters, and everywhere cripples with limbs missing, mud on their faces, teeth shattered, eyes filmed over in old yellow tears, crawling ignored through the streets. Freaks. Outcasts. Beggars. No one in Nanjing had survived untouched. The Japanese still held the city, patrolling the streets and victimizing whomever they pleased. There was no longer a place for martial virtue, for righteousness, or for heroism.

SAIHUNG WAITED IN an inn's stuffy second-story room for hours. This had started out as a martial crusade. He had been the gentleman-warrior bedecked in jade and silk, petitioning the martial world to bear witness to the great cause he would champion. He should have opened his eyes in Qufu. Half of the elders had been businessmen, and even the army was in it. He had battled bravely and heroically when the foes had subscribed to the same ideals. But now he saw that the world belonged to men like Du Yueshen and that warriors were now hacks with guns and artillery.

Saihung shook off these thoughts and recalled himself to the present. He looked out his window and across the balconied courtyard. The walls of the inn had once been white, but now they were streaked with rain stains and soot. He glanced at Wuyung and Wuquan. They were quiet and grim, and their swords were unsheathed. Butterfly was in a room across the way. It was only a matter of time.

At twilight, there was a flurry of activity, and several men came out of the room. One was Butterfly. Saihung jerked his head to signal his companions. They crept out and edged around the balcony wall. Saihung emerged from the room holding a four-foot-long blowgun. He looked at his brother and paused. Then he inhaled, a deep, long breath like the one before a sob. He felt his ribs open, his diaphragm strain, his throat tighten. Then all his regrets, all his ideals, all his emotions, exploded into the slender tube.

The drugged dart burst silently through the air and struck Butterfly in the neck. The men cried out in confusion. Saihung quickly reloaded and shot two more, as Wuyung and Wuquan sprang forward. Pistols were hurriedly drawn, and Saihung threw himself down to escape the fusillade. He took quick glances through a latticework opening. The two swordsmen quickly killed the gangsters. Saihung anxiously checked to see what had happened to his brother. He saw him standing at the edge of the railing. Butterfly pulled the dart out, but it was too late. He reeled unsteadily. As the swordsmen rushed him, he tried to jump down and escape. But his consciousness drained away and Butterfly fell into the garden below.

During the journey back to Huashan, Saihung argued bitterly with Butterfly. It was the voice of one betrayed. Saihung had once idolized him. Now, he had shot him off a balcony and was dragging him back for judgment.

"You see what's become of me, Little Brother?" asked Butterfly.

Saihung looked at him in the rocking train. His hands were bound behind his back, his feet bound eighteen inches apart.

"You said many fine words before," replied Saihung. "I believed you. Then you continued on."

"Each of us must make a choice," said Butterfly as he looked out the window. "Sometimes it's wrong. Real life isn't heaven. We can't all act like immortals."

"Real life is always a test," replied Saihung. "Entering heaven requires doing right. It's worth it in the end."

"Perhaps if you lived my life you wouldn't say that. Don't be like me. Learn from my mistakes. Study hard and discipline yourself. Be good and righteous."

"I can't believe this. You're the one who did wrong and you're trying to correct me?"

"It's only because you're my little brother."

"And what do you intend to teach me? More slop like what you fed me at Divine Eagle's home? I'm never going to listen to you again!"

"Don't be stubborn. There may come a day when you'll find that you've made some terrible mistakes. When that time comes, don't feel guilty. Don't hide it from yourself. Just do better in the future."

"Well, you'll have a chance to put your words into action now. When the Grand Master sees you, he won't be affected by your silver tongue."

"I'm not afraid of punishment."

"Wait until you get there."

The train slowed to a stop and Wuquan jerked Butterfly roughly to his feet.

"Here we are at Huayin Station," barked Wuquan. "Let's go, bastard."

They climbed the sheer heights of Huashan in a day and reached the South Peak Temple in the late afternoon. What a contrast monastic life was. The air was clean, the earth itself was unsullied by garbage, feces, or corpses. Ancient pines stood in grand silhouettes above the clouds; roaring cataracts spilled from inaccessible cliffs. Cranes and swallows dotted the skies, songbirds warbled in sweet tones. Although poor and old, the monasteries were clean and still. A feeling of peace enveloped Saihung as he savored the orderliness and tranquillity. Something in his heart grew calm.

Inside the temple, he could hear the chanting that he had heard since childhood. It was funny to him how something he had sometimes hated now filled him with sentiment. He inhaled the smooth, cool air with its undertones of camphor and sandalwood. It was good to be back.

His master and classmates were sitting in the main hall, lined up like judges.

Saihung, Wuyung, and Wuquan fell to their knees. Seeing Butterfly's defiant attitude, Wuquan pulled on the ropes binding his ankles and forced him down.

The room was silent.

The Grand Master motioned them to a small room at the side of the hall and they went in. It was a simple cell with only a window and tiny altar table. Used by the priests to rest between rituals, it was completely bare of any other adornment.

Only the two acolytes followed the Grand Master into the room. The Grand Master stood eye-to-eye with Butterfly, but said nothing. Butterfly, his hands bound tightly behind him, stood with his head cocked at an arrogant angle.

The silence was excruciatingly tense for Saihung. He looked at Butterfly. The orange half-light of sunset lit his back and threw his face into purple shadows. The sweat from mountain climbing left a sheen on his skin, and strands of hair fell over his face. Saihung wondered what Butterfly was thinking as he tested his will against the man who had raised him.

In contrast to their wretched state, the Grand Master was immaculate in his black robes. The creases fell in perfect and orderly folds, the hat was unsullied and adjusted to a studied perfection. His white beard contrasted sharply with his dark clothing, and not a hair was out of place. Saihung wondered what he was thinking. Did he feel regret that his adopted son had come to this? Was he sad, angry, or bitter? Would he forgive Butterfly?

The two stood for agonizing moments in complete stoicism. No emotions passed across their faces; nothing moved in their eyes. They were like two statues set face-to-face by destiny.

Suddenly, the Grand Master's eyes turned red. He took a step forward and smashed his palm over Butterfly's heart. For as long as Saihung had been a fighter, he had never heard the sound of a human heart bursting. Blood gushed out from Butterfly's mouth and nostrils, and his eyes rolled to complete whiteness.

"No! No!" screamed Saihung.

Even the swordsmen were stunned as they caught the falling body.

"Why did you do it?" cried Sound of Clear Water.

"Yes, why did you do it?" echoed Saihung as he knelt in grief beside the crumpled body.

The Grand Master only folded his hands and turned brusquely away. He left the temple hall alone.

Ashes

T HE INCENSE WAS still smoking. The candles blazed brightly, their melting wax
dripping like blood. The flowers were bright, fresh, even cheery,
but Saihung knew that they would soon wither, choke, and yellow. He solemnly dipped his hand into the urn he was carrying
and felt the gritty ash and pieces of bone. As he wandered over
the slopes like some lost ghost, he slowly scattered the last remains of his cremated elder brother.

It was difficult for Saihung to accept Butterfly's death, although everything had reinforced its reality. Saihung himself had
washed and clothed the stiff and heavy body. He himself had felt
the cold and turgid flesh as he had anointed it with oils and

sesame seeds. He had stared at the body for a long time, thinking even during the funeral that he saw it move. But it was only settling, sinking, accepting its final pull to earth.

It had never occurred to him to cry. He felt no sadness, only a shiver of recognition at the absolute nature of destiny's rule. He felt exhausted, empty, tired. He had been striving and struggling a long time, and now it was all over. Although he had groomed himself for the role of a knight, he had never considered the aftermath of a quest. He realized that he had been so involved in the pursuit that he felt drained without it.

Conflict and fighting, even the cruel pranks he once played on others, were normal, even oddly comforting, things to him. They still signified a relationship. Now, the perfect circle of master and disciples was now irreparably shattered. He only knew a feeling of crushing loneliness.

The Grand Master had never mentioned Butterfly again, leaving Saihung with many questions he did not dare to ask. His master had never failed to brilliantly answer anything about heaven or earth, but when it came to a personal matter, he withdrew to the loftiness of his supreme authority. Although Saihung could say and do anything to his master, no matter how outrageous, he now felt isolated by the older man's silence.

O VER THE FOLLOWING weeks, Saihung tried to fit back into temple life, but his confusion and disappointment hampered him. The contemplation of ascetic austerities discouraged him. He looked at the older priests. Although they had starved, sacrificed, and devoted themselves earnestly to lives of purity, it was still uncertain that they would succeed. They looked bad: wrinkled, stooped, but carrying on year after year with undiminished faith. As far as he could see, they had nothing to show for it. Saihung decided to leave the mountain.

He wanted to travel and search, but he knew that he needed a goal, a guiding star, a role. He considered martial arts, but there were no more knights. He considered returning to his family, but the life of the aristocracy was fading. He finally understood that all he really wanted to be was simply an independent traveler, a connoisseur of art and life. Here was his goal.

He would make of his mind a palace, a rarefied place where the utmost goal was beauty. This mind-palace would be a vast place to stroll in tranquillity and appreciation. He would have gardens to linger in, rich foods to savor, collections of fantastic art objects, exquisite furniture made by expert craftsmen, and unusual and accomplished people to talk to. Room after room would be dedicated to the pursuit of some special activity, each one a sensitive balance of beautiful furnishings, each one filled with art for contemplation.

For him, beauty transcended the mediocrity of the world. If he feared anything, it was to sink into the morass of banality that normal people called "the good life." He abhorred the possibility of a life without rich beauty. He could not contemplate living without appreciating and absorbing the highest achievements of humanity, art, and knowledge. He wanted to possess both, to collect them, keep them, and arrange them in his palace.

Art could be bought. Fine porcelains, rare antiquities, paintings, old books, handmade furniture—all could be bought and skillfully placed in his orderly interiors. Knowledge was a little different. It had to be studied, learned, and experienced in order to be possessed. It was elusive. It could fade away if not maintained, whereas an object would just gather dust. He needed that stimulation.

All the pieces of his life seemed to fall into place. All the diverse interests could be organized. He could finally see how everything would have a fine proportion in his life. His body would be the landscape, his thoughts the vermilion walls, his eyes the Gate of Heavenly Peace. Within the pavilions and courtyards, he could practice his martial arts. In the high towers, he could even meditate. In the splendor of his mind, there would also be people, those who especially helped him or those whom he simply met in his travels and brought back to live with him. Each one would have his own pavilions, his own gardens. There would be his master and classmates, indeed the whole of Huashan in one part of the palace. His family would be in another. People like Du Yueshen would be there because they had above-average lives. Butterfly, the Tigress, even the Tang poets, would come alive again. All that mattered was that each piece of art, each person, would be uniquely beautiful.

Saihung wrote a letter to his master stating his desire to leave monastic life. He then followed his petition with a formal audience.

"I need time to go out," Saihung said humbly. "My spirit is not at peace. I should not be on a holy mountain or with the gods. I need more experience."

"There are many moments in a man's life when he has a trying time," replied the Grand Master. "Even if he has a strong calling, he may still have misgivings. It is wise to consider such feelings. A man with a calling can go out into the world in an attempt to resolve misgivings, always knowing that he has something to fall back upon. But one should not wander without philosophy: Keep the strong foundation of your youth. Leave your intent fixed in one place. Go out knowing you'll come back."

"Perhaps I was never a committed priest," said Saihung. "I was drawn to it when I was young and without comprehension. Training doesn't have to be lifelong for it to be a part of me that I shall carry all my life."

"Don't be misled by the trappings of priesthood," countered the Grand Master. "Sutra recitation is fine, but one must do good deeds in one's life. It is your life that counts. It is by your life that fate and the gods judge you. You must always strive to live your life for the sake of good. Many people are only good out of fear. Others engage in charity only for the sake of prestige and the identity it affords them. Countless people do 'good' for a variety of reasons, but they all end up being actors playing roles. Don't be attached to the role of a holy man. That makes you no better than the rest. Just do good for true compassion."

"I don't feel that I have anything to prove. I'm not trying to be an example to others."

"That would indeed be unwise," commented the Grand Master. "Don't try to prove anything. Just act the way you want, and don't be a hypocrite. No one is perfect, not even the immortals and gods. Even the Monkey King was naughty. Tung Fengshiu was a thief. The Northern Sea Immortal was once banished from heaven as punishment for misdeeds. What is important is that you have a goal that you strive for. You must try to be good purely as a challenge, an adventure. Then the pursuit of the challenge will become discipline. Just take purity as a goal. If you really want it, you will put all else aside to achieve it."

"I'm unsure, Master. I feel discouraged."

The Grand Master paused. "There's nothing about you that accepts mediocrity."

"True," agreed Saihung.

"Then accept this challenge. Take purity as your goal. This will make you extraordinary. An ordinary person lacks willpower, fortitude, and strength. An unusual man is one of supreme determination. Once he puts his mind to it, anything can be done. The sages say a rock can come alive if one worships it with total belief. That is the mind's power. As you wander, turn that power to one goal: purity."

"Purity for what?" asked Saihung glumly. "Good men and bad men seem to end up the same: dead and buried. The priests here on Huashan try to be pure, but have they ever seen the gods? They live for decades in absolute faith and still there's not one shred of evidence that they will be rewarded."

"Don't try to be good for the sake of the gods," said the Grand Master patiently. "Be good for your own sake. Then you will also actually be doing good for the sake of the holy, for the gods are within you. The highest divinity exists within all of us. Don't look outside for it. Look within. But look with the gaze unpolluted by dishonesty, greed, lust, and attachment. Remember that everything we do, we do ourselves. The gods don't intervene; one's friends cannot really help. You can be what you want to be. Be extraordinary not for the sake of holiness, but only as a personal goal."

"Why not let me be anything? Why should I try to be so religious?"

"I said nothing about religion. Religion means other people are on your path too: They'll drag you down. No, you must be your own person, and you must resist following others' ideals. Filling yourself with the thinking of other people limits you. You must realize your own nature by yourself. Self-disciplinary realization is the key. You say you want to be free to be anything, but you can't. You must only be free to be yourself. You must know yourself, bring what is within yourself to fruition.

"My only purpose is to see you fulfill your life. You are about to go into the world without the structure of the priesthood. I am trying to show you an inner structure, a method of facing the confusing plethora of influences in the world."

"Yes, Master," said Saihung. He felt more receptive. "Please go on."

"Life is a game, a drama, mere theater. In this epic comedy, the stage is crowded with an amazing number of characters, each with his plots and subplots, each mired in his own petty and pathetic circumstances. How will you make your way through this eternal play? Will you be a clown? A hero? A tragic prince? A dupe? You must have principle and philosophy."

"I will be a man of principle," asserted Saihung quickly.

"But what about philosophy?" asked the Grand Master. "You must have a philosophy that truly perceives the reality of life and understands human feeling. Carefully observe everything before you enter any new phase. Consider before you decide. Use your reason, your powers of discrimination. Understand the reasons why good and evil exist. Understand how neither is indestructible and how they are even interdependent. Be flexible. Let your philosophy change and evolve. Be aware of how your thoughts progress and take different forms as you age. Think in terms of your whole life, not just the present. Make sure what you do will last a lifetime."

The Grand Master looked at Saihung before he went on. "Little Butterfly, only one thing counts in life: You must look deeply into the structure of your being."

"Thank you for your advice," responded Saihung emotionally. He suddenly realized that he was leaving for an indeterminate length of time. Intellectually, his decision had been so right. But his heart had not had time to catch up. He steeled himself to conclude the conversation.

"May I have permission to descend the mountain?" he asked.

"Yes, but with one condition."

Damn, thought Saihung ruefully. That old fox was never going to stop imposing restrictions on him!

"Everyone must have a task in life. Everyone who leaves Huashan especially has a lifelong task that he must fulfill."

That sounded like a quest to Saihung. Maybe everything

would be all right. As he built his mind-palace, he could use it as a fortress from which to sally forth on this quest. It could be quite exciting, he told himself; a last charming souvenir of Huashan.

"What is the task?" said Saihung.

"I will assign you a task from the *Seven Bamboo Tablets of the Cloudy Satchel*. Will you vow to fulfill it?"

"What is it?"

"I thought you were a knight, an uncompromising champion. What does it matter what it is? Aren't you courageous enough to accept it?"

It's a trick, thought Saihung. Another attempt to control me. But he was also curious. He decided to accept it—in case it was something really good.

"I accept."

"Good," said the Grand Master with a twinkle. "This is your task: Whenever you meet someone who is suffering and it is within your power to help them, then you must do so at all costs."

Saihung waited. The Grand Master was quiet but smiling gently.

"That's it?" Saihung was almost rude.

"Yes," replied the Grand Master placidly.

Saihung was not at all pleased. This was not a very glamorous task, and it was sure to interfere with his goals of becoming a collector, connoisseur, and martial artist. If he stopped to help the suffering, especially in China where literally millions were miserable, then he would never reach his own goals.

"Remember, you accepted this task, and you must fulfill it to the end of your days," said the Grand Master as he settled back in his chair. "Whenever you meet the suffering, you must help them."

With his descent from the mountain, Saihung was plunged into the restless, swirling ugliness of the world. The months that followed his departure from Huashan were convoluted ones filled with drifting and aborted searches for adventure. He put his master's advice far away, determined to pursue his own goals. Returning to his family, he was comfortable in wealth and luxury and spent a fortune collecting art objects and rare books. But he was restless and unsettled. He wanted adventure, to test his skills in the arena of life experiences. Saihung returned to Shanghai.

During Saihung's pursuit of Butterfly, Shanghai had seemed a bizarre place, a maze of danger, diversion, and evil. But now he saw it as the huge city it was: rich, bustling, cosmopolitan. The European buildings now seemed exotic—mountainous edifices of granite and steel, more massive than city walls, almost geometrically regular with their precise windows and their soaring Greek columns. He liked their domes and towers with slender white flagpoles hoisting flags high into the breezes that swept from the Pacific and the Huangpu. The buildings had none of the polychrome and rich detail of their Chinese counterparts, but he was now fascinated by the corners, buttresses, archways, and keystones that made sharp and monumental shadow plays across their facades.

From a distance they looked like a hundred fortresses set down against the wide, pale sky. The Chinese buildings—stores, apartments, theaters, opium dens, gambling parlors—filled in the cracks and sprawled away over endless, disorganized streets. They were brown, red, brick, mud, clay, and wood. They were crowded, noisy, busy with cooking, crying, cleaning, and commerce. The European presence was spectacular, flamboyant: It meant to have whole city blocks of the West grafted into the flesh of China. But the Chinese closed back in, bit by bit, until a strange urban symbiosis emerged.

In Shanghai, the peculiar meeting of East and West took on mythic proportion. All the stories of rich bankers, puppet politicians, ruthless soldiers, greedy gangsters, opium addicts, sexy women, hapless workers, sincere scholars, corrupt bureaucrats, hardy longshoremen, and ordinary people all existed in one way or another in Shanghai. It was in this fertile mixture of money, power, excitement, pleasure, graft, and drugs that Shanghai thrived. It was exactly in that rich urban environment that Saihung sought to exist.

He lived at a cheap boardinghouse in a room with six other men who came and went at all hours of the day. His possessions were locked in a trunk, and it seemed that he locked his past—both as a Taoist and a nobleman—in there as well. He suspended all judgment, forsook introspection. His personality was in a state of siege and was under the control of a dictator. That tyrant was youth.

Like many youngsters, he began a time of experimentation. Attracted to the easy money and challenge, he worked as a mahjong and domino dealer in the casinos. But he soon became disenchanted. He then tried being a guard at gambling and opium dens, thrashing troublemakers and patrons who refused to pay. This was more appealing. He became a cruel and vicious fighter who relied on a variety of weapons, his favorite being brass knuckles. Saihung gradually drifted over to the aesthetic of his martial-arts teachers: Choke a man until you see him bleed and his tongue rolls out. Punch a man's ribs and delight in the sound of cracking bone. Torture his muscles with twists and bone locks. Listen for his moans. Wait to hear his organs rupture. Each day he ate in the stalls and restaurants, slept a little by his locked trunk, and went out in eager anticipation of fighting in the dark, smoke-filled hollows of Shanghai.

He felt grim, severe, bad-tempered. But he liked it. He was feared, and to him fear was akin to respect. He did what he wanted, when he wanted. No one could oppose him. No one could restrict him. Those who blocked him were mercilessly brought to the ground. This was his hermitage now. The stone skyscrapers were the mountain ranges. Opium smoke was the poetic mist. Liquor formed the splashing brooks and sacred rivers. Neon and incandescent lights replaced the stars, sun, and moon. Pimps, junkies, gamblers, and whores were the masters, acolytes, and novitiates. His body was the temple, his legs the crimson pillars, his mighty hands the heavy gates.

Day after day, he went on, never backing down from a challenge, never failing to do his duty at the places he guarded. He stopped trying to understand life and himself. He would find himself in combat. Although he was aware of different feelings, and though he had reservations about the way he was living his life, he nevertheless refused to back down when the call to fight. It was a simple matter of survival, a case of injure or be injured.

BY WINTER SHANGHAI began to turn cold. Saihung tired of the boardinghouse and his shadowy existence. He decided to visit an old martial-arts teacher who had moved from Beijing to Shanghai.

The day he went to Wang Ziping's mansion was the first snow of the year. As a servant brought him into the courtyard, Saihung saw the middle-aged teacher stripped to the waist and doing bicep curls with steel and stone barbells. Saihung admired the rippling muscle and determined look, the heaving chest that sent regular bursts of frosty breath into the air. He could see that Wang had not lost any of his hardened six-foot-four-inch frame, nor had the years brought much humor to his severe, bearded face.

"Ah, Little Two, what brings you here?" said Wang, using Saihung's family designation. Wang was good friends with Saihung's family and knew him as the second-eldest son.

"I've come to join. Will you accept me again?"

"Why aren't you on Huashan?"

"I've descended the mountain for experience."

Wang let out his booming laugh. "Fine, fine. I'll take you in for your grandfather's sake. He'd never forgive me if I didn't look after you. Go fetch your things."

"Thank you, Master," said Saihung. He was relieved. There was something in him that needed a master, martial or spiritual. Though he wandered and rebelled and strove for independence, he was surprised at how comfortable he felt with the prospect of a master again directing him.

Wang was born in 1881 in Hebei Province. Originally, neither his father nor his grandfather favored his interest in boxing, even though the two of them made their living as professional fighters, teachers, and bodyguards. Wang trained on his own by lifting rocks. He became a troublemaker, and stories told of banishment from his hometown for being a "boxer bandit." That might have been the end of his talent, for without a master, it was impossible to become a martial artist. Brawn and courage were not enough. One also had to have technique and even the financial support of a school in order to have the time to learn.

Wang had an exhibitionistic character, however, and this was the way that he found his teacher in 1901. Boastfully demonstrating his might to a group of onlookers, Wang had used his bare hands to stop a large water-driven millstone. After that feat, a man stepped out of the crowd and offered to accept Wang as a disciple. Wang had knelt immediately, the traditional sign of respect for one's teacher, and had become a student of the famous Yang Hongxiu.

Aside from duels fought within the confines of the martial world, Wang Ziping was publicly known for exhibition matches with foreign strongmen. From the invasion of China by the British during the Opium War, the humiliation by the Western Allied powers in 1900, through the Sino-Japanese War in 1927, the Chinese national character had suffered a tremendous inferiority complex. Wang became a hero by standing up to foreigners. He accepted any challenge that came from Westerners or Japanese in fighting bouts well documented in the journals of the day.

Saihung lived with Wang, learning with the boxer's live-in disciples, assisting in Wang's osteopathic clinic, and attending the academy with which Wang was associated, the famous Jingwu Athletic Association. The chief virtue and radical innovation of the Jingwu Athletic Association had been its destruction of the rigid stylistic divisions that had hampered the development of martial arts. Whereas traditional teachers were secretive about their styles and forbade their students to learn the techniques of other systems, Jingwu advocated the combination of all the best features of China's martial styles. Dozens of masters taught at the red-brick compound in Shanghai, and students were required to master dozens of styles—like Shaolin, Taoist, and Eagle Claw—and many weapons.

But Jingwu did not stop at Chinese fighting skills, though it was first and foremost a martial-arts academy. The open-minded masters soon incorporated Western boxing and wrestling, football, weight lifting, swimming, and chess into the curriculum. This willingness to accept all things of value regardless of their origins was the hallmark of *Mi Zhongquan* (the Lost Track Style), the centerpiece of Jingwu's martial systems and the specialty of its founder. A synthesis of many other kinds of boxing forms, *Mi Zhongquan* was in itself a universe of techniques: It demanded mastery of fifty sets in order to gain proficiency. *Mi Zhongquan's* virtue was in the elusiveness of its movements, which caused one's opponent to lose track of the practitioner's movements.

As one of Wang's five closest disciples, Saihung simultaneously learned a separate and secret tradition of *Mi Zhongquan*.

273

This treasured teaching of Wang Ziping demanded the mastery of 108 weapons and the absorption of two sets. The first was called "Chasing the Clouds with One Thousand Steps," a comprehensive set reputedly created by taking the single best technique from one thousand different schools of martial arts. The second set, called "Climbing the Mountain with Ten Thousand Steps," had a peculiar logic to it. The set had been created in such a complicated and lengthy system that it could neither be completely mastered by a single person nor could it ever be humanly possible to complete a total performance. Each disciple selected a section from manuals and specialized in that part for life. The system had had its origins in three Qing dynasty masters and had been codified throughout ten generations of fighters.

Saihung often went into the streets to test the techniques Wang Ziping taught him. He favored an apple hat then, rakishly pulling it over one eye in the universal sign of the troublemaker. But he sometimes lost fights and would go home to complain to Wang that his techniques were impractical. The thought of one of his students losing invariably brought a loud and obscene oath, and Wang would coach Saihung for a return match.

Fighting was a daily certainty whenever Saihung accompanied Wang, for the master kept his skills sharp by brawling with street thugs. If anyone got in his way, or touched him slightly, it triggered an unreserved rampage. In China, where the streets were crowded and the majority of people walking the streets were rude, there was no avoiding such confrontations.

That temper also expressed itself in restaurants. Wang loved to eat at banquets—after all, his devoted students were required to pay. Many were the times he would be offended by the poor quality of the service. He did not hesitate to express his irritation, no matter how minor the infraction. Countless times, he overturned an entire dinner table with one push before stalking out. His embarrassed students had to file out behind him, paying for the damage without complaint. The journey back to the school was always doubly traumatic: Not only did they have to endure Wang's anger over whatever offense had happened at the restaurant, but they also had to bear his displeasure over being hungry.

Saihung and the other students stayed with Wang out of duty, of course, for in those days the Confucian standard of loyalty to one's teacher was still intact. But their loyalty was reinforced because they wanted to learn from one of the supreme fighters of his time. Ironically, Wang Ziping's name meant "Child of Peace." Wang lived up to his reputation, but not to his name.

With a famous name and an established school, challengers came nearly every day to try their skills against his. Among the most formidable of the fighters was a Shaolin boxer.

This fighter was clearly confident of his ability. When he strutted into the gymnasium, even the more experienced boxers moved aside. He had a body like an inflated anatomy chart come to life. Every muscle was clearly defined and rippled with a palpable intensity when he arrogantly stripped off his shirt.

"Forget it," Wang scoffed in response to the man's request for a match. "You'll lose."

"I insist!" The fighter took a raw coconut and shattered it by gripping it in one hand.

Wang laughed derisively. He turned to his students. "Watch closely. I will show you something you've never seen."

"Attack when you like," Wang said as he faced his opponent. The man charged, and Wang struck with a strike so rapid that Saihung almost missed seeing it. The challenger paused.

"A weak strike!" He stepped back to puff up his chest. "I am unhurt! I've practiced the Iron Shirt for years!"

"No so," said Wang with a cruel smirk. "Look!"

The place where Wang had struck, just above the nipple, suddenly showed a dark spot. Gradually, both the fighter and the students watched as a fearful dark cloud of hemorrhaging blood blossomed across his chest. A sudden pain shot through the man, and he collapsed—still looking at his own body.

"Heal him!" Wang had told his students as he had walked from the room.

Wang also sometimes lost these impromptu fights. When the gatekeeper announced the entrance of a challenger, all the students expected a quick resolution. But this time, when Wang Ziping looked up and saw a wiry man about seventy years old, he paused. Saihung stole a look at his master. Wang could size a man up at a glance. This one had skill.

The stranger was tall and quite thin. His white hair was cut into a severe crew cut, and he had a long beard, the symbol of an elder. He evidently spent a great deal of time outdoors, for his skin was as brown as teakwood. Saihung noticed that his arms were rather long, and his fingers were slender but flexible. Wang Ziping was a heavyweight. The man was like a stick figure before him.

276

"I know your reputation," began the stranger politely. He held his clasped hands gently before him in the gesture of respect. "I do not believe in isolating myself in a mountain retreat. I believe in testing myself against other skilled people. If I win, then I know that old age has not yet bested me. If I lose, then I know the weak points that I must still correct."

"I have heard of men like you," responded Wang. "You are interested only in the pinnacle of skill."

"My abilities are quite poor. I am not here to bring shame on your school, and I would understand entirely if you were to deny me. But I would only like to see if I have made any progress in my practices. Would you please oblige me?"

Wang could not refuse such a request. His honor was at stake.

They began to circle each other warily. Neither made any flamboyant moves. There were no fancy postures, no talking, no tricks. Just two old men who were fighting to see who the better was. They were two dedicated martial artists who would, if nothing else, uphold the dignity of the challenge and themselves.

From the very first clash, Saihung could see that his teacher was at a disadvantage. Blows that would have felled a horse were easily dodged or received by blocking forearms. The stranger's posture was low; his stance was strong. Saihung could see that he was using the Elephant style.

The main feature of the style was to use the hands like the trunk of an elephant. This meant that the arms were very flexible and came at a variety of unusual angles. Whereas other styles might use open hands, chops, or jabs with the fingers, the stranger relied primarily on his closed fists. The Elephant style emphasized the Eight-Cornered Meteor. Instead of a simple punch, the style singled out every angle of the fist as worthy points of contact. Overhand raps with the knuckles, pounding attacks with the base of the fist, roundhouse swings with the thumb side, and use of different angles of the face of the fist were some of the variations.

The stranger hit Wang repeatedly, hard enough to make booming sounds but not enough to injure him. A man with Wang's reputation was expected to be able to withstand some punishment. Saihung also saw that the man touched lethal spots, places that were used to kill. If Saihung could see it, he knew also that Wang Ziping could feel that he was being spared at every turn. The itinerant master was satisfied with demonstrating his abilities and control; he was not intent on hurting his adversary.

They fought in fifteen-minute rounds. Wang was tiring. He had already lost his Moslem cap in the struggle, and it was one of the few times that Saihung had seen him out of breath and sweating. The older man was not even breathing hard. He only went to an unoccupied side of the gymnasium to wait courteously for the next round. Wang Ziping tried every technique that he knew, including secrets that he had never taught his students. He still could not best his challenger. In all, they fought four rounds for a bout that lasted over an hour. It was the challenger who stopped the contest.

"Thank you for indulging me," said the man politely at the end of the final round. "You were too kind in letting me off."

"No, no. It is I who must thank you," responded Wang breathlessly. It was the only time in his life that Saihung had ever heard his teacher thank an opponent.

The man came close to Wang as he strode out of the school. "You should continue to teach. You are still good enough to do that."

Saihung had pondered the man's vast superiority. Totally anonymous, without career or students, the old man cared only for his art. Yet nothing about his persona hinted at his attainment. True, he had a better posture than most men his age, and he walked in a way that was more vigorous than even young men, but nothing else hinted that he was so great. That was why, Saihung thought, one should not boast or demonstrate: There will always be someone unrecognized who will best the arrogant. But such humility was the last thing on his mind whenever he fought. Once, Saihung had even challenged Wang Ziping himself.

Saihung had beaten a rich young fighter. Winning certainly was acceptable to Wang; in fact, it was everything. But the playboy was the son of a prominent official whose previous opponents had lost because they had been paid. Only Saihung had ignored the convention. He had hurt the youth's body, but worse, had annihilated his pride. Wang had called Saihung to task.

"He deserved it." Saihung smirked. "I couldn't stand that weakling."

"Watch your language when you speak to me!" said Wang sharply.

"I'm not apologizing to his family."

"I order you!"

"Never!" Saihung turned to leave.

"Do not turn your back to me!" shouted Wang.

As Saihung reached the door he heard a whistling sound. Cocking his head just in time, he dodged a heavy ceramic brush holder. It shattered, tearing a chunk from the carved door. Saihung turned in a rage. He shouldn't have done it, but he attacked his master.

At that moment, a proud assessment of his own skill came into his mind. He could support six men on his shoulders and legs. He could snap a leather belt buckled around his biceps just by flexing. He had kicked in a two-inch-thick door through the acceleration of acrobatic flips. He could dispatch his opponents with a flying split kick.

"The man is fifty years older and I have more muscle," he told himself as he closed in with a combination of strikes. Not a single one touched Wang. Where he had been angry in discussion, the master was calm in fighting. He dodged and blocked, content to test Saihung's knowledge of boxing.

This frustrated Saihung. He lost all his composure and tried dozens of techniques. Vicious blows to the groin, quick elbow strikes, jabs to the eyes. Nothing connected. As Saihung tried less and less honorable techniques, Wang began to hit back. His every punch hit a meridian point, and they hurt badly.

The fight went on for five minutes. That was too long, and Saihung knew he was in trouble. He finally had to use his proudest weapon, the flying split kick. It was a technique he had developed himself. From a standing start, he could leap to head level and flash his legs in a perfect forward split. With all the momentum focused in the front leg, he had felled numerous opponents. Saihung was desperate to salvage at least his pride. He drove Wang back with a flurry of combinations. Uppercut, cross, elbow, jab, palm. At the last second, he leapt high and executed the devastating kick with perfect accuracy.

Wang Ziping had never seen the kick before. But his reflexes were so fast that he did the one thing Saihung's previous opponents had never succeeded in doing: He stepped back. Wang grabbed Saihung's ankle, and threw his student roughly to the ground.

"I will give you something to remember me by," said Wang savagely. He knocked Saihung unconscious, though Saihung blocked the punch with both hands.

It took him months to recover from the injuries that he had sustained in that battle, and only the constant supplication and intervention of Saihung's family and the Grand Master of Huashan patched up their strained relationship. It had been fortunate that Saihung had been able to continue his education, for one of the best things he eventually learned from Wang Ziping was fearlessness.

AFTER NUMEROUS BATTLES, any fighter could claim to be reasonably fearless. In spite of the great variations in personality, one might still predict most of the ways an opponent could react. Many fights were even won psychologically, when a fighter gauged his adversary's inner weaknesses and decided his best strategy. But Wang Ziping had taught Saihung fearlessness by pushing him onto an inhuman opponent, one who did not use the techniques created by the human mind. Wang had taken his class into the fields to find a herd of wild boar.

One by one, his students were required to fight a boar. Some succeeded; others had to be saved from trampling. It was then Saihung's turn. He was allowed to wear only leather gauntlets and shin protectors. Some elder students selected a mean-looking pig and goaded it into a charge.

It rumbled menacingly at Saihung. He was stunned at how fast the animal moved. For a moment, he could hear the low grunt, see the red eyes, smell its bad breath, as it aimed its tusks at him. Saihung dodged and struck at the animal, making an ineffectual sound that only made the boar mad.

The boar did not fight in any particular style. It had no strategy to guess at. It could not be talked into making a mistake. It fought on pure instinct and relentless anger. The boar came again, and this time Saihung dazed it by striking just above its eye. This stunned it for a moment. It turned sharply, driving full speed toward Saihung. Using the power of its hind legs and shoulders, it slammed into Saihung's side and gored a deep, bloody gash. It slowed to turn, and Saihung grabbed an ear.

There was a squeal and a surge of energy from the angry pig. Saihung could not hold on. He leapt up and elbowed it hard, to no effect. The boar retreated a little, but that was only to gain momentum for the next charge. The pig bashed him again. He was badly bruised and bleeding. The boar was not tiring but renewed its attack. Saihung knew that he had to end the fight. He hammered a double-fisted strike to the top of the boar's head. It didn't kill it, but it did make the boar pause in pain. Close to exhaustion, Saihung hit the animal ten more times. Confronted by such a madman, the pig lost interest and soon sauntered indifferently away. "Sloppy," Wang said as he looked at the breathless Saihung. "But at least you're still standing."

Saihung turned away in exhausted frustration. He looked over the few students who had survived the test with their pride intact, as well as the equal number who had been badly injured. Wang ordered them to return to the city. He did not say a single word of approval to the victors, and he rebuked the losers, even though they were all champions. That was the way it was with martial artists. They knew only harshness and they looked only at a person's weakness.

Saihung's only social life was the pleasure of a new novelty, what was called "electric shadows": the movies.

Going to the latest Hollywood films at plush, rococo gilded theaters with red velvet seats was one of the most fashionable pastimes in Shanghai. Unfortunately, it was unacceptable for a young man to go alone to the theater. He had had to find some way to get his master to accompany him. Craftily, Saihung solemnly told Wang Ziping that these were "educational films" showing life in the United States and the ways in which American warriors fought. So master and disciple would go weekly to study the dubbed and subtitled movies of Douglas Fairbanks, Jr., James Cagney, Kirk Douglas, and Humphrey Bogart. Although these were the latest movies, and though there were always newsreels about World War II, the two of them still regarded the United States as an odd place of gangsters, pirates, Robin Hoods, werewolves, air aces, and cowboys.

Cagney was a favorite of Saihung's, and the tough-talking, streetwise character he so often portrayed was not much different from the personality that Saihung had developed. Nor did the cinematic world seem odd if he tried to understand it as America. The gangsterism, the money, the style, the masculine bravado, the streets of odd characters, impeccably dressed people, and shiny limousines seemed totally ordinary for Shanghai. Perhaps Chicago and New York were like Shanghai, he speculated. Maybe that was the reason that Hollywood knew the substance of a wickedly sophisticated city and why there was a man like Cagney who understood why a young man had to be so tough.

He took his master to theater after theater. Eventually, it didn't matter whether it was a rerun, a silent film, comedy, newsreel, or romance. Master and student loved to go to the movies, sometimes persuading other elders to sample this astonishing invention from the West. It was at just such an event, a screening of *Frankenstein,* that Saihung saw Liu, a fat Shaolin boxer and a contemporary of his master.

When the lights went down, the man sat peacefully and Buddhalike in his seat. He might even have been in total contemplation until the monster came on the screen. At that instant, the frightened man jumped up, smashing his neighbors' faces as he flailed around. Complete pandemonium broke out in the theater, but Saihung was delighted. Here's my next challenge, he thought.

Liu had a very big reputation in the city, but he was old, fat, and acted like a bumpkin. If Saihung could overcome him, why, just like those gunfighters in the Old West, he'd build a bigger reputation as a fighter. He would be, as they said on the screen, "a mean, ornery cuss."

Saihung challenged Liu the next day in a formal letter. The reply was swift, if a bit terse, and he was still chuckling as he arrived at the master's school the next day.

"Ah, you are Wang's disciple," said Master Liu.

"Yes," replied Saihung solemnly. "Forgive my challenge. I am brash and would appreciate some pointers." Inside, however, Saihung was thinking, Get ready, fatty, because here I come.

282

"All right, you may attack as you wish."

"You are a master. I need not hold back?"

"I shall be most disappointed if you do."

Saihung grinned. Here was the pig, and he was the butcher. He revealed two long, sharp daggers.

Master Liu tucked up the hem of his gown and smoothed the few lonely hairs on his scalp. His thick lips pressed together, and he stood proudly, not bothering to find a weapon for himself.

Pride won't help you, thought Saihung as he attacked.

He was amazed when the old man easily knocked the daggers from his hands in the first skirmish. Master Liu smiled broadly as he brought a ham-sized fist into Saihung's stomach.

But one blow could not penetrate years of training, and Saihung retreated. The master came waddling eagerly forward. Saihung hit him several times with full force. He might as well have been massaging a whale.

Unnerved, he ran behind a table to gain some time. He was shocked when the master jumped up and rolled across the table like a gigantic cannonball of fat. Saihung felt that he must use wrestling to win. Sidestepping the master, he pinned him from behind. Now, he had him where he could overcome him.

He heard a loud sound as the master farted a mighty blast. Saihung had never smelled a more noxious vapor. Nausea overcame him, and the master turned easily and knocked him unconscious.

When Saihung awoke, he was back at his master's mansion. A scowling Wang Ziping was applying medicine to his wounds. In the background was a concerned but gleeful Master Liu.

"Now, Master Wang will be angry for days that one of his students lost," teased Master Liu.

"You dunce," scolded Wang. "Master Liu is quite beyond your skills. You've disgraced me."

"Don't take it so hard, old friend," comforted Liu. "He is good. I was forced to use my secret weapon."

"No . . . not that!" exclaimed Wang.

"Indeed," said Liu proudly. He leaned over Saihung. "My boy, I trained many years to perfect this skill. I eat much meat, eggs, and special herbs. I'll teach you the method, if you like."

"Master is too kind," murmured Saihung weakly. He felt like throwing up.

283

"Just remember, my boy," said Liu with a twinkle. "A master always has a trick up his sleeve."

The two men went to the door, giggling like boys.

"See you at the theater," said Liu as he strolled out.

twenty six:

Butterfly
Dream

N EARLY TWO YEARS after departing from Huashan, Saihung stood in the wings of a Shanghai opera house. He had felt the need for a career. Joining the opera provided that chance. More important, it was a job during those war years. It was artistic, expressive, literary, and he met many interesting patrons in the troupe's travels. He liked the creativity of being in the arts. Not only was creativity akin to spirituality in its ability to give excitement and new impulse to life, but it also transcended mediocrity, the state Saihung most deplored. In fact, it was not all that different from the temple life or the martial world, just a rearrangement of motifs. He played the role of various gods and generals, and many of the plays had religious themes. He still had to utilize gestures and postures. He participated in plays that alluded to immortals, alchemy, renunciation (especially of historical officials who retired from society in order to escape Imperial service), the gods in heaven, and Lao Tzu himself.

Even his martial impulse was satisfied. He had to train daily for hours to prepare for his roles. He met many masters who coached him in acting, singing, and special theatrical martial-arts styles. He immersed himself in the classical literature that was the source of so many operas and explored their military themes from such books as the *Romance of the Three Kingdoms*, *Water Margin*, *Journey to the West*, and *Romance of the Yang Family Generals*. He had even had the opportunity to engage in real fighting, for there were always plenty of rowdy theatergoers interested in seeing whether the actors of warrior roles could actually fight.

It was the life he wanted. He had adventure and imagination. He was a star. People applauded whenever he performed. Unlike the frustration, restriction, and daily fault-finding inherent in monastic life, he was constantly celebrated. He realized his goals of collecting memories, experiences, and skills. His mind-palace grew into a rich sprawl of pavilions and mansions. Like the three-storied stage in the Forbidden City, his life revolved around opera, with its pageantry and the sheer fascination of lovely costumes, good music, fine acting, and talented song. This was good enough. Spirituality could wait for retirement. Then, like the scholar-officials, like his own master, he would return to the high mountains. But first he would finally get a lifetime's fill of rich beauty, enough to dazzle any eye.

In the center of the stage's dark atmosphere stood a solitary figure lit in a blazing spotlight. Blue in the cigarette haze, the beam shot the sparkling colors of the actor's robe throughout the house. He moved to center stage with a short, rapid step. Unseen musicians exploded in a frenzy of stringed sounds, and shouting came from the large and noisy audience.

The actor portrayed the well-known Taoist philosopher Chuang Tzu. He showed all the costume symbols of his character: maroon silk robe with the Eight Trigrams symbols embroidered in gold and silver, immaculately white water-sleeves, long black horsehair beard and stark white makeup startled by rouged cheeks, cinnabar eyeshadow, and arching eyebrows. He held a dragon-head staff in his left hand, and a fly whisk in his right.

"I raise the dragon-head staff," said Chuang Tzu. "My words shall strike fear into people's hearts. When we are alive we are promised everlasting love; but once dead, we are given only a fan to dry the grave."

He stroked his beard thoughtfully, a classic gesture of importance.

"Men's faces are readily seen, but their hearts are hidden."

He pointed to his heart and suddenly cocked his head toward the audience. A sharp strike of the sticks from the musicians punctuated his gesture.

"I am dead. Truly dead. I am the Taoist of the southern sea. I am Chuang Tzu who feigned death. . . ." The orchestra came in with a brief musical statement of support as he flipped the yak-tail whisk through the darkness like a shooting star.

The story was familiar to the audience, as were all scripts in Chinese opera. People did not go to the theater to see original works but instead went countless times to see the same themes and dramas. It was therefore the skill of the actor that was most under consideration, and the audience was uninhibited in shouting its approval or disapproval, or even a correction when a line was misspoken.

The Butterfly Dream was no exception in its familiarity to the crowd. In this play, Chuang Tzu, a scholar-magician, received permission from his master to descend the mountains for a reunion with his wife, Tian Xi. On his way, he met a woman fanning a grave. When he asked her why, she told him that she had promised her husband not to remarry until the dirt on his grave was dry. Chuang Tzu dried the grave with his magic powers. In gratitude, the woman inscribed a fan with the words "Wandering Taoist who pitied me: Tell your wife she would be no more virtuous than I." Upon returning home, Chuang Tzu gave the fan to his wife, Tian Xi, who indignantly swore her lasting fidelity to their marriage. In order to test her, Chuang Tzu, through yogic methods, feigned death and magically created a handsome

286

scholar. Tian Xi fell in love with him and, though still in mourning, married him. However, on their wedding night he fell into a coma. His servant, whom Chuang Tzu created from one of the paper funeral effigies, announced that only a medicine made from the fresh brain of a relative could save her lover. Since Chuang Tzu had been only dead a week, and though she had great misgivings, she eventually resolved to break open his coffin.

This was the plot known to everyone. As the second scene drew to a close, they saw Tian Xi, resplendent in white embroidered robes, before a simple altar. On the table was a pair of candles, an incense burner, and a tablet with Chuang Tzu's name inscribed upon it. Behind was the coffin itself.

287

"But stop!" she said in a nasal voice. "I was married to him. How could I do this? It's impossible! I could never do such a terrible thing."

She brought her palms up to her face and shook her head as she backed away from the coffin.

"What a bitter death is mine!" came the dead lover's voice from offstage.

"Ai! I lost one husband. Must I lose my second? I'll break open this coffin and save my young prince's life!"

As Tian Xi made her exit, the stage darkened again, dark as the scene in which Chuang Tzu had made his monologue. Behind the rear curtain, a stagehand held a bamboo pole. A paper butterfly suspended from it was made to flutter over Chuang Tzu's coffin. The servant boy, the one who was created from a funeral effigy, came on stage with a fan. Using acrobatic and martial movements, while still portraying the puppetlike gestures that suggested his origins, he chased the butterfly. He made a lunge for it, but it was jerked away. He closed his fan with a snap and, squatting low, shuffled across the stage in that position. The boy paused dramatically and then made a second attempt to catch the butterfly in both hands. But when he opened his hands to the audience, he showed them his failure. After more acrobatic footwork, he finally lost his patience. Going up on one leg, he snapped the fan open, flinging it wildly left and right as he made a third try. Again, he failed. Finally, he closed his fan in exasperation and marched offstage like a marionette.

The scene symbolized a famous story so well known to the audience that its lines were not included. It was enough to suggest it with the title of the play and the butterfly motif. The story was that Chuang Tzu once dreamed he was a butterfly fluttering here and there in enjoyment. When he awoke he was confused. Had he been Chuang Tzu dreaming that he was a butterfly? Or was he now a butterfly dreaming he was Chuang Tzu?

288

Saihung went backstage to the dressing room, passing all sorts of costumed actors. Properly arranged in their roles and in their correct dramas, they were quite understandable. But out of context, in the dim corridors of the theater, they became a bizarre and surreal parade of painted-faced generals in armor, lovely women (all of whom were male actors), strange clowns dressed like turtles and shrimp, caricature priests with dangling eyebrows, and a host of acrobats with innumerable stage weapons. Every color was in evidence. The rich hues of dyed silk—cobalt blues, blazing oranges, forest greens, sunset crimsons, along with tiny sparkling silver mirrors, gold thread, and iridescent pearls—made the dazzling carnival a procession of painted images come alive. Here and there he heard disembodied voices, singing, practicing scales, interjecting snatches of poetry from divergent eras of long-past events.

The noise of applause was a stimulant to Saihung. He could feel his veins gorge with excitement. He seldom experienced stage fright; there was something liberating about going in front of an audience with his face painted over. Although he, like most monks from Huashan, was shy in many personal encounters, his makeup gave him a mask to conceal his bashfulness. The stage was his freedom.

He stood up as Chuang Tzu rushed in with a sigh, threw his whisk to an attendant, and began removing his beard. Five maidens rushed to take their places offstage. Saihung picked up his spear and walked toward the stage.

The orchestra wound up to a clatter of drum beats and clappers climaxed by an interlude of warbling melodies. There were several strikes to the gong. It was his cue and, he mused, not too different from temple bells. He rushed onstage to embrace the excitement of performance and applause.

Aʀᴛ ɪᴍɪᴛᴀᴛᴇᴅ ʟɪꜰᴇ most ironically when Saihung performed in a little-known martial opera called *Purple Cloud Flower*. Its plot was a variation on the famous *White Snake* opera. A beautiful swordswoman, Purple Cloud Flower, finds that her lover has a serious disease. His illness will be fatal unless a medicine can be made with an herb found only on the summit of Huashan. She journeys to retrieve it only to be told by the Taoists who protect the herb that she will not be allowed to take it; the herb is exceedingly rare and precious and, as renunciates, they have no stake in the struggles of the mundane world. She attacks them with her sword. Though the monks are themselves superb swordsmen, she slays a number of them but cannot prevail over them all. The stalemate continues for three days, giving the actors many opportunities to demonstrate their flashy stage technique.

At the play's climax, the head monk finally consents to exchange the herb for her unique sword style. She teaches them her techniques, gets the herb, and returns home in time to save her lover.

One night he performed the play in Anhui Province. He did not know how many times he had played the role of the head monk, his face powdered white with the arching black eyebrows, heavy mascara, scarlet eyeshadow, and rouge. Dressed in his gray cotton robe and brandishing a stage sword, he dueled with Purple Cloud Flower, barely realizing that a former Taoist playing the role of a Taoist onstage was one of the oddest twists of life.

The audience was loud and restless. The play was staged in the midevening, before the literary operas full of long arias that the richer patrons favored. The first portion of the night usually featured little dialogue or singing, emphasizing action instead. This meant that a commensurately rowdy and illiterate audience came to see the early shows. They chatted and laughed among themselves, smoked, littered the floor with melon seeds and peanut shells, and shouted obscene remarks to the actors. Saihung ignored them as he came to the center stage.

The orchestra maintained dramatic tension with rapid beats of wooden clappers punctuated with rings of gongs. Saihung stood proudly at center stage and faced Purple Cloud Flower, dressed in lustrous silk that matched her name. She stood for his response with her left leg forward and crossed before her right, her tasseled sword behind her back, her fingers pointing toward him in the sword gesture. They looked like two life-sized dolls with painted faces.

"We Taoists are renunciates and care not for the petty concerns of mortals," chanted Saihung. As he spoke, he brought his palm down and made a gesture of dismissal. The orchestra followed the lead of his movements—his gestures and timing cued them.

Purple Cloud Flower changed her position, walked in a circle, and pointed once more at him.

"Nevertheless, I must have the herb!" she replied.

Saihung stepped forward, opening his eyes wide to catch the footlights. The eyes of an opera actor were supposed to glisten like jewels.

"Through three days, we have fought," sang Saihung. "Neither can prevail over the other."

There was another flurry of orchestral accompaniment.

"Equal value in trade," stated Saihung. "Give us what you most value—your art—and we shall give you the herb."

"Is this true?" asked Purple Cloud Flower.

"Yes. We are renunciates, followers of the Way. The cares of the mundane world hold no significance for us. Yet even hermits may be moved by compassion."

"Hey! Hey!"

Saihung was startled by the loud shout from the audience.

"What would you know about renunciation?" someone demanded.

Saihung turned his painted face rapidly. Purple Cloud Flower was preparing her reply, but he was intent on finding the speaker. Near the front of the audience were two old Taoists.

"Renunciation means to leave the mundane world," cried one of the Taoists, "but enlightenment comes from traveling through the world!"

Saihung was immediately intrigued and, as he continued with his acting, examined the two. It was unusual to see any holy men at an opera. But there they sat, in their dark blue robes, graying hair in topknots, and long, uncut beards. Their status was unmistakable.

At the end of his scene, Saihung found one of the stagehands. He ordered him to invite the two Taoists for an after-theater meal. Saihung was gratified to receive an affirmative reply.

Saihung was through with his performances a little past midnight. He changed into a dark blue gown and wiped his face one more time. That was the trouble with makeup, he thought. After a while, the white powder seemed to accumulate in the pores and folds. All veteran actors had ghastly complexions, as if their roles were slowly bleaching their personalities into neutral canvases for the colorful parts they played.

He found the two Taoists in the lobby of the theater and politely introduced himself with his family name. The two old men returned his bows with the familiar prayer gesture and bow of their calling. Free of the glare of the footlights and the layered veils of darkness and tobacco haze, Saihung could see them clearly for the first time.

The one who seemed slightly older was a very thin but tall man. This single fact must have seemed his primary rubric, for he introduced himself as the Slender Gourd Immortal. His face was a long oval with a smooth, pale complexion, and his avian eyes were large, serene, but invariably observant. His white beard was long and wispy, and his lips were pressed gently closed.

His companion was heavier, but not quite portly. Unlike the Slender Gourd Immortal, the Crystal Spring Immortal had an expressive, sunny face. He seemed to laugh and smile about everything, and punctuated his actions and remarks with sly twinkles of the eyes. His beard was full, his complexion ruddy, and his demeanor was animated and playful.

As Saihung escorted them to a nearby restaurant, he chatted casually. Mentally, though, he searched his memory. He had heard stories of two Taoists with these names. Reputed to be high-level practitioners, the two had earned the title of "Immortals" as acknowledgment of their great spiritual attainment. What the legends added was that the two had found in each other true soulmates and had been companions for at least two hundred years. It was true that they were already white-haired, and this made them look as if they were only in their mid-seventies. The ages were not unusual for Taoists to claim, but Saihung was a skeptic. He could only observe that the two men gave the air of being old, with their manners and white hair, but they seemed young and energetic in all other respects.

After they had been seated in a quiet upstairs room, the Two Taoists examined him in turn.

"You say you have some interest in Taoism?" asked Slender Gourd.

"Yes," replied Saihung modestly. "But I have been away from study for quite some time."

"Ah, well, life itself is study, is it not?" asked Crystal Spring.

"As you say, master," agreed Saihung deferentially. "I am ignorant. However, my two honored guests appear to be of great stature."

"Oh yes!" replied Crystal Spring in an outrageously immodest tone. He looked at Saihung with a broad grin. "We've mastered a fair number of things. Wandering here and there, we seek the Mysterious Portal. We've studied invisibility, flying, and we go to heaven all the time. Not bad, eh?"

Saihung looked at Slender Gourd. The man was quiet, with the merest smile. His eyes were fixed on him.

They're testing me, he thought.

"Ever learn to fly without wings, young man?" continued Crystal Spring.

"Yes, I have. Unless one can fly, how could one go to heaven?"

"Quite so. Quite so." Crystal Spring giggled.

Slender Gourd leaned forward.

"What is the technique?" he asked.

"The phrase 'to fly without wings' is, of course, a metaphor," said Saihung quietly. He saw Crystal Spring's stage chuckle disappear. "It means to bring one's spiritual essence up the spine."

"What is the secret of invisibility?" demanded Crystal Spring.

"The secret is to sit so still that one is like a lizard on a branch who is unnoticed because it is unmoving."

"Point the way to heaven," ordered Slender Gourd.

Saihung touched his forehead. "The term 'heaven' is a reference to the psychic centers within the skull."

"Is Lao Tzu in your head, then?" demanded Crystal Spring.

"Just so," replied Saihung steadily. "Even the holy one is a symbol of the psychic center associated with the pineal gland."

"Have you tasted Lao Tzu's Elixer of Immortality?" questioned Slender Gourd.

"Unfortunately not. My progress has slowed."

Slender Gourd sat back and stroked his beard thoughtfully. Crystal Spring looked at him and uttered a sound of satisfaction.

"You truly are what you say you are," concluded Crystal Spring.

"It is always an honor to meet a fellow follower of the Way," said Slender Gourd.

"Not at all." Saihung smiled. "It is I who am honored."

The table was quiet for a minute when the food came. Choice morsels of vegetarian cooking whetted their appetites.

"You are much too generous!" protested Crystal Spring.

"Please don't be so formal," said Saihung. "You honor me by accepting my invitation."

They ate quietly.

"May I ask your backgrounds?" said Saihung in a while.

"We have none," said Crystal Spring curtly. Saihung however, knew that the masters never discussed their personal history.

It had been so long since Saihung had been in the presence of spiritual people that the sensations seemed more exaggerated. Being with the two Taoists brought on a feeling of blissful tranquillity. He was caught in some human magnetic field, some intangible wave of reassurance that radiated from both of them. After so many months away from consecrated places, he had forgotten the power of other masters he had met, people whose mere passing stimulated instant joy, or made one immediately energetic, or brought sudden tears of happiness. Now, in the company of the two Taoists, he remembered, and felt. He knew that he sat with sages.

Long moments passed as the two Taoists finished eating with great gusto. Saihung felt content, at home. He wondered if it was merely being with Taoists. After all, he had lived with Taoists since the age of nine. It was quite possible it was all mere sentimentality. But he decided it was more than that. Somehow, the occasion was a small reminder that he had wandered a bit too far from his path.

"I would like to study with you," said Saihung. The two Taoists exchanged solemn glances.

"We do not live in a temple. We are travelers," replied Slender Gourd.

"I am willing."

"Our lives are very poor. Not at all like that of a successful actor," persisted the Taoist.

"I knew the ordination platform before I knew the stage."

"We are leaving tonight," said Crystal Spring.

Saihung was unwavering. "Very well. Please permit me to get my belongings and notify the troupe."

The two stood up.

"We will wait at the East Gate."

"I will be there in an hour's time."

Saihung hurried back to the deserted theater: Most had gone out after the performance, since actors favored the nightlife. A few were asleep. But this was a great opportunity for him. After deliberating a moment he wrote a letter, gathered up his things, and prepared to leave.

He stood for a few moments at his makeup table. In the indigo light, he could make out the specter of his own image. The dishes of makeup were huddled to one side. Dry smudges of red, gold, black, purple, and green edged the porcelain rims. He contemplated his letter, the translucent sheet with the black undulations that marked his turning point. To the side of the table was his headdress for the role of a general. The mirrors seemed dull; the fur balls dyed in vivid magentas and oranges did not move. He touched the three-foot pheasant feathers one last time. Pulling them down, he felt the quill flex with its own firm resilience. The memory of applause came faintly to him. He released the feathers, and they sprang into the darkness. Before they stopped quivering, he left the room.

THE NIGHT WAS cold. Saihung was glad that the waxing moon was growing full, for he had no lantern. The air made him shiver, but the sparkling spray of stars made his mind shimmer with hopes.

He found the two Taoists without difficulty, and they welcomed him. They set off immediately and, before long, came to a long wooden footbridge. As they crossed, Saihung thought that it was an appropriate image. He would not turn back.

Before they had crossed completely, Crystal Spring started laughing hysterically. Slender Gourd, who apparently never laughed, turned to look at Saihung with his sphinxlike gaze and half-smile.

"Listen!" Crystal Spring chuckled.

"I don't hear anything but our footsteps," said a mystified Saihung.

"Ours?" repeated Crystal Spring. "Listen again."

Saihung did. Only then did he realize that his were the only footsteps, and they were grotesquely loud. He paused, listening as the two Taoists walked farther. They were soundless.

When Saihung had clunked his way to the end, he found his two new masters still consumed with mirth.

"You have a long way to go." Crystal Spring laughed as he slapped him on the back.

They spent the rest of the night in a ruined temple, a favorite place for the two Taoists. The avaricious did not come because there was no profit, and the rest did not come because of superstition. Abandoned temples were ideal shelters.

Saihung was eager to be of service. He awoke at dawn, filled water gourds, and gathered wood for the fire. His delicate actor's hands were now splashed with cold morning water. The fine skin wore against splintered branches. But he was happy. How ironic, he realized, that he should like service so much now, where he had hated it on Huashan. As the two sent him into town for supplies, he fell readily into the role of student. It felt good. Only now did he realize the kinship of service and religious devotion.

The road was already crowded with people, though it was barely light. He passed children and adults on their way to early morning destinations—farmers with donkey-drawn loads of produce, woodcutters carrying impossible loads of cuttings. Saihung took a deep breath. He was back with masters, and he suddenly felt foolish. He wondered how much time he had wasted by ignoring the wisdom of his elders to strike out on his own. It had been three years since he had left Huashan, three years that he had spent with little spiritual counsel save the whispers of a too-often-shunned conscience. He had been a brawler, recording in bruises and painful breakages the exploits of his challenges. He had been an actor, absorbed in the glory of the art, the satisfaction of acclaim. He had become a young and wealthy gentleman and had built the mind-palace that he had envisioned. But only now did he see how empty it had been.

He cursed himself gently, reproaching himself for his short-sightedness. He reflected that impetuousness and brashness were his greatest faults. Saihung remembered times that his attention had wandered during entire lessons with the priests of Huashan. At the end of the lesson, they had stopped and did not repeat: Knowing that he had missed the knowledge, they would leave him without it. As he thought back, he knew that those precious secrets were gone forever, and the years that had passed since his departure from the mountain had been equal failures to apply himself to his spiritual task.

He was reminded of the task his master had set for him. He had done nothing to ease anyone's suffering except to throw a few coins to beggars. His own whims had been his only concerns. Fame and achievement had become obsessions. In his determination not to fail, to somehow equal in his own way the example of his relatives, classmates, and masters, he had sacrificed that last gift from the Grand Master.

Perhaps a chance still lay open to him. He had the opportunity to study again, to be a disciple again, to redeem himself. He knew that there was no such thing as forgiveness, no such thing as an apology that would negate his blunders: The past was irretrievably gone. The only chance was to look ahead and energetically apply himself to doing good.

Butterfly had been right, thought Saihung. In spite of the disaster that his elder brother had made of his own life, the comments he had made at the Divine Eagle's villa had been correct. The only medicine for guilt was to look ahead and persevere. Pursuing his destiny was all that mattered, and he knew his destiny was to be a spiritual aspirant.

He bought the supplies he had been sent for and started back. It was a two-hour walk to the temple. He could make each step an act of penance, each breath a bead in his human rosary.

IN THE MIDAFTERNOON, Slender Gourd took him to a shaded corner of the broken-down, weed-invaded courtyard.

"My brother and I will both teach you," he said. "I will first outline the method of cultivating the Way.

"Let me complete what I began last night. You must seek the Mysterious Portal. But it is guarded. You must have an offering to first bribe the guards and then the ability to be invisible so that you may slip through unnoticed. With these preparations, you must then learn to fly to heaven, surprise Lao Tzu in his chambers, snatch up the flask of golden elixir, slay the defenders, break down the palace walls, and return to earth an immortal!"

"This is like the opera *Monkey Makes Havoc in Heaven*," commented Saihung.

"Yes, but this is no opera," said the master severely. "Sit down and listen to me. The first thing is the bribe for the guards."

"What is that?"

"Gold and jewels do not move the demon generals. It is the human spirit. Your bribe is a vow that should you attain the golden elixir that will liberate you from this earthly plane, you shall not depart into the infinite before teaching others and continuing the lineage."

"I promise. I will do everything I can to walk the holy path," said Saihung. "Master, I will do anything to succeed."

"Not so fast," cautioned Slender Gourd. "You are obviously a man of determination, but you must maintain a certain perspective. For this brings up the question of flying. Flying means weightlessness. Such lightness means shedding weight. Your emotional burden is overeagerness to succeed and anxiety about failing. Gain and loss are not to be taken to heart. You must leave these attitudes behind. Do you understand?"

"Yes, Master."

"Invisibility, as you said last night, signifies stillness in mediation. With it, you can slip through the Mysterious Portal. This gateway is in the region known as the Precious Square Inch in the center of the head at eyebrow level. It is through this gateway that you will someday glimpse the divine light that is always there. When you can unify semen, breath, and spirit, you will soar to heaven—that is to say that you raise this essence to the Mysterious Portal. Snatching the golden elixir means that your channels are now open and that your energy breaches the Mysterious Portal. But at that final stage, the guardians will appear, and you will have to slay them."

"Who are these guardians?"

"Guardians are the agents of your own involvement with illusion. Your ego will not want you to succeed, for the resulting realization will negate your sense of self. Therefore, it will fight you and attempt to stop you from achieving your goals."

"Is the ego not my very self?" asked Saihung.

"The ego comes and goes, is born and dies. The self is eternal. It neither changes nor has substance."

"So when you say to slay the ego, then I suppose you mean that the true self subdues it."

Slender Gourd smiled. "Actually, the ego does not exist."

"If it does not exist, then how can it cause trouble?"

"There is an important inquiry! Ask yourself: Who experiences the trouble? The trouble is imagined. The ego is imagined. But we give ego substance, and it becomes the means to experience pain and pleasure. We are enslaved. If we inquire into the nature of ego, if we remember that it is our own creation, then ego, pain, and pleasure will disappear."

"Suffering is thus imaginary?"

"Yes. You suffer because you imagine yourself to be something other than who you actually are. In truth, you are the self alone. You are the *I* stripped of qualities. You are nameless and formless. Since you cannot grasp that fact, you cling to forms, emotions, and thought. Ego arises to give you form. By contrast, the man of wisdom simply *is*. He does not cling to thought. He is still and knows that he is god."

"I still don't understand how to slay the ego."

"Do you think there are two? Wake up! The ego is only imaginary. There is nothing outside yourself. You need only cast off the illusion, forsake your imaginary forms."

"Who casts off the illusion, then?"

"*I* cast off the illusion of myself. Yet I remain *I*."

"So the *I* must cast off the imaginary ego that binds me to illusion."

"Yes, we are all mired in the ignorance of illusion. You yourself are an ideal example. We found you on the stage. What could be a more perfect lesson than that? You were an actor, playing a role that people believed, and all the while both actor and audience were themselves victims of the illusion of reality. A play within a play within a cosmic farce: That was your past life. Don't cling to your individuality during meditation. This pathetic little drama we know as life is not reality. We are all just playing roles, put here for a reason, taken off when our roles are finished. But who is behind the painted face? Do not mistake your sense of self for your true nature. Instead, kill the guardians.

"This leaves only one task: to break down the walls of the mind-palace."

Saihung felt a sudden shock, and then an uneasiness.

"The palace walls must be broken down, for they will be the final barrier between you and the Source. Only by smashing the walls can we return to the Source. Once we merge with the Source, temporarily at least for our time of meditation, we surrender all sense of the world and our own individuality."

"Surrender?"

"Surrender is nearly impossible for a fighter like you, but that is actually what you must do. It means deliberately surrendering all actions, motivations, decisions. Even the form of meditation is transcended. The palace walls are the world of forms."

"How can they be smashed by surrendering? How can illusion be overcome like this?"

"Let me clarify that illusion is not falsehood. Rather, it is the active side of reality. This activity generates forms. From that variety comes illusion. Yet all this variation, all these changes, exist only in the mind. You look at me, look at the temple, look at the mountains, and forget your identity with these things. Focus on consciousness, not form, and the illusion of diversity and separateness breaks like a dream. Withdraw from the mind's interplay into stillness. Withdraw from activity to inactivity. Withdraw into the Source, and all illusion will cease. Then you will know that Lao Tzu, the golden elixir, the guardians, and palace walls existed only in your mind. The only truth lies in realizing yourself as the formless One.

"But talking does nothing. None succeed without effort."

He showed Saihung how to sit and repeated the steps for the meditation, and left Saihung in contemplation.

THE POOR TEMPLE room was a simple cell. Whitewashed walls had been so worn by time, so abraded by dust, and milky layers that they ceased to be dirty or coarse. They had acquired a patina of antiquity. A distant bell sounded and a faint scent of sandalwood lingered far in the background like an ancestral memory. The atmosphere was dense in its stillness. Quietude was a heavy, palpable presence. Serenity had pooled deeply within the confines of the temple and he submerged himself in it. He sank to its very depths and came to rest in a perfect pyramidal posture.

Perhaps this was what it was like to drown; to feel the liquid invade your nose, your mouth, every aperture down to your pores and soak to your bones in a few seconds' time. Only here, he breathed in the temple air, heavy enough to feel liquid. He became a rock. A large stone icon at the bottom of a sea of tranquillity.

Outside became inside. Inside became indistinguishable from outside. Nothing existed save the world of his meditation. Was time the cycle of the universe, or merely the measured cadence of his energy moving up his spine? He felt it was true when his masters had told him that the body was a microcosm of the universe. Wasn't he now the universe?

In the first darkness, it was his thought that created a thousand suns, a hundred galaxies. It was his breath that set the cosmos whirling. His universe evolved into the five elements, the ten thousand things. He could hear his body's functions. He could listen to his nerves firing and even detect the subtle electrical flows. He could smell different smells, some fragrant, some putrid, as they rose from the complex worlds of his organs. He could taste the flows of liquids and gases. The universe was not a mechanism. It couldn't be compared to the pathetic inventions of puny men. It wasn't an organism. It was eternal. It wasn't a divine being. It embraced both thought and nonthought, being and nonbeing. All those definitions and metaphors had to be inverted. The universe was of an infinite magnitude. He was a microcosm of the universe.

The masters said the world was illusion. By simple logic, if a human being was a microcosm of the external world, he also was

300

illusion, a phantasm imagining himself to exist in a nonexistent reality. He understood that meditation was not merely a state, but a vehicle to understanding. Existing or nonexisting, he commanded the forces inside him, concentrated them, directed them to one point. Illusion nevertheless had substance. He would pierce the veil to find the answer to this question.

The flow of his breath rose in his body, and he felt warm. He concentrated deeply, inhaling deeply. His mind seemed to dive deep into his body, down to its very base, stirring the sexual fluids. Conserved by a lifetime of celibacy, trained since childhood in meditation, it was easy to stir his basic chemistry. He unified semen, breath, and spirit—what the Taoists called "Uniting the Three into One," and directed the resulting essence upward like a flow of liquid light. The brilliance ascended to his skull.

301

His meditation was succeeding. He quickly realized that the ascension of energy meant that he was similarly rising toward the spiritual heights. The movement of energy was perfectly precise. He felt his psychic centers opening, whirling. Saihung felt great power.

All the abilities of his masters, which had seemed so unattainable before, now seemed within his grasp. In fact, they seemed absurdly simple. They were as easy to grasp as toys were for a child. He was ecstatic. But in that moment he understood that, even then, pride and ego had leapt up. By reveling in the power, he knew that temptation loomed all the more strongly. Balanced at the top of that slender shaft of high-voltage human energy, Saihung finally understood how easy it was to topple off.

The brilliance grew like a sun condensed, contained, but now bursting and burning. Glowing. Here was the golden light streaming through the Mysterious Portal. Here was the blinding stream of infinity. He felt a hesitation. A great inner tension. He knew these feelings were the "guardians." It was his self objecting to its imminent negation. He wanted to go, but something held him back. The light flickered.

Saihung saw the light again, flooding through the portal. It built in power. All he had to do was give in. All he had to do was let the light take his being over. He paused only a moment this time, and then plunged into the rising radiance.

He felt a brief but powerful sensation, like being torn by a great explosion. And then he felt nothing. There was no longer a *he* to feel. There was only golden light and the trace of his surrender.

Hours passed before he came back to awareness. He felt strangely disjointed. It occurred to him that he was dying. The more he thought, the more he felt that he was close to death. All his essence and concentration had been bound into that stream of light. But the rest of his body had been plunged into darkness. He had created a living day within, but this had left a cold and lonely night for the rest of himself. His spirit, confined for so long, had emerged like a beautiful white swan, breathing, awakened, joyous. It had left a trail of brilliant light and breath—a long, heavenly banner. But the rest of his body had begun to wither.

He began to perform dispersing movements that brought him back to reality and restored his own private little universe to proper circulation and functioning. He knew Taoists who had died spiritual deaths by meditating for forty-nine days. After what he had felt, he knew that forty-nine days of experiences such as his would have made him entirely spiritual. His body would have to die: Starved of life force for so long, it would be a wonder if it lasted that amount of time.

The energy drain was the reason for celibacy, diet, rest, physical practice, and sound thinking. He now saw them not as mere monastic affections, but as desperate measures to prevent a premature death during the struggle for enlightenment. He would have to balance his meditation with herbs, diet, and exercise in order to keep his tie to the earthly plane. The logic of his vow to help others became clear: If everyone passed into the infinite, no one would be left to point the way.

Saihung rested for a while, but still felt weak. He found the two masters sitting casually by the fire. They smiled when he recounted his experiences, commenting that he would soon regain his equilibrium. Meditation would then become smoother, and the body would be strengthened to support the critical flows of energy. Slender Gourd seemed uninterested in his feelings of death. Apparently, this was not significant to his quest. However, it did inspire the master to speak further.

"In order to understand the ultimate goal, we must understand death. Dying is life's only certainty. In one way, the Taoist seems intimately concerned with death because his priority is to transcend the mortal plane and escape the cycle of reincarnation. On the other hand, he can be quite unconcerned with death, since he views it as a mere cycle of change.

"There is the parable of the highwayman's victim. The fellow, believing his purse to contain a great store of gold, was horrified to be robbed. If only he had realized that his purse was empty! Then he would have surrendered it with equanimity. This is the true situation: The purse is filled with autumn leaves. The purse is the body. The leaves are the illusion of 'individuality.' There is something real to the human, however. It is a great deal more precious than gold, but it is not our possession. That something did not begin with our birth. It did not grow as we did. It will not cease upon our death. Death, to a Taoist, is nothing."

"I'm afraid that you've lost me," said Saihung.

"Butterfly Taoist! Butterfly Taoist!" Crystal Spring laughed. "Don't you know the parable of the butterfly?"

"Yes, I know it," responded Saihung. "But I do not see the connection."

"Let me quote," said Crystal Spring. "'I, Chuang Tzu, dreamed I was a butterfly. Now, when I am awake, I do not know if I was Chuang Tzu dreaming that I was a butterfly, or whether I am now a butterfly dreaming that I am a man.'"

"Yes, I am familiar with this tale."

"Then let me ask you this," said Crystal Spring with a sly twinkle. "What would an onlooker have seen?"

Saihung was bewildered. He had been thinking only of the paradox of Chuang Tzu and the butterfly.

"I don't know," he stammered.

"An onlooker would have seen no difference," announced the master triumphantly.

Saihung was thoroughly confused.

"Change is constant in nature," explained Slender Gourd. "But there is an unchanging principle underlying all change. Take water, for example. Water evaporates and becomes clouds. Clouds become rain, sleet, or snow. Lakes become ice. But throughout all these changes, water does not lose its essential nature. Some might say that when water becomes ice, it has 'died.' Or when it evaporates, it has 'died.' But this is absurd. In the same way, death is a mere transformation, not an end. We need not be terrified of it. In fact, our sentimental emotions are totally irrelevant."

"So you see," added Crystal Spring, "that Chuang Tzu is throwing us a diversion. He is neither Chuang Tzu nor the butterfly. He is both at once. What is important is not to be deceived by the dualistic question of whether he was one or the other, but to realize that there is some underlying essence beneath it all."

304

"Do not fear the sensations you feel during meditation," concluded Slender Gourd. "Let all phenomena come and go. Even death is a part of such illusion. Don't identify with phenomena, but instead look deeply into the Tao and its source. Forget the illusion of a separate existence. Cast off this imaginary limitation that separates you from the Way. Let your finiteness merge with the infinite. Far from becoming diminished, you will become infinite yourself. When you have this perception, you will then know the true secret of the sages: The mind of one who returns to the Source becomes the Source."

The
Golden
Embryo

S AIHUNG STAYED WITH the two Taoists for months of relentless travel. Their nomadic lifestyle took them over the length and breadth of China. They found inspiration in any event and any place they happened upon. Whether it was the mist-shrouded peaks of China's ethereal mountains, the parched plains of the northern deserts, or even the crowded and bustling urban centers, the two Taoists taught Saihung that everything was a part of the Way. They taught him that when one identified oneself with the universe, then the universe was real. If one perceived the universe as outside of oneself, then it was unreal. Illusion and reality were yin and yang and thus one and the same.

Swimming in the current of the universe was as important as still contemplation. Experiencing life, testing their learning and philosophy among people, and confirming speculations that arose from their contemplations were crucial priorities. Life experience, they said, would always be superior both to mere book learning and the artificiality of the cloistered world.

Their unconventional approach and their great insight gave their teaching an unusual character. While they would give their lessons the support of Taoist proverbs, they frequently interpreted them in startlingly new ways. They found precedent for their life of travel in the phrase "Without going out of my door, I can know all things on heaven and earth." Surely, Saihung thought, this was an argument for austere contemplation. But no, the two had countered with great delight. They interpreted the phrase from a greater point of view. "Without going out of my door" meant without dying too soon. "Knowing all things on heaven and earth" meant the completion of one's life task and the purging of all consequences of past lives. Therefore, the meaning they saw was that one should complete one's earthly destiny in a single lifetime. Such a goal could not be achieved by mere monastic living, for "know all things on heaven and earth" would require personal investigation.

They spurned traditional book knowledge and laughed at the efforts of scholars, though they were both educated, intelligent, and well read. Theories were merely the idle speculations of others. Stories could never substitute for real adventure, manuscripts and scriptures were inferior to direct transmissions from masters. The division and partisanship of schools and styles was useless. The intellectual was only valid when tested and proved upon one's own body and self.

Book learning was a violation of the basic human nature. Etiquette was a tiring yoke on the spontaneous will. Social duty only dulled happy spirits. Morality was repression. As they trekked through China, they sometimes came upon backwoods villages, or some of the even more socially primitive minority tribes. In the example of uneducated people free from the rigid socialization of mainstream Confucianist China, they found their ideal of a more pure and innocent human. Honesty, contentment, lack of striving, and simple lives close to the earth and seasons were the beautiful qualities of such people. The two Taoists pointed out that their unspoiled state was not derived from book learning, but the simple people still had wisdom.

Wisdom was a necessary pursuit for humans, not only because humanity had the inborn capacities for reasoning and higher learning, but because proper understanding could lead to spiritual liberation. Mastering a sufficient body of knowledge was a great challenge, because the Taoists demanded high degrees of excellence. Yet they used the ideal of the uncarved block as a balancing element. In the often frustrating search for perfection, it was useful to remember that the ideal state was not to be pursued, but uncovered. It was not to be searched for far and near, but to be found by realizing its presence within.

The two Taoists thus embodied a paradox of learning. They spurned education, yet they insisted that Saihung continue with his own.

They eschewed monastic living, yet they sequestered themselves daily for meditation. They advocated innocence, yet practiced complex arts. They lived wandering lives among all levels of society, yet they clung to very disciplined standards for their diet, thought, conduct, and actions.

"It is only on the extreme limits of knowledge that one encounters paradox," Crystal Spring told Saihung. "But if one would seek all knowledge, one must accept paradox.

"The conventional say that things must always be one way or the other. They would say that one must either be a monk or a layperson. This kind of dualistic thinking is why the Confucianists and Buddhists remain locked into dogmatic schools.

"That's why they hate Taoists. They dislike our nonconformity. But in fact, it is only due to their inflexible viewpoint that they fail to see the true substance and creative potential of our methods."

"So in essence," added Slender Gourd, "the paradox of learning is that you must be both artful and artless."

"That's it," said Crystal Spring. "You have to be both. Yin and yang together. Yin and yang oppose one another, define one another, complete one another, destroy one another. If you are to be learned, you must do the same. Embrace paradox, my boy. For unless you do, you will be doomed to contradiction."

"Pardon me?" asked Saihung.

"Contradiction!" snapped Crystal Spring. "Don't confuse that with paradox, or we'll never be done with this blabbering."

"I'm sorry," said Saihung. "Couldn't you just explain a little?"

"All I mean," said Crystal Spring, "is that those who don't embrace paradox in their knowledge will forever stumble upon the contradictions that will inevitably arise from their rational and logical calculations. Since they cannot account for these contradictions within the rigid framework of their doctrines, it renders their thinking completely sterile."

Knowledge and its history formed tradition, and tradition was also useful, even to the iconoclastic Taoists. They explained that traditional knowledge was an aid in shaping the early crude efforts of the beginner. It was a rich and varied source of all the tried processes, the improved methods, and even the dead ends of investigation. It stood as the delineation of the boundaries of the human imagination. Inviting spontaneous excursions inside its borders, or allowing reasonable attempts to expand its frontiers, tradition was the crucial matrix for an individual's efforts.

Since it was larger than any single human, traditional knowledge offered the seeker the choice of many precedents. Surely, the two Taoists told Saihung, tradition was superior to the efforts of novices, of the disdainful, or the ignorant. It was reasonable to learn as much as was necessary in order to reach the frontiers of reality; and then, from having saved one's creative efforts by profiting from learning, using one's creative efforts to make the leap into the unknown.

It was human nature to pursue learning, yet it was important to note that even the genius did not have truly encyclopedic knowledge. Human knowledge could not be mastered by a single person. There were twelve thousand documented herbs, but not even the most brilliant doctor used them all. There were more than ten thousand words in the Chinese dictionary, but not even the greatest scholar could explain them all. The pursuit of knowledge was the exploration of an infinite universe that

curved back upon itself, that frayed into paradoxes and contradictions at its extremes. All that was important was that Saihung
continue to learn and gather experiences, to stave off the mental
rigor mortis of the content individual and cling to the Way.

The two Taoists' attitude toward learning and skill was best
summarized in their maxim "Know magic, shun magic." Magic
truly existed, they taught Saihung. One should learn it—not to
use it, but to avoid it. Ignorance made one a victim. Knowledge
provided a defense. Only through understanding could one be
free of its influence.

309

They then took the example further, substituting all sorts of
words for magic: knowledge, tradition, martial arts, politics. The
equation applied to all those things and more.

Saihung had the chance to observe this philosophy when he
realized that he was never in any danger in the time he was with
the two Taoists. Bandits never attacked them. Animals did not
threaten them. Soldiers never stopped them. Without any structure or conflict, Saihung realized that there had never been any
need to fight while he was with them. His masters had gone beyond art and artfulness. Just as they could cross a bridge silently,
they could follow the Way without disturbance from themselves
or others. They wandered here and there fearlessly. They had indeed embraced paradox by being highly learned yet completely
spontaneous and natural. It came, no doubt, because they knew
magic yet shunned magic.

Saihung noted this observation, and the two Taoists merely
gestured toward a faraway temple.

"Magic is for simpletons. Idols are for the unthinking," said
Crystal Spring. "Truth is evasive and subtle. What you notice is
not the product of knowledge, but a sign of something much
greater. Yes, knowledge is essential, but it is not the ultimate
thing."

"What is truth?" asked Slender Gourd rhetorically. "What can
we put our trust in? Certainly not the world. Ultimately, the world
is an illusion. It is a stage play of elaborate costumes, bedazzling
sets, intoxicating music, and fascinating characters. It is full of
pathos, tragedy, happiness, and aspiration. But it is no more real
than the operas of which you once were a part. All that you experience, all that you see, is but a play of unseen elements. We see

the five colors, taste the five flavors, hear the five tones; we take this as reality, but it isn't so. 'Know magic, shun magic,' we tell you. 'Experience the world.' 'Travel to follow the Tao.' In the end, even these phrases are merely provisional. These just help you play your part on this ludicrous opera stage. The world is a farce, a kaleidoscopic play of shadows, colors, and reflections.

"All knowledge is infinite," said Crystal Spring. "Yet compared with the ultimate truth, it is an inexact approximation. Know knowledge to shun knowledge: You can put your faith in nothing but inner perception. Shall we base our truth upon the gods? Yet we know little about them. They are nothing of what they appear to be. The temples and scriptures are just religious theaters for the ordinary person. The gods are nothing like that. No, truth is to be based not on any ideal, no matter how purportedly divine, but on something else."

"But scriptures are holy," protested Saihung. "Aren't they truth?"

"The scriptures were written by human beings," explained Slender Gourd patiently. "They are useful as rough guides. The degree of truth they contain, when compared to the befuddled state of the average person, is extraordinary. But to the enlightened, the scriptures are mere funeral money and the gods but straw dogs."

"When I was on Huashan, they told me that mastering the *Seven Bamboo Tablets* was essential. I have never read it, I've never determined how far I have to go. Now you teach me that my efforts were illusory?"

"The *Seven Bamboo Tablets* were, according to legend, brought to earth by the God of Longevity," said Crystal Spring. "Even in antiquity, the earth was not spiritually cleansed, and the gods sent emissaries to help people. Sometimes they would bring scriptures and leave them as instructions for the worthy. The *Seven Bamboo Tablets* were such a gift.

"But the god left the tablets in a cave on a high peak in the Kunlun Mountains. Humanity had to prove itself worthy by sending a hero to retrieve the tablets. The sages selected a baby and raised him from childhood with his sole goal the seeking of the divine gift. This baby was quite unusual. According to legend, he was born from an egg that a farmer found while gathering wood. Since he and his wife were childless, he took it home. It hatched, and a handsome boy emerged. It was this boy who was groomed to take up the quest.

"He brought those tablets back many centuries ago. The original tablets still exist, but they were hidden away at Maoshan during the Opium Wars with Britain. Now all we have are copies with many commentaries attached by generations of masters. Additionally, there are different versions according to lineages and sects.

"In essence, The *Seven Bamboo Tablets* detail three hundred and sixty methods of attaining enlightenment. The number three hundred and sixty corresponds to the number of degrees in a circle. Thus, the entire range of methodologies is accounted for in this work. The methods range from the purely ascetic and meditative to controversial sexual techniques of dual cultivation. Philosophy, breathing, alchemy, drugs, ritual, ceremony, devotion—every possible means of achieving higher states is discussed, analyzed, and recorded for the sake of future generations. Even martial arts are a part of this sacred work, not as a fighting art, but as a complete way of study, discipline, and practice.

"The *Seven Bamboo Tablets* represent all that you must master, it's true. But don't mistake mastering the book for mastering the knowledge. What is important is that you fully complete your spiritual task."

"Look beyond this mere book," said Slender Gourd. "As it has three hundred and sixty ways, so must you become a complete and well-rounded man. Do not cleave to narrow doctrines. Take it as a framework, a scaffolding. But once we circle constantly back to tradition, we shall soar forth again."

"It matters not," Crystal Spring concluded, "whether you read the *Seven Bamboo Tablets* or not. You could read it and it might be as dull as a dictionary. In fact, that would be its exact appearance. But take its components, benefit from its tradition, use them as alloys to be blended in the crucible of life, and forge them into your own unique personality. Don't follow any book dogmatically, not even the most sacred scripture. It's stupidity to think any book is the word of the gods."

311

"Truth ultimately lies not in learning, for one inevitably reaches the limits of one's art," said Slender Gourd. "Therefore, one can attain truth only by transcending the self. The petty self is but a part of this grand comedy. The spiritual is the force that animates the play, and through mediation, one can merge with the spiritual. At the highest stages, the self is absorbed in a larger consciousness. Individuality is lost, accomplishments from skill become irrelevant. The pursuit of knowledge is vital to the continuing growth and health of the practitioner and is useful for helping others and cultivating attitudes of perfectionism. However, one's ultimate endeavor lies in the artless art of meditation, where all skill is finally transcended."

312

The truth. Something in Saihung awakened. All this time, he had searched to accumulate knowledge, struggled to complete methodologies, collected ancient manuscripts, studied with many great teachers. Despite years of experience and accumulated understandings bound by the monastic structure, he had been left with nothing. He thought again of the parable of the highwayman and the purse, and thought of the *Seven Bamboo Tablets of the Cloudy Satchel*. His masters had truly shown his purse to contain autumn leaves. And the Cloudy Satchel—what a monstrous joke, what a piece of compassion. All the knowledge of the sages was a tender way of leading the student to the realization that there was something beyond knowledge and facility, something on the other side of high learning. All of civilization was a mere shadow play, a crude projection from the light of truth that had need of neither conceptualization nor structure.

He stood up. What a thing to absorb. What a dunce he had been! But, he reminded himself, it was better to suffer a moment of embarrassment than a lifetime of shame. He strolled to the edge of the mountain and looked out, and thought of his master on Huashan with gratitude. The old man had begun the process, had worked for years with patience to prepare Saihung for this very point.

BEING IN THE mountains always calmed Saihung. Their loftiness gave him an entirely different perspective on life than when he was down on the plains. The pure grandeur dwarfed whole cities with their thousands of inhabitants engaged in their myriad pursuits. The exquisite splendor made his own emotions and anxieties seem superfluous. There on a high peak of pristine granite, he felt as if he were on the world's rim, only a breath away from heaven's borders. Whenever he looked to the wide horizon, he lost his frustrations and abandoned his mental troubles. His soul yearned to fly, to float, to become absorbed in that narrow band of mountains and sky. The day was warm and sunny. He sat back down in the shadow of a venerable pine to again listen to Slender Gourd's lecture.

313

"Our bodies, imagination, and breath are the only immediately available tools to we who begin spiritual practice. Deeper states and powers cannot immediately be tapped. We must first utilize those parts of ourselves that can most readily be brought under conscious control. These can then be gradually directed toward the attainment of more specialized abilities.

"The paradox is that these facets of ourselves can be our hindrances if left unchecked. Our bodies may deteriorate to the point that poor health makes practice impossible. Our imaginations can run wild, obscuring our true souls in wild and lurid fantasy. Our breathing, left only under the automatic control of our subconscious, can never become anything more than a way to provide oxygen to this physical shell.

"But the first stage of spiritual practice begins with the tangible. The body is disciplined by stretching, postures, herbs, martial arts, and meditation; its raw material and good health become the basis for further progress.

"The imagination is used to suggest goals and direct the movement of energy not normally under conscious control; its powerful message can overwhelm both mind and body. The breath represents not only the first organ that we can bring under our conscious control, but it is the physical link to the mind; its rhythms, ratios, proportions, and timing can cause the mind to respond with correspondingly altered states.

"Discipline makes achievement possible. Reins direct the wild horse; constraint directs the spirit. When a bow is pulled back, the arrow is aimed while the bow is at its highest constraint. Its release sends the arrow mightily to its target. Today, I want to teach you a very special technique vital to your development: the creation of the Golden Embryo."

"The Golden Embryo is our expression for creating a powerful force field in the abdomen. It fortifies the body and bolsters the organs. Loss of hair, wrinkling of the skin, stiffening of the joints, dulling of the eyes, diminishing of hearing, loss of memory, weakening of muscles, faltering of will, and decline of vitality all represent the progressive deterioration of the glands and organs. The Golden Embryo, if practiced faithfully, becomes a storehouse of energy distributing life force to rejuvenate the body."

314

"Does this make one immortal?" asked Saihung.

"Yes, but not in the sense of living forever in this mortal form," replied his master. "It does mean that your breath and lifetime will be extended and maintained long enough for you to gain realization. But it also is related to a very critical point: spiritual death."

"The spiritual death is not exclusive to Taoists," said Crystal Spring seriously. "The Buddhists call it *Nirvana,* the Hindus call it *mahasamadhi,* and the Taoists call it 'merging with the void.' Isn't that odd? At the moment we introduce the idea of an embryo, we must also discuss death."

They told Saihung that every human being had three selves: animal, astral, and spiritual. The animal self was the instincts, drives, lusts. Created at birth, it was trapped in the body upon death and decayed with the body. The astral self was the hereditary self. It carried with it the imprint of the parents, embodied their genetics not merely physically, but mentally and emotionally as well. This inherited personality determined a great deal of a person's destiny, for it established the basic parameters of potential progress and contained the metaphysical qualities of the parents. Education, parental upbringing, and the person's own actions would complete the elements of his destiny. Aside from that, the function of the astral self was to judge, reason, and learn.

The spiritual self was that element of a human that was on a journey, the immortal spirit that no physical force could destroy. Its sole aim was to return to the cosmic Source. In order to do that, it had to learn, be purified, purge itself of all negativity, in order to merge with the great One.

All three selves were active in everyday life. Whenever action was required, the three selves acted as a tribunal. However, one or the other self could predominate in the decision making, giving the person's actions a particular emphasis.

The two Taoists reminded Saihung that the critical thing in life was to die a spiritual death, to merge with the Void. In order to do so, one had to be free of the cycle of reincarnation. This meant absolutely no earthly ties. The important point was that having children automatically tied one to the circle of reincarnation. How could it be otherwise? By passing on one's metaphysical and physical genetics, one perpetuated one's earthly karma. This was why the sages had no biological children.

Assuming that a practitioner fulfilled all the requirements, he could, through his austerities, merge his three selves into one superdynamic new self. This composite spirit would emerge from the body at the right moment and would transcend the cycle of earthly reincarnation. It would then rise as high as it could to another plane of existence. There were few, even among the sages, who could return immediately to the Source. More than likely, the new Spirit would go on to an astral realm where there no longer was birth or death, but where everything was accomplished by thought alone. Then the spirit would go through more transformation in order to finally merge with the Void.

Superhuman achievement as it was to combine the selves and transcend the earthly plane, the two Taoists reminded Saihung that it was not enough in itself: They believed that one must pass through thirty-nine levels of existence in order to return to Nothingness. Earthly life was the very lowest level.

All this was relevant to the creation of the Golden Embryo, because this was the goal of practice. Otherwise, the technique was nothing more than a sophisticated health exercise. It was the Golden Embryo that supported the energy to maintain the adept and power his final ascension.

There was one curious footnote to the whole doctrine: A master could, just before death, project his Golden Embryo into the body of his student. This in effect made the student his child. The disciple then received incredible power, but with a catch: He also received his master's destiny, both good and bad. This meant that he then had to work off more destiny along with his greater power, and that his own master would return to earth again. Such a technique was rarely employed.

The Golden Embryo technique required that Saihung first master a complex system of *qigong* or breath control. A variety of options were open to him, such as the microcosmic orbit, meditation on the twelve meridians, or using *qi* to open the eight psychic meridians. Saihung had already learned these techniques on Huashan. They all opened the twelve regular meridians and the eight psychic meridians.

316

Once this had been accomplished, Saihung was to perceive—not simply imagine—the light of the Mysterious Portal. This light was pure life force. Then he had to direct it, to bring it down to the *dan tian*—the Field of Cultivation. He would then repeatedly raise and lower this light from his *dan tian* to the Red Palace just at the base of his heart. This current of energy created the Golden Embryo.

It was a dark, quiet night when Saihung first sat to practice this new meditation. He found an empty cell in the ruined monastery they had temporarily inhabited. How, he wondered, had this consecrated place been destroyed and its community dispersed? What danger or superstition kept it barren? Yet it was because of its wrecked status that his place made a perfect shelter for them. In the shattered shell of the aspirations generations before him had left, he sat down for his own attempt.

He sat cross-legged on a grass mat, without the luxury of prayer rugs and deerskin he had had on Huashan. He arranged his limbs exactly, clasped his hands in a particular way. He placed his body into an idealized alignment. His body and mind, so used to their everyday whirling about—mind racing and clicking into innumerable overlapping patterns, his limbs flailing and gesticulating—were contracted into a stable structure. His personality withdrew to an exact set of concordances. He breathed down to the root of life. The energy released could go nowhere but up into the channel he had left for it.

His meditation progressed according to a geometry of its own. The psychic centers of his body lay on a straight line. They each had their own colors and inner patterns. His energy flowed in lines, coursing through the meridians. Lines connected points. The network moved, glowing with high energy. Sequentiality came into the structure. Unfolding began.

He followed his masters' instructions exactly in order to direct the flow of energy. In daily life, energy and the distances between points in the body and mind varied and revolved. But now, by setting the structure of his personality into a particular form, concentration occurred. Energy was stepped up or down. Taoism knew no separation between materialism and spirituality. By beginning with the physical and tangible, he would pass into the metaphysical and ethereal.

He felt power. What a thrill it was! A confidence, an assurance, a danger. He knew that without meditation he would never gain spiritual maturity. Only by endeavoring to raise the energy high in his body could he gain the power to fulfill his quest. But the geometry into which he had set himself knew no morality. Patterns of lines and points embodied no ethics. He gained power through meditation, but, he realized, the choice of good and evil still was his to make. Nothing about meditation made an evil person good; it only put a formidable weapon into his hand, and good people found themselves tempted. This was meditation's safety device, its trap to catch the unworthy.

He built his energy higher, mindful of the danger, the temptation to linger in spheres that yielded great power and ability. He urged himself higher, into the realms above the heart, where he would feel indifference to the outside world and the realm of the senses.

All was still. The slightest external movement would alter the fragile route, snap the glowing strand. He breached the gate to the skull, the Jade Pivot, entered Lao Tzu's grotto, and his soul was bathed in a golden light. He took that light, like the life-giving glow of the sun, like the divine fire of a thousand stars, and embraced it, merged with it, loved it. Here was bliss; here was happiness. Here was god, or good, or whatever label there was for this force so divine and holy. Here was utter serenity and immortality.

How simple it all was, and how much like doting old aunties all his masters had been! He had thought them obtuse, secretive, and enigmatic people stingy with their realization. Now he knew them for the babblers they were, the caring, sentimental old fools who spent every day pointing out to their students what was absurdly obvious. Divinity and immortality were within us all. That could truly be known "without going out of the door."

His masters must have worn themselves out pointing out what to them must have been as obvious as the nose on his face. Now he saw. Now he realized that nothing in the external world could compare to this. Not martial arts. Not fine porcelains. Not great literature. Not a career or fame and fortune. Nothing could compare with this blazing glow of life force.

This pure energy, the pure essence of virility, was alive, and could give life and create life. It was inspiration; it was the movement that first set the universe into motion. It was that ray that first sliced through the dark chaos and brought reality into being. Now that ray flashed down through his body to the Field of Cultivation, to that place of fertility. It flashed like the warm rays of the sun; it stirred the rich soil of his soul watered by the fluids of his body. It warmed the valley, and he knew in time that creation would take place, and the Golden Embryo would emerge.

Words fail. They cannot describe the beauty of spiritual fulfillment. Emotions fail. They cannot encompass the profundity of birth. Men and women are filled with awe and wonder when they come together to create a child. How much more difficult it is to understand spiritual birth, where the mystery of life is ours to at once create and perceive. In the end, the intellect fails. Inevitably, this mortal shell too will fail.

For our lifetime, we live dependent on this physical cocoon. We love this vessel of flesh and blood, this vehicle of complexity. It is adorned, pampered, damaged by illness and violence, fed by consuming other bodies, joined in intercourse sometimes pure, other times unholy. In youth, we revel in its power. In old age, we curse its betrayal. Eventually, we see that over our lifetime, we have been imprisoned in a gradually rotting pillar of flesh.

The Taoists found the potential of the human. They found its potency, its fertility. They discovered ways to transform and direct that vitality so that what was immortal—the sliver of the spirit that was hurtling through millennia of the universe's existence—could be liberated from the physical shell. That was the purpose of the Golden Embryo meditation: to maintain the physical body until the immortal soul could emerge intact.

Hᴇ ʜᴀᴅ ʙᴇᴇɴ reborn, knew birth, knew creation. But life is nothing without death; and it was in the moment when Saihung truly began to know life that he also had to know death.

It was late in the year, just past the autumn equinox, that the three of them wandered toward Maoshan in Jiangsu Province. They went into the mountains and found a quiet and secluded cave. In the morning and at dusk, twice a day like some atmospheric tide, mists would roll through the passes and chasms. Like the ocean rushing between rocks, they obscured what lay below. On the solitary peak, there were no other people. Birds sang, the small stream nearby splashed a subtle rhythm, and the wind rustled the drying bones of trees. Saihung looked at his mentors. They were at peace.

"In a short time," said Slender Gourd, "we will leave this world."

"Who knows how long we've wandered this dusty vale," added Crystal Spring. "Alas, its charms are so ephemeral."

"Go into town, and buy some supplies," continued Slender Gourd. "Then build us a pyre."

Saihung bowed and turned toward town obediently, but inwardly he was disturbed. He had seen other masters on Huashan leave their bodies and had been a part of the witnessing students gathered to honor one of the greatest accomplishments possible for a Taoist. But it had never been one of his own masters, and he had always remained unemotional about it. Confronted with the imminent departure of Slender Gourd and Crystal Spring, he panicked.

They were going to die. Though a lifetime of study had taught him that a normal death was a mere transformation, and that spiritual death meant an ascension to a higher dimension of consciousness, he nevertheless felt a sudden loneliness. They were abandoning him, leaving him to his own efforts, depriving him of the guidance that gave him utter confidence that any sanctioned action was absolutely correct. He had become used to having masters again, indeed, he had never been free of that structure—even his rebellion was still tied to the authority it professed to reject. He wondered what he would do without them. Should he return to Huashan, the opera, or Wang Ziping? He found no appeal in any alternative except for the one he instinctively knew: that he would always be committed in some way to spirituality. Everything else was temporary and unsteady. Even as he split wood and spent days building a pyre, he understood that everything man-made inevitably comes to an end.

320

The dawn of the appointed day was cold and misty. Inside the cave, the two Taoists sat in meditation. At its conclusion, Saihung looked at them by the red light of the fire. Slender Gourd, thin but upright as a pillar, seemed older, a little more wrinkled. By the firelight, his fine white hair seemed like flaming lightning. But his eyes were still those limpid, enigmatic jewels. Crystal Spring seemed to sit with more presence. As he gazed dispassionately out through the mouth of the cave, his gentle visage was calm and heroic. Saihung found it amazing that these two men would be dead within a few hours. He wondered if they felt emotion or longing as they contemplated their voyage into the unknown.

"A sage knows how to send his soul into the great beyond," whispered Slender Gourd. "He has already seen higher planes of existence. Thus, at death, he firmly fixes his mind upon the place he wants to travel to. At death, his soul goes there."

"An ordinary person, however, has his three selves scattered," said Crystal Spring, "enmeshed again into the turnings of the wheel of life, they return again in a new form—but, sadly, to the same earthly hell. Remember to keep practicing, so that you may deliver yourself from this mortal plane."

"You are still young," said Slender Gourd compassionately. "It is a shame we did not meet earlier. But our time has come. Keep on with your spiritual path. Return to your master on Huashan. He will guide your progress with care and kindness."

"Do not feel grief upon our passing," said Crystal Spring as he noticed Saihung's reddening eyes. "This is only our physical shell. It is like a set of clothes that we discard. Our true selves shall emerge radiant and pure. Don't feel sad. Instead rejoice at our victory."

"Good-bye," said Slender Gourd as his eyes gently closed.

"See you on the other side, my boy!" said Crystal Spring. He smiled reassuringly, until his eyes closed too.

Saihung watched the two motionless bodies. But inside their stillness, he knew a dynamic movement was taking place. Within each master, a flow of energy mightier than any other each had ever manifested was rushing upward into the skull. Slowly, their bodies were passing into night. The arteries were pooling. The organs were stopping, drying up. The nerves were dulling. Every trace of life force was drawn upward. There, it was closed off. The body was in eclipse. The sun was contained in the head. The three selves became one, until in a powerful fusion their souls launched themselves away.

Watching, Saihung saw none of this. He knew the process took about twenty minutes, but he waited for twice that long, anxiously peering at his two masters. Were they gone? Or just still? All along he kept rehearsing in his mind what he should do next, as if that would give him some reassurance.

Finally, he rose to check them. He found neither breathing nor pulse. They were dead. They had transcended life, died a superhuman death; perhaps they had cheated the cosmic cycle itself. He was left behind on earth with only the memory of their extraordinary lives. He was left open to injuries, accidents, illnesses, tricks of fate, and weaknesses of character. He felt like a lost boy, stuck in a house with objects whose meaning he had never completely decoded, alone after the adults had left.

His masters had gone, leaving him with all his own physical and spiritual vulnerabilities to cope with. They had wordlessly left him with the responsibility not only for his own existence, but for his own transcendence. They had shown him a way to transcend death not for the sake of the burlesque that was religion, but for his own private moment. He knew he had to work out all his own problems, bear all his own injuries and illnesses, endure each brush with his own gadfly mortality until he too could leave the earth in a solitary and pure way.

He sat down. In respect for the moment, he tried to absorb it, to bear witness to it. A sense of his own mortality made him shiver involuntarily. He looked at the two Taoists again. Already they seemed a little smaller, a little less human. With the candles and incense, he could even have been in a little mountain shrine. They were like statues, unmoving, unyielding. After the two years he had been with them, he knew no more about their history or background than the night he met them. They were enigmas. With their passing, they had revealed nothing more and had left him with hundreds of unanswered questions.

The veil that had dropped between them could not be moved. It was opaque. He wished that they could talk to him from behind death's curtain. He wanted them to tell him what it was like there. What was on the other side?

The light in the cave slowly brightened. He realized that he still had his duty to do. It was a lucky thing for the living to have duty, he reflected. It kept them from being totally paralyzed whenever death made its appearance and took people irreversibly into its depths. Saihung carried each man tenderly out of the cave and laid him upon the bier.

He sprinkled sesame seeds all over their bodies to make them burn better. It occurred to him to wait. Maybe they would come back. After all, they looked like they were only sleeping. But no. He realized that he was only being sentimental. The two Taoists were gone forever.

He walked into the cave, picked up a torch, and set the mountain of wood aflame.

The fire was gentle and small at first. But it soon began to climb up the crisscrossed timbers, and the fountain of flame began to caress the two corpses. Panic rose up in him with the rising flames. It was shocking to see human beings burn. He had to stop himself from rushing to put out the fire. The taboo against watching helpless people destroyed was strong.

Soon, the bodies began to glow. The cloth was stripped away and consumed in the brightening inferno. The fire leapt higher, the wood cracking, splintering, sparks exploding as the blaze consumed it. Smoke rose up, and Saihung had to back away from the intense heat. He sat down to watch. The blaze dominated the quiet birdless morning.

Two days later, Saihung gathered the ashes, crushed the bone fragments, and scattered them in the forest. He returned to the cave and carefully obscured all signs of his presence. The scorched earth was swept over, and the rock was washed clean.

The way seemed traceless. Two men were gone as if they had never existed. He stood on the craggy cliff looking out over the silvery mists. It seemed as if his whole life had been a dream. He wondered if his master, the two acolytes, Butterfly, or he as the warrior, actor, or renunciate had ever existed. But then, who was asking the question?

It was he—he who had straggled off the Way but who, at least for the moment, had found it again. Following the Tao meant integration with it, all the time warding off confusion, emotionalism, and all other things that would oppose such unity. Through his life, he had had to cope with the difficulties forced upon him by his clan, his own mischievousness and wavering nature, his desire for fighting, his attraction to beauty, his dislike of discipline. Each time he had given in, he had lost his touch with the Tao; and when he had left Huashan for the streets of Shanghai, he had been no different than Butterfly in his fall from grace.

Slender Gourd and Crystal Spring had helped him to see beyond emotions. Their instructions had helped him understand his swings between enthusiasm and wild rebellion. They had helped him to leave behind his feelings so that it might truly be possible for him to fly without wings.

The two Taoists had taught him to look beyond mere technical knowledge, intellectualism, and even the substance of sacred literature. His body was the temple, and the divine was in him. Once that simple reality was grasped, all learning was a superfluous burden.

All his slipping from the path, all his returns to try once more, all his perceptions of the elements both good and bad that shielded his perceptions were unavoidable events in his progress. He had striven, fallen, ascended. He had found the Way again, and having plunged so far from it, was better prepared to stay with it. He truly could feel something growing within him—not just the physical field of energy promised by practice, but a new shining nature.

It was his original true self, finally bursting forth with clear brilliance. He glimpsed what it was to be "the uncarved block": pure, unmarred by emotional turbulence, misconception, or socialization. Through the grace of the Tao, there would grow in him a Golden Embryo of light and innocence, eternally in touch with the truth.

As the day began to brighten, he started down the mountain path. The trees were a vibrant green, made all the brighter by their white trunks. Some leaves were turning red and yellow, and the forest floor was carpeted by tiny maple leaves with slender stems pointing straight into the air. He took a deep breath, noticed the smell of the rich moist earth, caught the scent of botanical respiration. The sun broke through the clouds, and he smiled. He wanted to travel.

three

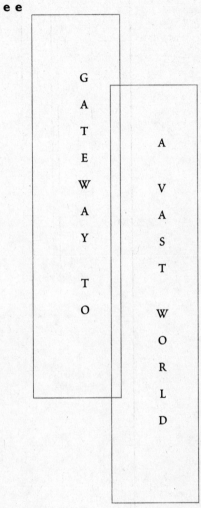

GATEWAY TO

A VAST WORLD

Beyond
Immortality

L ATE SPRING SNOW swirled around Saihung as he climbed the steep forest trail. Old pines cradled thick layers of ice on their green-needled boughs; barren branches of leafless trees were like smoke in the gorges. He looked through the diaphanous mists above him. Rock cliffs burnished by centuries of winter melt rose to nearly vertical heights, but he could not see their summit. They were obscured in storm cloud.

He began his climb up the cliffs. Soon, Saihung could pull himself up only with the help of heavy iron chains spiked into the hard granite, or by holding knotted ropes that had frozen stiff. The gloves on his hands stuck to the icy links, and they did

not keep the cold from chilling his fingers. A harsh wind sometimes pushed him onto the stone. He reached repeatedly for narrow ledges and climbed carefully over hand-hewn steps
contoured with ice.

At one point, he came to depressions in the rock. These in-
dentations, packed with snow and a few maple leaves that had
melted silhouette recesses, were believed to be the imprints of
ox hooves made when Lao Tzu had renounced the world to ride
westward. Now, Saihung also felt his distance from ordinary society as he scaled the seven-thousand-foot towers of stone.

He stood for a moment at the top of the first one thousand
steps, his chest heaving for oxygen at the higher altitude. Looking through the snow, he could barely make out the distant farm-
lands of the Shaanxi plains. As he climbed higher, the enfolding
parapets obscured all details that the ocean of mists did not. Ordinary life was insignificant from this spiritual citadel. There was
only the pure tranquillity of the mountain, the incomparable silence, the relieving calm. Troubles and tribulation seemed far
away; worldly involvement was gone.

The cold air was sweet, clean, tangible. Saihung filled his
lungs hungrily, greedily, though the freezing atmosphere dried
his lips and hurt his throat. Each exhalation changed the breath
within him, washed away the stagnant smoke of human society.
It was wonderful to be back. His body relaxed; his soul opened
like a flower. He felt safe, serene, and happy.

Wrapped in layers of quilted cotton clothes, a cloth cap tied
around his head, and wearing straw-bottomed shoes, he tried to
ignore the bone-chilling cold. The thrill of being on the mountain overran his senses. He hiked beside streams so clear that
they would have been invisible save for their ripples. Icicles that
hung like slender crystal spikes caught his eye as they shimmered on swaying branches. He watched a few maple leaves,
thin and brown from being frozen all winter, float from rounded
rock down into viridian pools. The water rushed sharply over the
gray rock, the jade-green liquid becoming a thousand shining
swords. Saihung imagined his own body as clear and subtle as the
water. He let his mind grow tranquil, immersed it in the frothing
sublimity of the pool's color. In the world of men, he was restless
and competitive. In the forest quiet, beside the living stream, his
soul found release and joy.

Five years ago he had lived here as a mountain hermit. Now in his thirties, he was a wanderer returning home. No matter how wild the trajectory his life had taken, his center was Huashan.

He eased the tension of the two Taoists' deaths by wandering. Accompanying an uncle who was a wealthy fur trader, or going alone by bicycle, he had toured Germany, France, and Eastern Europe, even though World War II was in progress. He found charm and beauty wherever he went, and had taken sentimental likings to the Black Forest, bridges over the Danube, the sound of Chopin. He loved to stay in alpine villages, and appreciated the hospitality that people proffered even to strangers. Though the land had been devastated, he took it all in, and the enchantment of a foreign land was mixed with the enthusiasm of his youth. For a time, he had even wanted to move to Europe, but his only friends were members of a dying aristocracy. They could offer him no solace.

329

Saihung returned to China. He was studying at Yenching University as the People's Republic came into being in 1949. One of his essays had caught the eye of Premier Zhou Enlai, who habitually recruited aides from the schools. Zhou summoned him, discussed ideas with him, and invited him to travel. Little by little, he assigned minor responsibilities to Saihung, covertly watching how the young man acted. Only when Zhou was satisfied that Saihung was a potential asset did he invite him to become one of his many undersecretaries. This role was classically Chinese. Saihung had gone through an initiation ritual in which he had ceremoniously knelt down to become Zhou's disciple.

Saihung proved to be an excellent and ruthless politician. Before long he was sitting in the People's Congress—a pale, severe, calculating figure in a gray Mao suit—studying the results of stratagems he had created. Being a part of government, as Zhou taught him, meant the absolute use of power. Allies had to be cultivated, enemies had to be contained or destroyed. For one trained since childhood to be a martial artist, being cruel in politics was simple. He loved to anticipate the actions of his rivals and set up circumstances to thwart them. He enjoyed their squirming.

Cunning and brutal manipulations were matter-of-fact necessities in politics. All would have been fine had Saihung not had another side to him. Whether innate or fostered by the monastery, he had conscience and emotion. These two factors were as much a part of him as his ability to wield power, and they were liabilities for a politician. He brooded about his actions; sometimes he secretly sympathized with his victims.

He left the government in 1951. The danger of political intrigue, rivalry with Zhou's other disciples, and disenchantment with the impermanence of political reform were the outward reasons that he left. But the more true reasons were the tensions between his mercenary and sensitive sides. He could never bring himself to complete the ultimate act of power: the eradication of his compassion.

Saihung had remained a solitary man, troubled by his inner schism and uncertain about his own destiny. He wanted, if not peace, at least a way through his dilemmas. Only when the futility of his life of travel had worn him down, and his dangerous ambivalence about public life had become too prominent, did he remember the recluse who had raised him. His longing snapped into focus. He decided that he would return to learn the higher stages of Taoism.

For as long as he had traveled, he had never discovered the possibility of learning such secrets elsewhere. It was said that deepening meditative techniques would teach extraordinary, even supernatural, things. He wanted to soar into heaven, dive into hell, know all things seen and unseen. He wanted to increase his health and take it to the ultimate extreme of longevity.

The Taoist life was not glorious. It was all homespun cloth, patched robes, bleached wood, dusty brick, coarse gruel. Governments were never patrons, for a Taoist, even at best, was the least cooperative of all holy men. Patrons found the doctrines as abstruse as the peaks were difficult to ascend. Gods had no gold for the Taoists, and the real fact was that "renunciation" existed only as long as there were others willing to support such efforts. Few on the outside had any emotion for the dwellers of Huashan save for scorn, condescension, or superstitious fear. But spiritual richness still flourished in surroundings of poverty.

The monks he saw as he passed the Gate of Southern Heaven were a testimonial to the rigorous and disciplined men who found vitality in the harsh surroundings. Huashan was a little like a university, except that there was a quietness to the way people moved back and forth, a seriousness of intent on their faces. The younger ones were dressed in blue or gray, the older monks in black. He passed dozens of men who were either working or hurrying to classes. As mountain ascetics, each one was to attune himself to the change in the sky, the stillness of the mountain, the compassion of the earth, the ferocity of thunder, and the meditation of the lake.

Saihung crossed a rustic log bridge over a pouring cataract and began his final ascent up the South Peak. As he came closer to his master, he began climbing in greater excitement. Through a cleft in the mighty granite, above the tops of pines with trunks like bronze, he saw his master's temple. It floated like a dream in the falling snow, its black tile roof frosted white. He could see priests standing at the top of the trail, men he had known all his life. There was no embracing, no shouts of joy or welcome. He walked back into his home temple in solemn quiet. He could only bring his left palm to his heart—the thumb touching his chest, the fingers upright—in the gesture of greeting.

As he walked up the stone steps and into the dark gate of the shrine, he met Mist Through a Grove and Sound of Clear Water. Now in their forties, the two returned his bow deeply. As they stood upright, they performed a series of hand gestures that formed a secret sign of their sect. Saihung replied in kind, but the two men began giggling. By the time they were finished, they were overcome with mirth.

Saihung was annoyed. Here he had climbed seven thousand feet in anticipation of a homecoming, and he was being laughed at.

"You're not supposed to laugh in the temple," he whispered to them.

Saihung's reproach proved even more hilarious to them. His two older brothers looked at his disheveled appearance, the hat askew on his head, and his pants soaked from snow and the spray of streams.

"You're not supposed to come into the temple like that either." Sound of Clear Water laughed.

Saihung pulled the hat angrily from his head. The acolytes only laughed all the more: Though his hair was short, it seemed as if every single strand was plastered down in a different direction.

"You'd better arrange yourself before you see the Grand Master," admonished Mist Through a Grove. Saihung bridled immediately. He wondered if he would always be a child to his older classmates.

"I'll bathe right away," he said with all the dignity he could muster.

"Impossible," said Sound of Clear Water. "The showers are closed until evening."

Saihung was about to burst out in frustration when he heard the familiar voice of his master.

"It's of no consequence," said the Grand Master.

Saihung turned in the hall to see his master with two other elderly priests. They were apparently on their way from a discussion. The acolytes withdrew two steps in deference. Saihung bowed immediately by kneeling and touching his head repeatedly to the tile floor. He did not care that he was leaving a puddle from the water and sweat on his head.

Stroking his beard thoughtfully, the Grand Master greeted Saihung with a formal phrase. Beyond that utterance, his master acted as if he had not been gone at all. The Grand Master told Saihung to rise. For a minute, he looked deeply into his student's eyes. Saihung felt that his own thoughts had been interrupted. He could only stare back, mesmerized.

The coil of hair at the crown and the thick white beard were like fine strands of silver wire against somber black robes. His skin was brown from years of living on exposed and lonely mountaintops. Fine wrinkles from wearisome responsibilities wove a net around his quiet eyes. Saihung saw a hint of sadness, a trace of resignation. He always wondered whether this was regret for the past, or an acceptance of a future as yet unknown.

The Grand Master stretched his hand forward in blessing. He assigned temple tasks and a demanding regimen of contemplation as if Saihung had never been gone. "From this day forth, it will be your task to solve the mystery of the self," said the Grand Master. "You will find Sound of Clear Water and ask him to assign you to a meditation hut. You must answer this question for me: Do you exist?"

Saihung looked up at the master. What an odd question, he thought to himself. But he had little time to think about it just then, and he could not ask for further explanation. The Grand Master smiled slightly before he gestured to the acolytes to follow him. They left Saihung alone in the hall.

Turning into the darkness, Saihung saw the image of the Queen Mother of the West, one of Huashan's patron deities. He walked up to the altar and offered incense. It felt good to be back.

I N THE ENSUING days, Saihung returned to his classes and began to work on repairing the North Peak Temple. The weight of snow had broken several places in the tile roof, and the repairs could not wait until spring. Balancing precariously on ladders, he and other monks took advantage of a clear day to carry tiles up and cement them in place. It was a dizzying task, for a fall would have sent him plunging.

333

The high vantage point allowed him a wonderful view. As he scanned the valley below, he noticed a strange flash of metal. He had his duties to perform, but he was curious. Telling the supervising monk that he had to relieve himself, Saihung walked through the brick temple and made his way carefully down the trail. The storm-whipped ridge was bald of trees. He was thankful to get out of the wind and into a forest.

Saihung came to a rise that was covered with pines. He could hear two men talking, but he could not see them from where he stood. Saihung walked carefully over the snow to avoid detection. As he crept closer, he was surprised to hear his master's voice.

"I am a renunciate who has lost all hankering for fame," said the Grand Master.

"I am also a priest," Saihung heard a deep voice reply. "But though the world of Tao is apart from the mortal world, there must nevertheless be distinctions between high and low."

"Tragic indeed that you should take such a view," murmured the Grand Master. "True followers of the way do not care about their place in any hierarchy."

"You speak as the abbot of Huashan. Isn't that contradictory?"

"My office is merely a duty. I would forsake it if required."

"But the person remains who he is."

"For as long as my destiny lasts."

"It is the person that I seek, after all, not the empty identity. It is against you that I have come to test my skill."

Saihung could not help but inch closer to gain a view. There in a snow-covered clearing, he could see his master, but not the man with whom he was speaking. Conifers stood starkly in the snow; black rocks protruded from the white banks.

The Grand Master turned slightly. Saihung saw that he was holding a sword of brilliant steel. A long tassel of white horsehair was tied to the handle.

334   "I am a simple and direct man," said the Grand Master. "What use is it to duel with me? It will surely not add to your prestige to best someone my age."

The other man laughed. "I am a Taoist. I do not care for prestige. I only care about self-perfection. Your modesty is as admirable as it is inaccurate. You are one of the few true swordsmen left."

"Why not say the truth?" returned the Grand Master. "You are trying to discredit Huashan and usurp power for yourself."

There was a tense pause. The Grand Master must have known the man's true motivation, thought Saihung. He cautiously moved to see him.

He was surprised to see a dwarf. Dressed in the gray robes of a Taoist priest, with white beard and topknot, he seemed almost as old as the Grand Master. His head was large, and though his eyes were somewhat crooked, they still came to the sharp corners that were supposed to signify a man of intelligence. He was only tall enough to come to the Grand Master's waist, but his hands were large and powerful. The sword he held was unusually long. Nearly four feet in length, it was a blade of purple steel, a metal famous throughout the martial world for its flexible strength. His tassel was dyed black and red. The dwarf showed no emotion at the Grand Master's accusation. He only brought his blade before him in silent challenge.

"All fighting, whether by swordsmen, sorcerers, or gods themselves, is egotism," declared the Grand Master.

"Your wisdom was gained through contest," said the dwarf. "I crave the experience of testing myself against you."

"Must you?" asked the Grand Master. "Acts of power are acts of greed."

"Only one who has power sermonizes about greed," replied the dwarf testily. "I have not yet gained what I must. You bar my way."

"Sad . . . sad indeed that you should be so bitter."

"Sadness is an emotion. A good swordsman has no emotion."

"You believe that you are such a swordsman?"

"There is only one way to answer," said the dwarf, thrusting the point of his blade forward. The tip began to tremble with the energy he projected through it.

"Even when one renounces the world, trouble will still come," sighed the Grand Master upon seeing this aggressive gesture. "You are determined to go through with this?"

"Yes," replied the dwarf. "My honor is at stake."

"May you someday see how useless honor is," replied the Grand Master. "But since you will not relent, I must respond. As your fame precedes you, I will not lighten my stroke."

"Nor will I."

The two men were about twenty feet apart. As a prelude, each was allowed to go through a few saluting postures emblematic of their style. The dwarf brought his sword before him, circled his free arm with a flourish, and made several cuts and parries. His open hand was held in the sword gesture, a closed hand with only the index and second fingers extended. He ended his salute first by pointing his fingers at the Grand Master, then by leveling the tip of his blade straight at his opponent's heart.

It was the Grand Master's turn, and he ritualistically went through his own salute. He brought the sword across his chest, raised it high, crouched down into a low stance, and leapt up onto one leg before settling into a position of readiness. He also pointed his weapon straight to the heart. Like his opponent's sword, the tip of the Grand Master's sword began to vibrate from the force conducted through the razor-sharp steel. The dwarf scoffed.

"Green Dragon Sword style," he spat out, for he recognized the Grand Master's postures. "A rather common style!"

The Grand Master remained silent. There was a moment of utter stillness, each swordsman waiting for the other to commit himself first. Snow fell, and the flakes caught on the bare steel.

The dwarf charged with a loud shout. His legs were mighty, and he leapt high at the Grand Master. Without moving his stance, the Grand Master bent over backward to dodge the cut. His waist was so flexible that he sprang back right away and then twisted around toward his opponent. The blade just missed, but it kept the dwarf from counterattacking.

Saihung knew that the sign of expert swordsmen was that they never clashed their swords directly with one another. To block was a sign of poor skill. Rather, the best fighters were always able to avoid the other's weapon, no matter how swift the combat.

The Grand Master came with a downward thrust, but his opponent easily sidestepped, aiming directly at the outstretched wrist. The Grand Master turned smoothly in a circular parry and hacked downward. The dwarf dodged and thrust at the chin. Each fighter took skillful, nearly balletic poses—at one point, the Grand Master dropped into a full split, the dwarf leapt into the air like a whirlwind—as they both tried to gain an opening. But it was not easy. Saihung could see that the dwarf actually had an advantage because of his quickness and his height. The Grand Master was forced to turn wider circumferences to escape return thrusts.

The dwarf jumped up again, his body spinning rapidly. He was like a hurtling comet. His sword moved so swiftly that Saihung could not see it. He could only hear it slicing the air in a terrifying sound halfway between a tearing sheet and a shriek. The Grand Master spun, pausing abruptly behind his attacker. His movement was fierce, his blade accelerating past the range of visibility as he twisted it out.

The dwarf parried, opening the Grand Master's guard for a moment. He could not turn his blade in time, so he smashed the butt of his handle toward the Grand Master's heart. The Grand Master jumped to the side in a spinning hack that the dwarf dodged only by twisting his whole body in the air.

Brief flashes of steel seemed to fly out from centrifugal force. Saihung knew that their spinning movements, characteristic of high swordsmanship, were not wholly a consequence of muscular or acrobatic abilities. Both men had brought power gained from years of meditative cultivation into play. Internal energy moved in spirals and lightened their bodies, and this was why they leapt and turned in the drifting snowflakes.

This was the true meaning of their contest. Thrusting and parrying were secondary. Strategy and martial experience were only remotely relevant. What was being tested was their totalities as men, their attainment of internal energy. There were thirteen levels to swordsmanship, with the first level already hopelessly above the average knight. The two fighters were already in the higher echelons of this elite. For them, swords were mere extensions of their bodies, and their bodies were mere instruments. They were throwing soul against soul, using the utmost of their inner fires.

Finally, the dwarf lunged low and cut the Grand Master's thigh. The Grand Master dropped down, feigning a serious wound. As his opponent came in for the kill, the Grand Master turned and cut off the dwarf's topknot. He could just have easily cut lower. The dwarf hesitated a moment, and in that second, the Grand Master stuck him in the wrist. The sword fell to the rock with a sound like an iron ingot hitting the foundry floor. It lay immobile and dark in the snow: an effigy corpse for its master. The Grand Master leapt up and raised his blade heavenward, but the now-frightened dwarf ran away. Saihung's master did nothing to pursue him.

It was wrong for Saihung to have watched the fight. Duels were a private matter, not an affair for gawkers. He stole away, apprehensive of punishment. He guessed that his master might have been aware of his presence, but Saihung decided to say nothing if his master remained quiet about it. He hurried back to his duties at the North Peak Temple.

"How could one go so far and long to relieve oneself?" demanded the supervisor. He was a middle-aged priest with a military bearing.

"It was a matter of the 'large convenience,'" said Saihung with an exaggerated stammer.

"One should not use such vernacular in the presence of the gods," said the priest hastily. Now Saihung had doubled his offense.

"This insignificant one recognizes his sin," apologized Saihung. "Please relent, though I deserve punishment."

"It is of little consequence," said the priest. "Go back to your duties."

Saihung went back to carrying tiles, but as he swayed in the wind, he relished the memory of his teacher's fight.

T HE GRAND MASTER summoned Saihung two days later. His master did not limp from the cut, and he made no reference to his duel. The Grand Master merely nodded to Saihung and gestured toward the monastery gate. The two of them walked toward the crest of the South Peak, quiet and yet aware of each other.

"Asceticism is possible only away from people," commented the Grand Master as they came to the very edge of a high cliff. "Can't you feel it?"

Saihung nodded as he felt the sting of the wind. There wasn't a bit of humanity in sight, only pure nature stretching to the horizon. He felt aloof from all that was normally considered important. After years of training, he had come to the conclusion that perceptions were superior to doctrine and procedure.

"Only here, away from the pull of other minds, can one attain tranquillity," continued the Grand Master. "Tranquillity leads to stillness. In stillness there is the possibility of wisdom."

"You've said that meditation is the key," said Saihung, anticipating his master's favorite theme.

"But not simply meditation. Life is not simplistic. Tao changes. Our methods to know it must also have variety. Live your life with discipline and explore relentlessly. Do not limit yourself, even by meditation."

"Then why do you preach a life of restriction?"

"This enforces discipline. Self-indulgence is a liability. Tao is known by the free. Only the disciplined are free to chase the flow. Eternal flux rules the universe. Know the Tao by inaction. That is the way to know its secrets. Keep to action. That is the way to experience its outcome."

"'Be desireless to know the essence of Tao. Have desire to know its manifestations,'" said Saihung, quoting from the scriptures.

"Yes," responded the Grand Master. "But you should speak from your own experience. Quoting holy words is useless. They only point back on oneself. They all say, 'Look within.' The only real value lies in firsthand experience."

His master was tough, admitted Saihung admiringly. The Grand Master had a taste for severity and discipline. Longevity

338

was simply a procedure to extend the process of simplifying the personality through penance and self-sacrifice. It was pure drudgery, a life of restriction meant to force the explosion of human potential by sheer compression. They walked farther on and stood for a minute at another ridge. Small trees, stunted by the bitter climate, dotted the pristine stone sporadically. Stronger trees stood starkly against the gray heavens.

"Look! Look!" urged the Grand Master. "Do you need a book? Look! Feel! The Tao surrounds you!"

There before them a vast panorama of aged peaks, their edges still proudly sharp and lofty even after centuries, stretched to the horizon. They were like many dragons, the rising mist like a swirling surf. Snow frosted the tops of the mountains where the aerial tide had ebbed. Clouds swept through like charging armies. The wind came in gusts and shook the tortured sentinel pines. Nature was supreme; nature was pure. It changed constantly, its transformations surrounded them.

Huashan dwarfed the puny men who stood so insignificantly on its ledges. They were nothing here. Their aspirations were mere glimmers, their bodies stupidly fragile. Their life spans were only moments in infinity. They stood in their transitoriness; master and disciple who were like footnotes to the epic of heaven and earth.

"Knowing the Tao is essential," said the Grand Master. He turned toward Saihung and smiled reassuringly. "Meditation is the way to know the Tao. Please tell me what progress you've made."

"I am not sure . . . the question that you posed to me is not easy to answer."

"What is so hard?" returned the Grand Master gently. "The question was only three words long."

"That's true. I have been meditating on it since my return. Nevertheless . . . "

"I will restate it," said his master. "I simply asked you: Do you exist?"

Saihung was silent. Somehow, he felt that he would say the wrong thing no matter what his response.

The Grand Master urged him on. "Are you speechless? You who are so fond of debating and arguing? You who have been to the university and traveled far and wide? Answer! Answer!"

"Yes!" burst out Saihung. "I exist!"

"Do you? Then where is your self? Show it to me."

"Why, I am right here before you."

"Are you? Are you so sure that I exist?"

"Master!" exclaimed Saihung. "Yes!"

"But I have no self to show you."

"I see you," said Saihung. He wondered if his master was getting senile.

"You see only a body, a borrowed vessel."

Saihung looked at his master in an effort to understand what was being presented to him. The Grand Master's life of deep cultivation had worked his face into eccentric beauty. Both the warrior and scholar showed, and tensions between the two extremes were resolved in the visage of the hermit. Did this man exist? For Saihung, he certainly did. Saihung was confident in his position. He would not be so dumb as to limit the self to the material and the physical. He took up the debate again.

"Of course there is something unseen, besides the body."

"What is that?" asked the Grand Master.

"The mind. The immortal soul. These exist. The scriptures tell us that there are three sheaths within us. The soul, the mind, and the body."

"You are a good schoolboy," said the Grand Master mockingly. "But I don't hear your own experience in those words."

"Master," replied Saihung in a patient tone, "I've meditated for years. I know the mind."

"If you knew the mind, you would not speak so recklessly. Those who truly understand the mind know that it is both friend and enemy. Don't you realize that it is the mind that subverts you?"

"The mind is real," declared Saihung.

"No, the mind is not real," responded the Grand Master with equal emphasis.

"I have seen too much of the mind's powers to accept that it is not real."

"Powers!" The Grand Master cut him off. "What have they done but obscured your true nature?"

Saihung felt irritated. He felt his teacher was being deliberately difficult—even hypocritical. The man had ten times Saihung's abilities, possessing skills bordering on the divine. It was ridiculous for him to suggest that powers were a hindrance. Saihung would have pounded any other man who had been so contrary.

But this was his master, and there was no possibility of hitting him. He was forced instead to consider what his master was saying. His master had referred to Saihung's true nature. He looked at himself for a clue.

"The mind is powerful," began Saihung again. "I know that it is not my body. Though I practice martial arts, I have also traveled outside my body. I have soared to other places, holding on to your sleeve. Don't you remember, Master?"

"How trivial!" declared the Grand Master. "A few insignificant flights and you think that establishes the self? I see nothing impressive about a mere wisp of smoke flitting here and there."

"The mind is my true nature," responded Saihung stubbornly.

"And since you've learned a few mental circus tricks, you assume that you're explaining the self?"

"Well . . . yes."

"That merely traps you in your mind. Pursuing power and intellect, astral travel and clairvoyance—these only strengthen your trap."

"Then why did I learn them?"

"Because you are greedy for power. You should learn them to understand their uselessness. Know magic, shun magic."

Saihung refused to be bested in the discussion. He tried a new direction.

"What about the gods, whom we revere? Surely they exist." He knew his master was devout.

"Even worse!" The Grand Master refused to take the bait. "It may sound like blasphemy, but the gods are also trapped in their minds. They live for eternity clinging to their identities and their roles. The Jade Emperor is omnipotent, omniscient, omnipresent, and no more."

"No more?" interjected Saihung. "Can there be anything else?"

"Yes, there is something else. We Taoists believe that there is something besides the gods. The Jade Emperor is only one being. He is not all beings, and he is not the universe, or all universes. The gods, in this respect, are as pathetic as humans in their delight for powers. This is their limitation: They still believe in the self."

"Well, if scripture is not enough, my mind is not enough, even the gods are not enough, then there can be no Tao."

"You are wrong," said the Grand Master, finally fixing him with a steady gaze. "When there are no scriptures, there is no mind, and there are no gods; then there is Tao."

They were silent for a time. The Grand Master closed his eyes while Saihung stood awkwardly in the bone-numbing chill. This habit of closing his eyes in the middle of a conversation had always unnerved Saihung. He was never sure whether to stand there or leave. As always, he decided to wait. This time, he considered himself lucky that the Grand Master began to speak after only an hour's lapse.

"Do you understand death?"

"I believe so," replied Saihung, as he tried to keep his teeth from chattering. He had seen many die during wars, famine, and in fights.

"Is death final, or is it merely a transformation?"

"The self of instinct decays with the body. The self of the mind and the soul are reincarnated," stated Saihung from his lessons. "If one practices spirituality, there is the potential to transcend death with one's individual awareness intact."

"Is that what you want?"

Of course it was. But he thought it best to be cautious in admitting it. "I have been taught that this was best."

"You are correct, but far off the mark. Your only concern should be liberation."

"Indeed it is."

"But liberation not just from life and death, transmigration, and one's own desires, liberation from one's own mind as well. The mind itself is capable of transcending death: We believe that one will go where one wills at the moment of death. Those who are confused will pass into oblivion or float in limbo: Sometimes they are not even aware that they have died. Others can, through the practice of good deeds and austerities, become gods. The majority, however, fall in between: Still clinging to a desire for life, or having been so unfulfilled, they come back again and again. Like the Butterfly Lovers, who were reincarnated sixty times before they could fulfill their love and gain release, the average person is repeatedly reincarnated to complete his destiny."

The Grand Master looked at Saihung. "All these people have something in common: They are prisoners of the mind. Whether they are the dunce too muddled to comprehend death or the sage who has been elevated to a god, they still cling to their identities. There is still something higher."

343

This aroused Saihung. The Grand Master knew his student well. Saihung would always reach for the best.

"The best is emptiness," said the Grand Master. "You must strive to be empty. Learn longevity, yes. But don't try to be immortal. Even gods die. Live long enough to fulfill your destiny."

"How does one do that?"

"By having a goal in life. Have a purpose, and your life will be purposeful. Have a meaning, and your life will be meaningful. Make a decision and stick to it, not dogmatically or rigidly. Persevere and be flexible. Once a goal has been selected, nothing else must interfere. Cut all that is ordinarily considered essential in order to find meaning. If one has a powerful motivation for living, then choices are clear-cut. With discipline, sacrifices are made for a higher goal, and one acts with confidence and directness. Then you will go into the source satisfied that you've completed your life on earth. Nothing will pull you back. You are free."

"Master, what is this source?"

"I will not tell you now. You must find out and tell me. Then I will know that you have truly found it."

They walked back toward the temple. The evening bells had begun to ring. Saihung continued to ponder his master's words.

twenty nine:

Contemplating
the
Void

S AIHUNG WALKED INTO the icy night, his way lit only by a paper lantern. His evening devotions were complete. In the remaining hour before midnight, he was to take advantage of the time when yin was at its height for his fourth meditation of the day. As he made his way toward his cell, he noticed the throw of golden light. He remembered the old saying: "The wise man who seeks the way carries a candle before him." That candle was supposed to be knowledge, but it only showed the way. One still had to walk step by step.

His present regimen of meditation required that he live alone in a small cottage. He had been assigned to a one-room place large enough only for a bed, table, and bookshelf. Only his teacher could visit, and all eating, study, and meditation were to be conducted in the tiny, solitary house perched on an undercut cliff.

Typically Taoist, the brick, wood, and tile hut was built on a ledge that was barely an aberration in the rock wall. Generations of monks had gained their realization in this fragile shelter, and it was said that years of such meditation had soaked into the very particles of the building. By opening his being in meditation, Saihung was to ride the reverberations of those people's enlightenment to the same states of consciousness.

The interior was of rustic plaster, whitewashed. A few scrolls of landscapes hung from the walls, but otherwise there was no decoration. The wooden eaves were exposed, gray and rough timbers barely stripped of bark. He hung a sign on the exterior that stated "meditation," so that he would remain undisturbed, and closed the pine door tightly against the wind. Taking a bundle of straw and kindling, he renewed the fire under his brick bed. Only layers of thick cotton quilting and the warm platform would prevent him from freezing during the night. He decided that it was too cold to undress; he would go to sleep fully clothed, with a hat tied to his head and a scarf over his nose.

He felt his hair by pushing his hand beneath his hat. It was shoulder length. Soon he would be able to pin it into the Taoist symbol. He went to a wooden trunk and took out a piece of silver. This hairpin was shaped like a straight blade about one-quarter-inch wide, narrowing over a six-inch length to a blunt tip. On one end was an intricately wrought dragon head.

He looked at the pin, topaz-colored in the lantern's light. It was the pen his master had given to him when he had been initiated. No other person had ever touched this hairpin. It had been consecrated and bestowed personally, just as his spirituality had been sparked by personal transmission. He had worn it through years of asceticism and had kept it during years of travel. It was the symbol of his renunciation and a sign of the strength of Taoism. He put it away, looking forward to the day he would wear it.

Saihung took out a book and a fountain pen, to avoid the tedium of grinding ink and preparing paper. He wrote down all that he and his master had discussed that afternoon. He pondered the conversation with some anxiety. He did not quite understand all that the Grand Master was teaching him. In fact, he had a fearful doubt that in the concept of emptiness, the Grand Master may have been offering only something without value.

He finished his recording without insight and arranged himself for meditation. Sitting on the platform, he had a momentary feeling of wistfulness. It felt good to be on the mountain, but it was a little lonely too. He sometimes wished that his relationships with the masters were less formal, that he could be playful or just joke with them. Saihung smiled. Such things were not permitted. But this was what he had come back for, no matter what the hardship.

He sat. This was physical stillness. He arranged his body. Cross-legged. Hands atop his knees. He became a mountain.

In deep silence, he let his master's words return to him. In profound quiet, the solitude that existed nowhere in the whole world save his heart, he heard his master's injunction: Meditate on the transitory. He was to investigate, with the mind he had so proudly proclaimed, the fact that nothing in life lasted.

Obeying this dictum and following a memorized procedure, Saihung first examined his relationship with others to understand how everything was temporary. This was one way that he could pare away attachment that bound each person to worldly things and avoid establishing his life meaning in ties to other people. This was not easy for him. He was sentimental.

He thought of his grandparents, whom he idolized. An image of his grandmother came to him. At six feet in height, she was a ruthless woman warrior. Her martial-arts name was "Buddhist Butterfly," though she was dainty only in appearance and name. When Saihung had scoffed at her feminine tassels, she had torn through his vest and gown with one stroke, leaving a red welt on his body. She had not even used a blade, or her full strength. In spite of his years of training, his grandmother was one fighter Saihung never dared to challenge.

Saihung once saw his grandparents fight assassins from the neighboring Wu clan. Disguised as birthday well-wishers, the assassins approached the patriarch in the courtyard. Saihung's grandmother was sitting in a pavilion, playing the harp. As soon as she saw the flash of a dagger, she pinned the hand of the assailant with a dart that she wore as a hairpin. Her husband immediately struck with a palm blow so violent that it shattered the man's jaw.

Another drew two sabers, but the elder easily disarmed and killed him. The last two fled, running quickly through the garden gate. Saihung's grandfather sat back down with his guests. He was magnanimous, and it was his birthday. He saw no reason to slay them.

"No!" his wife cried. "One must cut the weeds and pull the roots!" With that she leapt after them and killed them herself.

He was of his grandparents' blood; he sprang from their lives. But they were gone, lost to the shifting of circumstances that even they in their heroic might had been unable to resist. By contemplating their temporalness, absorbing the significance of their passing, adjusting his orientation until there was no sentimentality, he saw the tyranny of attachment and delusion. Nothing in life was permanent. Nothing in life could be depended upon for one's own existence.

The Tao changed constantly. It was not fixed. There was no reason to cling to loved ones, to cherished notions, perhaps even to one's own body. Saihung shifted the focus of his meditation. He viewed his body. As much as he had shaped it into athletic supremacy, he realized it would not last. He wanted longevity, but even if he lived for eons, he knew decline was inevitable: His fingers would stiffen, his limbs would fail, the organs would dry. His body was only a temporary thing—the five elements congealed together on some fundamentally unseen level. Held together by consciousness, the uncountable fine particles would scatter once his mind let go. Whether there was heaven or hell or nothing, no one ever carried his body beyond death. It was useless to cling to it. It would not even carry him to the next world; why should he be tied to it in this one?

Saihung thought of his master, who seemed older than old, who would pass from this life. He would be but a tiny firefly changed into night. But his master held that death was but a transformation.

Death. Yes, he had seen death. He wanted only life. He wanted immortality. But as he looked at all the people gone from his life, he wondered if the mind and soul were permanent. Could the mind actually transcend death and possess immortality?

He heard his master question him again. Where was the mind?

He searched interminably. Each possibility dissolved into nothing. Was the mind on some very minute atomic level? Was it hiding in some particle? Or was it as big as the universe?

All his resistance had stemmed from simple uncertainty about the unknown. He saw a new perspective, a thrilling, wide-open possibility: All the struggles, all the ideals, on which he based his life might be surrendered. Every bit of himself—created by others, and created by himself through instinct and ambition—could be allowed to float away. The mind that so furiously held his body and soul into a dense conglomeration called Kwan Saihung could simply relax, and everything he was—from physicality to imagination—would explode like a nova.

He vacillated on the cusp of this understanding. There was still a glimmer of mind, a faint breath of a human being left to contemplate its inherent nonreality. So many times his masters had told him, "The world is an illusion." Not wanting to unbalance him, they had waited this long to let him now realize, "*I* am an illusion."

I was made up. *I* was a by-product of the binding together of consciousness and matter. *I* was the microscopic fragment of some cosmic thought that itself was a fluke, a random occurrence, a mere ripple among an infinite number of never-conceivable universes.

The
Hairpin

W HEN THE WEATHER grew warmer, Saihung was assigned two responsibili-
ties: gardening and fish farming. He was glad to have these
duties, because he loved to tend living things. Watching them
grow was one of his delights.

He went out in the early morning after his devotions and meditations to dig in the rich earth, to pull the weeds. Saihung
checked the greenhouses that sheltered and warmed spouting
shoots. He transplanted some of the seedlings into precise rows
and watered them tenderly.

Small fields for more mature vegetables were in sheltered
places to protect them from the harsh winds. The Taoists had

placed these gardens wherever there was sufficient light through the gorges and clefts of the mountain. Through sheer determination and hard work, they cultivated the meager fields, nurturing crops to feed the many monks.

After working for several hours with the plants, Saihung next went to check on the fish. In naturally skylit grottos, the Taoists had built wooden troughs to hold carp and pike in various stages of growth from fingerlings to adult fish. He found that ice had glassed over the surface as so often happened during the cold mornings. Saihung broke away the crystal layer and scoured the troughs to remove dirt and algae, and adjusted the inflow of water through the system of bamboo pipes. He checked to see that water was still flowing freely at the inlet of the pipes. Returning to the troughs, he fed the fish a combination of insects, grain, and chopped fungus.

As Saihung trudged back up the trail toward the temple, he reflected on the machines that had slowly begun to appear on farms. He recalled his own essays on collectivization and mechanization of agriculture, which he had written as a government official. But the monks couldn't afford machines, even if they had favored their use. For them, the measure of work was still the labor of people.

Work was a potential time of spiritual growth. They were working with nature, not against it. They were taking and giving from the earth, not shamelessly exploiting it. The harvest that they worked for was not simply for a crop of fish or vegetables, but a harvest of the Tao. When Saihung plunged his hands into the damp earth, he held the Tao. When he touched flowing water, he touched the Tao. By following the seasons, he followed the Tao. Any moment might have brought enlightenment. Realization did not come from a prayer rug, an altar, nor even from holy scripture. It was a part of life, a gift of life, and to consider realization as something separate was a fallacy. One carried the muck of fish ponds as much as one carried devotion to the gods.

In the purity of the mountain air, in the honesty of hard work and the serenity of meditation, Saihung found a refuge in which to cleanse himself of worldly things. Perhaps this time his restlessness would not return and he could spend his days in contemplation and the devotions that he now joined the other monks in performing.

He went into the Temple of the Three Pure Ones. Putting on clean robes, he washed himself at a stone basin. The cold water numbed his fingers, but he was too intent on his holy duty to care. His ablution complete, Saihung went into the darkened interior. Without greeting anyone or engaging in conversation, he stood in a row with dozens of other monks. Sandalwood incense drifted languidly through the room, candles punctuated the blackness with dim glows that reflected on gilded carvings. Behind embroidered silk curtains, in shrines that amounted to small buildings within the temple, sat the life-sized figures of Taoism's highest gods. Saihung still thought of his childhood days, when he had been afraid to enter the temples: These deities seemed alive, might have spoken to him, or moved, or punished his sins. He remembered these feelings because there was still some of that primal awe in him.

He chanted. Mist Through a Grove, dressed in bright silken colors, sang the major lines, while Saihung and the chorus took up the refrain. Their worship was almost operatic, with the use of bells, chimes, drums, and cymbals. Recitation brought the gods down to earth, balanced the powers, and above all brought humanity into balance with all natural and divine forces. Without the devotion of the human heart, the Taoists contended, there would be no balance for evil or simple entropy.

Saihung sang unreservedly. Reverence and devotion were crucial expressions to him. Through the form of scriptures, through the ceremony of standing in a consecrated building, he brought forth the best that he had to offer. What he gave was not the highest talent that he had, or glibness of speech, but the simple and honest essence of his soul.

The ceremony lasted nearly two hours. At its conclusion, Saihung went before the altar. He knelt and bowed, stood up, and knelt again. Nine times he prostrated himself before the deities. Then he slowly backed away and turned to leave the temple.

Outside, he felt the frigid evening air approaching. He looked into the blackening sky, shimmering crimson at the horizon, deepening to black at its highest vault. He could already see a star, and the moon was already visible. It seemed to lead a current of icy cold down through the peaks and canyons. He shivered. It would be time for padded clothes again.

Autumn would be coming soon. The maples had already turned red, and the higher parts of the mountain had already seen some snow flurries. He saw the orange reflections of new snow on the mountains surrounding Huashan. He knew that he would have to prepare soon. Once snow set in, descending the mountain was impossible. Any slip on the ice might send him plunging thousands of feet.

He went to the kitchen of the main temple. This large, cluttered room with hanging herbs and pots was nearly the only warm place around. Cooks rushed to prepare the evening meal, their long hair wrapped in cloth. Some were stationed at enormous pots, standing on the brick stoves to stir vegetables stews. Others quickly fried gluten and more vegetables. A few tended to the ovens, for bread, not rice, was the staple in the area. Young novices fed the wood-burning fires.

Saihung carried a bowl of noodles and vegetables in one hand, a lantern in the other. It was a holy day, so the priests could not have any fish. Sometimes it seemed to the constantly hungry Saihung that there were all too many such festivals. He wanted to return to his hut and eat alone that night. By absorbing the quietness, he hoped to renew his efforts. Nearly every day he thought that he had the answer to satisfy his master, and each time he was rewarded with gentle chiding or a rebuke.

The room was bitterly cold. He lit an oil lamp and piled wood into the bronze brazier. As he was about to eat his meal, he was startled to see his master at the door. Saihung rushed to kneel. The Grand Master stepped lightly into the room. He was immaculate in his black robes.

The Grand Master stood for a while without saying anything. For long moments, Saihung felt as if there were no other presence in the world for him. He regretted that his grandfather was dead. He wished that his master were more like a grandfather, that there were more warmth and intimacy to their relationship. But in the temple, the roles of master and student were severely defined.

He was unaware how absorbed he had become until the Grand Master ended the long silence with an announcement.

"Your destiny is incomplete," declared his master. "You must not seek it here in China, but across the oceans."

Saihung was surprised at the abruptness of his master's pronouncement.

"Master, all I want is to serve you," he said.

"You cannot, yet. You must fulfill your quest."

"Then I'll do it and come quickly back," replied Saihung immediately.

"No. Don't come back."

Saihung was silent.

"I may not be here when you come back," added his master.

"What are you saying? Why won't you be here?"

"Don't question! Go out to fulfill your quest."

"But, Master! What is my task?" There was a tone of desperation in his voice.

"That is for you to find out," said his master firmly. "I know both the question and the answer. Do not return until you can tell me." The Grand Master turned and left.

A few moments passed before Saihung realized that he was sitting with his mouth agape. A burst of anger came up in him. He seized his bowl and flung it against the wall. He jumped up, staring angrily about, cornered. Saihung pulled the silver hairpin that pegged his hair and brought it before him.

Saihung punched the window open and threw the hairpin off the mountainside.

Chinese
of
Pittsburgh

S AIHUNG STOOD WITH a friend on the Sixth Street Bridge. The Allegheny River was below him, midnight reflections undulating on its inky surface. Central Pittsburgh, Pennsylvania, a dense pile of decaying brick buildings, was behind him. Cars rumbled steadily over the humpback span, shaking the girders and dirtying the snow that had fallen only recently. Saihung steadied himself against the stinging wind and gripped the twine handles of his shopping bag. Even with gloves on, the heavy groceries seemed to cut into his palm. His friend Sam Lee offered to help, but Saihung refused. This was the first time they had walked home together after work.

Sam was a slender man in his twenties. His Chinese name, Lee San, actually meant that he was the third child in his family, and the community had simply transliterated his name to an English one. He pulled a scarf more tightly around his neck. "Have you been in the United States long?" he asked.

"About two years," replied Saihung. It was 1953.

"Then you should have much experience with this country."

Saihung thought a moment. "No, I have never quite become used to this nation. The people are not always easy to understand. Some treat you well once you get to know them, but most can be mean. Everything is so different here." He wanted to add that he still felt frightened and lonely.

"Yes," agreed Sam. "It is a struggle to be here. This is not an easy life. One has to go where one can to make a living. I was just a farmer in the hills. If my uncle had not sponsored me, I might still be scrounging for a living in the villages."

Saihung had long ago made the decision to keep his past a secret. "Yes, me too. My uncle and aunt, the Yees, sponsored me here. Now I not only have to work to survive, but to repay and support them as well. They are getting old and have no one to help them."

"A Yee?" asked Sam with a rueful smile. "We're not supposed to be friends."

"My uncle and aunt aren't blood relatives," replied Saihung. "But I know that the Lees and Yees are sworn enemies."

"Oh, who knows why they fight?" said Sam. "I know only that my grandfather hated the Yees. No one actually remembers what the feud is about."

"This is America," said Saihung. "What difference does it make now?"

"Yes, that feud is a part of home," said Sam as he gazed across the river. "And home is very far away."

They stopped for a moment at the highest arch of the yellow-green suspension bridge. Lee was considerate enough to let Saihung pause in as much solitude as was available on a nighttime highway. He was good company, Saihung thought as they walked toward the North Shore where they both lived. Both had longing memories of home and hopes that were ill-defined dreams.

As he stood stoically over the water, he wanted to cry out, to lament in terrible tones to his heaven that was gone. Instead of living in his paradise, he was now an outcast. He felt hapless, wretched. He was condemned to wander in search of some un-named destiny.

He let out a silent sigh that registered as a cloud of breath before him. He had been exiled from Huashan with no further explanation or instructions.

"Are you thinking of General Yang?" asked Lee softly.

Saihung turned to look at him. Lee's thin and crooked face was made alternately pale and black by the passing headlights. He referred to a cook who worked with them. General Yang had introduced Saihung and Lee to each another.

"No," replied Saihung honestly. "I have always loved bridges. I like to look over them at the water. It always seems so peaceful."

"Ah, back home, the bridges are like that," agreed Lee. "Like the moon bridges, so perfectly round. I also liked to walk over them, especially when I was a boy. They told me that ghosts could not cross water. I liked that. It's a lie, though, isn't it?"

"Why talk this way?"

Lee looked at him with an expression at once terrible and sympathetic.

"Didn't you hear at work? General Yang killed himself last night. He jumped from this bridge—split his head on the river bottom."

He looked out at the rippling water. The news stunned Saihung as a dredging barge slid beneath them. The bridge was not that high. He wanted to say "No!" to the news, but he had learned to accept death silently, no matter how suffocating that was.

"It's hard to believe," said Saihung, gazing toward the point where the Allegheny joined the Ohio River. "One day a man is here, the next day he is gone. It's like a dream." He thought of Yang's military bearing, his pacing the kitchen as if he were still commanding the battlefield. "He lost too much," Saihung mused. "He lost his faith in a Nationalist China, lost his rank, lost his wife. He loved only gambling and his son."

"He died because of his son," said Lee quietly when Saihung finished his recollections. Saihung had seen a photo of the twenty-year-old, bespectacled youth. The picture had been like a votive object in the general's wallet.

"How could that be?"

"The son caught tuberculosis. He needed medical attention."

"He should have come to me."

"As if you're rich?" asked Lee sadly. "He had to raise more money than any of us have."

"What did he do?"

"Gambled," said Lee bluntly.

"Oh no." Saihung could see it coming.

"Yes," Lee continued. "He gambled all last night. He lost nearly all. He risked everything on the last gambit. He lost that too. Yang was so desperate that he even asked the dealers for a loan, some help. But you know how merciless gamblers are. They found him this morning. The family associations are going to take care of the funeral."

"It's a little late, isn't it?" said Saihung bitterly. "That money could have saved two men."

"They don't think that way." Sam shrugged as they started walking again.

They walked through a railroad underpass and crossed Sandusky Street at the corner of East Ohio. There was a soldier's monument on the corner. At the foot of the weathered marble were dozens of flowers—many artificial—and a brown, somewhat tattered, American flag. It was what might have passed for a roadside shrine in China, a place where he might have prayed. But there was no place here to pray for a man's soul.

He looked down East Ohio Street, the shopping thoroughfare for the neighborhood. It was a darkened corridor of brick buildings, mostly built in the late 1880s. They were cramped Victorian Gothics, sagging, holding each other up, sheltering dim and shabby storefronts, snow and shadow pooling deeply in the windows and doors. Most had ornate Romanesque decorations that had long ago lost their charm to the erosion of ice and time.

Saihung was still brooding about Yang when they came to Sandusky Park, a large, tree-scattered field about two blocks in area. On sunny days, he had sat there with Yang. Though the park was

357

nothing but bench, lawn, and tree, the two had tried to imagine a tranquillity beyond the roaring traffic.

The park was the interceding zone between the downtown area and their neighborhood. It was fastest to walk through the park. Saihung had never thought much of it. But Sam was suddenly nervous.

"Kwan, I did not tell you something," he told Saihung in a trembling voice.

"What do you mean?"

"Every night I am chased through this park. They beat me. I run all the way home, bar myself inside. They have painted my windows with tar, threatened to attack my wife."

"Calm down," said Saihung. "I see no one. Perhaps they won't come with two people."

"I hope so," said Lee dubiously. He anxiously lit a cigarette.

Tall leafless trees made the area gloomy. Cars drove by, but the traffic was not reassuring. Clearly, no one would get out of their cars to help if trouble came; perhaps they wouldn't even notice. The autos circled all four sides of the park. They were anonymous steel shells.

As Lee feared, three men awaited them. Saihung scanned their bodies by reflex. There was one large fat one, with greasy hair. The one standing in the middle was tall, heavily muscled across the chest and shoulders. The third was more lanky, but had the cruelest face. Saihung noted their characteristics with satisfaction. The key to his way of fighting was to ascertain all his opponents' weaknesses before words were spoken or blows exchanged.

"Hey, Chink! Brought a friend?" asked the tall one with a sardonic tilt of his head.

Saihung was quiet. He knew there was no way that Lee could understand what was being said to him. But threatening countenances were perhaps more traumatic than words.

"What's the matter, Chink? Cat got your tongue?" said the fat one.

"He doesn't understand you, stupid," returned the tall one. "Try ching-ching-chong-ding-dong!"

They laughed.

"Come here, Chinaman!" said the tall man, grabbing Lee by the shirt.

"Stop!" ordered Saihung, putting down his shopping bag.

"Shut up, asshole! We'll get you later."

Saihung liked to get close to someone when he fought. "I didn't hear," said Saihung, stepping right up to the man.

"Jesus Christ!" exclaimed the tall one. "This shithead doesn't know how to mind his own business!"

He let go of Lee and reached out to grab Saihung. Bringing his hand up to intercept, Saihung laid his wrist on top of his opponent's arm. One touch was all a good fighter needed to assess the strength of his adversary.

359

"Pretty bold, aren't you?" shouted the man.

Saihung said nothing. He only looked steadily back. His eyes did not blink, but his face changed. A look of hunger and eagerness came over him. He was like a predator looking at a tiny victim.

"Hey, dumb shit," continued the man threateningly, "I'm going to wipe that stupid look right off your face."

"I don't think so," replied Saihung as his eyes opened in anticipation.

The instant that he felt movement, Saihung's forward hand struck the tall man's abdomen with a blow so violent that it doubled him over. Saihung followed with a rapid blow to the neck. The muscular man staggered forward, gasping for air.

The others came at him, but Saihung used the first as a shield. Dazed, the cruel man was easily maneuvered. Saihung did not drop him until he had taken a good many fists and sticks from his companions.

Saihung dispatched the fat one with a rapid knee to the bladder followed by a blow to the heart. A thrill, a power, surged through Saihung. He stepped head-on as the hard-faced one charged again. Saihung blocked his blow and hit him hard in the ribs. Stepping behind him, he brought an elbow down. A satisfying thud smashed his opponent to the ground, but the man got up immediately.

"I'm going to kill you!" he cried.

Saihung stepped back. "Listen. I let you get up. That's a first for me. If you come again, I'm putting you in the hospital!"

"You full-of-shit-motherfucker!"

He tried to ram Saihung with a head-butt. Saihung side-stepped and brought a forearm into the midsection. Elbow around the neck, Saihung threw him again onto the ice-layered cement. A kick brought the snap of cracking ribs.

The tall one grabbed a stick and brought it through the air. Saihung whirled around. He blocked the arm while it was still up and brought his knee up, stooping the man over. Two quick combinations brought a spray of teeth and blood.

He fell on Saihung, panting and heaving. By reflex, Saihung would normally have struck him ten more times before his assailant hit the pavement. Instead, he caught him involuntarily.

So adept at improvising movement, so sharp were his abilities, that his touch instantly registered numerous options for further mauling the man. He paused. The jaw, against his bicep, was slack. Blood and spit blotted through his sleeve. The head felt surprisingly heavy. Here was a man. His to kill.

For the sake of women, children, and his homeland, he had gladly volunteered for war, willing to accept that consequence. As for martial duels, he and his opponents both acknowledged death as an integral part of the arrangement. There was a certain nobility and honor to his fighting. But here, there were only racist bigots, idiots. He disdained them. There was no glory in killing them. Saihung threw the man down and found the shaken and pallid Lee.

"We won't mention this, will we?" said Saihung.

"No! No!" agreed Lee hoarsely. "I hope this ends it. I had no idea you could fight."

"Forget it," said Saihung. "A little exercise before bed is healthy."

Saihung saw Lee to the door of his home before walking the three more blocks to his home. Though the fever to fight had worn off, he still thought about his confrontation. There was nothing heroic or principled about this type of fighting. He had not changed anyone's mind, had not remedied anything. It had simply been a primitive assertion of will. But worse than regret for the battle, he disliked being forced to consider issues never mentioned in scripture, sermon, or even in politics. Frankly, he had had few decisions to make on Huashan, and he liked that. The masters made all the decisions. They knew what was right and wrong. But since he had left China, he had had to make all his own decisions and make judgments with no precedents in his life.

360

S AIHUNG RETURNED TO the park the next day, on his way to Chinatown for supplies. There was no sign of his nocturnal struggle. He watched a few mothers escorting warmly dressed children to the park's community center and then went directly to the bridge. Walking southward through the main business district, he came to the settlement situated on the north and south sides of a small rectangular block. A few buildings faced onto Third Street, dwarfed by the height of the imposing Grant Building, and a few more faced south on the next street over, their view of the Monongahela River obscured by the wedge of a highway on-ramp.

361

The one single building identifiable as "Chinese" was the headquarters for the Peaceful Harmony Labor Organization, a three-story brownstone with fake tile roofs and wooden balconies that echoed the buildings of Canton. A Chinese restaurant on the ground floor proclaimed itself to be "Chinatown Inn." Beneath it was the single word "Cuisine."

A few doors down was Big Mrs. Lee's store, New Horizons. It was a four-story nineteenth-century brick building that had housing for old, unmarried men. New Horizons was the only place to go if he wanted to buy tofu, dried goods, herbs, or preserves from China. Mrs. Lee imported Chinese vegetables from New York. These were usually frozen or wilted, but they still satisfied the craving for familiar flavors. They were displayed in the crates that they had arrived in, propped open in front of the store. Saihung took two brown paper bags off an iron rack and began to pick some snow peas and cabbage.

At the front of the store was the cash register. Mr. Lee, a slender, bespectacled man with graying hair, was stationed there. He was slow-moving, his mind always on some abstract thought. He had been a scholar, and still loved to discuss the classics with the men, or his children with the women. He boasted endlessly about his son the doctor, his favorite married daughter, how well the younger ones were doing in school. He still retained the romantic notion that business was an improper activity for an academic man. Accordingly, he could neither add nor subtract. The shrewd Mrs. Lee rushed to wait on Saihung as soon as he entered the store. She was terrified that her husband would err at the cash register, as always, in favor of the customer.

Mrs. Lee was fat and fair-skinned, a woman with a golden smile. By design or poor health, every tooth in her mouth was pure gold, accentuated by crimson lipstick. Her hair was perfectly coiffed in a permanent wave. Her friends would come to pay homage to her every week, and comment on her good health. She would only reply with uncharacteristic self-deprecation that she was overweight. They would always say it was because she was blessed with fortune and happiness. Mrs. Lee was landlady, proprietor, mother, helpful savior, and, of course, town gossip.

362

There were no oracles in Pittsburgh, but near or far, she seemed to know everything as it happened. Marriages, births, affairs, deaths, hidden secrets, were all parts of her oral history. She talked constantly with the old women who sat in rosewood chairs at the side of the store. In winter, they warmed themselves by a wood stove. In summer, they languidly cooled themselves with eagle-feather fans. Their discussions formed a constant commentary on community events.

As he shopped, Saihung could hear Big Mrs. Lee and her chorus gossip.

"Did you hear about the poor boy drowned by his university classmates?" Saihung heard one woman ask another.

"Yes, that was Fifth Lee's son," replied another. "It's a tragedy! He received scholarships to engineering school. They were obviously jealous."

Big Mrs. Lee stopped weighing Saihung's vegetables.

"Shouldn't someone go to the police?"

"They won't take the word of Chinese over whites," said Saihung.

"That's true, Ox Boy," said Mrs. Lee, using the nickname the community had given the muscular Saihung. "Still, it's terrible. He had so much promise. The companies would have hired him right out of school. Imagine! A Lee! A professional!"

"But dead," said one of the old women bluntly. "Stupid kid! He was so excited when they invited him to a picnic. What a fool to go boating with them when he knew that he could not swim."

Mrs. Lee returned to Saihung's vegetables. "Tragic! Tragic!"

She bagged all of Saihung's purchases and looked at him.

"Don't you be so trusting," she told him.

"I'm not that way," replied Saihung.

"Oh yes, we've all heard about you." Mrs. Lee smiled.

"What do you mean?"

"We all know how you defended Sam, the dishwasher," said Mrs. Lee admiringly.

"Please don't mention it," said Saihung, blushing.

"You're too modest!" she exclaimed, slapping his arm insinuatingly. Saihung retreated in embarrassment. It was one thing to knock men to the ground. It was another to face the talkative Mrs. Lee.

363

Saihung left the store cursing the dishwasher. Everyone thought that martial artists were heroes. Children wanted to emulate them; older people looked upon them as knights for a cause. But he himself knew that being a martial artist was no easy matter. He had sustained many injuries over the years, blows that had distorted his body, struggles that had tired him to the soul. He had paid a high price to reach the point where a brawl in the park was an easy matter.

He walked back toward the Sixth Street Bridge. The afternoon was graying toward a chilly evening. The air was thick with dust, coal, smoke, car exhaust, and oddly enough, the smell of catsup; the Heinz 57 factory was on the North Shore. Snow was bright on the railings, dirty on the ground. The street lamps, rusted stalks, had not been lit.

He stopped in the twilight to read the bronze plaque on the courthouse that was inscribed with the Pledge of Allegiance. The Constitution, Declaration of Independence, Pledge of Allegiance, and the history of the Revolutionary and Civil Wars had all influenced him to emigrate to the United States. He had pictured dense forests stretching to the ocean shores, distant mountains of lofty magnificence, Native Americans of all the different tribes, people dressed in colonial costume as well as the modern clothes that he had seen in movies. As he thought over his fight and the drowning, the last line of the Pledge took on a new irony.

He wondered if he had made the wrong decision to come to the United States. He was in a huge, grim city dominated by the sound and smoke of steel mills, walking on paved streets beside cars, living in squat, geometric buildings that had arteries of galvanized plumbing and nerves of electric wire. There was no place in the city for jade, silk gowns, books written on delicate mulberry paper, fans with calligraphy, proud horses, or flutes of purple bamboo. All that he had of himself was in his heart, or locked in a chest at home, or to be shared with a few acquaintances.

Saihung walked down East Ohio Street to a black-painted entrance of Romanesque columns and an archway, and climbed the stairs to a small second-floor room. There were a few vinyl booths and a diner-style counter with stools. The chrome edges and stool supports were tarnished; the upholstery repaired here and there with plastic tape. The ancient clock had a yellow film over it, and its tail of electric cord was twisted and cracking. As usual, there were no customers.

A short man in his fifties greeted him. Uncle Feng was like a fireplug on legs. His neck was thick and stiff, and it supported a balding head with a face interested purely in expediency. He was dressed in white cook's clothes. Short sleeves showed heavy forearms and rough, thick-fingered hands abundantly scarred from cuts and burns. Uncle Feng wasn't actually his relative; it was just how a younger man addressed an older one. Saihung was glad to know some people who represented something familiar, and he could not be comfortable with the gabbing women at New Horizons.

"Hey, Ox Boy! It's cold outside!" said Uncle Feng.

"Yes, it is," replied Saihung, wondering about the Chinese habit of greeting others by announcing the obvious.

"Come in, and take your coat off," said Uncle Feng as he walked back into the kitchen. Saihung could hear something sizzling in the wok.

Saihung hung his things on one of the antlerlike metal coatracks and followed his host.

"Old Poon is late as usual," grumbled Feng. "He's never on time. And I have made some of the finest delicacies from our home province. Here. Help me cut some vegetables."

Saihung picked up a cleaver and stationed himself at a chopping block that was a simple cross section of a log. He quickly sliced carrots, celery, cabbage, and chard. In the meantime, Uncle Feng began cooking at a wok fired by leaping flames. His spatula beat a quick cadence on the iron. The vegetables in the pan roared like firecrackers when water hit the hot oil. Oil, wine, and soy were his main seasonings, and he produced beautiful dishes glistening with just the right amount of sauce.

Within twenty minutes, they sat down to a feast of catfish steamed with black beans, a crispy fried chicken, sauteed scallops with vegetables, braised pork, and hot steamed rice. Saihung shared everything but the pork. This always provoked a comment from Uncle Feng.

365

"A man who never eats pork! It's abnormal!"

Saihung only shrugged as he ate mouthful after mouthful of the fragrant and juicy food. No one knew he was a Taoist. Only he knew why he practiced certain restrictions.

Uncle Feng filled a glass with Johnny Walker. He motioned to Saihung to have a drink, though by now both knew it to be formality.

"I get tipsy," Saihung explained ineffectively.

"Youngster!" Feng laughed. "That's okay. There's just more for me and Old Poon."

There was a noise at the stairs.

"That must be the bastard now," said Feng, his face beginning to redden from the liquor.

"Did you two begin eating without me?" bellowed a voice from the door.

"You never eat with us anyway!" retorted Feng with the voice of an insulted cook.

"Huh! It's just that I have my preferences." There was the noise of a bicycle kickstand.

"Don't mar the walls!"

"Relax before you have a heart attack!"

Uncle Poon came charging up the stairs. Though he was nearly sixty-five and white-haired, he was straight-backed and vital. He made his living as a mover. Heavyset, he had large hands that he usually kept at his side as if at attention. He had been a seaman most of his life, and his expertise with knots made him one of the most sought-after men among the Chinese of Pittsburgh. Whenever anyone sent a box or trunk to China, it was Uncle Poon who bound it with manila rope. Saihung had seen him carry a steamer trunk on his back, and there was almost nothing he couldn't move with ropes, levers, or most frequently, his own brawn.

His pants were held up by a length of rope, and he wore the same wool coat in summer or winter. It was long, with the eccentric tailoring of many odd pockets sewn to the interior. These pockets might hold a slip of paper, a bit of twine, sometimes even a coin, but they were usually empty.

366

He came to the table and pulled his coat back to display his muscular girth. His head was as massive as an elephant skull, his skin brown, tight, and shiny. Incongruously, he had a tiny mouth and delicate wire-rimmed glasses balanced crookedly around his wide face.

"So why are you late?" mumbled Feng.

"I was held up," said Poon in English.

"Held up doing what?" asked Saihung.

"No, not held up, busy. I mean *held up*."

"You mean you were robbed?" asked Saihung with concern.

"Yes!" roared Uncle Poon with a knowing look at Feng. "After all, I'm old and yellow-skinned. Those American boys think I'm an easy target!"

Saihung smiled. He knew Uncle Poon was a veteran of waterfront brawls.

"So what happened?" asked Saihung obligingly.

"He stopped me as I was getting on my bicycle. He wanted my money. He had a knife."

"Stupid kid," muttered Feng.

"So I stood with my arms out. That idiot went through every one of my pockets—and even *I'm* not sure how many pockets are in this thing."

Uncle Poon paused dramatically, as if to give his two friends time to mentally tabulate the possible number of his pockets.

"He was mad when he was all done. Then I smashed him! I just made some dentist rich," Uncle Poon concluded as he walked into the kitchen. He shot out a fist the size of an anvil. Uncle Feng began laughing with delight.

Saihung and Uncle Feng returned to their dinner as they heard Poon light the burner. He had his own peculiarities in eating. Uncle Poon loved to eat something never gotten in China: T-bone steak. He heated the wok until it was smoking, quickly poured oil in, and threw the big piece of meat down. He seared it quickly over high heat, turned it over, and it was done.

Uncle Poon came to the table with the sizzling hot steak, rice, and a few seared vegetables. He poured some catsup and steak sauce and immediately attacked with knife and fork. Hot blood ran over his plate, staining the rice red. The steak was not rare. It was warm and raw.

"Barbarian!" said Feng disgustedly.

"Just pour the whiskey, you old miser!"

Feng did so, taking the opportunity to fill his own glass again.

"I'll have to catch up," commented Uncle Poon.

"Don't worry," replied Uncle Feng. "You can drink Ox Boy's share."

Poon quickly devoured the steak with great pleasure. "Ahh, except for steak, I wish I was back in Foshan," said Uncle Poon.

"Oh, the food in Foshan, Ox Boy. You've never tasted anything like it!" agreed Uncle Feng.

Saihung thought back over the many banquets and feasts he had tasted in rooms of sandalwood. Yes, Cantonese food was delicious, he acknowledged. Hadn't Emperor Qianlong disguised himself just to travel and taste southern cooking?

"Yes!" said Uncle Poon enthusiastically when Saihung mentioned the emperor's name.

"That Emperor was smart. And he was a good fighter too!"

"But cruel," interjected Feng. "After all he burned down Shaolin!"

Saihung immersed himself in sentiment as the old men drank. Where was the China of pageantry and beauty? Where was his master, his temple, his classmates? Where was the life he had aspired to, the life of wandering in a landscape thick with webs of historical association? In China, any given spot might hold tales both real and mythological. There might be stories of friendship, a famous duel, a spot where a god had come to earth, a place where lovers had met, a river where dragons slept.

"I'm old," said Feng as he got more drunk. "But if I could, I'd go back."

"I wouldn't," announced Uncle Poon firmly. "I'd be even poorer in China."

"Would you go back, Kwan?" asked Feng.

367

"I don't know." How could he tell them he had a quest to fulfill?

"Why don't you go back? Get married."

"Married?" Saihung smiled. "I'm not the type."

"Every man is the type!" Feng laughed.

"Well, you two are single," retorted Saihung.

"You think it's so easy in this country?" asked Feng.

"It doesn't matter," said Poon glumly. "Too old. Too poor. Too ugly. If one had even one saving quality, it would be all right. For example, if you're rich, you could buy a bride no matter how old and ugly you were. But us? As they say"—and here he switched to English—"three strikes and you're out!"

They all laughingly agreed.

"So did you just come to get rich, like all of us?" Feng asked Saihung.

"Well, I heard America was a different country," replied Saihung honestly.

"Different than what?" asked Poon in a perplexed voice.

"I read the Constitution and the Declaration of Independence. I thought it would be a wonderful place."

"Stupid idealistic bookworm!" cursed Feng.

Uncle Poon drained his glass. "Well, I certainly hope you got those notions out of your head!"

"You're drunk!" warned Feng.

"I am not!" insisted Poon. "And anyway, does that invalidate what I've said?"

"Ox Boy here is sensitive and idealistic," returned Feng. "Why spoil it?"

"So he reads books." Poon shrugged. "I'm trying to give him a real education."

"Suit yourself," said Feng. "I'm going to do the dishes."

Uncle Poon turned shakily toward Saihung. He leaned over close enough for his scotch breath to roar across the table.

"Let me tell you what a Caucasian man once told me," said Uncle Poon forcefully. "Ten Chinaman aren't as good as one nigger!' You know how they treat blacks. Guess the rest!"

Saihung only smiled and poured more whiskey for Poon. Perhaps it was inevitable that drunken gatherings always turned ugly. He picked up his dishes and helped Feng with the dishes before he ventured into the night frost. Saihung was still young enough to dismiss Poon's remark as mere cynicism.

S AIHUNG LIVED WITH his aunt and uncle a few blocks away from Feng's on Foreland Street, in the eastern half of a sagging wooden duplex. Two stories high, with attic and gables, it had been built after the Civil War, and its yellow paint had never been renewed. Saihung walked up the few steps to the door and inserted his key into the nearly useless lock. Warm air flowed at him from the dark hallway. That was the nice thing about staying with retired people, he thought. They kept the house a comfortable temperature.

369

He hung up his outer clothing and crept down the hall as quietly as possible. His aunt and uncle had their bedroom on the first floor. There was nothing else on the main floor but a small shrine to Guan Yin, the Goddess of Mercy. The original house was one-room deep, with the kitchen in an added-on section. In fact, the rear of the house was of several different supplemental structures, all added at various occasions with no regard to the surrounding architecture.

He walked into the kitchen, no longer noticing how its floor tilted at an angle different from the hall. Thoughtfully, his aunt had left a table lamp lit in the kitchen, and Saihung headed toward the slit of yellow light showing through the partially opened door. He smiled. The couple had surely argued about the cost of electricity versus the meaning of a gesture.

The kitchen was painted yellow over often-repaired plaster. The huge, streamlined white-enameled stove and refrigerator dominated the square room. Pink and green countertops were cluttered with tins of flour, tea, and other goods. In a corner, on the green linoleum floor, sat a twenty-five-gallon glass jar filled with rice.

Saihung put some water on the stove to boil, watching the flower of blue flame bloom with a *poof* under the old steel kettle. He reminded himself to grab it off the burner before its indecent whistle shocked the neighborhood.

As he turned toward the Formica table with its chrome legs, he noticed an envelope. There on the thin paper was his master's familiar calligraphy, along with a shaky English address written by someone else. He sat down to read it. He was careful: The kitchen chairs were some modern zigzag S-shape of chrome tubing and red-vinyl-covered plywood. He was forever in danger of pitching back in the silly things.

The letter was short:

> *I am leaving the mountain.*
> *Come back to help.*

It ended with the official seal of the abbot of Huashan.

Saihung put the letter down. His master's calligraphy was as beautiful as ever, but he was not impressed by the message. His first reaction was that he would go immediately. His second thought was: Why should I? After all, he still felt a little hurt. They had raised him from a youth but had pushed him out when he had most wanted guidance. He had the jealous suspicion that his master's acolytes and his other classmates were all learning the secrets of immortality while he was waiting on tables in some chop-suey house.

He read the letter again. It wasn't all that easy to travel to the other side of the world. It wasn't cheap; it wasn't quick; and it wouldn't necessarily be a happy reunion.

Saihung opened the back door to the garden and stepped through the black opening. The neighbor's dog barked immediately. A soft moonlight fell on the worn wooden porch. The house seemed to hold years of melancholy. He descended the cracked and moaning steps.

The midnight cold stung him. His skin contracted involuntarily with the shock, and he could feel the blood flood his cheeks as his body made an effort to maintain its warmth. The snow beneath his feet crunched with each step. He stuck his hands into his pockets.

The garden was small, just the leftover space after the haphazard additions to the duplex. There was a lawn in the summer that was usually brown from the southern exposure; but now it was covered with a three-foot layer of frosty white. In the middle of the expanse was the skeleton of a peach tree. Saihung had planted it there when he had first moved to the city. Still barely beyond a sapling, it stood straight but lonely in the snow.

There was not a leaf on it. From the outside, he might not have even been able to tell that it was alive. It seemed dead, withered, cold. No buds showed; not even an insect crawled on the nude branches. There was no way to know whether it was going to survive the winter. Spring might come, and it might still stand there just as forlorn and devoid of life. If it sprouted again, it meant that this botanical corpse had enough consciousness to have patience. There was faith that it would survive the winter, that it could even forego its life-supporting leaves in the knowledge that light and warmth would come again.

371

He asked himself if he should go back. Perhaps if he were back in an intact China, he would have consulted a fortune-teller or cast the yarrow stalks of the *I Ching*. But he was without such crutches. He had to do what the elders had taught him to do since childhood: read the patterns in nature. A tree stood on a spot of power. Its branches took on their formation for a reason. They reached out to the power spots in the atmosphere. Thus, one could "read" a tree. It had lessons to give, even power to transmit. Its branches were calligraphy. He stood in the dim moonlight, looking at the apparently dead tree. He thought of his own desperation, his own resentment of being separated from Huashan. Somewhere in all this madness, this working in restaurants, this being attacked, this living in a foreign land, was supposed to be some answer for him. He had believed that there would be a key of reason that would illuminate all his strivings.

Saihung thought back over his fight in the park. He wondered how long it would be before he would start thinking like everyone else. Drink. Gamble. Get married. Beat up on others until someone stronger brings you down. He had been raised with the ultimate goals of education, wealth, and spirituality. That still did not guarantee that he could live gently and grow. He had been provided with philosophy and guidance, had known whisperings from divine voices. Now, those were swept away by profanity and trauma.

He reached out and touched a branch. He had started out from something small, had been but a seedling. Had his master not nurtured him and pruned him and cared for him, he would never have reached this point. His master had sent him into the world. Saihung resented it. But he remembered the old expression: The seedling does not grow tall in the shadow of a larger tree.

He went back inside without expression. The dog barked again. Saihung turned out the light and climbed the stairs to his room. He took a shower, washing his crew-cut hair.

As he prepared for sleep, he looked at the letter again. Going back to China was not going to be salvation. It was going back to run an errand. Still, as much as he half resented his master for propelling him on these wanderings, he knew he would go back.

The
End of
Huashan

S AIHUNG TRAVELED FROM Pittsburgh to San Francisco by train, crossed the Pacific on the American President Line's SS *President Wilson*, went quickly through Hawaii, Yokohama, Hong Kong. A boat to Guangdong, and a series of train rides first through the province of Jiangsi, then the cities of Hangzhou and Xian, took him hundreds of miles into the interior. He crossed nearly the whole of Shaanxi Province by rail to reach the foot of Huashan. It was spring of 1954. Travel was slow, and it wasn't easy.

He gave himself all sorts of excuses during the month-long journey. He would be seeing Huashan again. Worship at all the old places. Get away from America. Maybe save some sacred books, find secrets in some forgotten manual. It would have been proper for him to return out of unselfish devotion. He reminded himself of loyalty and duty. He hoped he was not returning because of sentiment, or nostalgia, or love. That wasn't supposed to enter into the master-student equation.

It took him more than four weeks to reach Huayin train station from Pittsburgh. The tiny station seemed shabby, dirty, and poor. Certainly, compared to the terminals in the West, it was a mere ticket booth and turnstile. But it was the first tangible sight of the familiar place where so many of his past journeys had begun and ended. Beyond the crumbling building, Huashan rose up in expansive and grand proportions. Its lower flanks were hidden in cloud; it might have been an island floating in heaven.

Living rock. Pure water. Pines that reached inspiringly upward. For the first time, his perspective included his experiences in the United States. There was no immigrant struggle here, no thought of family life, no fighting with midnight hoodlums. Only rock, water, trees, and light.

As he reached the summit of Huashan, he recognized uneasily that the mountain itself had changed. There were dramatically fewer monks. No one stood guard at the gates, no one cultivated the fields, no one attended the altars. The ridges were eerily deserted; buildings and pavilions were abandoned. The legendary hoofprints of Lao Tzu's ox had been chiseled away. Soldiers had invaded the mountain only two months before, forbidding ceremonies, desecrating shrines, sending monks away. Huashan had not been invulnerable to political power, or the barrels of guns.

The uninhabited temples were already crumbling from disuse. Some had been wrecked by vandals. Halls once fragrant with sandalwood incense now smelled of urine. Offerings of flowers and fruit lay withered on bloodied altars. Gods had been smashed or shot or stolen. Walls where holy song had once reverberated were now covered with obscene graffiti. The shrine of Lu Tungpin the Immortal, a small brick building with slender columns, was battered open. Doors lay splintered in the dust. The life-sized figure with its face of pale marble and royal robes of silk was gone. Sculpted eaves had been broken off, gilded fig-

374

urines with gold and pearl dresses had been stolen, stone like-
nesses of mountain gods, sacredly nameless, had been cata-
logued for museums.

He found a tattered poster, a political diatribe against religion,
an appeal to join the glorious revolution. Shell casings littered
the floor. Charred furniture lay in the courtyards.

Had he not come himself, he would never have accepted that
this rare and extraordinary sanctuary was fading with barely a
trace of notice by the outer society. Huashan had been, for him, a
near utopia. How shocking to realize that human troops could
march into heaven and turn it into something earthly, vulnerable—a minor bit of history to be concealed by petty bureaucrats
and never learned by schoolchildren.

Saihung trudged past the Jade Maiden Peak, through the last
narrow canyon that led to his master's temple. When he got to
the walls of the compound, the gates had been left strangely
open. Saihung went into the littered courtyard, where a bronze
incense burner had been overturned. He saw several pairs of
shoes and, finding it odd, went closer to inspect. Inside he found
sheets of paper with writing. The soldiers had torn holy writings
apart, had placed them in the shoes, and had forced monks to
walk on the words that they most revered.

He ran up the steps to the main hall, hopeful that his master
had escaped injury. The Grand Master was capable of many unusual things, but Saihung knew that resisting gunfire was not one
of them. He went into the deserted building, ignored the dese-
cration of his childhood holy environment, and called loudly for
his master. He was relieved when the Grand Master walked quietly out, his two acolytes standing behind him.

His master walked unbent. His silver hair was impeccably
combed, his face calm and dignified. He looked at Saihung
steadily, wordlessly, as the light caught his eyes. The middle-aged
acolytes, their hair beginning to gray, looked pale and anxious.

"Master, I'm back," said Saihung as he knelt upon the stone
floor. Saihung indicated gifts that he had brought, but the old
man regarded them indifferently.

"There's no longer a need," said his master with a graceful
wave of his long sleeves. "The world has changed."

"Are you unhurt?" Saihung shifted a little in place. He had not been on his knees like this for years.

"Don't worry." His master smiled bravely. "I've seen dynasties and nations fall."

"But this is different. It's a way of life. It's Taoism." Saihung frowned.

"Everything has its time. Then it must move aside for the next stage. The Tao is creative and relentless. The circle goes on. It cannot be resisted."

Saihung stood up and greeted them. He looked at their traditional robes. He was a shocking contrast in his Western clothes, short hair, and sneakers. His master was quick to notice his thoughts.

"Even you've changed," commented the Grand Master.

"But not inside, Master!" said Saihung with emotion.

"Inside?" queried the master, smiling slightly for the first time. "You still need to clarify that."

Saihung was silent.

"If the Tao changes, so will you," continued his master. "Accept that. I've always told you: Your destiny will lead you on many distant journeys."

"I wish I could come back here." Even with the carnage, he was glad to be with the men who had raised him, who represented nearly infallible wisdom.

"There is no Tao here. Taoism is dead."

Saihung was stunned.

"The Tao is eternal." The Grand Master looked at him dispassionately. "But the Taoism I practice has been destroyed. They've forbidden me even to meditate, and they would rather I died. But I will not go so easily. If I die, it will be my way. That choice is still open to me."

"Is spirituality at an end?" asked Saihung.

"As I know it, it is," replied his master. "But the Tao continues on. It is still something for you to follow."

The master turned away, and the acolytes followed in automatic unison. It seemed to Saihung that the old man was always turning his back to leave. For once, though, Saihung regarded this odd habit with some sympathy. His master evidently felt comfortable enough to indulge in old habits. It was a silent approval, for he knew Saihung would arrange things.

"Go with your brothers," said the Grand Master from the door. "Prepare for our departure."

Saihung turned to the two acolytes, Mist Through a Grove and Sound of Clear Water, and they bowed to each other solemnly. But as soon as the Grand Master was gone, they smiled broadly and welcomed him. Saihung was quizzical. It always seemed that the acolytes laughed whenever they saw him.

"How is it in America?" asked Sound of Clear Water excitedly. "Is it true that the streets are paved with gold and that everyone there is rich and happy?"

"Yes, is it true?" said Mist Through a Grove. "Though I hear that some of the Westerners can be quite savage: They have the tails of foxes, and they eat their young!"

Saihung looked at his elder brothers with amazement. They had once been his tutors, and he had been the naive one. Now, the situation was the opposite. What could he tell them? How could he say that he lived in a country that barely tolerated yellow-skinned people and had places just as desperately poor as China?

"It's not like that, brothers," said Saihung gently. "There is no gold in the streets. The place is like here. Everywhere, people are rich and people are poor. The United States is no different."

The two acolytes looked confused. Saihung realized that they had never seen a newsreel, never heard a radio, never read the newspaper. They were true renunciates, innocent and pure. He felt dirty next to them, but somehow he did not regret it. He felt it better to see the world even if it soiled him. Being so innocent would have made him feel insecure.

"I'll tell you about my experiences," said Saihung. "But I have come a long distance and have climbed all the way up this mountain."

Sound of Clear Water rolled his eyes at Saihung's pleading look. "Have we ever known you not to be hungry?"

"Coming back makes me comfortable," joked Saihung.

"Come on, Little Butterfly," said Mist Through a Grove. "We kept some steamed bread on the stove."

After snacking with the acolytes, Saihung went to his master's chambers to estimate the scope of work to be done. He walked into the rough and tiny cell. Whitewashed walls reflected a soft and gloomy light onto the dusty tile floor. The only furniture left behind by the soldiers was a meditation platform and a desk. Both were too big to carry down the mountain. They would also have to leave them. All that would go would be small personal items. The Grand Master designated a few clothes, his books, robes, a prayer rug, and a carved wooden statuette of his personal deity as the only things that he wanted.

378

Saihung left his master and went down the trail to see how his meditation hut had withstood the invasion. The small whitewashed building was still standing on the cliff's edge. He went in, picked up a table that had been knocked over, and sat down on the cold brick bed. The floor was gritty under his feet from dirt that had blown in. Dead leaves lay withered in the corners. It was quiet. Not even the whisperings of the wind were audible.

He found it difficult to accept the impersonality of Huashan's demise. He looked toward the temple, where he once had directed his prayers.

He looked into himself, no longer with the formality of prayer rug and pyramidical meditation posture. Had he been able to pit his might against soldiers, the alienation he now felt would have been forestalled. Even defeat was better to him than this mute necessity to accept circumstances. At least that would have been personal, more like the essence of the old order, where supplies were carried up the mountain by men, craftsmen made wares by hand, and painting, poetry, song, calligraphy, were all individual endeavors, and even a duel had an opponent to whom one was introduced.

But the modernity that had finally swallowed Huashan was faceless.

THE DAY OF their departure was cold and clear. There was snow in patches, and small icicles dangled in the blue shadows of trees. The wind blew steadily across the pale sky; the distant rivers were lost in haze. The four of them walked calmly out of the monastery walls. The Grand Master was borne by porters and a sedan chair; his students followed on foot. No one was there to see them off, or secure the broken gates.

Saihung and the two acolytes each carried backpacks of clothing and a few possessions. Their real problem was the master's wooden trunk. Saihung and Sound of Clear Water suspended it by a pole and carried it between them. But descending Huashan meant descending vertical towers of granite.

"You go first," Saihung said to Sound of Clear Water. He let the acolyte lower himself hand-over-hand down an oxidized chain.

"I am at the next section," the acolyte called back in a while. Slowly, Saihung lowered the trunk by rope, the wood banging against the stone, the rope burning his palms. He thought of Uncle Poon, and wished that the old man were there to tie the ropes.

The trunk pulled at him, and his arms and shoulders ached from the load. He looked up, blinking to keep the sweat out of his eyes, saw only blue sky.

"I've got it!" The rope suddenly went slack, and Saihung leaned back against a boulder in relief. He glanced at his master, merely a dark profile in a sedan chair. Mist Through a Grove, standing with the porters, urged Saihung to go on.

Saihung tied his pack on and swung himself down the chain. He scrambled toward the trunk that was a mere speck below him. The next one to descend was Mist Through a Grove, and finally, the Grand Master in his sedan chair. If he was frightened to be suspended over a gorge by ropes and the brawn of four porters, he gave no sign. Saihung watched anxiously as the fragile wooden container brought his master down the first cliff of the mountain. They would have to repeat the procedure over and over again before they would reach less dangerous heights.

Lingering ice made their job all the more dangerous. Both the porters and Saihung had to brace themselves against whatever tree or outcropping was available; sometimes, they even tied themselves to chains and iron pegs to prevent plunging thousands of feet.

It was afternoon before they reached the pavilions where pilgrims had once paused to have meals and tea. Halfway down the mountain, they stopped at one of these places so that the bearers could renew themselves. The Grand Master walked to the edge of the terrace with Saihung. Below them was the rushing river that had its source on the South Peak.

"The Tao is like that river." The Grand Master gestured toward the cataracts. "But don't think that following merely means drifting."

380   He reached out and pointed to the water. Below them, the stream continued to flow downward. There were rocks that had barred its way for centuries. It overran them and continued its course. "What if that rock was not there?" continued the Grand Master. "Then the course would change. What if we place more rocks in the path of the water? The course would change again. Sometimes we can change the course of things merely by removing or placing obstacles. Sometimes, when confronted with obstacles, we must go around them and adapt."

The Grand Master reached out again, but this time toward Saihung. He blessed him. Saihung glanced briefly at the man he most cherished in the world, and for a moment he felt the normally stoic master smile at him in benediction. It was the last time that they would stand together on Huashan.

As they waited at the train station, his master never turned to look at Huashan again. They boarded the train crowded with gawking peasants, ducks and pigs, and rude conductors. His master was firmly silent.

They took a train to Beijing, a journey that would take them days on the inefficient train system. Though it had been frigid on the mountaintop, it was just beginning to warm on the plains. Trees had sprouted their season's leaves; peasants were already at work cultivating the fields. The fields outside Beijing were flat and the crops meager. There were signs left from the war; some buildings still lay blasted apart, bomb craters had become fish ponds. About fifty miles from the capital they got off the train and were met at the station by an old bespectacled man and his servants.

"Master! Master! How good to see you!" said the thin man eagerly.

"Not at all, old friend. It's kind of you to extend your hospitality," replied the Grand Master.

Mr. Chen was a wealthy scholar, a retired professor from Nanjing University who had been an admirer of the Grand Master for many decades. He had a villa outside Beijing and, for the moment, was still lucky enough to have property and servants. His spacious mansion was the epitome of the scholar's home: oriented to the south, high garden walls, meticulously pruned trees and flowers, graceful architecture of carved eaves and peaked tile roofs. He led them to a guest house just beyond a gazebo and an enormous reflecting pool. The Grand Master was welcome to stay there as long as he liked.

The sky began to cloud over until it was an opaque gray. From horizon to horizon, it obscured the sun and sky. A harsh north wind blew into the pavilions, shaking the budding willows. The streams and ponds shivered with ripples.

A few heavy drops came on the crest of the next windy wave. As the Grand Master and the two acolytes walked beneath a covered garden path, their robes fluttered like flags on a mountain peak. Saihung pulled his coat around him, even as he carried the trunk. The sudden arctic temperature made his face pale.

The guest house was nearly as cold as Huashan, although it was much more ornate in its appointments. The plaster walls were painted a pale lavender, and the sandalwood lattice windows were a warm accent. Heavy, elaborately carved rosewood furniture stood around the room. The scholar's own paintings of peonies decorated the walls. Saihung and Sound of Clear Water set the Grand Master's trunk down on the thick carpet. That was all there was to represent their beloved mountain.

The rain became a heavy downpour, sending unbroken rivulets streaming off the eaves. The constant percussion became a loud hiss. The plants of the scholar's garden did not endure the beating unbroken. Leaves and buds, never fully opened, fell to the ground and drifted forlornly in the black puddles.

Saihung walked down the outside portico, watching the curtain of rain, the slashing white of falling drops. Water was pure, his masters said. It washed away evil, and evil could not cross a running stream. Water washed the body. Water nourished the body. Water, in its patterns, formed an endless cursive calligraphy full of messages for the wise.

He walked back to the guest house and found his master also staring at the garden. The intricate lattice cast an indistinct lace of shadows on his face.

"It's done," murmured his master softly. "Those times shall not come again."

"There shall no longer be that kind of enchantment," agreed Saihung, turning to look out the window as well.

"Enchantment?" repeated the Grand Master. "No. There is no longer magic in this world."

"How did magic ever leave this earth?" wondered Saihung aloud.

"The folly of man, of course. Everywhere they rush to build homes and tall buildings. Across wildernesses, they string miles of electrical wire. Beneath the earth, they bore impractical tunnels. The skies are violated with planes, oceans polluted with wastes. What is their hurry? They are only suffocating the earth. Do they imagine that the only useful thing about this planet is to exploit its resources? If they understood the ideas of emptiness and impermanence, then they would see that virgin wilderness also sustains them.

"A person was made to fit into nature. In the forests and in the mountains, there are ten thousand forces that can sustain you at any single moment. The whisperings of eternity are audible, and nature nourishes through all five elements. Water, wood, fire, earth, and metal rotate in their proper orbits. We derive our power from attuning ourselves to it.

"But people imagine that wood is only good for building and burning. Fire is to drive machines. Earth is to be exhausted for its treasures. Metal is for tools of destruction. Water only receives civilization's defecation. They think all that exists is what we see. They feel that nourishment is what they buy in a store. They think they need attune themselves solely with ambition, greed, and selfishness. They glorify their pettiness, but if they would only stop to think, they'd realize that this world sustains them. When their time is up, it will swallow them mercilessly.

"Of all the creatures on the planet, only humanity was made to reason. Animals go through life without ever separating from their natural destinies. They live by instinct.

"Human beings should use their intelligence to turn away from their instinctive lust and greed, and turn their faces to the sun of holiness, the light of divinity. When the bright Way appears, one should be moved to reverence. Instead man has used his cunning to glorify his senses and cater to his greed. In the holy light, they shade their eyes and cling to the shadows."

383

The Grand Master turned to Saihung.

"This is your last lesson in China," said his master.

Saihung nodded solemnly.

"It's important to understand how to cope with life. Taoists understand life in a certain way. We have evolved a philosophy as an approach to life. But this philosophy will not always work in another culture."

"The West is completely different from China."

"I know. When you are in the West, you must try to understand it. Don't simply try to stay Chinese. Blend in with that culture. Understand it. Every culture works. When you are in it, you must do things their way."

"It's difficult to remember all that I am. In America, I am sometimes immersed in conflict. I cannot always keep my composure. You are telling me that these times are evil, yet you tell me to blend with it."

"Why be complicated?" asked the Grand Master. "Yin and yang and the ten thousand things mean separation. Separation means discrimination. Discrimination means discord. You must not cling only to the positive. In life you must also accept the negative. Those who do not accept both sides are the ones who become angry. Life is an oscillation between good and evil. Let it oscillate. There is creation and destruction, good and bad. Life will proceed on its own. Try to blend with it. Remain simple."

"How can I?"

"I know how you live," said his master with a slight tone of reproach. "But though you must blend, you must also remember who you are within. Search for your destiny. There are no more soothsayers. One must prophesize one's own destiny. That is unique. Who says that the only way to seek Tao is on a mountaintop? The Tao is change. Every day new people are born. Every day people die. If people didn't die, nothing would change. It is people who change, and so they imagine that there is progress. Past, present, and future all coexist. Movement in life is natural. The question is, where are you in this movement?"

"If only I knew . . ."

384

"I will not tell you. I'm not you. Your god is within you. Your god is your self. That is the source of your destiny."

"But I no longer have access to the teachings of our sect."

"You are afraid. That is unbecoming. If you give in to fear, you are like common people who do not understand the Tao. Hatred and anger come from fear. For the common people who are bound in such emotions, enlightenment comes only at the moment of death. Then their eyes and mouths open wide in amazement. They want to act, but death takes them just a moment after realization. You don't want that. You want your enlightenment while you can still act upon it. Put aside fear. There must be faith."

"But how can I now seek my enlightenment?"

"Life is but a wisp. It will be gone in a flash. Try to get as many moments of enlightenment—little realizations, tiny insights. Build up. The Tao is not fixed. Neither is enlightenment."

The master scrutinized him. "There is ambition and drive in you. That means you are incomplete. Some mystery drives you."

"But I don't know what it is."

"Of course not. That's why it's a mystery. If a man's life could be reduced to a road map, it would be quite worthless. You're a human being, in all your complexities and mysteries. Your personal scripture is inside you. You must decode that for your realization. I know you feel cheated. You want to become an immortal. But that art is trivial compared to the more essential issue of *why?* Why do you exist? Or do you even exist? If you can answer the why of your existence, then you have found your purpose. Your time with me was merely preparation. Your life is the time to exercise your learning. Spirituality and realization are personal. Practice through your whole life to gain realization. When you gain that realization, it should be cherished, treasured, and hidden. Keep it to yourself. Once you understand, you will see that whether you are priest or waiter is immaterial. These are only identities."

"I do see that clinging to the roles of the mind can be a detriment," offered Saihung.

"You recognize that to a limited degree already," agreed the Grand Master. "You reject the fixed identity of these various roles. But there is one final role you still cling to: your self. Only when you can leave that behind can you say you have glimpsed the Tao."

385

"Master, you do not know what it is like out there. I must believe in myself to survive." He could see no practical way to live in the United States in a state of selflessness. The tension between the simplification of the self and self-belief worried him.

His master seemed to lose patience. He turned away from Saihung. "So? Am I supposed to be sympathetic?"

"If only I could have more of your guidance. If only you would let me come back. I'm sure that I could leave all those roles behind."

"That is impossible until you fulfill your task," said his master severely.

"Why don't you and the acolytes come to America? I would work day and night to support you. Only please do not abandon me."

"Can our link be affected by distance?" asked his master.

"I am not so strong that I can know the Tao with no further teaching. I am only a tenth of the way there." He meant it.

"I made it. You make it." The Grand Master turned to look at him. There was a fierce look in his eyes. "Do you think I am going to make it easy for you? My masters never did me one favor. I had to achieve everything on my own. You have no time to indulge yourself any longer. The world is swiftly moving toward the dark side, but you are still attached to your idea of your self. Go! Go and explore and experience the world. Only when you are world-weary will you realize the answer. Until then, you must strive and suffer and persevere like everyone else. No one carries another being along the Way. No one."

Saihung did not dare to say anymore. He knew he would have given anything to avoid going back to Pittsburgh. But he could not argue with the orders of his master. He withdrew to stay with nearby relatives. The Grand Master was under surveillance by government cadres, and to stay too long in a group encouraged suspicious investigation.

Saihung walked through the front gate of the estate. He opened a bamboo and oil-paper umbrella against the rain. The clouds were dark, dense, moving swiftly. A sound like a thousand drumbeats came from the umbrella. He looked up. The clouds were like a mirror of the ocean. In the deluge, it seemed like an entire sea was falling on him.

No
Song to
Sing

SAIHUNG RETURNED TO the United States with fresh memories of China. He could still see twilight's last rose rays on white stucco, indigo shadows of poplar trees angled across yellow dirt threshing floors, brilliant green gourds hanging from bamboo trellises. He retained the impression of old men playing stringed instruments, not caring about an audience, only the pleasure of playing as they sat alone in doorways. He remembered smoke from distant fires against cobalt skies, even cherished the memory of walking through the straw and stubble of fields. The images were vivid in him. Even in the apparently barren fields, he was aware that so much was alive, the trees, the wind—breath of nature—small frogs in the field, birds, flies, a snake.

Time was slow in China. It was a pulse beating a muffled, un-hurried pace. A day was a mark anywhere; but in his culture, the cycle of change was double what it was in the United States. The division of hours was two times sixty minutes, so that people only divided a single day and night into twelve periods with poetic names. The months followed the cycle of the moon. The year was thought of as twenty-four seasons, and people looked expectantly to the fulfillment of that particular time: Coming Rain, Big Heat, Little Snow, Beginning of Spring. No rushing—working hard, yes, sometimes being hungry, or caked with dirt blown by a yellow wind—but at least life was honest and direct. People lived close to the earth, an ear to the slow rhythm that was a gentle echo of one from deep in the planet's core.

Life was faster in Pittsburgh. The earth was paved with asphalt and concrete and stabbed through with steel posts. Trees and nature were relegated to precise holes in the suffocating pavement, animals were categorized in zoos. Men rushed in buses and cars to their appointed eight hours a day. Eight hours. A job. Numbers. No poetry. Eight. Be at work at eight, work for eight, under the glare of fluorescent light, in the wind of a forced-air system, with clothes of chemicals, eating foods that had probably never breathed, or walked, or felt tender roots in the grainy anchorage of soil.

Was home to be a kitchen of familiar foods, a new family that spoke with voices from the homeland? Of black hair, round faces, amber skin, onyx eyes, laughter? A dumb joke with an untranslatable pun, stupid, innocent, and just like home. Food was food, but that special feeling just of talking, forming delicious syllables from childhood, playing roles observed from elders, pulling together in tragedy, making that special gesture indicated by a custom so ancient as to be genetic—all this was the special seasoning that was fragrant, maddening, that made eyes roll heavenward in delirious remembrance.

For the Chinese in Pittsburgh, they still unwittingly followed a pattern begun in the nineteenth century, when men came to the United States for the railroads, the gold mines, agriculture, and fishing. A few had been kidnapped; others came just desperate for money. Through the decades, fleeing poverty, they worked to earn their fortunes. Some dreamed of returning as rich men. Others worked to bring wives and families to the West.

No one escaped the dichotomy of homeland and workland, the difficulty of having love and value far away. All held the idea that hard work and sacrifice would enable them one day to realize their dreams. Saihung fell into the same immigrant pattern. He too sent money faithfully back to support his master and the two acolytes, for he was now their primary source of income. He too labored under the idea that he was working for some deferred goal while separated from beautiful memories by an ocean.

389

Even when Saihung got up on a Sunday morning, he kept thinking of the landscapes of his childhood, of happy moments in his grandfather's garden. He went into the backyard. Warm air with a trace of the river's scent flowed around him. The peach tree was almost in full leaf now, and he noted with satisfaction that it seemed healthy. Behind him, Uncle William slammed the back screen door, and walked down the path to the garage.

Uncle William was a portly man in his late sixties, with a round head, graying hair, and silver stubble on his roughskinned face. He called Saihung to help him with the car. He never let anyone touch his Buick, but Saihung obliged his elder anyway. The older man simply enjoyed displaying the centerpiece of his possessions. Though he called Saihung to close the garage door, it was evident that what he really wanted was an attendant for a nearly royal event. Uncle William wiped the fenders carefully, and checked the whitewall tires. Methodically, he raised the hood and checked first the radiator and then the oil. Satisfied that all was in order, he climbed into the driver's seat and started the car carefully.

The gleaming jade-green car rolled into the sun, and Uncle William drove it through an alley to the front of the house. Saihung was left to close the door and return to the house to announce that all was ready. Aunt Mabel, wearing a gay and colorful dress, took up a picnic basket and went out to the front.

In this short time, Uncle William had already turned the car off. It wasted gas to leave it idling, he always explained, before warming it up again. No matter how often Aunt Mabel urged him to keep the car running while he waited for her, he kept them waiting as witnesses to his exactly timed five-minute warm-up period.

The first stop was always the dairy near Schenley Park.

"Again?" exclaimed an exasperated Aunt Mabel. "We always have to go for ice cream! Every Sunday, it's always the same!"

Aunt Mabel, a rather large-boned and formidable woman, liked to complain. Married to her for over forty-five years, Uncle William adopted the archetypal male strategy: silence. He knew when to keep quiet—he had often whispered to Saihung that it was this sense of timing that was responsible for his long marriage—and there was no ultimate argument as long as he was driving. Saihung kept quiet too. He liked ice cream.

All three had their cones at the dairy. Despite her complaining, Aunt Mabel seldom failed to get ice cream. Her favorite was strawberry, though she and Saihung often experimented with the many available flavors. Uncle William was a true classicist and staunchly ordered a double vanilla each and every time.

Uncle William had worked in restaurants nearly all his life, first as a waiter, then as the owner of several unsuccessful ones. Retired, he still worked from time to time in restaurants during busy seasons. He always insisted that he could have run his own business, but his individualistic temperament and his unwillingness to compromise were his undoing. Had it not been for the financial help and planning of his wife, he would have easily slid into poverty as he chased his dreams.

It had been Aunt Mabel who had first urged a retreat to China during the 1929 depression, shrewdly waiting until it was again economically advantageous to return. In the years that followed, she earned her living as laundress, eventually opening her own shop on East Ohio Street. They had bought several pieces of property with her savings, which made their retirement more comfortable. Uncle William was content to tend their properties—disinterestedly—and ride around the North Shore in his Buick.

As his aunt relaxed, she took on an almost girlish demeanor. During the week, absorbed with taking care of the house, property, and Uncle William, she often seemed distracted and worried. She had once been a very stout woman of peasant proportions, but had begun to stoop and shrink in her aging. The laundrywoman's constant soaking in water had encouraged an arthritic condition that twisted her hands painfully and pulled her body inward. Saihung massaged her frequently with liniments of every conceivable nature, but there was no reversing a lifetime of exposure. Years of hard work showed on Aunt Mabel's wrinkled face, graying hair (which she permanent waved but refused to dye), and bent spine. Only when she was out on Sunday did she seem to cheer up. She smiled and laughed, gazing happily at the deep green trees.

Panther Lake was a small reflecting pond in a city park. There was a monument to George Westinghouse at the far side of the pond. This semicircular art-deco screen, painted gold, looked strangely similar to monuments in China. There was a sculpture of a boy facing the bas-relief screen in a central and symmetrical fashion. Large rocks lined the pond, like the gardens in Beijing or Suzhou. Golden carp swam languidly in the water. Irises, weeping willows, and magenta-tipped Chinese magnolias lined the shore. A warm honey-colored sunlight washed down through pines on the hill that overlooked the tiny hollow. The benches were massive black granite in simple post-and-lintel arrangements. They had no way of knowing whether the garden's designers had intended such an oriental feel, but it suited their nostalgia.

Aunt Mabel laid out the picnic basket. She helped Saihung and her husband to the lunch of homemade dim sum and poured tea from an old chrome thermos. Aunt Mabel enjoyed serving them, liked watching them appreciatively devour her creations. But once the lunch was over, she walked over to another section of lawn by herself to sit and look at the flowers and, Saihung knew by the faraway look in her eyes, dream of her life back in China.

Sitting on a granite bench, looking up at the sky through bright willow green, he could feel the cool stratospheric breezes as they had been on the summit of Huashan. He could hear the clean water rushing over rounded stones, and smell subtle fragrances of pine, earth, and sandalwood incense. There had been haughty cranes, regarding him with avian disdain, monkeys trying to steal fruit from the altars. There had been kindly old men who had inspired him to grasp the knowledge and art of living in nature. They had drawn him to know himself through meditation. They had instilled an awe for life and had then expanded that to the dizzying exploration of contemplative space.

Huashan had represented all that he had valued of tradition. He remembered the many religious relics on the mountain: begging bowls, rosary beads, scrolls, and books that were so delicate that he had to use bamboo tweezers to turn the pages. Huashan had been his unbroken link with the past, his image of antiquity. He was part of a continuous lineage, in touch not just with his master, but with a living tradition. As long as he lived, that inner link would last, but he still envied the churches and cathedrals around him, the news stories of religious relics being moved with great devotion: a bit of a saint's clothing, a tooth of Buddha, a desert scroll. Many people throughout the world had their beauty, the object of their worship. He had nothing but himself and memories of his old country.

He smiled and then sighed. He had been taught that externals were insignificant to the real qualities of inner cultivation. The masters would have burned temple, relics, even their own robes, to demonstrate what they had taught him repeatedly: The Tao is to be found within.

He was determined to preserve his spirituality. He resolved that he would earn enough money to make himself independent. Huashan might be gone, but he would still maintain its legacy. He looked at Uncle William, strolling on the opposite bank to feed the fish. He turned to his left. Aunt Mabel was pretty in the afternoon sunlight, sitting on the grass, arms and head propped on her upraised knees. They were living as successful and gentle an old age as they knew how. Saihung wanted that too, though that did not mean a Buick and a wife. He wanted to pursue his quest, fulfill it, and return to his master.

H E BEGAN A new job at a restaurant named Lotus Garden. It was quite far from Foreland Street, across two rivers. He had to walk a mile downtown to catch a bus that would take him to the South Shore and the community of Brentwood. The restaurant was on a busy highway, one of the main thoroughfares to Pittsburgh from southern Pennsylvania.

Situated between an auto-repair shop and a glass shop, with an ample parking lot in between, the gray brick building must have begun as a simple rectangular box building, like all the others on the semi-industrial strip. Now, it had fake oriental tile roofs grafted onto its roof line, and window frames with some flimsy version of latticework. Both the eaves and the frames were painted with shiny green and red enamel. The owner of Lotus Garden was apparently modern and progressive: He had a large illuminated sign proclaiming the name of his establishment, the letters written in a silly Chinese calligraphy style. Below it was the legend GOURMET CHINESE FOOD.

393

The interior was quite dim, even dark after the glare of the streets. Only a bit of sunlight came in the front door and two windows that faced the street. A slightly pudgy man came to meet him. He was vain and combed his hair back with just enough hair dressing to impart a smooth sheen. He was taller than Saihung and left the impression of an athlete gone slightly to ruin. Boss Lee was in his late thirties, only a few years older than Saihung. In culture and temperament, however, his prospective employer was quite different. He was Saihung's earliest encounter with the Americanized Chinese.

Boss Lee had grown up in the United States and did not expect to find his life's fulfillment by going back to China. He was a shrewd and ambitious businessman, but his expectations of success were a home in a good section of the city and Western education for his children. He was a proud veteran of the U.S. Air Force and liked to affect a leather bomber jacket. A few pictures of him and his Flying Tiger were hung behind the counter.

The restaurant was one long, narrow room. Green vinyl booths lined the walls. Square tables, set on the diagonal, and covered with white tablecloths, filled the center of the room, and there were several large, round tables for banquets. Aside from a monstrous stainless-steel station for refilling tea, there was little else on the walls except for a few token paintings and a single audio speaker softly playing big band music.

The kitchen was a small room, painted a shocking chartreuse mitigated only by years of scrubbing. Saihung saw that there were four woks and stainless-steel prep counters, sinks, and a dishwasher. The equipment did not seem to be enough to support the room, but Saihung refrained from voicing his judgment. At least the kitchen was very clean, he commented to Boss Lee. His employer told him that the city inspected the restaurant more often than white-owned businesses. Bribes were part of the cost of doing business.

Boss Lee introduced Saihung to the head chef, but Saihung already knew him from the rumor mistresses in Chinatown. The cigarette-addicted cook was named Devil Lee. Notorious for his bad moods and vicious tongue, the women at Big Mrs. Lee's store viewed him as pure evil. He was an ugly man with a crooked mouth; his face had been badly scarred in a fire. No one had called it an accident. They all said the gods had marked him as a monster as a service to humanity. Devil Lee's main perversity was refusing to cook when the mood struck him, often at the time when the restaurant was most busy. He grudgingly shook Saihung's hand and blew a stream of smoke into the air.

At four o'clock, Saihung changed into his uniform of white cotton shirt, black pants, and bow tie. Within two hours, the room filled up quickly. All the patrons were white, and most were from the neighboring wealthy districts. Some came even in chauffeur-driven limousines. They were greeted by the maître d', a slender and obsequious Japanese incongruously named Big Duke. Most of the customers had favorite waiters, and asked Duke knowledgeably for the table in their preferred sections. They were equally certain about their favorite dishes: egg foo young, chow mein, pork chop suey, wonton soup, sweet and sour pork, moo goo gai pan, egg rolls, barbecued spareribs. Those who considered themselves connoisseurs ordered half a roast duck with gravy. Children often ordered from the "American" menu, and had jumbo shrimp, barbecue pork sandwiches, or chicken-gravy sandwiches.

The youngsters not only liked the strange versions of home cooking, they liked two waiters in particular. The waiter Lee Shi had a large pointed head, greased-down hair, broken nose, and a normally rude disposition. He lived with the sorrow of his only son's death. A bullet shot in the air during a village celebration came down into the crowd, striking only the son. Lee brooded constantly about this accident and had lost all his faith in the future. He was savage to customers and workers alike, and it was only with children that he ever smiled or expressed a gruff consideration.

His confederate was the oldest one there, dubbed Ancient Lee. No one knew his exact age. He dyed his hair (Devil Lee always accused him of using black shoe polish), and kept it combed in a cresting pompadour. The sides swept into shiny fenders above each ear. When it got hot, a long strand fell down one side of his face, and he loved to fling it upward with a flip of his head. He looked as if he had no neck, and his shoulders were hunched up. He liked to make jokes that the children loved but that no adults understood. He never laughed at them either.

Saihung did his best with the tables left to him. Already an experienced waiter, he took the orders and delivered them as promptly as Devil Lee would cook them. The sound of the restaurant reached deafening levels, as patrons talked, babies cried, and the waiters shouted to take orders. Each time that Saihung hit the swinging double doors was like a drumbeat; each time that the porcelain plates slid across the steel counters was like the clanging of gongs. Devil Lee, his lips firmly clamped around a drooping cigarette, kept four woks roaring with sizzling food, his iron spatula moving like the piston of a train. Whenever the cook lifted a pan, yellow flame shot up to the fan hood, steam burst from the boiling sauces, and fragrant aroma exploded into the kitchen. The pace was maddening, with Devil Lee shouting for orders to be taken, the waiters yelling for new dishes.

Two dishwashers worked furiously in the corner. During the day, these two black women shared in the hard work of mopping the floors, setting up the tables, receiving supplies, and preparing the food for the evening crowd. They carried supplies down to the basement where there were additional stoves to pre-cook the ducks and chickens, tables to peel and cut vegetables, and even facilities to sprout mung beans and make bean curd. During most of the evening, they kept steaming-hot water streaming over the heavy plates and bowls.

Bessie was thin, with large eyes and a completely anonymous demeanor. She crept into work each day, like a mouse walking tentatively across a room. She spoke to no one, did her job impeccably, and left promptly at quitting time. But her partner was her complete opposite. Her nickname was Lucky. She easily weighed 350 pounds. She took short steps on enormous barrels of legs, and her girth and body were so large that she moved

395

through doors at an angle. A trip to put away dishes left her breathless, and she piled dirty dishes close in the sink so as not to let them get beyond reach. Lucky took a special liking to Saihung. Even in the heat and the clamor and the frantic pace of the kitchen, she sang gospel songs at the top of her voice. Perhaps because Saihung was the youngest one there, she always gave him a wink and a reminder that it was "never too late to accept the Lord."

396

ONE OF THE patrons who always asked for a table in Saihung's section was a large heavyset man with a shaved head. He came weekly with his wife, a quiet and shy brunette. The man ordered the same dishes with religious regularity. Egg roll, egg-drop soup, sweet and sour pork, fried rice. With identical regularity, Devil Lee would get the order wrong. The man always wanted lichee instead of pineapple with the pork.

One night, as patron and restaurant went through this ritual, Saihung engaged the man in conversation. Saihung had never forgotten the habit of sizing a man up. There was no doubt that this six-foot heavyweight was a fighter. It was clear in the way he walked, the way he dominated the tiny booth, even the pugnacious way he ordered his meal. Saihung felt sure that he had seen the man elsewhere.

"I know who you are," said Saihung one night in a casual tone. It was late, and Saihung was tired from working. When he had remembered where he had seen his customer, he had forgotten propriety.

The wife looked with concern across the table. The man looked up with annoyance.

"Now who do you think I am?"

"You're the Batman." The Batman was a masked wrestler on TV. Saihung and the others sometimes watched on Saturday mornings as they washed the floors.

"How the hell did you know that?" asked the Batman. "No one is supposed to know my true identity."

"It's not hard."

"Well, I didn't think you were so smart."

"There's a lot you don't know," replied Saihung. He immediately regretted it. It had been a hard day. He had argued with Devil Lee.

"You shrimp!" roared the Batman. "If you're so smart, how come you can't get my dinner right?"

Saihung threw down his tray in exasperation. The restaurant suddenly became quiet. Saihung felt the sudden discomfort of having a hundred people staring at him. Duke and Boss Lee rushed over.

"Is there some problem?" asked Duke nervously. The Batman was fully a head taller than Saihung. Duke was ridiculously dwarfed between them.

397

"This is between him and me," shouted the Batman.

"Hey, anytime," replied Saihung.

"You?" bellowed the Batman. "What can you do?"

"Like I said before, there's a lot you don't know."

"Don't fight!" urged Boss Lee in Chinese. "It's bad for business."

"Don't fight, Edgar, honey," said Mrs. Batman.

"Edgar?" snickered Saihung before he could stop himself.

"Hey, watch it!" growled Edgar Batman.

"Look. I've had a long day," said Saihung. He tried to remember what they said in movies. "Either put up or shut up."

"Why you punk!" cried the Batman. "I could flatten you so fast."

"Come on! Come on!" yelled Saihung, shaking his hands at his sides.

Edgar Batman charged Saihung. It was not a sight that Saihung took heedlessly—seeing a man both wider and taller bearing down would give anyone pause. But Saihung had always loved testing his mettle in combat.

Saihung sidestepped and threw a palm blow into the Batman's lower abdomen, but he pulled the energy. It would not be good to rupture a customer's stomach, but it might be nice to have a little fun. The big man went up on his toes as if he had had an electric shock. Saihung quickly reached under the armpit and threw him.

As the Batman rolled, Saihung jumped up and rolled with him in a perfect somersault. As the disoriented Batman pitched to the end of the throw, Saihung was right there beside him. There was a brief instant for Saihung to grin triumphantly at the dazed giant before his swift elbow strike knocked the Batman unconscious.

"So sorry! So sorry!" apologized Duke to the other customers.

"Ai!" exclaimed Boss Lee. "You'll drive all my customers away! Quickly! Revive him!"

Saihung did as he was told. In his training, it had not been enough just to learn how to knock a man out. He was also taught how to revive and heal people. He sat the Batman up with some effort. The man was heavy, and his head filled Saihung's hands like a huge bowling ball. Saihung massaged his neck and then slapped him hard on the back. The loud whack brought the Batman back to consciousness. Saihung helped him into the small booth. He saw that Mrs. Batman was too concerned to speak.

"I'm very sorry," said Boss Lee. "It won't happen again."

"Forget it," panted Batman. He turned to Saihung. "How did you do that? Show me! Show me!"

Just then, Ancient Lee tottered out with the Batman's order. There were still pineapples instead of lichee, but the Batman took it in good humor.

The other staff members told Saihung that they had all earned regular customers who requested them by name. Each one of them had a story. But none, they told Saihung, had been impressed because they had been knocked out.

Saihung laughed, but inside, his thrill always gave way to introspection. Soberly, he knew that the fight had not been necessary. Perhaps that kind of contest had been excusable in his youth, but now he began to see that he had exposed a little bit of his own identity. He thought back to the meditations that he was striving to master just before he had left Huashan. He was supposed to be erasing his ego, he thought. It would take a great deal of hard work to do that.

Hard work. Over the years that he was at Lotus Garden and among the Cantonese immigrants of Pittsburgh, he worked hard not simply at his job, but at his practices as well. He began to see a fascinating parallel between the persevering habits of his coworkers and the perseverance demanded by his sect. If there was a single tenet that the immigrants had, it was a word that is inadequately translated as "struggle," with the added connotation of "work hard" and "ability to bear suffering." It implied that one who knew how to "struggle" would succeed in the world. That was the way of both the immigrant and the ascetic. Struggle, suffer, work hard, until success came.

From the moment that he saw this common cultural element between holy and worldly life, Saihung found much greater comfort in the Chinese community. After all, except for the differences in their goals, they were all struggling for a future that held out no promise of reward. In a way, the society of men in the restaurant was almost monastic, and leaving the restaurant was as fun as leaving the monastery on festival days had been.

399

I N LATE FALL, Saihung joined his uncle and aunt on a rare outing to the countryside. Uncle William drove his reliable Buick to a beautiful spot over a lake. Big Mrs. Lee and her family, and friends of his aunt, Jean and Henry Chan, joined them. All along the shore, the maples were turning into a crimson seen only on the rarest of silks. The women unpacked plenty of homemade dim sum, along with tea and beer. There was much laughter as they ate, but Saihung was moody and quiet. His aunt suggested that he go off by himself. She understood his moods and the importance of solitude.

Saihung excused himself and went down to the water's edge. On a whim, he rented a rowboat. Gripping the thick oars tightly in his fists, he made a few tentative dips into the water before he fell into the rhythm of pulling and pushing. The blades made regular sweeps into the blue-green water, and soon the bow of his boat sliced the smooth lake in a perfect path.

He put his whole body into the rowing. His legs steadied and tensed with regularity; his abdominal muscle contracted and rippled with each stroke. His back muscles pulled, testing themselves against the thick water, and his arms pumped gratifying with blood.

He found himself breathing to a regular cadence. At least in its physical aspect, this rowing was almost as good as the *qigong* that he faithfully cultivated. It filled his lungs with clean, sweet air and excited the nerves and blood vessels of his body. Who cared about esoteric technique? This was still giving him health and experience.

The water was placid, calm. He looked at the ripples as they fell away from his boat. Abstract lines shimmered for a few moments, then faded into nothingness. Like the Tao that allowed some facet to come to the surface only to withdraw it again into its depths, the wake of his boat was constant; but never the same. It came into existence it passed from existence.

Soon, he had a sensation of his body meshing perfectly with the movement of the boat, with the swaying of the water, the gentle undulation of the lake. He remembered his master's words, that life was oscillation. There was creation and destruction. There was movement. He had to blend with the life, just as he was doing now.

Rowing a boat was so simple. It was just rowing, and thus it was his perfect Taoism. He rowed on. Pulling. Pulling.

Serenity passed into him. "Enter stillness." These two words were one of the most sacred mantras in Taoism. He became aware that his rowing was silently repeating this mantra. His oars dipped again and again. They entered and rose. Entered and rose.

He hadn't meditated for a long time. How could he, working and living in Lotus Garden? But now, unexpectedly, he recognized himself falling into the familiar state of meditation. Somehow the outer experience of rowing on a lake reflected inwardly in him. His outer senses were stilled, and he found himself looking inward. Certainly, his eyes still saw, but his mind saw only within. His mind stilled, his soul emerged, beautiful and pure.

His spirit intact and shining, he reached the shore and beached his boat. He walked into the woods. Saihung had always loved forests. Perhaps, he considered, he had been a forest dweller somewhere in a past life. Whatever the explanation, he knew that the feel of unobstructed earth beneath his feet was a great comfort, and the feeling of trees surrounding him made him feel safe.

He thought over how naive he had been when he had first come to the United States. He had expected Iroquois and Sioux, hunters, cowboys. He had thought of trees coming down to the water. How could he have known that America was a country that did away with its past? In China, nothing was thrown away with evolution. People lived substantially as their ancestors had. America was not even two centuries old yet. In China, there were family bloodlines, guilds, restaurants, farming methods, and schools of painting that preceded Columbus's discovery. He could not have known that things changed so quickly and thoroughly here.

The woods were quiet. Sunshine fell gently down through parted boughs; birds sang intermittently in high-toned warbles.

Listening to them, he suddenly remembered a very special song. This was not a composition made for entertainment, but a mystical one of sacred syllables. It was a song for people interested in mystical history. If one went to a particular place and sang the song, then the guardians of that place had to show it to the singer as it had been in the past. Time would be pierced—it was only in nestled circular layers anyway—and the beauty that had once been would be revealed. It seemed a little like making water flow backward, but that was exactly what the song did.

401

Saihung had used it in China. History for him had thus not always been the reading of books, but the nearly direct experience of having seen it all. He had seen poets, warriors, the Seven Sages of the Bamboo Grove. He had seen things as clearly as the trees before him now. Time, he had been taught, could flow in either direction. He decided he would sing this song. He could begin to learn from the natural world of this place, absorb the softly blowing wind, the pristine water. He could find the Tao anew here.

He sat for a time in contemplation, an inner ablution, a turning to the sacred. Then he stood, and in the gestures and movements that accompanied the words, sang the song. The wind stilled. The birds stopped. Even the trees trembled in response to his voice.

He waited expectantly. Nothing.

He reviewed his procedures. It had been a while since he had sung, but it was not a melody easy to forget. He sang again. Still no response.

By the third attempt, he understood that the song would not work outside of China.

Discouraged and sad, he turned toward his boat. As he rowed back to the waiting picnic, he realized his boat ride was just a boat ride.

Child
of
Peace

S AIHUNG RETURNED TO China in 1963. Hearing that he was going to the homeland they all cherished, many people gave him red packets of "lucky money." Big Mrs. Lee, Uncle Feng, Uncle Poon, Ancient Lee, even Devil Lee, gave him something for his journey. Saihung was moved. Even on Huashan, there wasn't this kind of support and camaraderie.

The reason for this trip was a request from Wang Ziping. He had always been viewed favorably by the Communist government. When Mao Zedong wanted to improve the people's health with martial arts, Wang was among the masters invited to reveal their arts.

Wang Ziping had accompanied Premier Zhou Enlai on a diplomatic visit to Burma. Saihung had no doubt that it had been Zhou's own expert sense of diplomacy that had led China to utilize martial arts as a tool of international relations. He suspected that Zhou was secretly sympathetic to many classical things purged in ideological conflicts. But characteristically, Zhou did not champion anyone's cause if he was being attacked. Instead, he waited patiently until he could resurrect the people and ideals that he wanted. Keeping his motives hidden, never showing his loyalties to anyone, he kept people guessing until it was impossible to undo the groundwork that he had laid.

403

Saihung felt that Zhou was behind this new interest in martial arts or, as it would come to be called in the West, *wushu*. The encouragement had all the hallmarks of the premier's manipulations: He liked strategies that even his enemies would have to applaud. Improving public health was a noble ideal that no one could quarrel with.

When Saihung arrived in Beijing, he was well prepared to face his master. But he was surprised to find a considerably less expressive Wang Ziping. The man had become circumspect, even quiet. It was true that he was eighty-three years old, but he still was more robust and heavily sinewed than men a quarter of his age. Though his hair was completely white, his eyes still showed undimmed ferocity. Wang greeted Saihung formally and even more curtly than usual. He motioned with his eyes toward a little man in a green Mao suit. Saihung knew instantly that the Communist cadres would be surveying everything.

Saihung had no private time with his master. He instead concentrated on rehearsals and learning prearranged sparring routines with other returned students. Wang Ziping had trained so many of those who had been called for the demonstration that almost none of them knew one another. It was instructive that nearly all had now returned from outside China. Proud individualists, these martial artists had not stayed in China past the early 1950s.

Constantly monitored, the martial artists learned their routines in sullen silence. They disliked the restriction but endured it for the sake of their master. They rehearsed at Wang's school, an old gymnasium with pale green walls and high windows that let in a bright, flat light. There were mirrors, punching bags, wooden men for target practice, ropes to climb, and acrobatic equipment. The air had a distinctive smell, a musty and pungent odor not from the training men, but from something in the building materials. They trained for eight hours a day under Wang's strict supervision. Each move was practiced repeatedly. If perfection angered the gods, then Wang was determined that they be madly furious.

The stadium was filled to capacity the night of the performance. Mao Zedong, Zhou Enlai, Zhu Deh, and other officials sat in a special box. Saihung looked at them skeptically. Once they had proclaimed martial arts as feudal. Now, they thought it might be useful for the sake of health and as a performing art to show to other countries.

The old martial artists came out to thunderous applause. There was the Monkey Master, who fought in movements inspired by apes; the man dubbed the Rat, who fought with a thirteen-foot cavalry spear. Wang Ziping himself showed his still vital skills by demonstrating the spear and the monk's spade.

When it was Saihung's turn, he came out dressed in a simple blue cotton shirt, white cotton pants, and the domestically manufactured version of tennis shoes. He had tied a sash tightly around his waist. In rapid succession with two other students, he showed the double meteor maces, the double daggers, and the Swimming Dragon Sword Form—a style handed down by a woman who had tried to assassinate the Emperor Qianlong. The audience cheered at his every dramatic move. Saihung used his experience as an actor to add facial expressions that complemented his shadowboxing routines.

Finally, his last solo performance came. He gripped a spear and looked out at the cheering crowd. Wang had not said a thing to any of his students, which was as close as they came to approval. The performance was going well. The leaders of the government seemed pleased.

His spear was made of the trunk of a young sapling. An inch and a half at the butt and tapering only slightly, it flexed gently whenever it was thrust out. The spear tip came to a sharp point and its ferrule was wrapped with a long tassel of red horsehair that tossed eye-catchingly with every moment. The tassel was not just for show. In combat, it distracted the opponent from the tip, and it could also be used to trap other weapons. The style was named the Blood Spear, because the spearman started battle with a white tassel and let it be dyed with his enemies' blood.

He gripped his weapon tightly as his name was announced. "Kwan Saihung. Blood Spear." Saihung walked out onto the stadium floor. He stood for a second as the audience calmed down. The spear was straight, with its butt resting on the ground. Its white wood suddenly reminded him of a spine. He brought his left hand over his head while he inhaled slowly. As soon as he gripped the spear with both hands, he raised it up mightily and launched himself into a performance that showed exactly how a man would fight. As if he was surrounded by many opponents, Saihung blocked, dodged, thrust, and leapt into balletic attacks. He wanted the audience to believe that he was actually fighting invisible enemies. Even Zhou applauded his performance. He wondered if the premier remembered him.

Other schools demonstrated before Saihung returned for prearranged sparring performances. Bare-handed, Saihung faced the director of Wang's Shanghai school, a stocky, solid, crew-cut man in his sixties. He held two real daggers.

"Attack!" shouted Wang. Saihung disarmed his opponent in five seconds. One: The man attacked. Two: Saihung dodged. Three: He hit the back of one hand. Four: He knocked the dagger from the other. Five: He returned to his ready position. The audience cheered.

"Too slow!" Wang cried. Wang, who had sometimes leapt into the ring whenever a losing student threatened to ruin the reputation of his school, wanted everything to be perfect for this event. He took Saihung's place, saying, "Three seconds should be enough."

The dagger man attacked again. One: As he charged, Wang stepped into him. Two: He struck so rapidly with each hand that both knives dropped to the ground. Three: Wang was back into his original position. Not only did the stadium erupt in admiring applause and shouting, but Mao himself gave Wang an ovation.

As the performances went on, Saihung reflected soberly. Once, he had wanted nothing more than to be a martial artist.

Growing up, he had seen former Imperial knights and had aspired to their heroism. But modernity and the Second World War had forever changed what it meant to be a warrior. Guns and armies became more important than skill and chivalry. There were no martial artists as in the old days. Those who fancied themselves so were only romantic hallucinators. What was left was a special heritage that tough men like Wang or his instructor from Shanghai were trying to preserve.

Now, the old arts were being sought by Mao and his government. The arts that the warriors had kept hidden were being exposed and exploited for political reasons. Of course, the decision had not been up to him. Wang had decided to cooperate, and Saihung had returned to China in obedience to his master's request. But he would not have exposed his art to the eyes of the curious under any other circumstances. He had always been taught to keep his skill hidden until the last possible moment. Yet from then on, the martial arts that represented principle, honor, discipline, and individuality would be transformed into a performing art and sport. They were giving away the legacy they so cherished.

Isle
of
Anonymity

Two days after the performance, Saihung took a train westward. As he traversed the countryside, he could see the makings of the new China: factories, a little more mechanization in the fields. The nation was on the verge of industrialization. It would be good for economics, the military, the balance of trade. He could see that people suppressed by his own former aristocratic class now had a chance of advancement. But with the passing of the old social order came the fading of the ancient, classical culture he so treasured. Imperial houses were now museums. Scholars were now working for archives if they were lucky, or in fields if they were not. Huashan itself had but a few monks and nuns (women were never occupants on Huashan in Saihung's time) imported by the government from other areas to act as caretakers of exhibits for tourists.

Saihung disembarked at dawn from the train he had ridden for two days. He walked from the station to a lake. Waiting for the boatman, he stood at the water's edge, a tiny figure dwarfed by the sweeping surface of the water. Gray and blue profiles of distant hills and mountains could barely be seen against the overcast sky.

Across the lake was a dark, crown-shaped island. No other details were visible from the distance, just the punctuation of stone and tree upon the still water. He knew that his master was there—could even detect a subtle presence—but there seemed to be little other life around the lake.

As he stood for some time, a group of swallows swooped down over the pale water, diving and turning with acrobatic finesse. He wondered if they were returning from some nocturnal journey, or whether this was an aerial dance to greet the rising sun. With wings like swords, speed that took the eye and mind long moments to comprehend, they cut their eccentric paths and were suddenly gone.

He listened to the gentle lapping on the sand, the soft swelling impulse of the ripples. On Huashan, the impassive mountain had represented absolute stillness. Movement was hidden in its living caves, its subterranean streams. On this lake, there was still the combined image of stillness and movement. The calm surface was like the meditating mind. As long as there was solitude, there was a chance for the Tao to come.

The boatman arrived and, after some bargaining, agreed to pole Saihung to the island. He helped Saihung load the boat, asking if he was a merchant. Saihung only laughed, replying that he was a visiting relative. He looked like a homecoming traveler gone a bit mad. He had brought dozens of gifts, and he had been purposefully excessive: flowers, fruit, cone-shaped wheat bread, peanuts, pickled vegetables, dried tofu, noodles. The presents filled nearly the entire boat.

He was happy to see the two acolytes waiting by the tiny dock, standing in the violet shade of a willow tree. They had kept their long, coiled hair and Taoist robes. He greeted them with a bow and quickly loaded them with his presents. For a minute, he felt a little awkward, even shy.

Sound of Clear Water dispensed with the elaborate ceremonial hand gestures and giggled. Saihung stood awkwardly and uncertainly.

"You look odd." The acolyte pointed to Saihung's American clothes.

"Don't tease him," said Mist Through a Grove with exaggerated protectiveness. "He's a world traveler."

Saihung shifted uncomfortably. He didn't know what to do. If he were still the man from Pittsburgh, he would have shaken their hands, but that gesture was foreign in China. If he were still a monk, he would have bowed and gone through the elaborate rituals of greeting. If he were still the child they thought he was, he would have hit them both.

"This is the style," Saihung remarked defensively. "I have to fit in." In his mind, he began to see his fellows as country bumpkins.

"A Taoist concerned about style!" howled Mist Through a Grove, his topknot coming nearly undone. "I can see that you are truly progressing."

Saihung lost his temper and was ready to brawl when all three noticed their master standing at the top of a knoll. They looked at one another sheepishly. Picking up Saihung's things, they started up the hill.

The island was smaller than a city block and was studded with willows and pines. It had a commanding view of the lake shore, with several mountain ranges visible in the distance. The Grand Master and his acolytes had been exiled there by the government. No worshipers came. No students were there to learn.

It was rumored that Zhou Enlai himself had arranged this sanctuary, yet the refuge was also a prison. The Grand Master was too famous to be shot, but the government nevertheless wanted to ensure that he would not advocate religion to the masses. Although he was a renunciate, he was famous enough for them to fear his popularity. It was far better to isolate the older man in an unknown shrine.

The temple was the only building on the island and was nestled atop a knoll. It faced south, the traditional orientation for most shrines. Much of it was in ruins or had been torn down. The remaining area was tiny, with only a main hall and a few smaller adjoining cells. Brick walls were plastered and whitewashed, the tile roofs were an ashen-gray clay. The eaves had once been painted, though they were now bare and weathered, and moss and grass had begun to fill the crevices. Temples usually had a plaque at the lintel giving the name of the hall, but this one's was missing.

410

The acolytes showed Saihung through the open latticework doors. There was so much dust and earth worked into the grain that they might have been slabs of stone. The wood was cracked, as if vertical fault lines had shot through the mud-colored doors. There were no statues, no altar, not a single trapping of religion.

The Grand Master stood before the hall. He was at once familiar and yet, after Saihung's ten years in the United States, he seemed like an apparition. Saihung made his obeisance before his dark-robed teacher. Few words were exchanged; no excitement was expressed.

"You were kind to bring such generous gifts," murmured his master.

Saihung had not thought that it would be such a thrill to hear his master's voice again. "I am honored to return," he replied softly.

"You can see that I have been reduced to rather poor circumstances."

"Your richness lies elsewhere, Master."

"Obviously, it was not enough to save me or those who stayed with me out of loyalty."

"You exaggerate," said Saihung. "We are your students for life."

"And what is this life but a dream?" whispered the Grand Master.

"Yes, and one that is over all too quickly," replied Saihung.

"That is why my only teaching to you is this: Understand impermanence. Contemplate the transitory."

The Grand Master gestured to the acolytes. "He has come a long distance. Let us sit down to a meal together."

They sat at an ancient wooden table in the middle of the dusty refectory. The acolytes busied themselves in cooking. By etiquette, it should have been Saihung's job as the youngest, but he was now the guest, and the Grand Master sat with him to talk. Saihung found his master's state of mind clear.

"Taoism cannot be practiced now," said his master seriously. "Stay in the outer world, but keep Taoism alive and pure within you."

Saihung nodded in acknowledgment as he sat on the hard bench.

"Don't think that Taoism will save you," continued his master. "You have to save yourself. Taoism is a part of life, but life will not happen by itself. Each person has to go out and actively pursue life. In the same way, Taoism will not come to the passive person. Neither life nor realization comes without effort."

"It's a double effort, though," interjected Saihung. "I have to survive, and I have to follow the Tao."

"In the past," responded his master, "time was slow. There was less pressure, less competition. But now, your life in the West is different. You must meet it head-on, but you mustn't become involved with it inside. Tread the Way. Maintain and cultivate the five elements. Yield to the currents of life."

"It may be difficult to maintain balance." Saihung poured tea into his master's cup, grateful for the chance to listen.

"Not if you understand the difference between modern and ancient," replied the Grand Master. "The modern man does not know the unity of yin and yang. He wants only what is positive and pushes the negative aside. He doesn't realize that bad comes with good. In an effort to advance constantly, he turns to technology and accelerates his progress. Sadly, he does not realize that the greater his progress, the faster negative things will come. To the modernist, efficiency and practicality are paramount."

"And the ancient way?"

"The mind of one who follows the ancients is like a gnarled tree. Ugly. No one wants it for wood, but it provides shade. It is both good and bad. Thus, it survives, remains strong and self-sufficient."

"Constant striving only for positive results leads to destruction," reasoned Saihung.

"Exactly," said his teacher. "Modern man doesn't understand this. If Taoism is ever adopted by the modern West, it will mean the end of this philosophy. Taoism was developed in a particular place, and practiced by people who understand it. It goes very deep, has innumerable cultural roots. One would have had to be in China, living day by day, year by year, in order to be Taoist."

"Then Taoism will remain in China?" asked Saihung.

"No. It shall not even survive here. Modern architecture, medicine, and technology are all being eagerly adopted. Now, there are radios, television, watches, cameras. Progress. Advancement. China is becoming more like the West, pushing only for the positive, ignoring the negative. China cannot absorb so much. There will be disease, illness, and mental imbalance. They have forsaken their native wisdom."

The acolytes came with the food. Saihung saw that the meal consisted almost entirely of things he had brought. There was the bread, fresh vegetables, various forms of bean curd. He wondered if this was out of politeness or necessity.

His master blessed the food, holding up the plates and offering it as if there were still gods to see it. They ate in silence and Saihung noticed that his master ate very little, as was his custom. Toward the end of the quiet meal, his master gestured with his chin as a way of urging Saihung to eat more.

"One cannot eat the way monks do while in the outside world," commented his master. "You must do what you can to sustain yourself. Society is not a monastery. There is no shelter from the pressures and demands that will come your way. You must have fire and strength. Being Taoist does not mean passivity. It means that you meet life directly on every level demanded of you."

"What do you recommend?" asked Saihung. He tried to be gracious, but after such a long time, he did not need urging to fill himself up with the food of home.

"There are two rules to Taoist dietary practices: moderation and variety." The Grand Master observed Saihung's undiminished appetite. "First is moderation. Do not overeat, do not undereat. Do not go to extremes of fasting or overemphasis on any one food. Each meal should have moderate amounts of meat, vegetables, a starch, and a beverage. Avoid pork, duck, wild fowl, and shellfish, as we regard these as having toxins in them.

"Variety means that one eat according to the seasons. In winter, eat foods that will build the kidneys and the blood, such as lamb or veal. In summer, the cooling fruits, vegetables, and melons should predominate in your diet. Whatever the meal, try to have a minimum of three vegetables at every meal: one red, one green, one yellow. Do not have great amounts of single ingredients with your meal, but have a great variety of foods instead. If you follow the way of the ancients, you will have the strength to meet your challenges.

"Food is a primary source of energy. Thus, it is foolish to restrict it. It is wisdom to control it, however, for this can be a significant factor in the cultivation of energy. One's *qi*, the very vital force of the body and soul, is formed from the essence gleaned from food. One might even go as far as to say that the foods you eat can be used to manipulate the consciousness."

Saihung marveled that his master would combine the most abstruse metaphysics with the most concrete of dietary recommendations. It was all part of the same subject to the master.

They were quiet again as the acolytes took away the dishes. Saihung insisted on helping. His master remained seated in the dining hall. As Saihung reentered the room, he looked at the man who had been his mentor for decades. The Grand Master had his back to him and sat upright on a bench. He was still, not meditating, but just sitting quietly. His thick white hair was gathered into a coil on his head and pinned. His dark robes made him seem almost formless.

He wasn't supposed to have any emotions if he had truly realized the doctrine of impermanence. If his current feelings meant that he had not reached a high level, then he accepted it for the time being. He saltily observed that even his master did not live without companionship, and that both he and his master still benefited by the partly emotional ties that were between them. Ironically, his master and his lineage were his assurance of finding freedom from his inner turmoil. For the masters were like the chains that he had once used to climb Huashan's steep crevices: Link by link, they guided him through the dangers of life until he reached freedom. He had no doubt that he would be lost without that chain.

The acolytes came out, and Saihung observed them silently attend to the master. Again, he compared himself to them. They were what he could be if he did not have this mad combination

413

of compassion and cruelty, sentiment and cunning, faith and cynicism. As he looked at Sound of Clear Water, the direct and honest carpenter, he realized that he might have been like him. Sound of Clear Water was a man of pure heart. Had Saihung stayed and become such a monk, he too might have found peace and tranquillity. But he knew that he had been too complicated and ambitious a man.

414   Saihung compared himself to Mist Through a Grove. Clever at strategy, deeply intelligent, and a wonderful musician, he represented what Saihung believed that he himself could have been had he not had an ambitious side. Had life been different, Saihung might have sought a life as a painter or poet.

Saihung wondered whether there was some analog to his own political manipulations and was surprised when his eyes immediately focused on his master. Saihung flatly admitted to himself that the temples had been just as political and prone to the manipulations of power and position as the worst government assemblies that he had been to. At one time, even the Grand Master's own senior students had tried to usurp his master's position. Saihung knew that the Grand Master was quite capable of intrigue.

As he stood there watching the three men who had guided him since childhood, he understood himself a little better. He saw what he might have been had his personality been balanced just a little differently. He was also reminded of the politics and intrigues, the drive for position and power, that he might have dealt with had he stayed in the Taoist hierarchy. But whether through fate or his own stubborn will, he had gone a different path.

He refused to see that as something inferior to the way that his master and classmates had gone. He felt that he had gone through many of the same phases in life, exercised the same skills, faced the same pitfalls. The context was different, and that was all. Had he not fought on the streets of Pittsburgh, it would have been elsewhere, perhaps even against the soldiers who had invaded Huashan. Had he not involved himself with intrigue in government, then he would have striven for leadership within the temples. Had he not learned to find wonder and beauty wherever he traveled, then he would have learned it on the mountainside.

His master had sent him away to work out the same dilemmas that he would have had in the monastery. The only difference was that he was put in a wider field with more pitfalls and more bewildering choices to make. Perhaps he should never have been named Kwan Saihung, "Gateway to a Vast World." Perhaps the name would keep him a wanderer in search of his destiny.

415

S AIHUNG LEFT THAT evening and returned a few days later with more supplies. He could stay on the island only for short times. They knew that the cadres were watching them constantly, and they did not want to cause any suspicion.

"Master, let me stay with you," insisted Saihung impulsively when they met again. In the nights away from the island, he recognized his master needed his service, and that Saihung needed his master's instruction. But the Grand Master again refused him.

"You cannot," said the Grand Master gently. "The government will never permit a young man like yourself to stay here. The acolytes and I are elderly; we are a threat to no one. But you are young: a potential subversive."

"I only want to come back."

"They'll know," said the Grand Master. "There are government observers everywhere."

"It's despicable."

"You still are very individualistic—and you've not lost your anger," observed his master. "China is not the place for you."

"America isn't either," replied Saihung. He thought about his circumstances in Pittsburgh. Humble surroundings were neither poetic nor spiritually rich there. He wanted the island.

The Grand Master strolled to the front of the temple. Saihung followed. Though physically large, Saihung was still a head shorter than the willowy sage. His master's robes trailed behind him as he walked with an ethereal grace. Saihung, in his everyday clothes, walked just on the ground. He was reminded of his boyhood days when he walked behind the old man, sneaking candy, disinterestedly meeting men of wisdom now vanished from the earth.

The sun came softly through the dusty and broken lattice-work. The paper windows had been patched repeatedly. In a corner, one of the acolytes had put some fresh patches up in a tentative attempt to improve the building.

The master pushed the doors open, and fresh air and light came in. A breeze came up, and falling plum blossoms swirled lightly into the gray hall. They began to walk down to the shore. The gravel under their feet made a slight crunching sound.

"You are a man of many ambitions and of great energy," said his master. "You must exercise it and learn where it will lead you. You cannot yet practice complete emptiness. You cannot practice impermanence yet, for you have not yet had your fill of all that life has to offer. Go forth and strive mightily. When you learn the futility of your ways, you will find the key to your destiny. When you have fulfilled your destiny, you will be satisfied. Once you are satisfied, your soul will rest. Only when you rest will you know stillness. In stillness is returning. Only in returning is there emptiness."

"Master, there is still so much for me to learn." Saihung came face-to-face with his master and made his appeal as sincerely as possible. "I am lacking. Please instruct me more."

"There is no time for that," said the Grand Master. He looked far to the distant horizon. There were diesel boats going across the water. "Your place is elsewhere; your destiny is beyond the borders of China."

"But Taoism is Chinese. How can I follow the Tao else-where?"

"You must solve that difficulty yourself. I can only give you one word of advice." He turned to Saihung and paused for a second before delivering the single word: "Persevere!"

Saihung looked up at his master. The eyes were clear, farsee-ing. The day made his hair and beard seem like strands of sunlight. He wondered how his master could deny him. Surely, ten years in the West was enough. He hated the advice. The word for persevere also meant "bear it." He had the hideous image of working as a waiter for decades, all because of that one horrible word.

"Master . . ."

"Say no more," said his master as he gazed at a boat in the distance. "You have been away, but you have not determined your destiny. I told you long ago that I was awaiting your answer."

"But I've barely been able to survive."

"The answer!" demanded the Grand Master harshly.

"I—I don't have it."

The Grand Master turned from him. His face was strict, almost cold. "Then you should persevere."

The Grand Master looked up. "There is a boat nearby," he observed. "I think that we are being watched. You had better leave."

Saihung was reluctant. Of all the things he hated, he hated saying good-bye most of all. In the past, different masters had had to trick him into leaving when his period of living with them was over. One had even blessed Saihung in his sleep, for he was bound to leave once he had received a farewell benediction. As Saihung faced the Grand Master, he felt the same sadness of separation.

"Master," he said. "Come back with me. I'll work to support you."

"You need to support yourself," said his master. "I cannot leave China. My five organs are the five sacred mountains. The rivers are my blood, the air my breath. I could not reconstruct myself in a foreign land. Whatever my destiny holds, I must meet it on my native soil. Yours is different. You are destined to wander. I await you here, on this island. Now go."

"Master," said Saihung as he knelt down. He could see that there was no use in pleading any further. "Please take care of yourself."

His master said nothing. He waved his hand before Saihung in the gesture of blessing. The Grand Master looked for a few moments more at Saihung, then he turned back to his temple.

A S SAIHUNG TRAVELED away from his master, the new civilization quickly presented itself. There were hundreds of distractions. Some were interesting, like new trucks, faces, attitudes. Some were annoying, like going through customs. Some were frightening, like being on his first airplane. By the time he was once again flying toward the United States, his master and the two acolytes seemed almost fictional. No one had the slightest knowledge that there was such a sage on an anonymous island. The government would cease to acknowledge them. The Taoists would never cooperate with the political world. They would become shunned, regarded as nonexistent.

The curious would never find them. Certainly, Saihung would never lead anyone to them, nor would the Taoists expose themselves. They liked anonymity. They did not like modernity and cared only for self-perfection. Showing themselves would only pollute them and lessen their chances for spiritual success.

418

Golden
Gloves

H E RETURNED TO the United States with a feeling of loneliness. He found himself in a world where everything he most valued was now irrelevant. Maybe he needed a change. As much as he found comfort in Pittsburgh, he sensed that there was no future there. He'd try someplace else. He was getting older, and felt the need to make some more conservative decisions in his life. Having repaid his debt to Uncle William and Aunt Mabel, he wanted to establish financial independence. Saihung determined that he would save enough to return to a daily schedule of training and perhaps even found a school. That would take years of hard work and saving, but he felt ready to do it.

He went to New York to work for Uncle William's brother. Uncle Lenny was a balding man whose penchant for plaid shirts and worn, misbuttoned cardigan vests was an act of self-sabotage. He loved big cigars, shouting, and talking about his money and real estate holdings. His skin was spattered with dark spots, and his shaving was usually uneven. In spite of all this, Uncle Lenny mustered enough charm to maintain a smart-looking redheaded mistress.

420

Unlike his Pittsburgh sponsors, Uncle Lenny had no intrinsic affection for Saihung, and he treated him like all the other employees. That meant that his workday ran for ten hours, his pay was fifteen dollars a day minus taxes, Social Security, and meals, lodging was a tabletop in the storeroom, and showers were a hose of cold water in the garage. Saihung read many books during that time, if for no other reason than that they made a good pillow.

He decided the first thing he would do would be to improve his English. Reading was no problem—he had mastered that quickly enough—but speaking was another matter.

His solution was to go to movies every day off and reward his efforts with a cold milk shake. Some New York theaters showed as many as six movies for a dollar. He sat in the dark theaters, among the passed-out winos and necking couples, and studiously repeated the dialogue.

"My name is Bond. James Bond."

"Go for your guns, cowboy!"

"Th-th-that's all folks!"

His next effort was to discover how American society was structured. In China, the Confucian order ordained a definite place for every person in society—father to son, husband to wife, children to elders. Old people wore dark black and blue. Young people wore bright colors. Old people were supposed to walk a certain way; young people were allowed to be carefree and energetic. But after much examination, he was astonished to conclude that there was no difference between young and old in America.

Seeing no way to integrate himself into society, he sought refuge in an institution more familiar. He began weight lifting and sparring at a gym on Canal Street. The building was on the

northern side of the street that was the border between Little
Italy and Chinatown. Though it was understood in those days
that the two ethnic groups were unwelcome in each other's territories, Saihung was a northern Chinese. His features were different from the Cantonese, who were more common in New York,
and the ambiguity of his racial features was an asset.

The gym was on an upper floor. On the hot and muggy summer days, they left the windows open, and the traffic, honking,
and shouting came up from the crowded streets. There were two
small rings in the middle of the loftlike room. Many of the ropes
and buckles were covered with black tape. These numerous layers of repair were common on the punching bags that hung from
the ceiling, and the ubiquitous tape was even used to affix the
posters of favorite boxers. Like images of patron saints, the faces
and fists of such men as Joe Louis, Jack Dempsey, and Rocky
Graziano overlooked the sweating, silent boxers.

He had been there a week, tentatively jabbing at the leather
bags that were different from the ones he had worked with in
China. No one was coaching him. He just imitated some of the
moves that others did. A big heavyweight with a face like misshapen bread dough came up to him.

"What are you doing?" The man wore trunks with the name
"Barry" sewn on them.

"Just fooling around," replied Saihung.

"Yeah, that's what it looks like." Barry looked down derisively.
He outweighed Saihung by at least twenty-five pounds and was
six inches taller. Saihung was irritated.

"What's it to you?" said Saihung rudely.

"I don't like you."

"So what? That makes two of us."

"Why don't you quit screwing around and step in the ring with
a real man?"

Saihung assented without hesitation. Someone strapped big
sixteen-ounce gloves and a headguard on him. Barry did the
same. They climbed into the ring as the others in the gym gathered around to watch.

Barry came on savagely, catching Saihung in the face several
times. Saihung didn't know what to do. He couldn't use any of

his techniques with the big gloves on his fists, and he didn't know any of the footwork.

He tried desperately to fend off the incoming attacks, blocking the best that he could.

"Jesus! You move weird," said Barry. He caught Saihung with a good combination to the body and a heavy uppercut. Saihung backed up and Barry pushed him to the ropes.

Saihung tried to hit back, but his padded hands did not seem to have any effect on his opponent. Barry laughed at him and pounded him down to the canvas.

"Look, I don't know if you're a Spic, a Chink, or what," Barry said as he stood over the stunned Saihung. "But fucking get out of this gym. You're a bum!"

Saihung looked up at the puffy face, the flattened rectangular nose, the mop of black hair, the crooked blue eyes. He felt a raw hatred in him but could not act upon it. Helplessly, he watched his tormentor leave the ring.

Everyone else went back to their activities without so much as helping him. As he sat up, he saw through his sweat-stung eyes a group of gray-haired men. Day and night, these old men sat in the gym like the retired masters that they were. These battered and scarred pugilists shared friendship and passion by living in the boxing world. With their cauliflower ears and broken noses, they were a grotesque lot. They had no pretensions; they had earned their positions. These veterans, who ranged in age from the fifties to the late sixties, never hesitated to enter the ring with arrogant men young enough to be their grandsons. More often than not, they brutalized the youngsters with their superior instincts and enormous fists.

Saihung went to them the next day to learn boxing. They were observant and wise when it came to the ring. They didn't care what words came out of a man's mouth, only how he moved, how powerful his body was, and how smart he was in the art of attacking and protecting. Saihung bribed them extravagantly with meals and liquor.

Saihung liked this study. He could throw himself into this training: roadwork, the heavy bag, the speed bag, conditioning with medicine balls, sparring, shadowboxing, calisthenics. But from those simple elements, an infinite world emerged. Boxing was at the very root of life whenever he was in the process of punching, aiming, looking, stalking.

There was no judgment against violence in boxing. All that counted was moving, attacking, replying to the opposing movement. The fact that there was only one victor in a match did not invalidate the loser's action. Pain was not the same as it was for normal people. For the boxer, pain was an acceptable part of life. He was capable of going on in the face of excruciating agony, even of staying on his feet and punching while nearly unconscious. He inflicted violence, and his opponent inflicted it in return. No other connotations. No metaphors. No intellectualizing. Simple action with the brain and the body. Nothing else.

423

Boxing brought him to his absolute physical and emotional limits. Beyond the study, beyond the daily training, beyond the pursuit of the skill to fold an eighty-pound leather bag with the force of a single blow, was the thrill of the contest. No one was stupid enough to say if he would win or lose, not if he was honest with himself. He would only find out in combat, in testing, in answering the challenge with all the skill gleaned from the alchemy of talent and training. Each blow that he received to the head and the body pummeled his ego into silence.

Only his belief in himself, his reliance on his knowledge, his powerful determination to keep on with somebody constantly battering at him and punishing his every second of carelessness, could account for his survival in the ring and his fascination for fighting. His will was all that kept him from giving up, from obeying the instinct to flee from pain.

Never in the ring, or in the gym, did he ever question this will. But outside—away from the blood, and the sweat, the bitter cries with spit welling in the throat and hurt burning between the ribs—he sometimes questioned this powerful force that brought him through the rounds. It was precisely this will that barred his way to spiritual fulfillment. As long as he depended on this self, he could not realize its essential emptiness. At the same time, he knew that emptiness could not be realized without totally plumbing the depths of a self that was a phantom in ordinary circumstances. Fight on, he decided. He would not be able to transcend anything until he reached its limits. And boxing brought him brutally, harshly, and undeniably to his limits.

His coaches, an old Italian named Gus and a German named Alex, soon decided that Saihung was ready for the ring, and he began to fight in Golden Gloves matches. It was three simple rounds in front of crowds partisan to particular fighters or ethnic groups. No one ever came to watch Saihung fight. He was always a lone champion, an unknown whose name was applauded only accidentally or by drunks. Even that name was unreal. "No one is going to come see a Chinaman," Gus had said bluntly. "We'll put you down as Frank Kahn. Maybe at least the Irish will cheer you."

That didn't matter much to Saihung. He stood in the ring, nearly naked, his hands tightly wrapped, his fists bound in leather. He shifted his mouth guard impatiently as he eyed his opponent, a big Italian. They announced Frank Kahn. He turned in a circle. There were apparently few Irish in the audience. They announced his opponent's name. There were cheers and screams. They went out for the referee's instruction, touched gloves, and retreated. Then the bell.

Saihung went out and immediately received several stinging lefts and a tentative right uppercut. He cursed. He could not kick, he could not use acrobatics. It was just him and his fists, just him standing on his feet upright. He counterattacked with several combinations. He felt the man's muscle through the gloves, felt the heat of his breath, heard his insults.

A blow got into his body, and he felt his breath leave him for a moment. It hurt. The crowd cheered loudly. His anger welled up inside him. There was no need to hold back, no way to plan. There was only the consciousness of combat.

Saihung was a left-handed boxer. He threw two rights and then came in with a heavy left. His opponent covered up. Saihung went to the body, hooked into the kidneys. He heard a groan. He grunted in satisfaction and renewed his attack. But his next few blows were picked off on the man's gloves, and suddenly, his opponent bore in on him with a few quick jabs.

Saihung sidestepped and connected with a straight punch that sent a shower of sweat off into the dark room. It was not enough. There was a turn, and the fighter bore down angrily.

The crowd screamed. There were insults, shouts of command from both corners. His two coaches yelled at him, ordered him to renew the attack, and told him to use particular blows. He only shut them out. He had to concentrate. By the time he acknowledged their instructions and transmitted them to his hands, his opponent landed ten blows. He punched and dodged, hit back, tried to form some strategy. His breathing accelerated. He hit his opponent over and over, but the man still came, desperate and grim.

The round ended and he walked to his corner. They wiped his face, gave him water. Alex leaned over and uttered a string of obscenities in his heavy accent, mixed with his instructions. Saihung only nodded. He decided to use every bit of his knowledge.

425

The bell rang again, and he went out, hands held high, to guard his head. Boxers liked to go for the head. They figured that if they hit a man in the head long enough he would fall over. Saihung decided that his approach would be different, more systematic.

He faked high. His opponent's hands went up. Saihung came in with a devastating straight punch to the abdomen. He had folded a heavy bag. Now, he folded the body over. He followed with two more punches and saw the man's heels come off the ground. He heard a familiar wheeze as the boxer struggled for breath, watched the blood rise to the face. The man fought to keep control of his body. He had felt the pain, and that was nothing. But the lack of response, his inability to answer the call of the attack, brought a desperate look to the man's face.

Saihung came with another series of combinations. He whipped the forearms away, exposed the heart, came in on his opponent's left side. Ribs were only a fragile cage to Saihung, and he hit them hard enough to jar the heart. The face reddened more; the eyes bulged. Saihung threw a stinging left above the nipple as the man tried to inhale. That interrupted his breath. A soft right set the head in position for the final knockout punch. He watched his victim fall heavily to the ring's floor.

"I don't know what the hell you're doing," commented Gus, "but it sure seemed to work." Saihung could only reply with an exhausted nod as he climbed from the ring. They took his gloves off and cut the bindings from his hands.

"Good work, man!" he heard as he walked to the showers.

"I lost money on you, asshole," he also heard. But he didn't care. At other times, he might have avenged such a remark. But he was too tired.

He stood in the showers, the water stinging hot. He at least hoped that it would wash away the smell of the other man. Turning his face to the water, he let it run over his swollen eyes and down his neck before he picked up a piece of soap. He rubbed a few places where he knew there would be bruises the next day.

As Saihung stood in the shower, he felt good at having his first bout. Boxing had its good points and its drawbacks. It lacked the variety of Chinese martial arts, and it was not as well integrated into the culture. But its training for pure punching power was undeniable, and much of boxing was, after all, predicated on the ability to hit hard and fast. In that there was no discussion of superiority of systems. All that mattered was how dedicated, disciplined, and talented a fighter was.

He marveled at the difference between a Western boxing match and a martial duel. Fights here were open to the public. Duels were not. The audience in New York consisted of teenagers and frustrated older adults. The audience in China consisted of all boxers. There, matches were on a simple platform with no ropes. Instructors sat on the main floor. Masters of schools sat on the first balcony. Grand masters sat on the highest level. The judges were the best in the martial world. These men, usually in their fifties, earned their office by fighting, not by democracy. They watched the match and decided the victor.

A referee was always present in the ring, and he had the right to intercede at any moment. Due to his expertise, he could usually anticipate a foul. Many was the time that Saihung saw a fighter stopped in midstrike by some elderly referee. In at least one instance, the referee's grip had left a bruise where all the opponent's punches had not.

Victory was awarded after one man or woman conceded or fell (in the martial world, men and women dueled with each other on equal terms). There were no rounds, just continuous fighting. Unlike the bouts in the United States, there was no cheering, no lusty moving around. The masters watched in stillness and silence. The outcome was likewise received in silence. There was never applause, never any word of encouragement or insult.

Whether in China or America, boxing was a fundamental and primal reality, the ritual of primitive consciousness on an altar of bone and sinew.

THE MORE PUGNACIOUS Saihung became, the more restless he was in daily life. By the summer of 1964, he could no longer stand living in a storeroom eating mostly rice and a few vegetables and the scraps from Uncle Lenny's plate, which he always refused. He went to an employment agency and got a job as a cook at a restaurant in Queens; and at the same time, he moved in with a cousin at Eldridge and Broome Streets in the Bowery.

The building was a five-story brick tenement. There was a strange stoop with a Greco-Roman archway, and a battered steel door with one tiny window. Narrow stairs wound up from the ground floor and zigzagged up to the roof. The walls were painted a dull flesh color; the doorways were dark brown. All the doors were solid metal. No matter what time of the day or night it was, there was never an open door or anyone else in the dim hallways, only peeling paint and scurrying roaches. There was, however, plenty of noise. There were sounds of arguing, crying children, loud Latin music, people making love.

The apartment was one squat, four-square room with two windows and a blistered linoleum floor with a pattern like men's underwear. The brown-and-yellow wallpaper was torn in places, and underneath the plaster was cracking. The bathroom had seen its best days before Saihung had even been born. There was more black mold between the tiles than there was grout, and the faucets had been worn to the brass. The kitchen was a simple open place against the wall, just off the main door. There was a sink, a stove, a refrigerator. A single bare light bulb hung down from the ceiling in the center of the room.

It was oppressively hot. Saihung tried to open the window. It would not budge.

"Don't open it," said his cousin, a young man named Wing. His name meant "Eternal Beauty," but Wing was as plain and thin as a stick.

"Why?"

"Because the Puerto Ricans and the Cubans will come in."

Saihung looked out the window. He saw the alleyway down below, where the tenants of the next building kept their garbage cans. Iron fire escapes were layered with years of paint and rust. The windows facing his had decorated arches that hinted at a time when landlords must have had more pride in their buildings. Most of the panes were dirty, scumbled with a layer of grime that obscured the small interiors. Some had potted plants; at a few windows, there was drying laundry. The setting light was orange through the chimneys and television antennae. The street dialogues were constant, punctuated with screams and shouts, curses and gunshots.

Saihung turned and looked around the room. There were five locks on the door and a special steel brace to wedge in the floor. There was little furniture: a table, some wooden chairs, several steamer trunks covered with clean but tattered towels. Wing pointed to some fold-up army cots. "This is all we have to sleep on. We put them away during the day."

He went to a trunk and pulled out a bar of steel a little over a foot long. "Take this with you whenever you go out. Wrap it in a newspaper. You will need it."

Saihung nodded as he took the cold blue metal in his hand. He had seen the street toughs eyeing him on the corner, the groups of noisy men playing dominoes in front of stores. Certainly, the sound of gunfire was even more alarming. He turned the weapon over in his hands. Survival mattered.

"I'm going to work, now," said his cousin. "Our roommate doesn't get home until the morning."

Saihung watched him pick up a bag lunch and wrap his steel bar. His cousin walked out the door and reminded Saihung to lock it behind him immediately. This Saihung did, carefully wedging the brace in its brass socket.

He took off his shirt and changed into some shorts and an undershirt. He was sweating so much that the cloth stuck all the more to his skin. Breathing was an unwelcome necessity. He went to the kitchen, washed a glass, and poured boiled water from the teakettle.

He sat down in the tiny kitchen. The floor sloped disconcertingly, and matchbooks and napkins were wedged under the legs of the table to make it level. A few dusty mousetraps lay sprung in the corners. He positioned a drab green electric fan in front of his face, but the propeller could do no more than to blow hot air in his face. Coming from a mountain temple, he was not unused to poverty-stricken conditions. But this slum was different.

He sat for many hours, just thinking of the future. He looked down at his hands, which had once been folded in contemplation beside mountain springs. The fingers, slender and tapered, had once caressed the strings of a lute. Now, they were rough from the hot oil that splattered on them when he was cooking. The heat and the constant handling of four woks had put thick calluses on his palms. He had been trained to hold a writing brush; now he was always holding metal—if not the spatula in the kitchen, then the handrails on subway cars.

There was a chrome thermos bottle on the plastic laminate table, and he saw his reflection. He looked older. When he had seen himself on Huashan, his face had been fresh, young, hopeful. As he looked at himself in the polished silver, he saw the face of a man in his forties, features that were set, weary, a bit cynical. Though a stranger would not have placed him at more than half his age, he knew better. He saw every scar that he carried, noted the nearly invisible lines of disappointment.

He decided to go out. There was no use sitting in a tenement that smelled of baking plaster and melting asphalt. He went to his trunk to get a change of clothes. As he opened it, he saw a letter from Aunt Jean. She had moved from Pittsburgh to San Francisco. Writing wonderful descriptions of a friendly city, she wrote of the significant Chinese population and how they would welcome him. Saihung pondered her urgings, but he found in himself a new cautiousness. He couldn't even afford to go out to see the city. It was better to be patient, work hard, save money, and establish a life in which he could return to his spiritual aspirations. That was his goal.

Saihung moved some books aside and found a long cloth bundle. He unwrapped two long knives encased in special leather sheaths made to strap to his forearms. The blades were slightly curved, like the contours of a saber-tooth tiger's fangs. The metal was a flawless steel alloy, and the blood grooves that ran the

429

length of the knife were deep and polished. Deeply etched ideograms caught the light in the slender, brilliant strokes. It had been years since he had worn these, but if life was to be as rough as his cousin said, he wanted protection.

He undid the brace on the door and descended the narrow stairs. He went out the front of the building. It was a little cooler outside; the sun had long gone down. He was the only man on the street wearing a windbreaker and carrying a newspaper. The young Latins loitering on the stoops across the way were dressed only in tank tops or no shirts at all. They spoke in Spanish, and he could not understand them. A few looked him up and down with stoned eyes, heads cocked back at an arrogant angle, lips curled up, implied sneers. Their music was loud, blaring an insinuating beat of congas and trumpets. He glared back, never one to back down.

He looked up at the buildings around him. Old brick Victorian-era buildings were built tightly against one another. Their surfaces were etched by soot, rain, car exhaust. Cornices and archways were amazingly intact, considering the obvious age and decay of the buildings. The windows were opaque rectangles. At the roof line, he saw chimneys and water tanks, smokestacks, a jumble of rusted wire. The street was all blacks and ochres, red-brick melting to dark grime, harsh yellow street lamps casting a lone spot per block. He walked north. The Chrysler building was a tiny tower, crowned with triangles that glowed in small points against the onyx sky.

A block away from his apartment was a movie theater. For a dollar, one could see up to three movies. Saihung could not resist. Perhaps he could forget about his troubles for a while and practice his English. He went in.

He found his way through by the flickering blue light from the movie screen. Half of the audience was asleep. Some were old men whose age or drinking had caught up with them. Others were passed-out junkies who had sought a refuge in the dark, sweltering cavern. There were some families, and children ran screaming up and down the aisles, bumping him. He found a seat on the side section and sat down in a chair that sagged at the back.

He saw only horror movies that night. All he remembered after nearly seven hours were monsters trampling Tokyo, creatures emerging from swamps, and aliens blasting people from office buildings. He did not learn much English, and there was mostly the sound of screaming and explosions. It was getting close to midnight, and he had to go to work the next day. He went back into the night, and still the men were talking and laughing and watching him.

Even the next day, it still seemed dark whenever he was outdoors. He left for work before the sun came up, and it was night when he made his descent into the catacombs of the subway station in Queens. The tunnel was smoky, and the air was thick with humidity. He was a man alone on the platform, waiting uncertainly for the next train to arrive. He spent long minutes staring down the straight corridor, counting the receding cadence of pillars, listening for the metallic sound of an approaching train.

He heard some laughter and some shouting. There was the sound of people jumping the turnstile. A group of young Cubans approached him.

He thought when the moment came that they would ask for money. They didn't. They were apparently only interested in the pleasure of beating him. Five of them surrounded him menacingly. One waved his hand provokingly in front of Saihung's face. There were urgings among themselves in their native tongue, but no one bothered to address the intended victim.

Saihung examined them quickly. He found them curiously short, but noticed that a few of them had weight lifter's bodies.

There was the click of a stiletto, and Saihung discarded the newspaper.

One man grabbed his hand, and Saihung promptly brought the bar down and shattered his assailant's wrist. He spun around and caught another youth just above the ear. A blade cut toward him, and Saihung dodged one of the heavy men attacking swiftly from behind. Swiveling away from this dangerous position, Saihung rushed furiously forward. He covered his assailant's whole face in the grip of his hand and squeezed hard enough to feel blood. Lunging forward, he pushed his struggling victim onto the tracks. As he put his foot back to the concrete, he rammed the end of the bar into the throat of the dagger man. The man staggered forward, and Saihung seized his wrist. A sharp twist dislodged the stiletto.

The biggest one tackled Saihung around the waist, but Saihung stood his ground. He did not let go of the knife-wielder's wrist but brought the steel sharply down onto the head of the attacker. Blood wet his hand.

432

Only one man was left and, seizing him by the wrist and twisting, Saihung pulled him up. The man yelled loudly with the pain. Saihung put the bar against the elbow, and threw the man harshly to the ground with a mighty flip. A snapping kick broke his jaw.

They dragged themselves away. It was another twenty minutes before the gunmetal cars came down the track. Saihung gladly boarded and sat down in the loud and rocking car.

When he emerged from the subway station near his home, he was followed by a tall man. He might have to fight more. He walked swiftly up the street, stepping quickly over the few passed-out drunks who lay unmoving in his path. He had not settled down from the fury of fighting in the station, but he did not want to fight again. He was afraid that he would not remember to hold back. These were not desperate people who needed something to eat. These were men who got their enjoyment by hurting people.

He turned the corner on to Eldridge and stopped. An enormous dark man stood in his way. He was wearing a blue short-sleeved shirt with tropical colors. His ebony skin glistened with perspiration, and his crooked teeth were stained and brown. Saihung turned. The shadow he had picked up at the subway station was right there. Saihung saw the flash of brass on the fist that came out of a pocket. There was not even the chatter of Spanish as there had been earlier, only the menacing closing of the trap.

Saihung lashed out with the bar, but the shadow grabbed it. He loomed over Saihung and shot his hand out for his jaw. Saihung intercepted it, grabbing a finger and bending it back. He twisted the arm in its socket and hit the man on the front of the rotated shoulder, dislocating the joint.

Saihung heard a sound and cocked his head in time to avoid a heavy blow. But though he protected his head, the iron links struck him full on the back. He turned and ducked the backhand return of the chain. Saihung whirled in close and hit the man hard enough to send blood and teeth into the gutter.

They staggered angrily toward him. He backed up a few paces. With a great deal of swearing, they made a few lunges that he sidestepped. Finally, it seemed as if he had no other choice. With his back to the door of his apartment building, he pulled out one of his own daggers. The crescent of steel was almost incandescent in the night. The men paused.

433

"Come on! come on!" shouted Saihung. "I'll give it to you right here!"

They turned and fled. Saihung unlocked the door and rushed in. He checked under the stairs for anyone hiding there and ran up the stairs to his room. There was no one else inside. It was oppressively hot. He looked out the dirty windows. They remained closed.

Renunciation

T HERE WAS A park on the southern edge
of Chinatown. Saihung had acquired the
habit of going there since he first arrived in
New York, and he still went there in the early morning to work
out. He came in darkness and usually left before the sun came
up. A Romanesque granite building that looked like a cross between a dance hall and a grandstand bordered the park, and Saihung fancied it to be like the pavilions in China.

Other men came to work out in the park as well. They practiced different forms that they favored, manipulated staffs and
swords for the exercise. Some even knew *qigong*, and Saihung
could see their solitary figures doing deep breathing or standing
in contemplative postures.

It was hot in August. Even the dark summer mornings seemed warm on his skin. He stood in the black shadow cast by the pavilion's upper level and made himself absolutely still. He thought of his *dan tian*, a spot of concentration in his lower abdomen. According to the classics of Taiji, this was the moment analogous to the void that preceded the universe. It was *wu wei*, Nothingness. He held no thoughts.

The first moment of the universe, when time and energy and matter were all set into motion, was believed to have been triggered by thought. In the same way, he decided to begin. This was volition. There could be no movement without it. He inhaled, and the breath stirred the respiratory of energy in his *dan tian*, just as the first ray of though that flashed through the void had generated breath.

His arms rose. The energy rushed up his back and out to his hands with a tingling sensation. His fingers filled with blood. Breath and blood and consciousness all flowed from his center out, as the universe had first expanded from a single point of infinity. He lowered his arms, bent his knees, and the energy sank back to his *dan tian*, descended to the bottom of his feet. He established upper and lower, rising and falling, expansion and return. In the movement of two arms, he distinguished yin from yang. All this occurred in the first movement of Tai Chi Chuan. It did not need discourse or philosophical speculation; it taught by doing. It taught on a level that the conscious mind did not acknowledge.

He began to move his arms and take a variety of stances. Outwardly, the postures seemed similar to other styles of martial arts. After all, the science of footwork and strikes was already well established before Tai Chi had ever been created. It was a relatively young martial art, which had reached the zenith of its forms only within the last one hundred years; it was natural that it should resemble other styles. But inwardly, it was much different.

Other styles had features that were outwardly apparent. This was part of the reason that a fighter like Saihung could observe the patterns of a style and adapt even during the heat of battle. Taiji, however, could only be appreciated by the person doing it.

So much of its qualities lay within the mysterious arrangement of its movements, the slowness that encouraged healthy circulation, the deep breathing that became automatic when the postures were done correctly. What was hidden in Taiji was the secret that only the practitioners knew: Energy could be circulated in a special way if one took the trouble to keep certain alignments of the body.

436 These alignments were a straight back, rounded shoulders, pelvis tilted upward, head straight, feet firmly planted, and body relaxed. This simple set of concordances set the gates of the body open; and if one had not clogged the pathways of the body by poor diet or indiscreet living, the energy would spontaneously move on its own. The first thought in the first posture set it into motion. Throughout the rest of the movements, it would flow on its own. No ordinary person could see this on the outside, but inside, the practitioner could feel the movement and enjoy the sensation of life force itself. By relaxing and letting go, he gained everything. He loved feeling the movement deep beneath his skin.

Here in the process of Taiji was the sensation of life itself. It was not just blood flow. It was not just the simple tingling of nerves. It was the unmistakable feeling that a force was flowing like a tide throughout the body. Not only did this force leave one feeling fresh, alert, and renewed, but it also responded to consciousness.

The quality that made him a living human being was not simple energy like electricity from a socket. It was something more subtle, more complex. It would respond to his thoughts, and it could be disrupted by his thoughts. That was why there was meditation. The more focused one's thinking was, the more one could direct and learn from the forces within.

When the energy flowed, the channels were purified, the organs were regulated, and the subtle channels of the nervous system were cleansed. Consciousness had set the universe in motion. The motion in Taiji did the opposite. It could affect the consciousness of the individual. Both sides of the body were moving, the eyes were following the hands, the spine was continuously being rotated and stimulated, and it was inevitable that both sides of the brain would be opened at the same time. All of this happened through the gentle movements of a set of more than one hundred postures.

He practiced other martial arts, reviewed the weapon techniques that he relied upon to save his life in his neighborhood. He went to the park every day to stand in the quiet time before there was even morning light. At work, he was someone to be ordered around, a body to cook meals for the sake of business. In the ring, he was a fighter against a man whose face was often obscured by a headguard. In the streets, he was the target of men whose language he did not learn. Only there in the anonymous dark did he feel that which was within him.

437

TWO YEARS AFTER he had begun boxing, Barry, the fighter who had beaten Saihung in the gym, appeared again. Once more, he watched Saihung at the bags, asked who he was. He had forgotten Saihung, but Saihung had not forgotten him. He watched the man with the bloated face walk toward him.

"What are you doing?" Barry asked him aggressively.

"Just fooling around," replied Saihung noncommittally. He wondered if this was a rehearsed routine with Barry.

"Yeah, that's what it looks like."

Saihung decided to cut the ritual short. "I don't like you. Step in the ring or get out of my face."

"Asshole!" Barry leaned over Saihung menacingly. "I'm gonna make you ugly!"

Saihung looked over at Gus. The grizzled senior coach nodded his approval.

"All right," shouted Saihung. "I want four-ounce gloves!"

Barry knew what that meant. Four-ounce gloves had no padding at all. He hesitated a moment, but his pride was too strong. "Okay, chump. It's your funeral."

"You bastard!" Saihung's face turned crimson with fury. "I'm going to piss on your grave!"

Saihung went over to Gus, who taped his hands, slipped on the gloves, and put a headguard on him.

"I know you're mad," said Gus, as he made sure that everything was cinched up. "But you keep your head out there, okay?"

Saihung said nothing in response. He nodded. He never took his eyes off the pale-skinned Barry. Gus pulled one of the ropes down and pushed Saihung gently into the ring.

Barry looked at him eagerly. Saihung could see that his reach and weight gave him confidence. Barry grinned maniacally.

The bell rang, and the other men began to cheer. The first time they had fought, men had watched silently; no one knew Saihung. But this time he had acquaintances who shouted their encouragement. Barry charged at him with a barrage of heavy blows. Unwarily, he threw his might into the first skirmish without any tentative punches. Saihung counterpunched and stung some hard jabs to Barry's arms. The punches hurt enough for Barry's guard to falter. Saihung noted with pleasure the sudden look of bewilderment on Barry's face. Two years of hitting the heavy bag had given Saihung's punches a new authority.

Barry tried to punch Saihung toward the ropes, but Saihung moved to the side and hit Barry's face several times. He saw a swelling. Barry came in again and tried to maul Saihung, and Saihung punished the move with heavy hooks that caught the side of the face. He followed with a straight overhand that pushed Barry's jaw far to the side.

By the second round, Barry circled Saihung a little more carefully. Saihung took some hard lefts but then opened up several cuts on Barry's face. Blood began to smear on the front of Saihung's gloves as he threw punch after punch. He felt the heavy impact of his knuckles on bare skin and bone. People began to yell from the sidelines, and Barry began to curse loudly as he came in with a heavy uppercut that nearly knocked the wind from Saihung's lungs.

Saihung pushed him off and looked at Barry angrily. Saihung swept aside his reservations, and for a few exchanges, he and Barry stood toe-to-toe slugging it out. Saihung hit him with a right, made sure Barry was looking, and then dropped the guard of his own left hand while feinting again with his right. Barry took the bait and threw a crushing right hand, which Saihung dodged. Before Barry could withdraw the hand, Saihung stepped inside and came up with the hardest left he could muster. Barry went down, his jaw and nose nearly bent out of human proportions.

438

Saihung stood over the fallen man without grace or composure. He shouted obscenities and spat on his face. "Now who's
uglier?" he demanded of the bloody and immobile face. Gus
rushed up to drag him away. The ring filled with men.

"You're getting a little crazy," Gus whispered. Saihung said
something obscene in response. Gus shrugged. "Hey. I'll talk to
you when you've cooled down."

It was not until hours later, sitting alone in the light of the lone   439
incandescent bulb that hung above his locker, that Saihung
began to reflect on the fight and Gus's pronouncement. It was
the first time that he considered whether he had gone too far
from his path.

S AIHUNG CORRESPONDED REGULARLY with his aunt and uncle
in Pittsburgh. Toward the end of 1968, they wrote that their
house had been bought by the city. The site had been part of
land designated for a freeway. They had no choice but to move.

Aunt Mabel and Aunt Jean, who had once worked in the same
laundry, had been corresponding. Aunt Mabel wanted to move to
San Francisco, or at least any place that did not aggravate her
arthritis as the winters in Pittsburgh did. Surprisingly, Uncle
William did not want to move from the city. He had lived there
for forty years and had grown quite attached to it.

Uncle William feared old age. His letters constantly appealed
to Saihung to return to take care of the elderly couple. Saihung
did not object to helping them, but he did not want to move
back. He, too, thought seriously of San Francisco. He could not
continue forever with his New York life. He was getting varicose
veins from all the standing that he had to do as a cook; he was
never sure if one of the street toughs would get lucky with a pipe
or zip gun, and he had been wondering about his emerging savagery.

His final matches as a Golden Gloves boxer were fought in
Madison Square Garden, which represented the achievement of
a certain plateau to him. But as he sat in the dressing room after a
fight that he had won by knockout, he accepted the fact that he
had changed. He was off course. He had boxed enough to be
able to decide when to knock a man out. He had begun to enjoy

the sound of ribs breaking. With some fright, he saw that the eagerness for triumph had obscured all his other priorities.

Gus came into the room.

"Hey, Frankie Kahn!" exclaimed Gus. "You were great out there! Did you ever think of turning pro?"

"No," replied Saihung before he could consider what he was saying. "I'm quitting."

440

"What the hell do you think you're talking about? You don't quit like that!"

"I do what I want!"

"Hey! Cool down! It's an old problem. I've seen lots of fighters go through what you're going through. It's a postfight letdown. Give it a rest for a couple days. You'll come around. And when you do, son, there are some people interested in you."

"I'm going to hit the showers. I'll think it over."

"Sure, sure," said Gus. "You'll come back."

"Yeah," said Saihung offhandedly. But he knew that he would go back only to clean out his locker.

That night, he walked to the waterfront. He pulled out his daggers. Though he had never used them, he had threatened plenty of people with them. Superstitiously, he felt that carrying them invited trouble.

The martial principles that he had learned emphasized virtue, chivalry, and honor. Only two people who were on the same level dueled. Sometimes they only fought for respect. Defeat came to all fighters. No matter how great, every one had felt what it was to lose. Perhaps a fighter even answered a challenge knowing that he was the inferior one. But in the martial world, it was good enough that one was valiant. Losing did not necessarily compromise one's honor.

Saihung felt that there was no honor in the fighting he had done. He did not honor his opponents, and they did not respect him. That was not the type of fighting that he had trained for decades to do. Martial arts was for discipline and dignity, not for sweating and shouting and bloodying and slaughtering.

He turned the blades over. Their curve echoed the crescent moon. He held them up one last time, remembered that they had been custom made of the finest metal available, that he had consecrated them with the appropriate runes and mantras. Weapons had power. Weapons had spirits. But power and other spirits could possess a man. He wanted to stop fighting. He already had tickets away from New York. Saihung flung the daggers as far as he could into the river.

Gate

of

Liberation

442

S AIHUNG, AUNT MABEL, and Uncle William took the train out to San Francisco. Movers would ship most of their possessions after they had established themselves. This was done easily with the aid of Aunt Jean, the pleasant middle-aged friend they had known from their Pittsburgh days. His aunt and uncle moved to a small apartment on the eastern slope of Nob Hill. Saihung found a single room on Stockton Street above a butcher shop.

His first days in the often foggy San Francisco were unusually sunny and warm. He happily walked street after street in exploration of his new home. He walked from Chinatown through North Beach and then began to climb steep steps on the sidewalk toward Coit Tower. The surrounding bay made the city seem especially tranquil to him. As he first climbed Telegraph Hill, and then Russian Hill, he could always see the serene blue of the distant bay, placid and wide. He felt welcome.

The people seemed friendlier, open, and more relaxed than those whom he had met in Pennsylvania and New York. Though he soon discovered that there was racial tension even here, it was not so immediate or so savage as what he had experienced before. Perhaps it was because the city was simply not so densely populated. As he walked up to the crest of Hyde Street and looked down a steep hill to the piers at the bottom, he met very few people. Compared to China, where sidewalk traffic was like a major parade, or New York, where people were on the streets at any hour, San Francisco seemed almost intimate.

He wandered into a park past some tennis courts and then down several flights of concrete stairs. He could see hill upon hill, and beyond the waters even more hills, like the spine of a dragon lying on the horizon. He walked by some recently painted green park benches where a few people sat casually reading the Sunday paper. Strolling to a lower level, he found an empty bench with a view of the Golden Gate Bridge.

There was just a hint of salt in the air, mixed with traces of pine trees. He was able to see the Marin headlands, the straits leading to the Pacific Ocean, the almost indistinguishable squares of houses on the slopes to the north. Not since he had been on Huashan had he had the opportunity to feel that he was standing on a high vantage point. It felt good. It made his recent past seem all the further away.

He sat there contentedly for a long time until he realized that he was due at a welcoming banquet. Saihung walked back over the hill and down Jackson Street to his aunt and uncle's apartment. He rang the bell and smiled when his aunt came out in a blue coat and a hat with a veil.

"Auntie," said Saihung. "It's quite warm outside."

"Wait until you're seventy." His aunt laughed. "You'll wear a coat too."

She walked slowly down the stairs. Saihung noticed that she seemed a little more stooped, a little tinier.

443

Uncle William locked the door behind him. He wore a brown striped suit and a camel-colored hat.

"Ah, Ox Boy! It's good of you to escort two old people."

"It's not natural for young people to be with old," commented Aunt Mabel.

"Yes," agreed Uncle William. "We aren't too slow for you, are we?"

444

"I don't mind," responded Saihung. "We're all new to this city. Why not stick together? We are practically relatives."

"You're kind to pretend," said his aunt.

"Are you finding it easy to get settled?" asked Saihung.

"I'm making many new friends. Jean is showing me the city, and I've met some of her co-workers. Your uncle has been down to the family association quite a bit."

"So you like it here after all?" Saihung asked as he turned to his uncle.

"It will do," said Uncle William gruffly. "But I miss my Buick."

"Oh, forget that thing," said his wife scornfully. "Both you and it were getting too old to drive around together anyway."

"And ice cream," continued Uncle William, studiously ignoring his wife. "There don't seem to be many ice-cream places here."

"I'm sure there are a few," said Saihung.

"Where?" demanded his uncle.

"I don't know . . . I'm sure we could find one."

"Yes," said his uncle emphatically. "It should be done before the next Sunday."

"Stop ordering him around," said Aunt Mabel. "Ox Boy has his own life to live. Besides, how can you talk about ice cream when you have a whole banquet ahead of you?"

Uncle William shook his head. He leaned over to Saihung.

"I envy you," he whispered. "You were smart not to get married."

"I heard you!" said Aunt Mabel in a tone of mock outrage. Uncle William began to laugh, and his wife was soon laughing at his teasing too.

The banquet turned out to be a rather modest affair. There was roast duck, a whole steamed rock cod, beef with broccoli, sea cucumbers. Aunt Jean sat across from Saihung. She was a short, plump woman in her fifties. Her skin was wrinkled at her forehead and mouth. Her eyes were narrow and closely set, so that she seemed slightly cross-eyed, even when she was looking far away. She dyed her hair jet black, and it was hair-sprayed into a virtual helmet. Gaudy gold and jade bracelets dangled on her wrists. Though she wore a *cheongsam*, the traditional Chinese high-collared silk gown, she had an old cardigan thrown over it. Comfort was what was important, she reminded Saihung.

445

Her husband, Henry Chan, was a large man with a brown and sagging face. He had large, puffy bags under his down-sloping eyes, and thick lips that usually were wrapped around enormous cigars. A full bottle of brandy sat before him, and the only thing he drank it with was a glass. He never laughed, though his idea of dinner conversation was to make fun of other people under the pretense of good humor. He enjoyed blowing smoke magnificently over the table.

"Hey!" he shouted to Saihung. That was Henry's typical form of address.

Saihung looked over.

"How you like it here?" Uncle Henry did not speak much Chinese. His English, on the other hand, was outrageously accented. Saihung wondered just which language his uncle was comfortable with.

"I like it fine," said Saihung, straining to be polite as more cigar smoke came his way.

"Hey! Your Aunt Jean went through a lot of trouble to get you here." He stubbed his cigar into a glass ashtray.

"Yes, I know. We all appreciate it."

"Okay. Hey! Eat more. This food's expensive, you know." Henry gestured expansively over the table and looked at Saihung with red-rimmed eyes.

Saihung held his temper. His uncle's comment certainly did not stimulate his appetite.

"You know how I can afford to do this?" Uncle Henry continued without any encouragement. "I worked hard. Saved my money. Invested it. Chrissakes, look at you. It's time that you did something too. Don't just throw your money away on women."

Saihung did not know what to say.

"Hey, I know. Young guy. They all do it. But if you want to get ahead, you save. Got anything?" Henry waved his hands at Saihung. A large, gaudy jade ring gleamed on his little finger.

"Yes, I do," said Saihung with as much dignity as possible.

"Put it in the bank over on Grant and Jackson. Best interest rates." He turned to look into his glass of whiskey.

Saihung said nothing. Henry looked up suddenly, his droopy eyes opening in surprise.

"Chrissakes!" he exclaimed. "Don't tell me that you stuck it all in a mattress somewhere?"

No, he hadn't. He carried it with him.

His uncle spoke Chinese for the first time. "You stupid country bumpkin! Don't be dumb. You never heard of interest?"

Of course Saihung had heard. But he wasn't sure how finances worked in the United States. His embarrassment prevented him from responding.

"You want to make your money grow, you invest it," explained his uncle. "Take me, for example. I got a deal coming up to open a big restaurant. All the investors are getting together and we'll make a nice profit. Hey, you could do it too."

"I don't know that end of the business," said Saihung.

"That's the beauty of it. You get the experience of others to work for you. Think it over. Get a deal going like that."

"Henry," interrupted Aunt Jean. "Stop talking about money all the time."

They finished the last course of the dinner, and Saihung was thankful that his two uncles found enough in common for him to be left out of the conversation. Eventually, Uncle Henry stood up unsteadily. "Hey! You enjoy yourselves. I'm going to the bar!"

Saihung went the next day to a Chinatown employment agency and applied for a variety of jobs. He found that there were few positions available: cook, waiter, laundry, houseboy. He wanted to stick to restaurant work; that was what he knew best. The first job he got was as an ice-cream scooper across from the topless bars on Broadway. It took several months of applying before he got a better position as a waiter at a downtown men's club. It was back to eight hours a day, but at least he was away from the Chinese employers who paid little for long hours. He continued to save and added that to the money that he had brought with him from the East Coast. Within a year of his arrival in San Francisco, he had put together a sizable sum of money, enough to have bought an entire house for cash. But he did not want a house. He wanted enough money so that he could still persuade his master to come live with him. He remembered Uncle Henry.

"How did that restaurant do?" asked Saihung when he met his uncle on the street.

"Fine," said Henry. "Sold it already." He lit up the stump of his cigar.

"So fast?"

"Hey! There were three partners. We each made thirty thousand." He blew cigar smoke out of his mouth and watched it drift down Stockton Street.

"I've got money to invest," said Saihung in a quiet voice.

"How much?" His uncle did not even turn to look at him.

"As much as what you made on the restaurant."

"You should buy a house. Get married," advised his uncle.

"I'd rather invest it."

"With me? Forget it. I don't do business with relatives." He looked with a bored expression at the glowing end of his cigar.

"But I don't know who to trust."

"Well, maybe," said his uncle noncommittally. "I'll call you if another deal goes through. You need people who can handle everything. Do you know how to get permits? Do you know the guys in city hall? It takes a lot of wheelin' and dealin'."

Saihung knew nothing about such things. That was why he needed help. "You'll call me?"

"Yeah. Doesn't Jean have your number?"

Saihung nodded. Eventually, Uncle Henry helped him invest in a restaurant.

UNCLE WILLIAM DIED two years after they moved to San Francisco. Saihung did his best to comfort Aunt Mabel and personally arranged for his uncle's burial. A year after, Saihung came back to his hotel room and found a message that his aunt was ill. Alarmed, he walked immediately to the community hospital.

The interior was dark, a narrow hall lit in sepia tones. A rubbery-faced nurse with a double-pointed white hat looked at him indifferently. "No visitors!" she said curtly.

"It's not ten o'clock yet," replied Saihung patiently. "And I am a relative."

"So what?"

Saihung moved forward threateningly. "So I want to see her. Now!"

She jumped a little. "Name?" she said, a little more meekly.

"Mabel Yee."

"Room 402. You've got five minutes."

He raced up the stairs. The wooden steps creaked with each step. The air was very warm and smelled of camphor and alcohol.

The doors to the individual rooms were painted with a heavy red paint. There were wooden bins on the doors for charts. Some overstuffed chairs were in the hallways, as if to provide places for convalescing patients to rest as they tried to walk. The corridor was dim; the light bulb hanging from the ceiling was bare. He found his aunt's room and went in to find a man dressed in black standing over her.

"Who the hell are you?" demanded Saihung protectively.

The gray-haired man turned around. He was tall, ruddy-faced, blue-eyed. Saihung saw the white collar around his neck. The priest was holding a rosary and a Bible.

"I came to help your aunt."

"Ox Boy . . . " whispered his aunt weakly. "Make him go away."

"She doesn't want you here," declared Saihung. "Please leave."

"I understand that you might be upset at this moment. But it is often a comfort to hear the word of God."

Saihung restrained himself from being rude. "My aunt has her own religious beliefs."

"There is only one God."

"I'm not in the mood," said Saihung, grabbing the priest by the arm. He shoved the man out the door and closed it firmly.

He pulled the curtain across the room and sat down beside his aunt. She was elevated in an overstuffed hospital bed. Dressed in a pale gown, she lay small and still under the stiff white sheets. A lamp cast yellow light low on the bed. Some flowers in an old porcelain vase had already begun to wilt in the heat.

Her hair was laid out around her head in small waves of silver. Aunt Mabel's face seemed to be more wrinkled, the eyes like jewels sunken almost entirely into the mass of her pale flesh. Her lips were dry, colorless.

"Where does the soul go?" she asked with childlike directness.

Saihung did not even think to engage in scholarly discourse. "It will be a comfort. The gods will take you. You will be reborn."

"Heaven is hard to imagine," she murmured. "It's harder than remembering China."

"Auntie, don't talk if it makes you tired."

"I've lain here all day. I want to talk. All I've thought about is my home in the village that I haven't seen for fifty years. How odd to think of it so vividly. Do you think my soul will go back there?"

"If you so will it."

"Ah yes . . . if I so will it."

A voice came from the hallway. "All visitors must leave!"

"I must go, Auntie," said Saihung softly. "I will come in the morning."

"Yes, come," replied his aunt. "Read me the sutras, so that I may find my way to the next world."

"I will be here," he promised as he adjusted the sheets.

As he walked into the foggy streets, he wondered about what he had so easily told his aunt. Aside from what was written in scriptures, there was no guarantee that the gods existed or that there was even such a thing as reincarnation. But he did believe that the soul could go where it wanted to go upon death. He had enough respect for the human mind to understand that it could transcend death.

If Aunt Mabel was determined enough, she would indeed go back to her village. If her prayers were fervent enough, she could be led to paradise itself.

He found sutra books and went to her side the next day. But she was unable to hear him. He sat there for a long time praying, the first that he had really prayed since he had left the temple.

He had been taught from childhood that the chants of the devout could lead the soul of the dying, guide them at the moment when they were most bewildered. He whispered his prayers sincerely over and over, determined to escort his aunt to the other side. She never awoke to see him again.

Only at sporadic moments did he see the sheets rise and fall with slight breathing. Breath was the very basis of life, but breath was slowly abandoning her. There was neither enough going in, nor even enough energy to take the air.

Saihung looked down at her hands, shriveled and gnarled roots lying on the clean white fabric. Twisted, curled, they had been painfully distorted for years by arthritis. She had been unable to straighten, in spite of medication and Saihung's massaging. Her profession had crippled her permanently. But as he looked at her spotted brown hands, he remembered the care that she had taken in making dim sum, the patience with which she used to mend his clothes.

He prayed there the whole day, determined that he would do whatever he could to lead her soul safely into death. With single-minded concentration, he repeated the chants, sent his most heartfelt feelings. Destiny could not be stopped, but at least he would do whatever he could to ease its final path.

Aunt Mabel died the next day in her sleep. Aunt Jean and Uncle Henry were there, and helped ease him through the confusion of all the arrangements. There were many old women at the funeral, friends that his aunt had made in San Francisco and young people who had escorted the elderly. They buried her next to her husband, on a grass knoll overlooking the bay. Incense was burning, candles flamed brightly over the grave, flags with holy words fluttered in the wind. Taoist priests chanted and prayed for her soul.

He looked down as a young man shoveled earth over the coffin. Where was Aunt Mabel? For all his training and his meditation, he could not see where she had gone. Uncle Henry laid a comforting hand on Saihung's shoulder.

"Don't take it too hard, son," he said in his rasping voice. "She is in a much better world."

Saihung looked up quietly. It was an idiotic thing to say. But he only nodded.

"Hey. Come by and see me and Jean when the mourning period is over, okay? It might be time to celebrate the restaurant."

"It's not respectful to talk about it now," said Saihung.

"Don't take it wrong. I only mean that it's too bad Mabel
won't see it." Uncle Henry rolled his eyes.

"I will come in a month," said Saihung. "When mourning is
over."

"All right. Watch out for yourself until then."

451

When Saihung returned to his room, he sat down on the edge
of his bed and thought about his aunt. It would be wonderful if
he could see her, if he could somehow know that she was all
right. As he meditated, he could not detect any presence of Aunt
Mabel. She was gone.

In China, he would have found a sorcerer and paid him in gold
for the service of guiding her soul into the next world, but he was
not in his homeland, and the government prohibited any sorcery.
Only in America did he consider for the first time that this might
not actually work.

He observed the mourning period anyway and then went to
see his Aunt Jean and Uncle Henry. Traditionally, that time
could have lasted up to three years. Instead he held a month-
long vigil. There were some blessings in modernity. The permits
for the restaurant were ready and the remodeling about to begin,
Uncle Henry had told him by phone. Saihung had seen the at-
tractive storefront out on Clement Street. He had invested all his
money, but it was for the best. He would have a secure future.

Uncle Henry and Aunt Jean's house was about an hour's walk
from Chinatown. It was a two-story Italianate building in the Ma-
rina district. Saihung appreciated the sun and the fresh air that
came to the front of the building. It was certainly better than
Chinatown. He went up the stairs of the white stucco building
and rang their bell. No response. He rang again. Saihung
shrugged. He'd leave a note and call some other time.

As he turned, the landlady poked her head out the other door.
She was a large Chinese woman who had plucked her natural
eyebrows out in favor of higher, painted ones.

"You're making a great deal of noise," she said fearlessly.

"My apologies, I just came to see the Chans."

"Too late. They've moved." She began to close the door.

"Moved?" Saihung reached out to stop her. His heart beat faster.

"Yes. Two days ago. And don't try to rent their place either. I already have other prospects." She glared at him until he took his hand from the knob.

"But where did they move to? Did they leave an address?"

"No. What do I care?" She slammed the door.

Saihung stumbled dumbly down the stairs. He reproached himself repeatedly. For all his time abroad, he had kept to himself, been very careful. He walked home from his aunt and uncle's house mournfully. There would be little hope of independence now.

He picked up his mail, climbed the long, rickety stairs, to his one room, and sat glumly on the creaking bed. He truly had nothing—only the money in his pocket. It would be two weeks to his next pay period, and working as a waiter would bring in little money.

Saihung had been in the country nearly twenty years. Twenty years in which he did not fit in, twenty years in which he had felt alienated from his master, his past, the country that surrounded him. Twenty years in which he had seen people dear to him die just working their whole lives away.

It was twilight. An orange light came over the crest of the hill, and the bells of the nearby cathedral began to ring. He drew the roller blind and looked helplessly around the room. He felt trapped in the cubicle. The brown and green wallpaper, yellowed by a film of nicotine from previous tenants, made the room seem smaller. The light was low—a brighter bulb would blow the fuses—and the sepia shadows seemed to wash in toward his feet. He kept the pale green portal of the door closed. It kept out the noise and the rats.

He picked forlornly through his mail, and brightened a bit upon seeing his master's calligraphy. He had written to his teacher, hoping for some wisdom, some guidance from the one he hoped would save him. Reverently, he turned on the gooseneck lamp on his battered desk and opened the envelope. He unfolded the white paper only to find one word brushed in powerful strokes.

452

"Persevere."

Saihung tore the letter up in anger.

He sat on the edge of the bed and tried to meditate. Nothing happened. All that came to him was a burning desire for revenge. There was no dodging this blow. He would suffer for a long time.

SAIHUNG NEVER FOUND his swindlers, though he tried. Over the next few years, he patiently stalked them through much of the western United States. But they always stayed a step ahead of him, and eventually left the country. A sense of futility overtook Saihung, though his hatred soon faded into a simple sense of desperation. He truly had nothing. He could afford to eat only some canned food roughly overturned on a bowl of rice.

In spite of the despair that gripped him during that time, he was intrigued to find that his meditations grew more deep in the next year. He had nothing. He couldn't go out; he couldn't find any happiness. He craved a serenity free from any conscious thought. He had to make a living, fight enemies, face his problems. He had discovered his drives and ambitions, his own implicit qualities, saw the storehouse of attributes that he had accumulated. If only he could empty his mind completely of those things, then he could undoubtedly enjoy great peace. In earlier years, he had enjoyed such serenity. He wanted to find that tranquillity again.

Whenever he was devoid of thoughts and appetites during meditation, he felt a great bliss. He began to meditate more. Every moment when he was not doing so was a moment of torture. Spiritual practice was addicting. It was a lie that holy men were all gentle and kind. Those he had known were among the most moody and angry men he had met. From hermits in China to sages in the Himalayas, they resented being torn away from their heavenly states. He never thought that he too would come to a point where everyday pain would increase his own need for meditation.

He wanted to be empty. That meant that the energy he cultivated, such as what he experienced while practicing Taiji, might then be used to empower introspection. For the Taoists, even looking within required an extraordinary amount of energy. No

453

normal person could have the stamina to make the long inquiry. And more to the point, the mind had a variety of dimensions that the normal person did not even suspect.

Everyone talked about the self, from the most egotistical lout to the highest holy man. But his aim was to subdue the self, that part of him that was aware of his pain. His master told him in letters that the self did not exist in the first place. Why, then, should Saihung be so troubled? The difficulty, after all, was only imagined. There was no actual self to suffer. But how could he be nonexistent and aware of his apparent unreality?

Return to the Source. That was all that the Taoists seemed to repeat over and over. What was that Source? It was supposedly a state of complete void. That was what he concentrated on day after day. Being a waiter was secondary. Being anything outside his room was nothing compared to what he was experiencing inside his mind. That room in Chinatown became his meditation cell, the place where he began to resolve all the various aspects of his life by first realizing that they were part of a whole that had never truly existed objectively.

He went on for months. In the profundity of these states of consciousness, he realized that his identity was fading. He had done it all. He had lived through the Sino-Japanese War and the revolution. He had been a Taoist, a politician, a martial artist, a waiter. Now, he realized that those had been mere identities. Instead of defining him, they had discharged some aspect of his personality. Only a tiny bit—a thread—remained to pull his soul back into his body.

Since his youth, Saihung had learned that one of the highest accomplishments was to leave one's body. If the practitioner had substantially liberated himself from the attachments of life, and if he knew the correct procedure, he could project his spirit away from his body forever. Saihung wanted to do that. He felt close to that point. It would just take a little bit of effort, and he could launch himself away from his misery and unhappiness. If he was successful, his physical body would apparently die, but the soul would be radiant, conscious, immortal. But there was a danger. After all, the universe and all the dimensions were infinitely vast, eternally complex. As wonderful an achievement as it was to liberate the soul from the body, there were many realities and many places of illusion; the fragile soul could be easily lost.

He needed his master. Even if he reached the stage of skill and eligibility, his master had to be on "the other side" to guide his soul to the correct gate. Otherwise, there would be enslavement by other beings or imprisonment in limbo. He poured out his troubles in a letter to his master, telling of his successes, begging his teacher to grant him the final act of grace. Expectantly, he entered each session of meditation, waiting for the last glorious moment when he would be shown the true portal.

For once, the Grand Master replied quickly. "I forbid you to leave. You have not determined your destiny, let alone fulfilled it. You have too many sorrows and regrets. Any one of those, unless resolved in actual life, can pull you back to earth. Resolve the turmoil in your heart." To add to the insult, he criticized Saihung's spelling and calligraphy.

Saihung promptly wrote back. "There is nothing in this world for me. I can see the gate and the world beyond it. I will go through whether you bless me or not."

The written reply was short and harsh. "No," the letter stated simply. "I will stop you."

Saihung furiously ripped up the last letter. He cursed his master as the cruelest old man who ever lived. It was easy for him, thought Saihung resentfully. The Grand Master could undoubtedly visit any part of the universe he pleased. Time, space, and consciousness were no barriers for him. He probably cavorted with the gods themselves. But when it came to using his power to lift his youngest disciple from the wretchedness of the world, he was stingy and uncompassionate.

To hell with him! Saihung decided he would leave the world anyway. He doubted that the Grand Master could stop him. The Grand Master had threatened to place a barrier over Saihung's soul, barring his exit from the world. That would have been a tremendous act of power, and Saihung judged that his master might not be capable of it. He decided that it was just a psychological threat.

Within forty more days, he came closer and closer to leaving his body. He quit his job so that he could meditate four days a

455

week. He ate very little, only enough to keep his body going. He would soon enter a stage where he would not eat at all or go out. He floated in a state of bliss, already halfway in the next world.

Nine days more and the process would be complete. He meditated on. The night of the forty-eighth day, his spirit rose up from his body. Radiant. Shining. Pure. Who could doubt that there was a self?

456

He was a bright star floating upward. He was pure energy, pure being. In the dark hotel room, he seemed to float as if in an aqueous medium. He looked down at his body, sitting there very still. He felt curious, wondering whether this was actually himself. Here he was, looking at his own body in the only way to do so besides using a reflector. What was sitting there couldn't be him, if what was looking was the consciousness floating above. The body was not the self, he concluded.

The dazzling light within him continued. The walls seemed to be nothing. They were only composed of matter. He was now pure consciousness, and nothing on the material plane could oppose him. They dissolved.

He was out in darkness. Saihung felt an acceleration, and he burst into a maelstrom of colors. Colors more vivid than dyed silk, more brilliant than the refractions from a thousand shattered prism spectrums. He flew through this vortex powerfully. After some distance, he came to an opening into a boundless space. There, across this ocean of molten rainbows, he saw the gate to liberation.

He floated in utter tranquillity, and it seemed that his entire soul trembled in the delight of experiencing a splendor that was holy, welcome, and peaceful. He was light, and he absorbed light, became brighter as he went closer. He felt a profound sobriety. It was an aloofness from all that was human, all that was associated with the misery of his emotions and the tyranny of his subjectivity. He was free simply to perceive the gentle thrill of being in a stream of infinity. He was with the Tao.

Saihung contemplated this opening in space. He wanted very much to go through it and leave the human world behind. There was a wide world on the other side, a paradise. It was not like the human world at all. It was no city, no place, not material. It was not even governed by the physics that people experienced. Nevertheless, Saihung felt himself overwhelmingly attracted to it. He let himself go with no regrets, no hesitation. Now! He would leave this human folly for all eternity!

He willed himself forward, farther than he had ever projected himself. Recklessly, he plunged farther. He strained his concentration, kept it at an absolute peak. The silver cord that attached him to his body, that was literally his very lifeline back to earth, began to stretch thin and fade in its luster. Saihung's eagerness was uncontainable. He flew toward the portal.

Suddenly, the jarring sound of an electric guitar chord cut his trajectory. He felt pain. The place where the silver cord was attached to his abdomen wrenched at him, and he turned in space. Again came the noise, jerking him back into his body so suddenly that he nearly cried out with the agony. He opened his eyes. He was back in the room. His neighbor had turned his radio up loud. Rock music blasted through the walls so acutely that the walls shook.

He lost all control. Saihung dashed from his room, his eyes glaring demonically. He splintered his neighbor's door. With a mighty grip, he pulled the startled man to his feet. The man wet his pants in terror.

"He's killing me!" The neighbor's eyes teared up with fear, and Saihung could feel his stiff neck trembling under his grip. Saihung squeezed a bit more to quiet him. Wire-framed glasses fell to the floor.

Other men desperately tried to separate Saihung from the frightened man. It took six of them to drag him into the hallway. He let them do it, for he had slowly begun to realize the absurdity of his actions.

The manager, an overweight ex-marine, told him to move. He would not have maniacs busting down doors. Saihung didn't care. That day was the forty-ninth. He would be gone by the evening.

He sat back down in his room. The floor was fearfully quiet. There was no doubt: He had to leave the world. But when he tried to enter into the special state of serenity, he found that it was impossible. In losing his temper, he had lost the delicate detachment that made him eligible to leave his body. The feelings of meditation, all that he had experienced, was gone.

Perseverance

THE ONLY THING that had stopped Saihung from leaving his body had been the radio. He found another flophouse hotel in which to live and went to work at a liquor store. He wanted to try again. But this time he would plan his physical environment much more carefully. Saihung resolved that he would find some consecrated ground where no interruptions would occur.

The ideal place would be a temple or hermitage. Saihung had a friend, the abbot of a Zen temple in Japan. He wrote to the priest, honestly disclosing his intention to leave his body. That request was proper, but not all holy people believed in voluntarily forsaking the world. It was with great relief that he received the reply. The abbot consented.

Again, the possibility of leaving the world became practical. Saihung went for a walk to think things over. He enjoyed the clear sunshine and found himself climbing the slopes of Telegraph Hill. He walked up the Filbert Street steps. It was distant from Huashan, he thought, but here he was, again climbing a mountain.

He walked the path that spiraled around Coit Tower. He saw a few tourists and couples in love. Children played in the shrubbery. He had a commanding view of the city, the Golden Gate, the shimmering bay. The moon had already risen, a pale white disk against the powder-blue sky. A pair of sparrows flew by him. They landed on the branch of a green bush with red berries and scrutinized him, turning their heads in short gestures. Life was not any less delightful, he had to admit, but it no longer had much appeal for him.

Saihung took the letter from his pocket and read it again. Yes, he decided, here was his chance to attempt another departure. Once he was in the serenity of a temple, he could achieve the proper consciousness. There would be no desperate circumstances, no noisy neighbors. He planned to save enough money to make the journey, make a donation to the temple, and leave enough behind to provide for the Grand Master and the two acolytes. He would leave the world with no doubts.

He considered that he had not completed his assigned quest. He had come no closer to saying the answer that his master expected. He still had no idea of what it might be—perhaps it wasn't anything verbal. The most eloquent answer would have to be his life. He had struggled and fallen from the path repeatedly. He had traveled around the world, known wealth and poverty, wisdom and ignorance. He had maintained his body in meticulous health, and it had served him in martial-arts duels, Golden Gloves bouts, and brawls in the street. He had shaped it into a cocoon, in preparation for his ascension.

He was the Butterfly Taoist. It perfectly expressed this climax to his life. Maybe the Grand Master had even foreseen it when naming him. Perhaps the Butterfly had prepared himself for a second birth. That was surely as noble a destiny as any.

He decided that this would be what he would tell his master. Hopefully, it would placate the Grand Master enough for him to

459

guide Saihung's soul away. After all, he wouldn't even be the first. Out of thirteen classmates, the Grand Master had already ushered eight from their bodies. It was unfair of him to deny Saihung alone. If Saihung could not join his master in China, then he would await him in the next world.

He sighed. Renunciation and liberation were only for the world-weary, he reflected. When he was younger, the world seemed so thrilling. The political shifting and acceleration of technological societies had coincided with his disillusionment. There was really no reason to curse progress. It was wonderful for those who could benefit from it and find delight in it. There was nothing wrong with it. But it had hastened his own alienation. For centuries, literature had alluded to the red dust of the world. The red dust had choked him long enough. He was ready to shake it off.

A voice interrupted his thoughts.

"Hey! Hi! How ya doin'?"

Saihung looked up, startled. He quickly put away the letter.

"Remember me? My name's Steve. I come to the liquor store."

"Right. I remember you," replied Saihung. He looked at the slender, handsome Eurasian. Steve had shoulder-length hair, black-rimmed aviator glasses. He wore Ben Davis pants and basketball shoes. His T-shirt had a peace symbol on it. Saihung knew him to be in his twenties, or at least he had a fake I.D. that said so.

Steve sat down casually on the bench without asking. Saihung hid his annoyance.

"What's your name, man?" asked Steve.

"Kwan."

"Hey, far out. Like the God of War, right?" Steve had an exaggeratedly mellow tone to his voice.

"Sort of," replied Saihung disinterestedly.

"Yeah. Hey, Kwan, want a toke?" Steve took a carefully rolled joint from a matchbox. Saihung refused.

"It's really good. Heavy with resin. You could really get off on it. Maybe see things, huh?"

Saihung only smiled weakly. He hadn't heard this type of talk in movies, and his curiosity about Steve's odd language was the only thing that kept him from being rude.

"Yeah, I like to come up here a lot," continued Steve. "Get my head together. It's like, you know, going to higher ground." Steve leaned back on the bench and looked wistfully to the horizon.

"Yes ... Yeah," Saihung replied, trying to imitate the kid's talk.

"So you wanna get high?"

"No," said Saihung with a weak excuse. "I'm allergic."

"Oh. Okay. Hey, I'll just take a walk and come back. Don't go away, okay, Kwan?"

"Okay," said Saihung without hesitation. He did not think to turn down such an innocent request.

He watched Steve walk to the base of a eucalyptus tree to light up. What a waste, thought Saihung. Instinctively, he scanned Steve's body. Steve was clearly no threat, but he seemed healthy. If only he knew how to take care of himself, he could realize his potential, thought Saihung. He wondered about Steve's Eurasian background and was reminded of men in the Chinese aristocracy who had arranged to have European mistresses. They wanted children with the minds and thinking of Chinese, but the strength and beauty of Europeans. Breeding superchildren was the way they hoped to perpetuate their class. Saihung had known some of the children while growing up and had watched with pity as they had been rejected by both cultures. Steve was clearly not the result of such a bizarre experiment, but Saihung sensed that he suffered the same problems of rejection.

"Hey, thanks for waiting, man," said Steve, returning red-eyed.

Saihung should have gotten up and left, prepared for his trip to Japan. He didn't know why he stayed.

"Feel better?" No use sermonizing, thought Saihung.

"Yeah. Great!" There was a pause as he savored his euphoria. "Did you see that movie down at the Great Star Theater? Man, those movies are fantastic!"

Saihung laughed. The martial-arts movies were a pale image of the great world he had known.

"I saw *Five Fingers of Death* ten times!" continued Steve enthusiastically. "I was trying to learn some moves. Like this. Check this out!"

Steven ran through some strikes and kicks with great seriousness.

"How 'bout that, Kwan? Does it look like the real thing?"

"Uh . . . I don't know." Saihung smiled and tried to be diplomatic. "Maybe the stance isn't very good."

"I couldn't see that part. It was a close-up."

Saihung laughed out loud. He didn't know what made him stand up. Perhaps it was Steve's innocence. He checked to see if anyone was looking, and when he saw that no one was, he launched into a short performance of Lost Track Boxing.

"Wow! Wow! Hey, Kwan, that's spectacular! Teach me! Teach me!"

"I don't know anything," said Saihung, regretting his lapse.

"You do! You do!"

Saihung vacillated. He shouldn't have shown anything. But the boy was so earnest. "Why don't you join a school?" asked Saihung.

Steve grew quiet. "Oh, I don't know . . . no money . . . wouldn't fit in . . . you know."

Saihung felt sympathetic. He paused for a moment. There was absolutely no rational reason why he should make any offer, but without consideration, he said, "I've got a couple hours off tomorrow. Want to meet here?"

He was gratified by a beautiful and appreciative smile. "I guess I should kneel down, huh?"

"Don't do anything like that," said Saihung hastily. "Let's just say we're working out together. We're trading knowledge. Maybe there's something that you can show me."

"I don't know anything," said Steve dubiously. "This doesn't mean you're not going to show me anything, does it?"

"Of course not," explained Saihung patiently. "But let me tell you something about myself. That way, no one's disappointed. Fair enough?"

Steve nodded.

"I'm a wanderer," said Saihung. "I can show you things you never even dreamed about, but that doesn't mean that I'm a mystical being. I'm only an ordinary man. Remember that, all right?"

"That's good enough for me," Steve said enthusiastically.

"Okay. I'll see you tomorrow." He began walking down the hill.

"Thanks, man," shouted Steve behind him.

Saihung had not had any martial-arts students since he had left China. He liked having students, but he had not considered

teaching for nearly three decades. He had wanted only liberation. That required having no commitments. Having students
was a big responsibility.

Taoists traditionally met students by chance. Even Saihung's
own study had come from such a seemingly random meeting.
The stories always spoke of the great difference that Taoist wisdom made on the recipient. He could recall no story where they
talked about how the Taoist felt.

The Taoist, upon meeting someone in need, was to share his
knowledge out of unselfish compassion. After the circumstances
in question were settled, they disappeared. A Taoist was nonat-
tached. Unconcerned about worldly things and human emotions,
the true wandering Taoist never sought to have a following or set
himself upon some throne of permanency. Presumably, he
walked away and forgot the whole incident. It was, after all, not
even real to him.

He wrote his master for advice after he began teaching Steve.
Should he leave his body or stay and teach? Steve would never
be a Taoist, and Saihung was undecided about what to do.

The Grand Master's reply was considerate and gentle. He felt
that Saihung would make a good teacher. Saihung was quizzical
about this. He felt that he had no patience.

"It is not your time to leave your body," the Grand Master reminded him. "Death is preordained, and we cannot alter that.
You are under no compulsion to teach. But it is noble to help another.

"You have the personality for it. You won't frighten your students. Teaching is not your ultimate destiny, but if you stop and
think, you'll realize that you haven't completed everything yet.
Complete your life before you try to leave it behind."

Saihung pondered his master's words. Leaving had been his
primary concern, and the only way to leave life was death. But
how to die was the question. Everyone had a different way, he
thought. Some died in their sleep; some died in violent accidents. Some died for a cause, others with whimpering and tears.
He had wanted to make his final worldly act the conscious and
beautiful act of leaving his body.

Yet that was still death. He knew if he had broken the Grand
Master's prohibition and had rushed into the void that he would

not likely have reached the gate. He admitted to himself that he would have been committing suicide. That would have been a waste, and it would have condemned him to rebirth—if his soul had been collected.

Saihung sat down to meditate. He would not try to leave, would not try to accomplish anything, he told himself. He touched his fingers together, his thumbs, palms, and overlapped fingers formed a circle. He let his eyes almost close and focused them on the floor a few feet in front of him. Gradually, he put his thought on his breathing, letting his breath settle into a slow and deep cycle. The more his inhalations and exhalations lengthened, the more his mind became calm.

Years ago, his master had asked him if he existed. He considered this question again. The body that had been his haven and his vehicle of martial pride was something he had been eager to leave behind. He had seen the spirit rise from the body. Thus, he concluded that the body was not his true self. It would fall as soon as he flew. Decay would begin immediately. It would separate into water, chemicals, particles. Surely then, the self might be the astral body that had risen into the room. But that spirit had consciousness and volition. He had been able to see his physical form, and he had been able to travel. In essence, the self that emerged had a mind, or more precisely, was the mind.

Where was his mind? he asked himself. Where was the source of his consciousness?

He waited. No answer.

Where was the mind? he asked again.

No answer.

He felt a shimmer in him. The soul. The mind and the soul were one and the same. Not just the mind of the brain, but the greater mind that was a little blob of life force from the universal One.

Finally, he knew that the brightness left after all other aspects of his life were stripped away was itself but a tiny distant reflection of the cosmic and almighty unity, a dewdrop away from the shining ocean. Did he exist? No. Not once he understood that the concept of his individuality was a mistake. Not once he accepted that he was a part of all and all was a part of him. Separateness was only an illusion.

464

As he met steve the next day, he realized what a pleasure it was to share, and he understood how long he had been without such a simple pleasure. It seemed to him that he had struggled in isolation since he had left China, and it had made him humorless and angry.

He watched Steve practice the beginnings of the martial movements that Saihung had learned from Wang Ziping. On the green lawn overlooking the bay, with all of the office buildings and the waterfront below them, Steve slowly began to piece together the punches and variations in stance. Saihung thought of the long road ahead for Steve. It would take decades before the young man could do what Saihung did as a matter of reflex and instinct. But that was all right. Watching his student was like watching a baby learning to walk. There was still something delightful, joyous, an event that filled him with wonder.

Steve moved to the side in a lunge and whipped both arms like a windmill. His fists came into alignment, one in front and one in back of him.

"Is it like this?" asked Steve.

Saihung silently went up to his pupil and raised the hands a little higher. He remembered how he himself would have been whipped with a split bamboo cane for such a simple question.

Steve moved into the next section of movements, moving in great sincerity, if not accuracy. He stopped.

"I don't remember this next part," he said apprehensively. It was a question that he seemed afraid to ask. Saihung did not want to tell him that he himself had also been scared to ask the same questions of his teachers. He decided in that instant that he would not teach the way he had been taught.

"It's like this," said Saihung, as he leapt forward like an archer pulling a bow. He swiveled quickly and punched, twisted into a jumping kick, and came down into a combination of thrusts. Steve smiled happily.

"Do it with me," Saihung urged. Steve followed him as best as he could, and they did it over and over until the youth was breathless.

"I guess I'm a little out of shape." Steve bent over and put his hands on his knees.

"You have no stamina. Smoking and drinking destroy stamina." Saihung tried not to lecture. He still thought of himself as a student. He knew very well what treatment he resented, how reproaches could be confusing.

"Don't you work in a liquor store?" The boy pushed his glasses back onto his nose and turned to look at him.

"It's a job. I do it to survive. But I don't drink, smoke, or fool around with women."

"Never?" Steve looked at Saihung incredulously. "Man, isn't that a little grim?"

"No, it isn't," said Saihung without hesitation. "In my time, there were many men like that. I had good examples. They inspired me to be this way. They taught me to walk this path, and I would never really consider leaving it. I have a master in China. He keeps me on the proper way. I control my diet, practice hygiene, exercise. That's it. Martial arts is only a hobby with me."

Steve straightened up. "Not a bad hobby. But what else do you do?"

"Meditation. That and philosophy are more important than fighting."

"I wish I could see you fight."

Saihung looked at Steve. "No, you don't. You don't want to see me fight. There's nothing pretty about fighting. It's not a movie, it's not opera. And I don't want to ever catch you fighting either."

"But then why am I learning this?" Steve looked at him with a pout.

"As a means of discipline," replied Saihung. "If you learn martial arts, it will improve your health and give you the discipline to do anything in life. The demands to master all the facets of martial arts will shape your personality and give you the resources to face all that fate sends your way."

"How will it do that?"

"If you acquire discipline, then you will have the freedom to do anything and be anything you want in life. Then you can walk through a whole wonderful world that you'd never suspect existed. That's not the world of boxing, it's the world of experience. Life is the best teacher, and I am trying to equip you not to fight, but to learn from the true teacher."

"I'm not sure what you mean, but it sounds all right. Will you help me?"

"Sure I will. But you have to put in the effort."

Steve nodded. "I will."

"Okay. Back to practice."

They worked out together until the sky began to flame with the setting sun.

"That's it for today," said Saihung.

"Will you be here tomorrow?"

"Of course I will." Inwardly, Saihung knew that he was taking on another obligation.

"Can I bring a friend?"

"I don't know," said Saihung dubiously. This was a little too fast for him.

"Oh, please." Steve gave Saihung a pleading look. "He wants to learn too."

He tried to be strict. "We'll see."

"Great! See you tomorrow at the same time?"

"Yes, the same time."

Saihung watched the lanky boy trot contentedly down the hill. He laughed at himself for the talk that he had given Steve. Wasn't that what he himself needed to pull out of his desperate outlook? With a student, life did not seem so bleak or lonely. More important, it was a thrill to share the art that he cherished with someone who was falling in love with it for the first time. That freshness was a source of renewal for him.

Saihung sat down on a bench to watch the sun go down. He saw the orange orb slowly descend to the gray-blue horizon, watched the deepening purple shadows of the streaked clouds. The sphere of fire was on the Pacific in a short time, but the combination of the two antagonistic elements seemed perfectly fine. He had a sense of harmony, and he felt his patience returning to him. He would continue to search for the answer that would satisfy his master, and in that process, find his own life's meaning as well. He stopped wanting to rush. There was time. And as he searched, he would show this boy, and perhaps others, some of the beautiful secrets of life. He would show them the way to a vast world.

Afterword

I STOOD ON a busy Chinatown street, waiting for Mr. Kwan. He lived in a small, dark hotel. He could afford nothing else. I looked up at the pale pink stucco building and saw the opaque windows, wondering which room he was in and whether he could see me. I had come to help him run some errands before the small class that he taught. Though the time was prearranged, I did not ring or go to his room. He was late.

Many of the arts that Mr. Kwan taught were only hinted about in books or labeled "lost" or "legendary." Since my initial research into Chinese martial arts and Taoism, I had heard of boxing skills like Eight Trigrams Palm, or Snake Boxing; health exercises like Eight Pieces of Brocade, Muscle Change Classic, and the Five Animal Frolics; meditations such as the Eight Psychic Meridians Standing Meditation and the Microcosmic Orbit. I had wanted to learn them for years.

I had read about the famous Song dynasty general Yueh Fei; now here was someone who knew his boxing style. I had read about the heroes of the classic *Water Margin;* now here was someone who knew how to use their strange weapons. I had heard of the famous Taoist strategist Zhu Geliang; now here was someone who had studied similar philosophies. Scholarly and military talents were the classical ideal in Imperial China. Mr. Kwan advocated that well, and he embodied a history's worth of ancient arts to support that.

Admittedly, my infatuation with martial arts was somewhat romantic, even idealistic. I was addicted to Chinese novels about chivalry, honor, knights, and heroes. Many of these stories had supernatural elements—ghosts, goblins, demons, sorcerers—and Taoists. Usually, these men were considered to have great skill, magic arts, and an otherworldly perception that held this world as illusory. Taoism was present in much literature—from Chuang Tzu and Lao Tzu as opera characters to the story of Han Chungli in the *Yellow Millet Dream*. A Taoist usually represented wisdom, nonconformity, and disinterested heroism. They often appeared in people's lives to intercede at just the right moment. With this cultural background, I was predisposed toward meeting a Taoist.

Mr. Kwan began from the simple premise that the body had first to be made into a fit vehicle for the mind and spirit. I learned calisthenics, stretches, different kinds of boxing. The breath needed to be trained, so I learned a great variety of breathing movements that attempted to direct the flow of physical energy in the body (*qigong*). He did not teach philosophy by discourse; I simply accompanied him and learned from his reaction to actual life experiences. Meditation would not be taught until he believed me to be thoroughly prepared (it would be years).

His metaphysical discussions were not only enlightening, but virtually invulnerable to argument. His depth of knowledge of Chinese culture was amazing. He knew things even my grandmother didn't know, and in some ways was even more traditional and conservative than she. Whenever I thought back on the times he had thrown or struck me during a demonstration, my doubts faded. Skill was always apparent. One could not fake talent.

Hearing of his travels in the United States, I knew he had had to make compromises, and inevitable mistakes. Perhaps some would have said that he was not even "spiritual." Someone who fought in the streets, worked as a cook and a waiter, who scraped for his existence like many other immigrants, may not have fit their preconceptions of a holy aspirant. But good fortune and a life devoid of doubt and conflict seldom happen to a person who faces life's deepest questions. Spirituality that is never tested by bitterness, that never has to face the dilemmas of contradictory experiences, can never be strong, true, or honest.

Such integrity was undoubtedly all that Mr. Kwan cared about. He made it clear that he did not consider himself to be special. Mr. Kwan said that his only secrets were that he kept to the way of his master's lineage, kept himself healthy, sought the reasons for his life, and helped those whom he met without seeking to bind them to himself. His Taoism was a hardheaded, practical, hardworking, and disciplined system. He advocated celibacy, ab-

470

stention from liquor, drugs, certain meats, bad thinking, and overinvolvement with worldly things. All there was for him was daily practice, discipline, dignity, understanding.

Following him required considerable sacrifice on the part of the prospective student. I was not surprised by the number of students who left him—dozens more than stayed. They refused to make the sacrifices and put aside enjoyments, relationships, or career goals. Mr. Kwan told me that since not everyone is ready to learn or stay, he can do nothing but let them go. I once thought this sad, but after many years I had to conclude that he was right.

I made my own sacrifices, though they were always gradual and voluntary. One of them involved drinking, which I loved. When I began to learn *qigong*, Mr. Kwan warned me to stop. Once purified, the body would reject all that was bad for it. I scoffed inwardly at this advice. Who could be sure if all this huffing and puffing and holding of breath would have an effect? I would wait and see. The desire to have my cake and eat it too was always an unfortunate tendency.

Before long, I found that I could not hold my liquor as before, and worse, the pleasure faded. It might just be psychological, I reasoned. Stubbornly, I refused to change until a crisis brought on a decision.

Mr. Kwan was far away on a long journey. I had just moved into a house and was due to have a big party the next day. I became violently sick, enough that I woke up in agony. The party could be canceled, of course, but I did not want such an embarrassment. Nevertheless, I could not see the possibility of recovery in time as I knelt at the toilet, waiting in high fever to throw up. I hated nausea. I hated vomiting. As I lapsed into dry heaves, I blamed Mr. Kwan.

"I know you're doing this to me," I said superstitiously. "Or at least someone up there is. All right. I'll make a deal. Let me get well in time for my party, and I'll quit drinking."

The next day, to my great chagrin, I was well. I decided to keep my promise—it was as good an excuse as any—and all my friends were shocked at my sobriety that night.

Once I made this sacrifice, it became a little easier to make others. Gradually, I tried to make my life more in keeping with

471

the way I was learning. I made many mistakes, of course, but perserved. Mr. Kwan always emphasized discipline. From my sacrifices, I realized that discipline was equivalent to freedom. Pure self-denial does not have any intrinsic value, but discipline and self-control allow one to set a goal and do the necessary things to attain it. I valued my relationship with Mr. Kwan, and that was part of the reason that I did not mind waiting ridiculously on a Chinatown street.

472

Mr. Kwan finally came down the stairs, and I put aside my reflections. He dressed in warm-up clothes and running shoes. His face was wide, rectangular, red. The feature that always struck me were his large, glistening eyes. As he crossed the street, my heart sank. I could see that he was in a bad mood.

"Sifu," I greeted him respectfully.

"These people don't know who they're pushing around," he began without preliminaries.

What had happened? Had he gotten into some trouble? It wasn't considered polite to ask.

"Are you having some difficulty?" I asked carefully.

Mr. Kwan caught himself. "Oh, never mind," he said. "I must be the only practitioner who has to scrounge for his own existence. But I have to talk to you."

I was surprised. He was seldom so direct.

"They've taken everything away from me in this country. I've been discriminated against. I've lost so much. But I want to give you something that can't be taken away."

"What is it, Sifu?" I hoped it wasn't too valuable. I had a tendency to lose things. Perhaps I could get a safe-deposit box.

"A spiritual legacy. You have a father. Someday he will give you an inheritance. That will be your material legacy. But a master is like a spiritual father. His heritage is spiritual. This is transmitted from the master to the student. It is inside. They cannot take it away, yet it is a great gift."

I could not believe what he was offering to me. "I will try my best, Sifu," I said immediately.

"Good. Let's go shopping."

We got into my car. He had asked me to make a commitment. I had made it. I should go into this new stage in my life with no doubts, I told myself.

"Sifu?" I asked before I started the car.

"Yes?"

"There's just one question I would like to ask."

"Okay."

"Did you do anything to make me stop drinking?"

The normally stoic Mr. Kwan turned scarlet from giggling.

"I would not use sorcery on you, even if I knew it," said Mr. Kwan when he had collected himself. "You are a young man, already half-formed. You know how to make decisions in your life. It would be wrong for me to bewitch you, because you would never understand the reason you were doing something. I can only make suggestions and hope you'll listen. If you were a child, it would be different. If the child does something wrong, the elder punishes the child. If I treated you the same way, you would only resent it.

"I need you to cooperate. You must make the effort. I'm not pouring anything into you. You are creating yourself. I am like a sculptor. He takes a little here, adds a little there, but he cannot change the inherent nature of his material."

I became the sculpture who participated in its own sculpting, and it was the beginning of a great deepening in my learning. It was said that one could not learn without the grace of the master. It was true. Though I might find a procedure published in a book, it didn't seem to work until it was taught to me—and invariably details were left out of the writing. I suppose this was what is called "direct transmission." It wasn't anything mystical or supernatural. It was the security and power of a lineage, the vitality of being taught.

Some of the best lessons happened spontaneously. I remember, for example, his lesson to me about yin and yang. We were sitting in my parked car and began discussing the fundamental duality of the universe. Though it was hardly the traditional poetic spot by a mountain waterfall, we fell into discussion. "Yin is like all these moving cars and rushing people," Mr. Kwan said. "Yang is like that phone pole."

I was puzzled. I quickly reviewed what I had learned about yin and yang—something I knew only from reading. I wondered what direct experience could lead him to say such a bizarre sentence.

473

All I knew about yin and yang was that yang was all things positive: light, hardness, fire, movement. Yin was negative: darkness, softness, water, stillness. There was certainly nothing in the classical references that would have led me to cars and phone poles. I really didn't understand him and asked for further explanation.

"Yin represents ambition, drive, movement," Mr. Kwan told me. "It is the female, the ultimate fertility. Yang, by itself, is so strong, but in its pure form it has no drive, no motivation. Thus it is static: Without yin, it cannot move. Without yang, yin will have neither direction nor form."

474

"Yin is movement, yang is stillness?" I asked. "You are saying the opposite of what is written in the books."

"That's why book learning is inadequate," he said dryly. "I only learned that lesson from two Taoists with whom I traveled. They told me that the lessons of life were far superior to the words of men. According to my masters, life is the only true classroom, and experience is the only reliable textbook."

Real-life situations were what Mr. Kwan liked best. The Tao was everywhere. Its understanding was to be imparted at any time. Theory was important, but a book could not shock one out of one's misconceptions the way a teacher could. This could happen anytime and anywhere—even after a movie.

"Casanova is the perfect Taoist," Mr. Kwan declared after we had seen the film *La Nuit de Varennes*. I was mystified again. How could a man like Mr. Kwan, raised in a monastery, advocating a lifestyle of meditation, discipline, and celibacy, call Casanova a perfect Taoist?

"Are you sure?" I asked him. "He seems to be a self-indulgent seducer."

"But he had insight," replied Mr. Kwan firmly. "He perceived his own nature and did not hesitate to fulfill his destiny. He was a freethinker and a man of high cultivation. That's why I call him a perfect Taoist."

Mr. Kwan's pragmatism sometimes meant that his lessons were on a martial level. At one point, there was an outbreak of muggings on buses. Mr. Kwan came to class one night with great concern. He had us set up chairs to imitate a bus, and we went through hours of drilling to cover every aspect of attack on public transportation. He even taught the women separate techniques, going as far as borrowing a purse to show its use as a weapon. Eventually, we moved to strategies that had evolved from his experiences in New York. Significantly, that was the first time we had even heard of his stay in New York. We still have a technique nicknamed "The New York Subway," instead of its original and more poetic name, "The Crimson Child Worships Buddha."

TODAY, THE GRAND MASTER and the two acolytes, Mist Through a Grove and Sound of Clear Water, live in obscurity, the only inhabitants of an island temple in northwestern China. Only five of the original thirteen disciples are still alive.

Du Yueshen returned to Shanghai in 1945 and, until the Communist takeover in 1949, revived the old Shanghai world. He fled to Hong Kong, where he died on August 16, 1951. His body was eventually interred in a tomb on Taiwan.

Huashan was overrun by the Red Guard. Monks were killed, temples burned, holy ground desecrated. Scriptures and relics were destroyed, among them one of the oldest surviving copies of the *Seven Bamboo Tablets of the Cloudy Satchel*. The original may still be on Maoshan, but that place is fearsome and shunned, and its priests are powerful sorcerers unlikely to bother with the world. Other versions are considered to be fragments overly laden with later commentaries.

Mr. Kwan's own struggle and quest continue. His master, still alive in China today, refuses to let him come home: He still has not got the answer. Whatever this task is, it is something far beyond mundane realization, enlightenment, or the completion of errands. I am not inviting the reader to guess what Mr. Kwan's destiny is. Rather, I invite you to think of your own. We must all walk our life's way, solve our own personal riddle. If someone like Mr. Kwan can persevere with undiminished determination, then surely the rest of us can put aside the petty and banal details of every day to pursue our highest goal.

All the special methods of Taoism are relevant only because they help to clarify and achieve that goal. A Taoist must endure suffering and misfortune like anyone else. The only difference is that Taoists believe in having many skills and resources to traverse this uncertain life. No one knows beforehand what circumstances will befall oneself. But whatever they may be, the Taoists hope to have whatever means necessary to maintain their purpose.

I'VE WRITTEN THE *Chronicles of Tao* to support Mr. Kwan and honor his tradition, to show that the antiquity he so treasures is being perpetuated. The fact that his system is still alive and vital is not the impossible replication of old Taoism. Rather, it is the nurturing of a seed from that great tree. Should it sprout and grow to maturity, it will be the spiritual legacy that he promised me.

Mr. Kwan has retired now, weary of his trials in the world, unwilling to advocate his calling publicly. He has withdrawn into seclusion for his final stage. But I feel fortunate. I have found a way of life that guides and sustains me. I value this heritage and finally understand why the masters would rather it died than permit its adulteration. I will walk my path as long as I am permitted, in reverence for the beauty being constantly born, and the way of the sages still vital to this day.

476